Chatuh Shloki

# Manusmriti

An English Commentary

Chatuh Shloki

# Manusmriti

## An English Commentary

**Nithin Sridhar**

Vitasta

Published by
Renu Kaul Verma
Vitasta Publishing Pvt Ltd
4348/4C, Ansari Road, Daryaganj
New Delhi-110 002
info@vitastapublishing.com

ISBN 978-81-19670-91-8

First Edition 2025

MRP ₹ 795



Edited by Kangam King
Layout by Somesh Kumar Mishra
Printed by Chaman Enterprises, New Delhi

*I place this work at the lotus feet of my Gurus and all the Pūrvācāryas in the dharmaśāstra tradition.*

# *Maṅgalācaraṇa*

॥ श्री गुरुभ्यो नमः ॥
वक्रतुण्ड महाकाय सूर्यकोटिसमप्रभ ।
निर्विघ्नं कुरु मे देव सर्वकार्येषु सर्वदा ॥
सर्वमङ्गलमाङ्गल्ये शिवे सर्वार्थसाधिके ।
शरण्ये त्र्यम्बके गौरि नारायणि नमोऽस्तु ते ॥
ईश्वरो गुरुरात्मेति मूर्तिभेदविभागिने ।
व्योमवद् व्याप्तदेहाय दक्षिणामूर्तये नमः ॥

श्रेयःसाधनिकं कर्म लोकेऽभूद् यदुपक्रमम् ।
यदुपज्ञं नृसोदर्यं शास्त्रं वेदार्थवन्महत् ॥
योगक्षेमकरं पुंसां यद्वाक्यामृतभेषजम् ।
तं नुमः पितरं नृणामादिमं पुरुषं मनुम्[1] ॥

श्रुतिस्मृतिपुराणानाम् आलयं करुणालयं ।
नमामि भगवत्पादशङ्करं लोकशङ्करम् ॥
भारतीकरुणापात्रं भारतीपदभूषणम् ।
भारतीपदमारूढं भारतीतीर्थमाश्रये ॥
विद्याविनयसम्पन्नं वीतरागं विवेकिनम् ।
वन्दे वेदान्ततत्त्वज्ञं विधुशेखरभारतीम् ॥
॥ ॐ तत् सत् ॥

# A Stutiḥ dedicated to Svāyambhuva Manu[2]

वेदोपदेशमधिगम्य पुरा विधातुर्
योऽस्थापयत् स्वकुलजेषु परम्परायाः।
राजर्षये निगमधर्मविवर्धनाय
तस्मै सुभद्रवचसे मनवे नमोऽस्तु॥१

यद्धेषजोपमगिरं समुपाश्रयन्ते,
आचारसंशयसमुद्भवमोहमग्नाः।
आर्षाः सुशिष्टमतयो भुवि लौकिकाश्च
तस्मै प्रशस्तवचसे मनवे नमोऽस्तु॥२

येनोपदिष्टवचनाश्रयमाललम्बे
कण्वात्मजा सभरता विभया सभायाम्।
भार्याधिकारविनिकृत्पुरुराजपत्नी
तस्मै सुशर्मवचसे मनवे नमोऽस्तु॥३

यत्रादृता हि महिला महिताश्च वृद्धास्
तत्रानिशं सुमनसः सगुणा रमन्ते।
इत्याज्ञया मनुजधर्मपथप्रदाय
तस्मै विशुद्धवचसे मनवे नमोऽस्तु॥४

आम्नायतत्त्वविदुषे विधिमर्मवेत्त्रे
पूर्वर्षिदेशिकवराय जगद्धिताय।
वर्णाश्रमेषु निहिताखिलकर्मगोप्त्रे
तस्मै सुधर्म्यवचसे मनवे नमोऽस्तु॥५

—Śrī Kushagra Aniket

# Contents

*Blessings for the Book* *xiii*
*Praise for the Book* *xvii*
*Foreword* *xxvii*
*Preface* *xxxi*

**Section 1**
Introduction to Manusmṛti and the Larger Dharmaśāstra Tradition 1

Chapter 1
Origination, Transmission, and Authorship of Manusmṛti: Is the Text a Patchwork or a Careful Construction 3

Chapter 2
Place and Function of Dharmaśāstra in Hindu Worldview 28

Chapter 3
Decoding Manusmṛti: Some Pointers to Make Sense of Dharmaśāstra Texts 53

## Section 2

# Blessings for the Book

I am happy to know that Sri Nithin Sridhar is bringing out a new publication on *Manusmṛti* entitled *Chatuh Shloki Manusmriti.* It is a commentary in English on the opening four verses of the original text and it also contains elaborate interpretations and observations related to our *dharmaśāstra* tradition from various academic and cultural perspectives. It is the result of much painstaking labour and diligence on the part of the author, who has delved into several important original sourcebooks related to Hindu dharmaśāstras.

The full text of Manusmṛti contains 12 chapters and approximately 2600 verses, some of which are considered highly controversial in the modern context which emphasises egalitarian and democratic values.

Manusmṛti is nevertheless a remarkable historical document because it reflects the social and cultural values that prevailed in ancient India during the early stages of the Vedic civilisation.

If this book and its modern approach to this ancient text can inspire students of sociology, anthropology and Indian history to read the original work of the sage Manu, along with the commentaries of Medhātithi, Govindarāja and Kullūka Bhaṭṭa as well as other important sources of Hindu dharmaśāstras, such as the works of Yājñavalkya, Parāśara, Kātyāyana, Āpastaṃba and others, it will certainly serve a great purpose.

It is hoped that, in years to come, the author will be able to take up similar works to continue this fruitful project of introducing India's ancient wisdom to the English-speaking world.

**Swami Tattwamayananda,**
Vedanta Society of Northern California,
San Francisco

To write a book about the Manusmṛti is a daunting task for three reasons. Firstly, many things including authorship and the timing of the work are disputed by scholars. Secondly, due to ill-conceived perceptions among contemporary scholars that regard Manu's treatment of socio-cultural issues as dated and therefore, at best, irrelevant for modern seekers of Hindu *dharma*, the book has a very controversial reputation to say the least. Finally, even though not many people have actually studied the Manusmṛti, quotes from the text's controversial views of women and their place in society are well known in all circles, leading people to dismiss the book in its entirety.

Nithin Sridhar has seemingly pulled off the impossible by writing an elegant and persuasive book on the first four verses of the Manusmṛti. His main purpose is to demonstrate the need for understanding the moorings of *dharma* for the purposes of bringing about a Hindu renaissance. I commend Nithin for undertaking this task of discussing Manu's treatment of *dharma*. The book is eloquently written and justifies the need for a deeper study of the Manusmṛti, which is an erudite and authentic rendition of the *Vedas*' position on *dharma*.

**Swamini Svatmavidyananda Saraswati,**
Arsha Vijnana Gurukulam,
Eugene, OR, USA

# Praise for the Book

This commentary by Nithin Sridhar is a rich primer on Manusmṛti. The author demonstrates the rigour and scholarship of a *bhāṣyakāra* by adopting the textual traditions: word-by-word examination of verses and elaborating on the subject and context in them, is one such. The *catuḥ ślokī* route to explaining too is a part of that tradition. An essential reader on Manusmṛti.

**Smt Nirmala Sitharaman,**
Minister of Finance and Corporate Affairs,
Government of India

I applaud Mr Nithin Sridhar for his outstanding scholarly publication *Chatuh Shloki Manusmriti* which effectively counters many common doubts, misperceptions and prejudices around the concept of *dharma*, integrity and importance *of* dharmaśāstras, particularly Manusmṛti. Adopting rigorous analysis of the tradition of textual condensation, abridgement, and expansion, Mr Sridhar demonstrates that the extant text of Manusmṛti is neither a patchwork, nor a gradual composition spread over many centuries, and underlines its unitary authorship and careful construction to maintain the underlying structural unity. Manusmṛti has timeless, universal relevance since it is primarily concerned with the eternal causal relationship between different categories of *karmas* and their *karmaphala*. It is not a law book or a constitution, nor a book of commandments in a biblical sense; it is for the individual to use own discretion and free will to interpret, internalise and act, and bear the consequences of one's actions.

Contrary to the Western egotistic obsession with identity of authorship, the Indic tradition involves interplay between *apauruṣeya* origination and the *pauruṣeya* textual composition: *ūrdhvamūlamadha: śākhamaśvatthaṃ prāhuravyayam*. Further scriptural texts themselves are not the end, but only a means to a higher knowledge. Mere reading/recitation of even *Veda*s without proper understanding is useless: *yastanna veda kimṛcā kariṣyati*. The ultimate reality cannot be grasped through extrovert senses. It requires *śraddhā* and practice of introspective, meditative, and yogic techniques by the individual seeker. The inward vision reveals harmony, interdependence and interconnectedness, weaving not only humanity but the entire physical creation in a single web: *ṛtasya tantuṃ vitataṃ driśe kam*. So, the *dharmic* worldview is fundamentally holistic, unified, and universal and not segmented, selfish, and anthropocentric. It does not impose any artificial, hegemonic notion of mechanical uniformity and equality, but recognises the diversity of creatures; their uniqueness; existence of many ways to see and describe the same object; and plurality of possible paths to reach the same destination. It provides a sustainable framework for harmonious co-existence in a single ecological abode, *eka nīḍam*.

I hope Mr Sridhar's work on Manusmṛti will inspire further study and research on Indian knowledge heritage without colonial prejudices, to evolve solutions for contemporary challenges.

**Sri Akhilesh Mishra,**
Ambassador of India to Ireland

Manusmṛti is a text rarely read, but routinely maligned. We are descended from Manu. As such, we are *manava*s. In the present *kalpa*, we are in the seventh *manvantara*, that of Vaivasvata Manu. There have been six Manus earlier and seven more will follow. The Manu of Manusmṛti or *Manava Dharmaśāstra* is Svāyambhuva-Manu. As it now stands, Manava Dharmaśāstra has 12 chapters and more than 2,600 *ślokas*. Of these, Nithin concentrates on four, the first four opening *ślokas*. He is one of our foremost scholars and his translations (as with *Īśopaniṣad*) go much beyond translations. They are commentaries, with in-depth research, typically with a comprehensive introduction. They remind me a bit of George Bernard Shaw's plays, where the preface is just as valuable as the main course.

Who composed Manava Dharmaśāstra and how was it transmitted? Among Sanskrit texts translated into English, Manusmṛti was one of the first. Accordingly, Western scholars have commented extensively on it, to criticise and condemn. The prevalent scholarly view is that the text evolved over a period of time, with constant collations and additions, thus explaining the perceived inconsistencies, reflecting different value judgements at various chronological points of time. In the comprehensive introduction, the author convincingly contests this customary proposition. This is first done by considering the internal evidence within the text. That internal evidence is fairly clear. The apauruṣeya subject matter of dharmaśāstra originated with *Brahmā*, who taught it to Manu, who became the pauruṣeya composer of this particular text. In turn, Svāyambhuva-Manu taught it to Bhṛgu and other sages. The version that has come down to us is thus the Bhṛgu recension. Next, external evidence from the *Itihāsa-Purāṇa* corpus is used to validate the argument that there were different recensions of texts for the three *puruṣārthas* of *dharma*, *artha* and *kāma*. Hence, on dharmaśāstras, there were the Bhṛgu, Nārada, Bṛhaspati and Añgiras recensions. Using *Nāradasmṛti*, Nithin persuasively argues for a transmission from Svāyambhuva-Manu down to Nārada, Mārkaṇḍeya and finally Sumati Bhārgava, from the Bhṛgu lineage. There is no particular reason to dismiss this evidence, though this also means we no longer possess the original text abridged by Sumati Bhārgava, having lost roughly one-third of the *ślokas* down the years. This has been the process of transmission for other texts too, *Kamaśāstra* and *Vedānta* being cases in point. I think this proposition, including that of the unitary narrative structure and deeper architecture, is very well argued and Nithin Sridhar's monograph is a great value addition to our understanding of Manava Dharmaśāstra.

This is followed by a rich discussion on such *smṛti* texts as *śabda pramāṇa* (one of the acceptable methods of proof) for pursuing *dharma* and on the illusory perceived conflict between *Śruti* and *smṛti* texts. Finally, we have translations of the first four *ślokas*. As with *Īśopaniṣad*, these are detailed commentaries, not simple translations. This requires serious research, driven by intensity and passion. While this is asking a lot, I hope, eventually,

Nithin does get around to doing something similar for all of Manava Dharmaśāstra. That's not an easy task to accomplish. But, if there is one person who is capable of accomplishing the task, it happens to be the present author. All too often, Western narratives on dharmaśāstra texts have been mechanically accepted and regurgitated. If a better narrative is to be stated, the work has to start somewhere and I hope this monograph is the beginning of what will become a multi-volume exercise.

**(Late) Dr Bibek Debroy,**
Renowned Economist and Translator of
Hindu texts including *Mahabharata*

Nithin Sridhar has explained in this work the eternity of the truths contained in the Manusmṛti. May this work go on to educate the deracinated Hindu population about the value of Manusmṛti, popularly misunderstood and misrepresented.

**Dr Jayashankar Rajagopalan,**
MA, PhD, DLitt. Former Dean of Languages,
Magadh University, and Former Advisor to the Prime
Minister of India on Education

*Chatuh Shloki Manusmriti* by Shri Nithin Sridhar is quite an interesting book on *dharma* in general and Manusmṛti in particular. This is a good example of a well-knit argument, a well-prepared treatise and a well-analysed idea in the light of modern canons of research methodology.

Nithin Sridhar will certainly lead the new generation to healthy academics. He is well known in academic circles as a devoted academician with clarity of thought and lucid presentation. Through this treatise, he very successfully generates interest in the study of dharmaśāstra texts like Smṛti, among the modern generation. He explains that the text that tells us what actions lead to happiness and what lead to sorrow can be called dharmaśāstra.

Nithin Sridhar explains, argues, substantiates and refutes many existing views in this treatise regarding the nature and position of texts of dharmaśāstra. He draws logical strength from many ancient commentators like Bhāruci and Medhātithi to Govindarāja and Kullūka Bhaṭṭa. He quotes in proper context the required statements from epics, purāṇas and other ancient Hindu texts.

This book will definitely be a much read and discussed one in academic circles in coming years both by those who like *Sanātana Dharma* and those who criticise it. I congratulate and thank Nithin Sridhar for this wonderful treatise.

**Prof Madhusudan Penna,**
Professor of Sanskrit, Dean,
Kavikulaguru Kalidas Sanskrit University,
Ramtek, Maharashtra

The Mānava Dharmaśāstra, also known as Manusmṛti or the Laws of Manu, is a Sanskrit text of the dharmaśāstra tradition. This is the most popular text, which was followed in India till two centuries before. From twentieth century, however, it was unnecessarily and wrongly caught in debates over a few verses; it was widely criticised and even burnt. Therefore, a scholar undertaking its translation and analytical interpretation needs to gather courage to face the uproar in society. The young critical thinker and author Nithin Sridhar has taken up this challenge and has presented the first four verses of Manusmṛti.

He has discussed at length the authorship of the text,

its value as a dharmaśāstra text, its authoritativeness, *prāmāṇya* and its presentation. The scholar has adopted the age-old Indian methodology of *anubandhacatuṣṭaya* and has discussed about the *adhikārin* of the author at the beginning, stating that Manu was the most suitable person to be approached by the gods for laying the code of conduct for human beings.

The presentation consisting of the original Sanskrit verse, its word-by-word meaning, free-flowing English translation, analysis of the content and discussion, is the most scientific and systematic method. Quotations from the commentators of Manusmṛti like Medhātithi, Kullūka, Govindarāja and other smṛti texts by Parāśara, Yama, etcetera have enriched the discussions. The appendix taking into consideration Surendra Kumar's Viśuddha Manusmṛti is commendable. Translating the entire Manusmṛti in this manner is a humongous task, a life-long project, perhaps. I wish Nithin all the very best and I hope this book will be a bestseller in the coming days!

**Prof Gauri Mahulikar,**
Academic Director,
Chinmaya International Foundation

Nithin Sridhar has brought this praiseworthy commentary upon the initial ślokas of the Mānava Dharmaśāstra at a time when new readings on classical texts are marginal, and above all, a new reflection on dharmaśāstra has been very rare. Here, Nithin strives to combine the traditional commentarial approach with contemporary text-critical perspectives, examining many of the claims advanced by current scholars. Not too long ago, dharmaśāstras dominated the sphere of *dharma* discourse, with the disciplines of *Vedānta* and Yoga limited to the quest for liberation from *Samsara*. Dharmaśāstras interacted with and influenced the making of secular law and guided people on moral and ethical issues. By revitalising the discourse on dharmaśāstra, I believe Nithin's work will invite a fresh conversation on the converging domains of secular and religious laws and engage on various issues of ethics that overlap jurisprudence.

**Sthaneshwar Timalsina,**
PhD, Professor, San Diego State University

*Chatuh Shloki Manusmriti* written by Shri Nithin Sridhar is an authentic, well-researched, scientifically and structurally expressed work on the first four ślokas of the Manusmṛti. It is evident that Nithin Sridhar has put in a lot of effort and spent a significant amount of time researching and understanding the intention of the *ṛṣis*. Manusmṛti is among the many *Sanātana* works that have been popularised as works of oppression and dogma by anti-Sanātana forces for extended periods. A well-researched and written work was needed for a more extended period. I congratulate Nithin Sridhar and express my gratitude for taking up such a herculean task of documenting the real intention of the ṛṣis as a follower of Sanātana *Dharma*. I wish Nithin comes up with more such works which could guide the younger generation. May *Parameśvara* guide him in his quest! *Jaya Jaya Śaṃkara Hara Hara Śaṃkara*!

**Vidwan Dr Jammalamadaka Srinivas,**
Scholar – IKS Courses,
Siddhanta Knowledge Foundation

Nithin Sridhar is one of the most important writers on Hinduism in English today. He is able to, with courage and clarity, portray the traditionalist *śāstraic* Hindu perspective in a modern context in clear, accessible English. This is laudable and necessary. This book is perhaps Sridhar's most important work to date. There isn't a more potent lightning rod for debate concerning Hinduism today than the mere mention of the Manusmṛti, a text that has been subject to gross misinterpretation and misunderstanding in terms of its societal and religious role and relevance. This book painstakingly details the evolution and transmission of the text, providing a compelling argument for the fundamental integrity and coherence of the text. Sridhar offers an elaborately detailed, word-by-word translation and explanation of the first four verses based on traditional commentaries. This is a great introduction to the text in English for those who may not be familiar with it.

**Aditi Banerjee,**
Author, Speaker & Attorney

Nithin Sridhar's book raises crucial questions to the field of Hindu Studies. Sridhar makes persuasive arguments about the authorship and structure of Manusmṛti, one of the most important dharmaśāstras we have today. His understanding of the significance of *dharma* in Hinduism is on point. If we truly understand the first four verses of Manusmṛti, then we will not be validating many of the questions that Hindu Studies ask today. Sridhar's comments on *varṇa* are in order since the dharmaśāstras' main concern is *varṇāśrama-dharma*. A great read for novices and scholars alike!

**Dr Sushumna Kannan**
Scholar-In-Residence, INDICA

# Foreword

This is a remarkable work that sets out to make observations in English in the traditional *vyākhyā/ṭīkā* style followed in Sanskrit writing for many centuries in India. Besides reflecting a respect for tradition, this sort of commentary is best suited for analysing the whole of the text synchronically along with the scholarship available on it so far.

Nithin Sridhar begins with discussing the problems of the origination, transmission, and authorship of Manusmṛti. He then moves to the three issues which have been wrangled upon too often: 1. Is the text a patchwork or a careful construction? 2. Place and function of smṛtis and dharmaśāstra in Hindu worldview 3. Decoding Manusmṛti: Some pointers to make sense of dharmaśāstra texts.

Needless to say, all these questions and the many debates about the authorship and validity of the textual recensions are initiated by Western scholarship conditioned by their familiarity with Greek, Roman, and medieval European texts. In these texts, the author of a given text is usually a single person. He is often locatable in a known time span and region. It is the individualised nature of the text that reflects the mind of a known person. The author, thus, may belong to a school of philosophical thought or be a known disciple of an earlier master, but nevertheless he is a distinct individual and thus a recognised historical figure.

In contrast to the authors of the classical Greco-Roman and medieval Christian traditions, the texts of ancient India emanate, not from an individual author but from śāstra traditions. In India, it was not the person or the individual scholar but an area of knowledge or a discipline (śāstra or *lakṣaṇagrantha*) which was important and in which the individual author located himself. He was not aiming to announce some fresh and distinct observations in the area of study but was merely offering a variation of information on a body of scholarship (in a specific area such as medicine, theatre, poetics, sexuality and so on) that had been ongoing for a long time. Hence, whereas the *Nicomachean Ethics* is a personal vision of Aristotle on ethical issues, the Manusmṛti is the product of a school of scholars trained in preserving a tradition or *saṃpradāya* of ethics. Whereas Aristotle wished to be original and distinct from others in his vision, the *śāstrakāras* of Manusmṛti only wished to further embellish a tradition. Whereas Aristotle was concerned with analysing, defining and prescribing *eudaimonia* or how to achieve uninterrupted happiness, the Indian codifiers were largely descriptive of how people had evolved patterns of ethical behaviour, and how these norms alter as time passes.

While the authorial voice of the śāstrakāras was constantly upholding the eternal principles of *dharma* or *ṛta,* it was shown to be achieved through a moral conduct or *ācāra* which was an evolving and diverse process to be followed according to the needs of a specific time, place, and person. Where the moral codes of the Bible, Quran or Hadith are stuck in a time frame and do not provide for modification that can be justifiably adopted with changing environment, the Smṛti principles of varṇa and āśrama though based on unchanging principles/*siddhāntas*, uphold the view that conduct/ācāra under these very siddhāntas will vary according to place/*deśa* and times/*kāla*. The force of time and place/region or *loka* was so powerful that so many rules of conduct followed in specific regions and given the name of *lokācāra* were allowed to set aside the conduct as described in the Smṛtis and called *śāstrācāra*.

Nithin Sridhar thus reconciles many seeming anomalies that plague a modern investigator of Manusmṛti about multiple authorship and contradictions in the content of verses as found in the different recensions. He shows that a tradition of a particular śāstra over time does not mean random collection of ideas but a unified vision which upholds some well-defined ideals. Assuming that even if there were later contributors, these contributors did not make random additions suiting their whims but in accordance to the main thrust of the dharmaśāstras and Manu in particular. Nithin Sridhar has given in detail his reasons for believing that the main recension in which Manusmṛti was preserved belonged to the *Bhṛgu* tradition/saṃpradāya. Thus, it is this unified vision of Manu that needs to be deciphered and it is to be seen how it served the four aims/puruṣārthas. Modern Indians, under a pseudo-reformist zeal have fallen shy of doing this. A traditional format commentary will help to get over this modern syndrome.

Nithin Sridhar has also pointed out very ably the comprehensive nature of the text. Most discussions on smṛtis in general and Manusmṛti in particular keep harping on the hierarchy of *varṇas* as foundation of discrimination and inequality. The Euro notions of equality, liberty and fraternity as envisaged in post-industrial societies have made the ancient world of Hindus look like a monument of Brahminical tyranny over all other sections of society. As a result, apart from the sections on varṇa, all the other sections of Manusmṛti that begin with cosmology and go on to establish the concepts of *karma*, *dharma*, *pañcamahāyajña*/five obligations of an individual, four āśramas/stages of life, dispensation of justice, rules of inheritance and governance, marriage and household duties, renunciation and self-realisation/*ātmatuṣṭi* as instruments of making Hindu life meaningful are seen as not even worthy of a cursory glance, let alone any serious discussion.

While the present work has given a commentary on the first four verses of Manusmṛti, the discussion on nearly all the fundamental notions in all the twelve chapters is made through the defining and analysing of each and every word of the four ślokas. The four ślokas not only happen to contain the essential definitional terms, but they are part of a plan—writing such verses at the outset that would introduce the cardinal terms. This was the methodology of śāstra*s* and also of the commentators and no less of the able teachers who taught these śāstra*s* to their worthy disciples. Those few who have studied these texts in the traditional system from an authentic guru would be able to recognise this method.

Thus, that this work for sure will promote a deep understanding of Manusmṛti is a safe guess.

**Bharat Gupt**
Former Faculty, Delhi University
Fellow, Sangeet Natak Akademy
Trustee, Indira Gandhi National Centre for the Arts.

# Preface

> For the man performing the *dharma* laid down by the Śruti and the Smṛtis obtains fame here, and after death, unsurpassed happiness.
>
> The *Veda* should be known as the Śruti, and the dharmaśāstra as the Smṛti'; in all matters, these two do not deserve to be criticised, as it is out of these that *dharma* shone forth.
>
> **Manusmṛti 2.9-10**

There can be no proper understanding of *dharma* without a patient, dispassionate and in-depth study of dharmaśāstra proper aka smṛtis. This is a realisation that has dawned upon me after half a decade of engagement with Hindu textual tradition, especially on topics that come under the broad umbrella of *dharma*.

Before 2015, my engagement with Hindu textual tradition was limited to a few *Veda*ntic texts and perhaps some secondary literature on miscellaneous aspects of Hindu *dharma*. It was not that I was totally unaware of smṛtis or that I was utterly uninterested in *dharma*. It merely so happened that in the broad landscape of Hindu textual universe, I had simply focussed more on other aspects.

It was in the aftermath of the Sabarimala temple entry issue in 2015-16, when I began to research for my book *Menstruation Across Cultures: A Historical Perspective* (2018), that I realised that the epistemological, ontological, ethical, theological, and teleological basis of much of Hindu beliefs and practices lie in a genre of texts (*Śabda Pramāṇa*) called dharmaśāstras with Śruti and smṛtis at the core of it. Since then, whenever I have undertaken a research project that has a bearing on Hindu identity, religious beliefs, and socio-cultural practices—be it abortion,[3] *satī,*[4] adultery,[5] or homosexuality[6]—I have kept going back to the dharmaśāstras to gain clarity and access to proper epistemic tools to understand the Hindu worldview and its practices.

In the last few years there has been a growing recognition of the need to develop Indic *dṛṣṭi* or perspective on all matters and a serious attempt to revive Indic Knowledge Systems, but unfortunately dharmaśāstras continue to be ignored even on important political, socio-cultural, legal, and religious matters. As a result of this, on important matters concerning our society, matters which are strictly under the domain of *dharma* such as whether and to what extent should abortion be permissible, the legal age of marriage, whether homosexual unions constitute marriage, etcetera, the only dominant narrative in academic and popular discourse is the one borrowed from the West.

The only way to change this trend and pave way for the development of an Indic dṛṣṭi on matters concerning Indian society in general and *dharma* in particular, is to revive the study of dharmaśāstra textual tradition.

However, such a study cannot adopt a historicist approach that views smṛtis as relics of the past to be used to have better knowledge about the past. Instead, it must be a philosophical study of the dharmaśāstra by accepting the larger Hindu epistemological, ontological, and theological landscape within which it functions. It is only through such a philosophical study of dharmaśāstra on its own terms that we will be able to understand the principles of *dharma* and contextualise the same to address contemporary issues.

However, such a task is easier said than done. As one begins to engage seriously with dharmaśāstras, one will encounter several obstacles in the form of misinformation, prejudice, hatred, propaganda, and confusions which are prevalent in contemporary discourse. However, the greatest obstacle is the loss of familiarity with the language and style of presentation of the dharmaśāstra authors because of the extended periods of physical and mental colonialism.

This book attempts to clarify some of these doubts and confusions, especially those related to fundamental questions such as definition of *dharma*, place and function of smṛtis in Hindu textual universe, integrity and importance of Manusmṛti, etcetera and introduces the dharmaśāstra landscape to a lay reader so that one can then engage with these texts in a meaningful manner.

This book is divided into two sections followed by appendices. The first section is the 'Introduction' which contains three chapters namely, 'Origination, transmission, and authorship of Manusmṛti: Is the text a patchwork or a careful construction?', 'Place and function of smṛtis and dharmaśāstra in Hindu worldview' and 'Decoding Manusmṛti: Some pointers to make sense of dharmaśāstra texts.' They examine the fundamental questions about *dharma*, the role of smṛtis, the correct approach to studying the *dharma* texts, and the integrity and transmission of Manusmṛti.

The second section is a commentary on the first four verses of Manusmṛti that deal with *anubandha catuṣṭayam*—the four aspects of a text—namely, the subject-matter of a text, the fruit or utility of studying the text, the intended audience of the text, and the inter-relationship between the three. In this section, I have adopted the traditional technique of *bhāṣyas* or commentaries which involves a detailed word-by-word examination of each of the verses and an enunciation of all ideas and themes connected to the subject-matter of the particular verses. This methodology ensures that the present work though contemporary, is well anchored in the textual tradition and hence, must be seen as a contextualisation and contemporisation of the teachings of the long dharmaśāstra tradition, rather than a new innovation.

There are three appendices. Appendix I titled 'Hindu conception of Varṇa: A multidimensional approach' and Appendix II titled 'Antarprabhāva in Surendra Kumar's Viśuddha Manusmṛti: A critical examination in view of its professed revisionist interpretation' together examine the Hindu conception of Varṇa-*dharma*. Appendix III contains the Stutiḥ dedicated to Svāyambhuva-Manu along with its English translation by Śrī Kushagra Aniket.

Why a commentary on only four verses? There is a popular convention in Hindu textual tradition to write works focussing on only the opening verses. For example, we have *Brahmasūtra-Catuḥsūtrī* wherein only the opening four verses of *Brahmasūtras* are focussed upon.

Likewise, we have works dealing with opening four verses of *Bhāgavata Purāṇa* called *Catuḥślokī Bhāgavatam*. This book *Chatuh Shloki Manusmṛti* is a continuation of that tradition.

A work like this could not have been completed without many friends and well-wishers contributing to it in multiple number of ways.

First of all, I would like to thank my teacher Vidwan Sri Venkatraman Hegde of Maharaja's Sanskrit College, Mysuru, under whom I studied some select portions of Manusmṛti along with Kullūka Bhaṭṭa's commentary. This study was crucial and helped me in gaining clarity on many fundamental issues.

Many friends helped me at various stages. Vidwan Jammalamadaka Srinivas was my go-to person for clarifying many doubts on many crucial points, especially related to Mimamsa. Manjushree Hegde, Giridhar Sharma, Aditi Banerjee, and Satyan Sharma were among the early readers of the manuscript and many of their inputs were significant and have been incorporated in the book. Friends Manu Kashyap, Sudarshan KS, Pravin Nair, Jayaraman Mahadevan, Sushumna Kannan, Maitri Gowswami and Angirasa Shreshta have helped in different ways. Kushagra Aniket was kind enough to compose a Stutiḥ for Svāyambhuva-Manu for the book. I have been discussing the Manusmṛti with many friends on social media platforms both publicly and privately and these discussions have been very insightful and encouraging. I am very thankful to all of them.

I am also thankful to all the acharyas, scholars and public intellectuals who read the book despite their busy schedule and kindly shared a note endorsing the book.

I am very grateful to Dr Bharat Gupt, whom I have looked up to as a teacher-figure for many years now, for blessing the book with a foreword.

I am also grateful to Dr Bibek Debroy who has been very supportive of my work and whose untimely passing has left a deep scar in my heart. In his foreword, Dr. Debroy had expressed his wish that I would write a similar commentary on the entirely of Manusmṛti. It is my hope that I would be able to fulfill his expectation.

I am also thankful to Sri Hari Kiran Vadlamani, my mentor and boss at INDICA Center for Moksha Studies who has always been very supportive of all my work. A shout-out to the larger INDICA family which has provided me with an ecosystem to write, share, and promote my work.

I am thankful to my publisher, Renu Kaul Verma, and her wonderful team at Vitasta for bringing out this book.

I am thankful to my wife, Pratyasha, and my parents who have been a constant source of support and inspiration.

Finally, no work is possible without the blessings of Gurus and the Great Gods. My *sashtanga-pranams* to them.

**Nithin Sridhar,**
Mysuru

Section 01

# Introduction to Manusmṛti and the Larger Dharmaśāstra Tradition

Chapter 1

# Origination, Transmission, and Authorship of *Manusmṛti*: Is the Text a Patchwork or a Careful Construction[7]

## Introduction

Starting from western indologists such as George Bühler and E Washburn Hopkins in the nineteenth century to Patrick Olivelle and Wendy Doniger of our own times, modern scholarship has had a long engagement with the text of Manusmṛti. Though their engagement has been long and at many different levels, one thing which they are yet to come to terms with is the sheer size of the text as well as the wide range of the subject matter covered in them.

Modern scholarship has generally held that Manusmṛti, like many other Hindu texts such as the *Mahābhārata*, was composed gradually over a long period of time. The predominant view is that such a composition was accomplished by collating and patching together various proverbial verses, moral sayings, and legal adages that were floating in the society over many centuries by anonymous authors, compilers, and copyists (Olivelle, *Manu's Code of Law: A Critical Edition and Translation of the Mānava-Dharmaśāstra* 2005).

Hopkins (1885, 268), for example, expressed such a view way back in his 1885 publication titled 'On the Professed Quotations from Manu Found in the Mahäbhärata':

> I draw the conclusion that the Śāstraṃ [Manusmṛti] was in great part collated between the time when the bulk of the epic [Mahābhārata] was composed and its final completion, that previous to its collation there had existed a vast number of sententious remarks, proverbial wisdom, rules of morality etc. which were ascribed, not to this treatise of Manu at all, but to the ancient hero Manu as a type of godly wisdom. These I conceive to have floated about in the mouths of the people, not brought together but all loosely quoted as laws or sayings of Manu and these sayings were afterwards welded into one with the laws of a particular text called the Mānavas—a union natural enough, as the two bodies of law would then bear the same title, although the sect had no connection with Manu except in name...According to my theory, these Manu-verses found in the Mānava treatise were simply caught up and drawn from the hearsay of the whole Brahman world, keeping their form after incorporation with the Mānavas' text (emphasis mine).

Echoing a similar view almost a hundred years later in her Introduction to her 1991 translation of Manusmṛti, Wendy Doniger (1991) writes:

> The *Laws of Manu* encompasses contradictions that may indeed be ultimately 'insoluble', but not necessarily irreconcilable, nor are its attempts to reconcile them necessarily 'frenzied'. Given the historical background, it is not surprising that Manu expresses a number of

> different views on many basic points. Different parts of the text were added at different periods (the portions dealing with legal cases are generally regarded as the latest) and, in the recension that we have, some topics are split up and treated in several different places, or in what seem to us to be the wrong places.

She further calls the text a 'patchwork',[8] woven using scraps inherited from ancient sources.

We can summarise the predominant view of modern scholarship on the composition of Manusmṛti thus:

1. It was a gradual composition, spread over many centuries; different parts of the text being added at different times.
2. It was a collation from various sources, predominantly drawn from hearsay, proverbial wisdom and prevalent rules of morality and involved the work of a large number of anonymous compilers, editors, and copyists.
3. Different parts of the text have been designated excursions and later-day interpolations.

There are many gaps in this predominant view of the modern scholarship and how the Hindu tradition itself has received and understood the text. These gaps have largely arisen due to the sidelining of the evidence available within the Hindu tradition, be it in the commentary tradition, or in the form of textual evidence found in other Hindu texts.

This paper intends to address the problematic areas in the above delineated conclusions of the modern scholarship from an emic perspective. It will further contend that the extant text of Manusmṛti is a carefully created text having unitary authorship but with a long history of knowledge transmission of the subject-matter through successive abridgement in different schools of transmission prior to its composition in the current form.

In the first section, I carefully examine the evidence available within the extant text of Manusmṛti regarding its origination and composition. In section two and three, an examination of the evidence available in the larger Hindu textual tradition regarding the transmission of the śāstra attributed to Manu will be taken up. In section four, the general mechanism adopted across different branches of Hindu knowledge tradition will be examined through a comparative study of transmission in the knowledge traditions of *Kāmaśāstra*, *Vedānta*, and Manusmṛti. In section five, the question of authorship of Manusmṛti attributed to Manu will be explored. In section six, the narrative structure and the underlying deeper architecture of the text will be examined to establish Manusmṛti as a carefully constructed unitary text.

## Origination and composition of Manusmṛti: Evidence from within the text

In the extant text of Manusmṛti, we find an account about its origination and its composition in the very first chapter which speaks about cosmogony. After giving an account of the universe—its creation as well as its dissolution—the text notes in verse 1.58[9] that 'After composing this treatise [śāstra], he [Brahmā] himself in the beginning imparted it according to rule to me [Manu] alone; and I, in turn, to Marīci and the other sages[10] (Olivelle 2005).' The list of sages to whom Manu taught the śāstra is available in verse 1.35[11]—Marīci, Atri, Aṅgiras, Pulastya, Pulaha, Kratu, Pracetas, Vasiṣṭha, Bhṛgu, and Nārada. Then, in verse 1.59,[12] addressing a different group of sages who had approached Manu for instruction on dharma of all varṇas and mixed varṇas at the beginning of the extant text, Manu says: 'Bhṛgu here will relate that treatise to you completely, for this sage has learnt the whole treatise in its entirety from me (Olivelle 2005).'

A question which naturally arises at this stage, and which has been satisfactorily dealt with by the commentarial tradition is this: If Lord Brahmā is the composer of Manusmṛti, why is it attributed to Manu? Why is it even called Manusmṛti? Anticipating this question, Medhātithi (ninth or early tenth century CE), in his commentary on verse 1.58[13] of the extant text, gives two possible resolutions for this. One, that the term 'śāstra' which is said to be composed by Lord Brahmā does not refer to any particular text or treatise, but to the entirety of the subject of injunctions and prohibitions that is the subject-matter of the Smṛti-s (G Jha 1920). That is, it refers to the entirety of the subject-matter of dharmaśāstra and not to a specific text. Second, that just as the *Veda*, despite being eternal and apauruṣeya, has sections referred to by names of ṛṣis such as Kaṭha; so also this śāstra can be referred to as Manusmṛti, though it originated from Brahmā (G Jha 1920).

In other words, the attribution of the text to Brahmā is merely in the sense of 'origination' of the entirety of the subject-matter of dharmaśāstra and 'not' in the sense of 'composition' of a particular text.[14] Brahmā is the apauruṣeya originator of all knowledge including the knowledge about dharma, while Manu is considered as the pauruṣeya composer or author of the particular śāstra attributed to Manu. Further, the account makes it clear that though Manu had originally taught the śāstra to not just

Bhṛgu, but to nine other sages as well, the extant text that is available to us has come down to us in the recension of or in the line of transmission from Bhṛgu. It may be prudent to note here that the Manu to whom the extant text attributes its authorship is Svāyambhuva-Manu and not the other well-known Manu-s.

We will take up the question of pauruṣeya authorship attributed to Manu and what it implies at a later stage.

## Different recensions of *Manusmṛti*: Evidence from Mahābhārata and Purāṇas

From the Mahābhārata and different purāṇas, we come to know that the śāstra on dharma has been transmitted over the ages through different schools.

In the Mahābhārata *Śānti parva*, Chapter 59, for example, it is revealed that the original work of Brahmā on dharma, artha and kāma consisted of one hundred thousand chapters. This was then subsequently abridged into 10,000, 5,000, 3,000 and 1,000 chapters respectively by Śiva, Indra, Bṛhaspati and Kavi/Uśanas (Debroy 2013). Again in Chapter 322 of the same Śānti parva, it is narrated how Svāyambhuva-Manu along with seven other sages (Marīci, Atri, Añgiras, Pulastya, Pulaha, Kratu and Vasiṣṭha) composed a grand treatise promulgating the dharmas in one hundred thousand verses with the guidance of the supreme being Nārāyaṇa himself, and how at a later period, Uśanas and Bṛhaspati composed their own works on the subject based on this treatise of Svāyambhuva-Manu (Debroy, The Mahabharata, Volume 9 2015). Since, both the accounts mention Uśanas and Bṛhaspati, most likely they refer to a particular school of transmission, which starts with the supreme being (conceived either as Brahmā or as Nārāyaṇa) and Svāyambhuva-Manu and was then transmitted through successive abridgements of the śāstra by Śiva, Indra, Bṛhaspati and Uśanas. The latter account which mentions Uśanas and Bṛhaspati as composing their own treatises with the guidance of and by quoting from the treatise of Svāyambhuva-Manu may point towards abridgement being not just an act of cherry picking of select verses from the previous larger work, but instead as a new creation, which is new in its form and presentation, but presents the sum total of the subject-matter of the larger work in a nutshell.

In the *purāṇas* also, we find evidence of the presence of different schools of transmission of the śāstra of Svāyambhuva-Manu. In a verse[15] attributed to *Bhaviṣya-Purāṇa* by Hemādri Paṇḍit (thirteenth century CE) in his magnum opus *Caturvarga Cintāmaṇi* as well as in other well-known works on dharma like *Saṃskāra Mayūkha* (Kane 1930, 138) and the same verse attributed to *Skanda-Purāṇa* by Rao Saheb VN Mandlik (1880, xlvii), it is mentioned that there are four acknowledged versions[16] of *Svāyambhuva* śāstra composed by Bhṛgu, Nārada, Bṛhaspati and Aṅgiras. Further, the fact that the extant text of Manusmṛti mentions Manu as teaching the śāstra to ten sages clearly points towards the presence of multiple recensions and schools of transmission of the śāstra even if we sideline the narrative aspect of the account as being allegorical.

Thus, the Hindu tradition has retained a memory of the presence of different recensions and lines of transmission of the śāstra of Svāyambhuva-Manu, among which, the four mentioned in the purāṇas appear to be prominent ones. Among them, the extant text of Manusmṛti likely belonged to the recension of Bhṛgu.[17] This conclusion is not only evident from within the extant text itself, but also from the colophons of the available manuscripts of the text. We already saw how in verse 1.59, Manu says that the rest of the treatise would be narrated by Bhṛgu who has learned the śāstra in its entirety from Manu himself. Again, in verse 1.119, addressing the sages who had approached for instruction, Bhṛgu says: 'Just as, upon my request, Manu formerly taught me this treatise, so you too must learn it from me today (Olivelle 2005).' Moreover, the colophons of the available manuscripts of the extant Manusmṛti designate the text as Mānava Dharmaśāstra in the recension of Bhṛgu (Jolly, *The Minor-Law Books* Part 1 1889, xii).[18]

## Transmission of the *Bhṛgu* recension of *Manusmṛti:* Evidence from *Nāradasmṛti*

The opening preface of the *Nāradasmṛti* has an interesting account about the transmission of the śāstra of Svāyambhuva-Manu. It says in verse 2-5.[19]

> Holy Manu, after having thus (composed) that (book) in a hundred thousand ślokas, and in one thousand and eighty chapters, delivered it to the divine sage Nārada. He having learnt it from him, reflecting that a work of this kind could not be remembered easily by mortals on account of its size, abridged it in twelve thousand (ślokas) and delivered it to the great sage Mārkaṇḍeya. He having learnt it from him, and reflecting on the (limited duration and) capacity of human life, reduced it to eight thousand (ślokas), and delivered this (abridgment) to Sumati, the son of Bhṛgu. Sumati, the son of Bhṛgu, after having learnt (this book) from him and considered what human capacity had been brought

> down to through the (successive) lessening of life (in the four ages of the world), reduced it to four thousand (ślokas). It is this (abridgment) which Manes and mortals read, whilst the gods, *Gandharvas*, and other (exalted beings) read in extenso the (original) code, consisting of one hundred thousand (ślokas).[20]
>
> (Jolly 1889, 2-3)

It must be pointed here that what Jolly translates as 'son of Bhṛgu' is the term *Bhārgava*, which simply means a descendant of Bhṛgu. That is, Sumati Bhārgava more likely was a descendant in the lineage of Bhṛgu rather than a biological son.

In any case, what Nāradasmṛti narrates is the account of transmission of the śāstra of Svāyambhuva-Manu through successive abridgement by Nārada (12,000 verses), Mārkaṇḍeya (8,000 verses) and Sumati Bhārgava (4,000 verses) until it was reduced from a large corpus containing a hundred thousand verses to a short manual containing only four thousand verses.

Though Nārada is mentioned as one of the sages doing the abridgement, the account of transmission mentioned in the text does not refer to the line of transmission of the Nārada recension. This is because, Nāradasmṛti itself notes in verse 6 of the opening preface that his text is an exposition on the ninth chapter of the śāstra of Svāyambhuva-Manu and thus, clearly points out the departure of the Nārada recension from the mainstream recension of transmission of the śāstra of Svāyambhuva-Manu. I argue that this mainstream recension whose account of transmission through successive abridgement is mentioned by Nāradasmṛti is actually the Bhṛgu recension, whose final version is the extant text of Manusmṛti.

But, there are two issues with this hypothesis, which need to be addressed. One, the account of transmission mentioned in Nāradasmṛti does not mention Bhṛgu. Two, while Sumati Bhārgava abridged the śāstra to contain 4,000 verses, the extant text of Manusmṛti contains only 2,684[21] verses.

Regarding the first, while Nāradasmṛti's account of transmission does not mention Bhṛgu himself, it mentions Sumati Bhārgava, a descendant in the Bhṛgu lineage, thus indicating that the school of transmission referred to in the Nāradasmṛti is indeed the Bhṛgu recension of the extant text of Manusmṛti. Further, Nāradasmṛti notes that the original śāstra of Svāyambhuva-Manu contained twenty-four sections and gives a list of these sections, which clearly correspond to the topics dealt with in the extant text of Manusmṛti (Jolly 1889).[22] Then, in verse 5[23] of the opening preface, Nāradasmṛti mentions that the opening verse in this śāstra of Svāyambhuva-Manu as transmitted through the successive abridgement by Nārada, Mārkaṇḍeya and Sumati Bhārgava reads thus: 'This universe was wrapped up in darkness, and nothing could be discerned. Then the holy, self-existent Spirit issued forth with his four faces (Jolly 1889).' This clearly corresponds to verses 5-6[24] of the first chapter of the extant Manusmṛti, with the first four verses providing narrative plot and the actual discourse beginning with verse 5. Also, as Jolly (1889, xiv) notes, the forensic law, which according to Nāradasmṛti, formed the ninth chapter of the original śāstra of Svāyambhuva-Manu corresponds to the discussion on law and judicature in the eighth and ninth chapter of the extant text of Manusmṛti.

Thus, we can clearly see that the account of

transmission through successive abridgement mentioned in the preface of Nāradasmṛti is actually an account about the transmission of the Bhṛgu recension of the extant text of Manusmṛti. The omission of Bhṛgu in the transmission account given by Nārada was perhaps due to the fact that the account only mentioned the names of sages who carried out the abridgement of the text in the Bhṛgu recension and not the entirety of *paramparā*[25] and all the sages, teachers, and others who were part of the process of transmission.

Regarding the second, i.e., the mismatch between the number of verses in the extant text of Manusmṛti and the abridgement of Sumati Bhārgava, scholars have expressed a variety of opinions. While Jolly (1889, xiv) has called the number 4,000 attributed to Sumati Bhārgava as a 'rough statement of the actual extent of the Manusmṛti', Kane (1930, 156) opines: 'When Nārada mentions the tradition that Sumati Bhārgava compressed the vast work of Manu into 4,000 verses, he is somewhat obscurely hinting at the truth. The extant Manusmṛti contains only about 2,700 verses. Nārada probably arrived at the larger figure by including the verses attributed to *Vṛddha-Manu* and *Bṛhan-Manu*.'

But, both these opinions are expressed with an assumption that the account of transmission narrated in the Nāradasmṛti is merely allegorical and is at best a 'rough statement' or 'obscurely hinting' at some truth. On the other hand, we have argued in this chapter for taking the native accounts of knowledge transmission as well as the memory of such transmissions available within the tradition more seriously. Proceeding along this line of approach, if we take the abridgement of 4,000 verses done by Sumati Bhārgava as a statement of fact and not merely an approximation, then there are only two ways we can account for the presence of only 2,684 verses in the extant text. One, to admit that there was a further abridgement of the Manusmṛti, which was not recorded in the extant text of Nāradasmṛti. Two, to admit that the extant text is same as the text abridged by Sumati Bhārgava, but has lost around 1,300 verses during transmission over centuries. The former seems less likely, since, the extant text of Nāradasmṛti is clearly posterior to the extant text of Manusmṛti, for otherwise, it could not have included an account about the transmission of knowledge in the mainstream Bhṛgu recension. Moreover, scholars like Jolly (1889) have established through a comparison of both the texts that Nāradasmṛti is posterior to Manusmṛti.[26] This leaves us with the latter possibility that the extant text is indeed the text abridged by Sumati Bhārgava, which has lost around 1,300 verses during its transmission before it was, in its current form, preserved by the commentary tradition.[27]

## General transmission of Indic Knowledge: Evidence from *Kāmaśāstra* and *Vedānta*

To better understand and appreciate the transmission of the śāstra of Svāyambhuva-Manu through different recensions and successive abridgement, let us briefly study how knowledge transmission in general is carried out in Indic tradition. For this purpose, let us look into the transmission of knowledge in two subject areas: Kāmaśāstra and Vedānta.

In Vātsyāyana's Kāmasūtra, we find an account about the origination and transmission of Kāmaśāstra. It says that *Prajāpati,* the lord of all creatures, after creating mankind, composed a treatise in a hundred thousand chapters for imparting instruction about dharma, artha and kāma (verse 1.1.5).[28] While Manu expounded upon the dharma portion and Bṛhaspati enunciated upon the artha portion, Nandī—the companion of Mahādeva—composed a treatise with a thousand chapters on kāma (verse 1.1.6-8).[29] Later, *Śvetaketu*, the son of Uddālaka, abridged this text into 500 chapters (verse 1.1.9).[30] This was further abridged into 150 chapters by Bābhravyaḥ[31] of Pāñcāla region who arranged it under seven heads (verse 1.1.10)[32]—*Sādhāraṇa* (General remarks), *Sāṃprayogika* (Amorous advances), *Kanyā-saṃprayuktaka* (On choosing a wife), *Bhāryādhikārika* (On a wife's duties and rights), *Pāradārika* (Relationship with wives of other people), *Vaiśika* (On courtesans), *Aupaniṣadikaiḥ* (On the arts of seduction, tonic medicines, and occult practices). Each of these seven themes were later individually taken up and elaborately dealt with by Cārāyaṇaḥ, Suvarṇanābhaḥ, Ghoṭakamukhaḥ, Gonardīya, Goṇikāputraḥ, Dattakaḥ, and Kucumāra respectively (verse 1.1.11-12).[33] Then, with passing time, Vātsyāyana's *Kāmasūtra* notes that owing to the creation of separate works on individual themes, these works were on the verge of being lost, and they had also lost the larger vision of the overall concept (verse 1.1.13-14).[34] Further, Bābhravyaḥ's comprehensive treatment of the subject had become inaccessible owing to the difficulties in its study arising due to its length (verse 1.1.14). To address these issues, Kāmasūtra notes that Vātsyāyana decided to abridge the work of Bābhravyaḥ (and others) into a short easily accessible volume in the form of Kāmasūtra (verse 1.1.14).

This account is very instructive by its parallel to the transmission through successive abridgement of the Dharmaśāstra of Svāyambhuva-Manu and the eventual composition of the extant text of Manusmṛti. Vātsyāyana's Kāmasūtra by its own account of its origination and composition is not an independent text standing in isolation. It is in fact a result of a long tradition of transmission of Kāmaśāstra through successive abridgement and expansion. From Nandī till Bābhravyaḥ, the Kāmaśāstra underwent successive abridgement. Then, through authors like Cārāyaṇaḥ and others, the said śāstra underwent expansion. Finally, as Vātsyāyana himself admits, since the expansion had become too bulky and hence difficult to read, he created a new abridged text in the form of Kāmasūtra. Post-Vātsyāyana, there was another phase of expansion of the Kāmaśāstra, not only in the form of Yashodhara's commentary *Jayamaṅgalā*, but also through the creation of new independent works like *Dattakasūtra* of King Mādhava II, *Ratirahasya* of Kokkoka, *Ratiratnapradīpikā* of King Devarājā and many others, all of which brought new insights into the knowledge field of kāma, but at the same time stood firmly on the shoulders of previous tradition. Works like Ratiratnapradīpikā of King Devarājā can in fact be considered as a summarised presentation of a few key aspects of the entire Kāmaśāstra tradition. Each text created in such a transmission of Kāmaśāstra, be it in the abridgement phase or in the expansion phase, is a new text, but the śāstra it expounds has been transmitted and received through a long lineage of transmission over a very long period. In other words, each person, be it an author of an independent work, or a commentator, or a person carrying out abridgement, all of them built upon received tradition, but more importantly also brought in their own new insights, latest findings, and new aspects of knowledge into the field. It is through such a complicated process of transmission that the śāstra tradition continues to remain ever flourishing and relevant to its immediate present.

This becomes even more evident in the transmission of *Vedānta*-śāstra. The *Upaniṣad*-s, which are the source texts of *pramāṇa* are very extensive and difficult to understand for the untrained. Bādarāyaṇa Vyāsa composed *Brahmasūtra* by condensing the teachings of the Upaniṣads into a concise format of sutras. Then, Ādi Śaṅkarācārya wrote his celebrated *bhāṣya* on the Brahmasūtra, thus elaborately treating the subject matter. On this bhāṣya, Vācaspati Miśra wrote his monumental sub-commentary *Bhāmatī* thereby further expanding upon the subject. Bhāmatī itself has a commentary titled *Vedānta-Kalpataru* by Amalānanda, which in turn has another commentary by Appayya Dīkṣita called *Kalpataruparimala*. There have been many other independent works like *Sarva-Vedānta-Siddhānta-Sārasangraha* of Ādi Śaṅkarācārya, *Vedānta-Sārasangraha* of Anantendra Yatī, and *Vedānta-Saṃgraha* by Rāmarāya Kavi, which have presented the entirety of Vedānta-śāstra in a very concise format. Thus, we can see both condensation and expansion phases in the transmission of Vedānta-śāstra as well.

It is important to note here that this condensation and expansion could either refer to condensation of a treatise in the form of abridgement and expansion of a treatise in the form of commentary and sub-commentaries; or it could refer to condensation of the general subject matter in the form of summarisation of the salient features of a particular knowledge field and expansion in the form of newer independent works detailing particular aspects of the knowledge field.[35] Further, while we notice a definite trend of condensation and expansion phases following each other successively resembling an 'hourglass', it may not always be the case. They can easily be happening in parallel as well.[36] All these various trends are intimately linked together making the Indic system of transmission complex, but very comprehensive.

In Figure 1 below, we have given a simplified representation of the transmission of knowledge in Kāmaśāstra, Vedānta-śāstra and Svāyambhuva-Manu's Dharmaśāstra tradition. We can see how in each of these knowledge fields, there are successive phases of condensation and expansion, thus forming an hourglass pattern with the extant texts available to us, be it Vātsyāyana's Kāmasūtra, Brahmasūtra or the extant text of Manusmṛti, forming the central narrow-neck. Just as in the case of transmission of Kāmaśāstra of Nandī where Vātsyāyana's Kāmasūtra is the oldest available text, so also in the transmission of the Dharmaśāstra Svāyambhuva-Manu in the Bhṛgu recension, the oldest available text is the extant text of Manusmṛti. Further, we can easily make out the complexity of the transmission process and how the condensation-expansion process is employed for the transmission of both subject-matter of a śāstra as well as a particular text or its recension. Also, except for the Vedānta tradition, wherein the Upaniṣads are still easily accessible; neither in the Kāmaśāstra tradition nor in the case of Dharmaśāstra of Svāyambhuva-Manu, older works i.e. works which fall in the upper-portion of the hourglass pattern are available. Further, both, commentaries on authoritative works as well as newer independent works, have performed the role of expansion of a particular śāstra—with respect to both subject-matter and a particular text. In many a sense, newer independent works building upon the subject-matter of a particular śāstra can be considered commentaries in the sense that they explore and expand the existing subject-matter.[37]

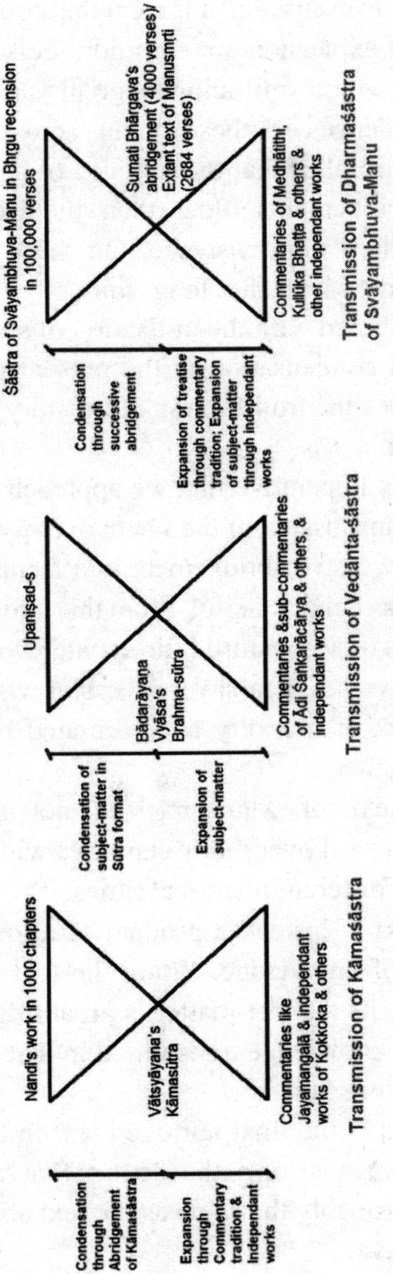


Transmission of Knowledge in Indic Tradition

Figure 1

From the above discussion, it is clear that condensation, abridgement, and expansion are common tools employed in Indic tradition to transmit knowledge in various fields. The wide prevalence of these tools across different knowledge fields implies that the absence of accessibility to texts and abridgements older than the extant texts does not prove their non-existence. On the other hand, the retained memory of the long line of tradition of transmission combined with the utilisation of similar tools of expansion and condensation in the present provides a strong indication of the truthfulness of memory preserved in native tradition.

Therefore, it is imperative that we approach the native accounts of the transmission of the śāstra of Svāyambhuva-Manu through successive abridgement as a factual account and not dismiss it as being fanciful. From this it follows that:

a. The extant text of Manusmṛti is not a patchwork created from floating verses, hearsay, proverbial wisdom, and prevalent rules of morality as speculated by Bühler, Hopkins and others.
b. The extant text of Manusmṛti is not a gradual composition spread over many centuries with different parts added at different historical times.
c. The extant text is instead a product of a long line of transmission of knowledge. While the text itself is a fresh creation, its subject-matter is an abridgement of the entirety of knowledge transmitted in that particular school of transmission.
d. The extant text is the final abridged text in the Bhṛgu recension of transmission of the śāstra of Svāyambhuva-Manu and is probably the same as the text abridged by Sumati Bhārgava.

## Authorship and Authorial Voice: *Manusmṛti* as a text of Unitary Authorship

The question of authorship is one of central bearing for understanding the composition of Manusmṛti.

In the preceding sections, based on the available textual evidence, we established how the extant text of Manusmṛti is a text composed as an abridgement of the śāstra of Svāyambhuva-Manu transmitted in the recension of Bhṛgu through a process of successive abridgements over a very long period of time. We also explored the identification of the anonymous author narrator, who does not directly appear in the extant text, and noted how it is very likely that this anonymous author is none other than Sumati Bhārgava mentioned in the Nāradasmṛti. Thus, if the extant text of Manusmṛti has not been produced in layers at different periods of time as alleged by many Indologists and is instead a text of unitary authorship as upheld by Indic tradition, how then should we understand the pauruṣeya authorship attributed to Svāyambhuva-Manu and by extension to Bhṛgu?

While the Indic tradition answers this question by considering Svāyambhuva-Manu and Bhṛgu as ṛṣis or divine seers who were manifested by Brahmā and Svāyambhuva-Manu respectively[38] and who in reality were the composers and early teachers of this śāstra; the modern scholarship has rejected this pauruṣeya authorship attributed to Svāyambhuva-Manu and Bhṛgu as merely an apologetic endeavour to portray the extant text as authoritative by attributing it a divine origin.[39] Since there is no way of verifying independently the truth or falsity of these accounts in a historical sense, we must consider these accounts as 'apodictic truth' i.e. 'it is so because it is said that it is so'[40] as suggested by Mircea Eliade (1959, 95) in his phenomenal work, *The Sacred and the Profane.*

Since the attribution of pauruṣeya authorship primarily to Svāyambhuva-Manu and by extension to Bhṛgu is an 'apodictic truth', a question that arises is whether there is a meaningful alternative approach for understanding the issue of authorship, without having to indulge in either asserting or denying the existence of either Svāyambhuva-Manu or Bhṛgu.

Fortunately for us, we do have such a framework, which has been extensively used by scholars like Alf Hiltebeitel for understanding the authorship of Mahābhārata attributed to Sage Vyāsa.

Distinguishing the real authors or composers of Mahābhārata from Sage Vyāsa, who is posited as performing the author function within the text, Alf Hiltebeitel writes:

> Vyāsa gives presence to authorial claims, processes, and literary experiments *in* the text. So does Vālmīki...The Mahābhārata poets have provided us not only with a fictional omniscient author, but *two* 'unreliable narrators' (Booth 1983: 158–159, 271–274, 295–296) as its main oral performers, two narrators (Saṃjaya and Bhīsma) given the 'divine eye' tọ handle two immense stretches of text, and various other authoritative sources, mainly Ṛsis.
>
> (Adluri 2011, 22-23)

He further notes at another place: 'The "bard" and all the others who figure in the epic's three frames are fictions of the text: fictions, let me propose, of real *Brahman* authors who must have enjoyed creating them in some complex image of themselves (Hiltebeitel 2001, 101).'

That is, according to Hiltebeitel, Vyāsa is a 'narrative

fiction'[41] in whom the 'composing committee (of Mahābhārata) cloaked its ultimate authorial voice'.[42] For him, the references to Vyāsa as the author as well as the allusions to the orality of the text mentioned within the text, are both 'literary tropes' used for conveying teachings about dharma.[43] Further, he posits Śuka, the enlightened son of Vyāsa as an 'evocative representation'[44] of Mahābhārata itself.

Whether one agrees with Hiltebeitel's characterisation of Vyāsa as fiction or not, the framework used by him for understanding authorship and authorial voice is quite ingenious and resourceful for approaching the question of pauruṣeya authorship of Indic texts, including the Manusmṛti. After all, as Hiltebeitel notes, the emergence of 'author function-s' with the 'individualisation of the authors—divine, fictional, or otherwise—first takes on literary proportions in early post- and para-Vedic smṛti texts… (Adluri 2011, 21-22).'

Applying this framework to Manusmṛti, we can distinguish between the actual author of the extant text, who we have identified as Sumati Bhārgava, and the author function performed by Svāyambhuva-Manu and Bhṛgu to whom the text's authorship is attributed. While, at one level, Svāyambhuva-Manu and Bhṛgu represent the authorial voice of the actual author of the extant text; at another level, the very choice of Svāyambhuva-Manu and Bhṛgu to represent the authorial intention and perform the author function can be understood as a result of the preserved memory about the origins of the śāstra.

Considering the extensive evidence about the memory of the transmission of the śāstra of Svāyambhuva-Manu through different recensions available in the smṛtis and purāṇas that we examined before, it cannot be merely an accident or a coincidence that the author of the extant text chose Svāyambhuva-Manu and Bhṛgu as the authorial voice of the text and not any other deities, sages, or other divine or human beings mentioned in various Vedic texts, nor simply made up his own fictional character as attributed author. Further, within the extant text, the dynamics shown between Svāyambhuva-Manu and Bhṛgu is that of *guru* and *śiṣya* and the entire narrative structure in the first chapter has been created to stress upon the fact that the subject-matter enumerated in the extant text has been received through a long line of transmission in the guru-śiṣya relationship.

Thus, the pauruṣeya authorship attributed to Svāyambhuva-Manu and to Bhṛgu can be understood as evidence for preserved memory about the origination and the transmission of the śāstra, which imparts unitary authorship to the extant text at two levels:

At the level of composition of the extant text, where the author by employing Svāyambhuva-Manu and Bhṛgu for performing 'author function' has shown how the text is a careful construction and a work of single authorship, or at best a work undertaken by a committee within a short span of time.

At the level of śāstra being represented in the extant text, wherein the choice of authorial voices of Svāyambhuva-Manu and Bhṛgu represents the fact that the śāstra has been carefully preserved and transmitted through guru-śiṣya paramparā over a long period of time before its current composition in its abridged version. That is, the extant text has been abridged from a carefully preserved śāstra with its subject-matter having a unitary authorial voice, and not a patchwork compilation of floating verses.

Even if one were to ignore the available evidence

regarding the origination and transmission of the śāstra of Svāyambhuva-Manu through successive abridgement and in multiple recensions; even then, one would have to accept the first of the two implications mentioned above that by using the literary trope of introducing Svāyambhuva-Manu and Bhṛgu for performing author-functions, the extant text shows that it is a product of unitary authorship, a text which has been carefully created for instructing its readers on dharma.

## *Manusmṛti* as a Carefully Constructed Text: Evidence from the Architecture of the Text

The evidence for the extant text of Manusmṛti being a 'carefully constructed' text is available within the architecture of the text itself.

To begin with, the extant text of Manusmṛti, much like the Upaniṣads, and unlike the older *dharmasūtras,*[45] embeds a narrative structure in the form of a dialogue between the sages who approach for instructions and Svāyambhuva-Manu and Bhṛgu, who impart the teachings. It opens with this dialogue, and till the very end, the text maintains this narrative structure, with the sages reappearing twice, once with a sub-question as in verse 5.1-2[46] and then with a follow-up question as in verse 12.1[47], and Bhṛgu's authorial voice answering these questions. The voice of Svāyambhuva-Manu is brought forward again and again in the text through phrases like *manurabravīt*[48], *abravīn-manuḥ*[49], *manuḥ-svāyambhuvo 'bravīt*[50], *manoranuśāsanam*[51], or *avatīrmanuḥ*[52]. Olivelle (2005), in fact, considers the introduction of the narrative structure and the usage of ślokas instead of prose as the two innovations of the extant text of Manusmṛti.

Apart from the inclusion of a narrative structure, the text's architecture also incorporates 'transitional verses' that help the reader to make a smooth transition from one subject to another. These transitional verses are central to the very architecture of the text as they not only demarcate one theme from the other, but also help us to make sense of the larger picture. Olivelle (2005) believes that these transitional verses are original and integral to the text as against the division into twelve chapters which he considers later impositions. He further notes:

> Such a technique is unique to Manu; it is not used in the Dharmasūtras and sparingly, if at all, in the later Dharmasāstras. Note also the use of the verb *nibodhata* in most transitional verses; this manner of expression becomes a signature of Manu. This device was, I believe, an innovation conceived by Manu and provides an insight into the plan he had for his book. By following the trail of these transitional verses, we can uncover the overall plan and structure of the MDh [Manu-Dharmasāstra].
>
> (Olivelle 2005, 8)

Using these transitional verses, Olivelle (2005) recognises four major themes dealt with in Manusmṛti—cosmogony, sources of dharma, the duties of the four varṇas, and the concept of karma, rebirth and liberation. Arguing that such a comprehensive architecture of the text points to its unitary authorship either by a 'single gifted individual' or by a committee with a strong chairman, Olivelle (2005, 7) writes: 'A deep structure that runs through the entire book…could not have simply happened over time as the text was being put together by different individuals separated by centuries.'

Moreover, there is a deeper mimetic architecture that runs through the extant text of Manusmṛti that imitates the cosmic cycles of *sṛṣṭi* and *laya*[53]. For example, Manu's discourse on dharma begins with an account of sṛṣṭi at verse 1.5 and ends with an account of laya at verse 1.57. Similarly, Bhṛgu's discourse begins and ends with an account of sṛṣṭi and laya at 1.61-62 and 12.125, respectively.

These features—the inclusion of a narrative structure with Svāyambhuva-Manu and Bhṛgu performing author function, the employment of transitional verses to demarcate different themes and the embedding of a deeper mimetic architecture—clearly show that the extant text of Manusmṛti is a carefully conceived and constructed text.

## Conclusion

From the above discussion, we can conclude that the extant text of Manusmṛti is not a patchwork created out of floating verses extracted from different sources, but instead it is a carefully constructed text having a unitary authorship, and a product of a long line of transmission of the sāstra in the guru-śiṣya paramparā through successive abridgements and through multiple recensions.

Further, it has been demonstrated that the attribution of authorship of the text to Svāyambhuva-Manu and Bhṛgu is neither accidental, nor done with an intention to give a divine status to the text, but instead its inclusion in the narrative structure of the text is intentional and serves the purpose of recording the provenance, history, and transmission of the said sāstra.

Chapter 2

# Place and Function of Dharmaśāstra in Hindu Worldview[54]

## Introduction: Current Situation

Śāstras play a central role in Hindu tradition and society. However, due to the effects of colonialism, Hindus have become deracinated and have lost touch with this core aspect of our civilisation.

The deracination is so deep that while detractors of Hinduism with ideological agendas continue to use Hindu śāstras as a tool to undermine Hinduism, the response from the Hindu side has been clumsy, disoriented, and one that involves denouncement of our śāstras as not relevant and outdated.

A good example of this is how texts in the dharmaśāstra tradition, especially the Manu-Dharmaśāstra (popularly called Manusmṛti), are often blamed by the detractors of Hinduism as the root cause of every ill they can find in the current society. There are many such examples.

This narrative against Hindu śāstras is one which has been carefully cultivated and promoted in academia, media, and popular culture. However, unfortunately, the typical Hindu response to this intellectual attack on Hindu śāstras is that these texts are outdated and we as a society have moved forward by reforming ourselves!

We can routinely find in social media as well as in opinion pieces on media platforms the following assertions about Hindu śāstras in general, and about dharmaśāstras in particular:

a. Hinduism is a way of life. It is not a book-based religion like the Abrahamic religions.
b. Hindus are not bound to any texts; real dharma is in following tolerance and compassion. All religions teach these.
c. We must be flexible and forward looking and not bound to any tradition or texts as they lead to dogmatism and orthodoxy. Texts like Manusmṛti have no place in a civilised and cultured society.
d. Manu and other dharmaśāstra texts are smṛtis which are based on time and place and hence are outdated today and no longer relevant. Instead, our constitution is the Smṛti of today.
e. Smṛtis are not central to Hinduism. Instead, it is the *Veda*s and *Bhagavad Gītā* which are central to Hinduism. Therefore, what smṛtis say does not matter.
f. Most Hindus today keep Bhagavad Gītā at home and not dharmaśāstra texts like Manusmṛti. Therefore, what dharmaśāstras say has no relevance today. A Hindu intellectual has apparently done a Twitter poll to 'prove' this.[55]
g. All problematic assertions in smṛtis are later-day interpolations done by some wily *brāhmaṇas* who deserve the choicest of abuses and hence, these texts are not worth considering.
h. Manu was never held in high esteem, nor was his text ever important. It was the British who brought

Manusmṛti on the central stage and did great distortions to it as part of a colonial agenda.

i. There is a great need to sanitise and purify our texts by removing all such interpolations by wily Brahmins, the British, etcetera. For example: a book titled *Viśuddha* Manusmṛti' was brought out a few years ago as part of such a sanitisation project.

The root cause of such clumsy and disoriented response from the Hindu side, which often involves denouncement of our śāstras as not relevant and outdated, is the result of ignorance and confusion regarding the place and role of śāstras in Hindu Dharma, in particular the role and function of texts such as the Manusmṛti, *Yājñavalkyasmṛti,* etcetera which constitute a genre of texts collectively called as dharmaśāstras.

This chapter seeks to understand the place of dharmaśāstra texts in Hindu scheme of things.

## Dharmaśāstra: A Definition

The term dharmaśāstra contains two words: dharma and śāstra.

The term dharma can be variously understood to mean ethics, morality, law, justice, duty, righteousness and so on depending upon the context of its usage. In the context of an individual, dharma refers to duties and the righteousness of actions. In the context of a society, dharma refers to social harmony and morality. In the context of governance, dharma refers to law and justice and in the cosmic context, dharma refers to cosmic order and balance.

Literally, dharma means that which upholds. *Mahānārāyaṇa Upaniṣad* (79.7) states that dharma supports the whole cosmos and removes all sins.[56] Similarly, Lord Kṛṣṇa in Mahābhārata (*Karṇa Parva* 49.50) says that dharma is that which upholds all created beings.[57]

A more practical definition of dharma that explicitly explains what this 'upholding' means is found in *Vaiṣeśika Sūtra* 1.1.2, which says that an action which yields *abhyudaya* and *niḥśreyasa* (of all) is dharma.[58] Here, abhyudaya means 'material wellbeing' and niḥśreyasa means 'spiritual emancipation'. Therefore, in the context of an individual, all those actions which lead to one's overall wellbeing is dharma and the opposite, those that lead to fall, bondage, and sorrow of the individual, is *adharma*.

The term śāstra also has multiple meanings. According to major *Saṃskṛta* dictionaries:

1. It can refer to an order, command, precept, or a rule.
2. It can refer to teaching, instruction, direction, advice, or good counsel.
3. It can refer to any instrument of teaching, any manual or compendium of rules, any book or treatise, any religious or scientific treatise.

Dr Bharat Gupt (2016) in one of his talks defines śāstra as *śāstram iti śasanopāyam*—a śāstra is an instrument to create *śāsana* or order within an area of human concern. That is, the purpose of the śāstra is to create order and systematically present different aspects of a particular field of knowledge. Śāstra is thus, a scientific or a technical treatise which enumerates the fundamental principles governing a particular field, defines what success is, how to measure the same and how one can succeed in that field. Every śāstra is written with a *prayojana* (purpose) in mind, be it a *kalā* or *vidyā*. It investigates a continuous process of achievement in its chosen field. They are written for the practitioner with the purpose of making *prayoga* (practice) reliable.

In short, a śāstra can be understood as a reference to 'a body of teaching, scripture, science'. For example, *bhautikaśastra* – physics, *jīvaśāstra* – biology, *arthaśāstra* – science of politics and economics. It is a body of work which imparts knowledge about a field of study through the medium of words and sentences.

Combining dharma and śāstra, we get dharmaśāstra: a technical treatise on dharma i.e. a treatise which reveals what actions are dharma and hence beneficial to us and what actions are adharma and hence not beneficial. They tell us what actions lead to happiness and what leads to sorrow. Any text which fulfils these criteria can be called a dharmaśāstra. This view is in alignment with Bhagavān Kṛṣṇa's instruction in Gītā 16.24, where he says that the śāstras are the basis which determine what actions should be performed and what actions should be avoided.[59]

In his *Mīmāṁsā Śloka Vārtika* (*śabda pariccheda* Verse 4), Kumārīla Bhaṭṭa gives the following definition of śāstra which is most relevant to our discussion:

प्रवृत्तिर्वा निवृत्तिर्वा नित्येन कृतकेन वा |
पुंसां येनोपदिश्येत तच्छास्त्रमिति कथ्यते ||

(D Jha, 1979, 493)

*pravṛttirvā nivṛttirvā nityena kṛtakena vā |*
*puṃsāṃ yenopadiśyeta yacchāstramiti kathyate ||*

'Scripture' is the name given only to such 'words'—either caused or eternal—as lead, either to the activity or to cessation from activity of certain human agents.

(G Jha, Slokavartika 1900, 208)

That is, śāstra refers to those texts which reveal about activity either in the form of direction to perform something, or in the form of direction to cease from some activity. And such texts can be eternal, namely *Veda*, as well as created, namely, smṛtis, purāṇas, etcetera. Therefore, for Kumārīla Bhaṭṭa, śāstra specifically refers to that verbal testimony which teaches dharma in the form of stipulations and prohibitions.

Alternatively, the verse can be understood as saying śāstras are those which either lead one towards *pravṛtti* i.e. practice of dharmic action or towards *nivṛtti* i.e. renunciation of action for the sake of pursuing mokṣa. This is the interpretation adopted by Vācaspati Miśra in his Bhāmatī while commenting on *Brahmasūtra-Śaṅkara-Bhāṣya* on verse 1.1.4 where he cites this *Mīmāṁsā* verse.[60] As per this interpretation, śāstras are twofold: dharmaśāstra and *mokṣaśastra*.

Hindu tradition recognises eighteen *vidyās* (fields of knowledge) and sixty-four *kalās* (fields of arts/skills) and dharmaśāstra finds an explicit mention in the list. For example, *Viṣṇu Purāṇa* (verse 3.6.28-29) says:

अङ्गानि चतुरो वेदा मीमांसा न्यायविस्तरः। पुराणं धर्मशास्त्रं च विद्या ह्येताश्चतुर्दश। आयुर्वेदो धनुर्वेदो गान्धर्वश्चैव ते त्रयः। अर्थशास्त्रं चतुर्थं तु विद्या ह्यष्टादशैव तु।। (Upreti 2003, 352)

*aṅgāni vedāścatvāro mīmāṃsā nyāyavistaraḥ | purāṇaṃ dharmaśāstraṃ ca vidyā hyetāścaturdaśa | āyurvedo dhanurvedo gāndharvaśceti te trayaḥ | arthaśāstraṃ caturthaṃ tu vidyā hyaṣṭādaśaiva tu ||*

The eighteen vidyās are: four *Veda*s, six *Vedāṅgas (Śikṣā, Chandas, Kalpa, Jyotiṣa, Vyākaraṇa, Nirukta),*

*Mīmāṁsā, Nyāya,* Dharmaśāstras, *Purāṇas, Āyurveda, Dhanurveda, Gandharvaveda, and Arthaśāstra.*

If all texts that impart dharma can be called as dharmaśāstras in a broader sense, what are the principal texts that come under it?

Manusmṛti in verse 2.6 calls *Veda* as the very root of dharma and further in 2.10 says: 'The *Veda* should be known as the Śruti and the dharmaśāstra as the smṛtis; in all matters, these two do not deserve to be criticised, as it is out of these that dharma shone forth (G Jha 1920).'[61] That is, Śruti and smṛti are the primary texts that constitute dharmaśāstras. The term smṛti includes the six Vedāṅgas as well as other smṛti texts like those of Manu, Yājñavalkya, etcetera. To the list given by Manu, Yājñavalkyasmṛti (1.3) further includes purāṇas (including itihāsas), Nyāya and Mīmāṁsā texts.[62]

Therefore, all these texts constitute the source of knowledge for understanding dharma. To fully comprehend and appreciate the function of dharmaśāstra in understanding dharma, we must first understand Hindu epistemology or Hindu theory of knowledge which explains how knowledge about any object arises.

## Hindu Epistemology or Theory of Knowledge[63]

Epistemology i.e. the philosophical study of the nature, origin, and limits of human knowledge is a vast topic, but central to understanding any philosophical and theological school of thought. Hindu tradition has six *Āstika Darśanas* (viz. *Nyāya, Vaiśeṣika, Sāṅkhya, Yoga, Pūrva Mīmāṁsā,* and *Vedānta*) with each school having its own theories of knowledge.

While a detailed study of them is beyond the scope of this book, understanding some basic principles that define Hindu epistemology is necessary for understanding the purpose and function of śāstras in Hindu scheme of things.

The fundamental questions that epistemology deals with include:

*What is knowledge?*

*How is knowledge produced?*

*Whether the acquired knowledge is reliable or not?*

*And what determines the validity or otherwise of the acquired knowledge?*

In Hindu epistemology, when it is said that we have acquired knowledge/cognised an object, there are four elements involved in the process: The subject/knower called *pramātā* who perceives the cognitions. The object of knowledge called as *prameya*. The method or means through which the knowledge was acquired called *pramāṇa*. And finally, the knowledge itself. This knowledge is called *pramā* or valid knowledge/valid cognition if it is correct knowledge and *apramā* if it is invalid or erroneous knowledge.

The definition of pramā or valid knowledge is given in different ways in different darśanas. *Nyāya Darśana* for example defines pramā as true presentational knowledge (*yathārtha-anubhava*) which is definite and assured (*asandigdha*). *Vaiśeṣika Darśana* adds 'memory' as well to this definition given by Nyāya. *Sāṅkhya Darśana* defines pramā as the reflection of the self in the intellect as modified into the form of the object. In *Bhaṭṭa Mīmāṁsā*, pramā is defined as primary and original knowledge (*anadhigata*). *Prabhākara Mīmāṁsā* defines pramā as immediate experience (*anubhuti*). Vedānta (Advaita) defines pramā as knowledge that is original and uncontradicted by other means (*anadhigata-abhadita*). Simply put, pramā is knowledge of objects gained from a pramāṇa which is not contradicted by other pramāṇas. The Mīmāṁsā and Vedānta definitions are especially relevant as they are directly related to *Veda*. Nyāya definition is also likewise relevant as it forms the logical basis of all vidyās.

Hindu darśanas broadly accept six pramāṇas or sources of knowledge. Pramāṇa can be defined as the unique operative cause of pramā or valid knowledge. It is unique because, though for the generation of pramā, all the three, namely, pramātā, prameya, and pramāṇa are required, existence of pramātā or prameya in itself will not lead to pramā. However, existence of pramāṇa invariably will be accompanied by generation of pramā. Further, pramāṇa is the immediate antecedent from which knowledge flows. Therefore, pramāṇa is the special operating cause that gives rise to pramā or valid knowledge as opposed to general conditions that facilitate this.

The six pramāṇas identified in Hindu tradition are: *pratyakṣa* (perception), *anumāna* (inference), *upamāna* (comparison and analogy), *arthāpatti* (postulation, derivation from circumstances), *anupalabdhi* (non-perception, negative/cognitive proof) and śabda (word, testimony of past or present reliable experts). Of these, Nyāya Darśana accepts four: pratyakṣa, anumāna, upamāna, and śabda. Vaiseshika Darśana accepts only two: pratyakṣa and anumāna. Sāṅkhya Darśana accepts three: pratyakṣa, anumāna, and śabda. Prabhākara Mīmāṁsā accepts five pramāṇas: pratyakṣa, anumāna, upamāna, arthāpatti and śabda. Only Bhaṭṭa Mīmāṁsā and *Advaita Vedānta* accept all the six pramāṇas.

However, what is common to all the Āstika Darśanas irrespective of how they define pramā is their acceptance of śabda, especially what is available to us as *Veda*, as a pramāṇa that reveals true knowledge. Even Vaiśeṣika Darśana which accepts only two pramāṇas accepts śabda as valid but as part of anumāna itself.

## Śabda Pramāṇa: The Source of Knowledge in the Form of Words

Śabda literally means 'verbal knowledge'. It is the knowledge of objects derived from words and sentences. However, all verbal knowledge is not valid. Therefore, Nyāya Darśana defines śabda as 'valid verbal knowledge'.

*Nyāyasūtras* of Akṣapāda Gautama 1.1.7 defines 'word' or valid verbal knowledge as the instructive assertion of an *āpta*.[64] A trustworthy person is referred to as an āpta and Vātsyāyana in his commentary on the above verse defines āpta as one who possesses the direct and right knowledge of things and is willing to communicate these tenets in the exact way that he has realised.[65] Nyāya Darśana further notes that it is not the perception of the words which imparts knowledge of the objects, but it is the understanding of the meaning of those words and sentences which leads to knowledge of the objects. Therefore, pramā or valid knowledge arises when the correct meaning of the statements of the āpta is understood.

Mīmāṁsā Darśana on the other hand defines śabda pramāṇa as that which provides true knowledge of the objects derived from an understanding of the sentences. They classify śabda pramāṇa into two divisions: pauruṣeya and apauruṣeya. Pauruṣeya consists of words of trustworthy persons and apauruṣeya consists of words of the *Veda*.

Vedānta Darśana accepts śabda pramāṇa as a statement of an āpta and posits it as knowledge derived from an understanding of the sentences or propositions which assert a certain relation between things and is not contradicted in any way. Sāṅkhya Darśana likewise accepts śabda pramāṇa as being constituted by statements of trustworthy sources that give the knowledge of objects which cannot be known by perception and inference. For them, śabda pramāṇa specifically refers to *Veda*.

Rāmarāya Kavi notes in Chapter 3 of *Vedānta Saṅgraha* that śabda-pramā or correct knowledge of śabda arises from *āpta-vākya* (statement of the āpta) through the fulfilment of four conditions: (a) *ākāṅkṣā* or expectancy, (b) *yogyatā* or compatibility/fitness, (c) *āsattii* or proximity, and (d) *tātparya* or the intention of the speaker.[66] R Balasubramanian and S Revathy who have brought out an English translation of the text along with their annotations on the verses, explain the four conditions thus:

> Sentence, whether spoken or written, is made up of a group of words. Any combination of words will not make a meaningful or significant sentence. We can construe the meaning it conveys only if it fulfils the four conditions mentioned above. A word by itself cannot convey a complete meaning. Only when it is brought into relation with other words, it will be meaningful. The moment a word is uttered, it generates expectancy in the mind of the hearer. For example, when someone says 'bring', the hearer wants to know 'bring what?' The expectancy can be fulfilled only when another word is uttered by the speaker; then the meaning is complete. Secondly, the relation between the words should be such that there is compatibility (*yogyatā*) between them. If, for example,

one says: 'Cool it with fire,' the sentence does not convey any sensible meaning, because there is no mutual fitness between the words. The third condition says that the words uttered should be in close succession or proximity (*sannidhi*), one following the other. Spoken words, which are separated by long intervals of time, cannot convey any significant meaning. In the same way, written words cannot form a sentence if they are separated by long intervals of space. Lastly, one should construe the meaning of a sentence as intended by the speaker or writer. Stated differently, to understand the meaning of a sentence, one should take into consideration its *tātparya* or intention by looking into the context (*prakaraṇa*) in which it is spoken or written.

(Balasubramanian 2012, 49)

S K Ramachandra Rao in his book *Ṛgveda Darśana: Sāyaṇa's Ṛgabhāṣya-Bhūmikā* Volume 14 comments:

And the validity of verbal testimony is contingent upon three factors: the testimony is from a reliable authority (*āpta-vākyatva*); the testimony is derived from a scriptural source (*Śruti-mūlatva*); and the testimony is augmented by rational considerations (*yukti-mülatva*). Further, scriptural knowledge becomes authentic only when it is in perfect accord with the facilities of the speaker, the listener and the occasion; the speaker (*vaktṛ*) must not only know correctly but must have the will to communicate what he thus knows (*vivakṣā* and presupposing it, *vivakshitārtha-tattva-jñānam*); and his organs of observation and understanding must be efficient (*kāraṇa-pāṭavam*). The listener (*śrotṛ*) must be capable of understanding what the speaker

> communicates (*tattva-jñāna-yogyatā*); he must be willing to receive the knowledge out of his love and regard for the speaker (*vaktṛ-prīti-viṣayatā*).
>
> (S K Rao 2004, 106-107)

In short, śabda pramāṇa is a source of knowledge in the form of words and sentences wherein pramā or valid knowledge of objects arises from a correct understanding of the meanings of words and sentences subject to fulfilment of conditions like the verbal testimony being uttered by an āpta or trustworthy person, has its source in the *Veda*, is logically sound and relevant, and the listener is competent.

Nyāya Darśana classifies śabda pramāṇa into *dṛṣṭārtha* and *adṛṣṭārtha* on the one hand and into *vaidika* and *laukika* on the other hand. The former classification is enunciated in *Nyāyasūtra* 1.1.8[67] and is adopted by early *naiyāyikas*, whereas the latter classification is adopted by later naiyāyikas.

Dṛṣṭārtha refers to knowledge regarding perceptible objects. For example: If a person gives a description about the Himalayas, or about how good a book is, it is dṛṣṭārtha. It can be verified or falsified by empirical means. Adṛṣṭārtha refers to knowledge about imperceptible objects. For example: The *Veda* says, if one does a particular *yajña*, it results in the performer attaining *svarga* upon death. The results are not perceptible to our sensory organs and cannot be verified or falsified by empirical means. Likewise, laukika refers to knowledge about worldly issues and vaidika refers to the knowledge revealed by the *Veda*.

Vedānta Darśana accepts the classification of śabda pramāṇa into vaidika and laukika. Rāmarāya Kavi notes in Chapter 3 that *vaidika vākyas* are of three kinds: those related to *vidhi* or injunctions, those related to *niṣedha* or prohibitions, and those related to *Brahman* or ultimate reality. While vidhi and niṣedha belong to early portions of the *Veda*, the teachings about Brahman belong to the latter portions of the *Veda.*[68] Thus, *Veda* reveals two-fold objects of knowledge: dharma and Brahman. And these can be known through śabda pramāṇa in the form of *Veda* alone and not through any other pramāṇas.

All the Āstika Darśanas accept *Veda* as the ultimate śabda pramāṇa when it comes to understanding non-perceptible objects like dharma and Brahman. However, the way they understand the authoritativeness and trustworthiness of *Veda* is different. While Nyāya considers *Veda* as being authored by *Īśvara*, who is the most trustworthy source and hence without any faults or lacunae; Sāṅkhya, Mīmāṁsā and Vedānta consider *Veda* as apauruṣeya i.e. impersonal, one which exists eternally and has not been authored by any being—human or divine, and hence is without any fault or lacunae, and possesses self-evident validity (*svataḥ-pramāṇa*). Commenting on this, Satischandra Chatterjee writes:

> In the *Sāṅkhya-yoga* system too, we find a recognition of śabda or testimony as a valid method of knowledge. But, while in the Sānkhya, scriptural testimony is regarded as impersonal and therefore possessing self-evident validity, the Nyāya takes it as neither impersonal nor self-evidently valid. It holds that the scriptures have been created by God and require to be proved by reason as much as any other form of knowledge...According to the Nyāya, scriptural testimony is personal, since the *Veda*s have been created by the supreme person or God. For the Vedānta, it is impersonal inasmuch

> as God does not create but only reveals the contents of the *Veda*s, which are eternal truths independent of God. So also the *Mīmāmsākas* look upon the *Veda*s as a system of necessary truths or eternal verities which are independent of all persons and therefore purely impersonal in character. For the Naiyāyikas, the *Veda*s as a system of truths embody the will of God. They express the eternal reason of the divine being in the order of time.
>
> (Chatterjee 2015, 352-353)

## Manu and Other Smṛtis as Śabda Pramāṇa for Dharma

While *Veda* is the ultimate pramāṇa for understanding dharma as enunciated by Mīmāṁsā Sūtra 1.1.1,[69] and has been accepted as so by all the Āstika Darśanas, we find smṛti texts positing themselves and other similar texts as valid sources for understanding dharma as well. Manusmṛti in verse 2.6 and again in verses 2.9-10 posits both Śruti and smṛtis as pramāṇas for gaining correct knowledge or pramā about dharma.[70] Yājñavalkyasmṛti adds purāṇas, Nyāya and Mīmāṁsā texts to this list as well.[71] Manu 2.10 goes to the extent of saying that when dharmaśāstras or treatises that enunciate about dharma and adharma are mentioned, one must understand it as a reference to the smṛtis.[72] However, the smṛtis are neither apauruṣeya in the sense that Mīmāṁsā and Vedānta posit *Veda* to be, nor are they authored by Īśvara per se as understood by Nyāya.

How then does Hindu tradition establish the authoritativeness and trustworthiness of these smṛtis with respect to their teachings on dharma? The Āstika Darśanas put forward two main arguments to establish the authoritativeness and trustworthiness of the smṛtis as a śabda pramāna:

1. Smṛtis are teachings based on *Veda*s and hence they are valid, because *Veda* being apauruṣeya is always valid. This is the argument put forward by the Mīmāṁsākas.
2. Smṛtis are teachings of trustworthy ṛṣis like Manu, Yājñavalkya, and others who can be considered as āptas as they have directly perceived what constitutes dharma and what does not through yogic perception. This is the argument put forward by the Naiyāyikas.

Nyāya and Mīmāṁsā Darśana provide extensive arguments to prove the authenticity and validity of smṛtis as śabda pramāṇa.

Jayanta Bhaṭṭa, the ninth century Naiyāyika in his renowned philosophical treatise *Nyāya-Mañjarī*, devotes an entire section in book four to this question and quotes the arguments from both Nyāya Darśana and Mīmāṁsā Darśana to establish without doubt the validity of Manu and other smṛtis as a pramāṇa śāstra for knowing about dharma.[73]

Jayanta Bhaṭṭa says that as per Nyāya Darśana, smṛtis are valid because they have been revealed by āptas or trustworthy people like ṛṣis. Nyāya proves the trustworthiness of smṛtis in three ways (Freschi 2012, 10-15, 31-33, 37-38):

1. The ṛṣis have directly perceived dharma through yogic perception and are hence reliable.
2. Agreement of other exemplary people. Jayanta Bhaṭṭa defines exemplary people as those who belong to four varṇas and four *āśramas* and are very well known in the *Āryadeśa*.

3. Running a partial test where possible (as in assertions related to dṛṣṭārtha) to test whether the assertions are verifiable. Earlier Naiyāyikas utilised this method.

Jayanta Bhaṭṭa says that Mīmāṁsā Darśana on the other hand holds that smṛtis are valid because they are based on Śruti or *Veda*. The Mīmāṁsākas prove this in two ways (Freschi 2012, 10-15, 28-31):

1. **By using arthāpatti or postulation which is a valid pramāṇa:** Mīmāṁsākas note that the teachings of Manu and other ṛṣis cannot be based on error, doubt, etcetera which are apramā or invalid knowledge because what they teach is not invalidated by any subsequent cognition. Further, since what smṛtis reveal is unique and cannot be accessed through other pramāṇas like pratyakṣa, by arthāpatti we can arrive at the conclusion that smṛtis are based on *Veda*.
2. **By reference to the fact that those who practice *vaidika karmas* also practice the stipulations of smṛtis**: Mīmāṁsā successfully shows that smṛtis cannot have any source other than *Veda* and that it is not a product of *rāga-dveṣa* using arthāpatti pramāṇa.

Jayanta Bhaṭṭa then makes an important assertion that since both Śruti and Smṛti have been revealed by āptas who have directly perceived dharma (the former by Īśvara who is omniscient and the latter by ṛṣis through yogic perception), in case of apparent contradictions regarding any issue, their prescriptions must be taken as valid alternatives, rather than one superseding the other. Therefore, there are no real contradictions between the teachings of Śruti and Smṛti. Further, *Prabhākara Mīmāṁsā* holds that *Veda* are of two kinds: pratyakṣa (perceived) & *anumeya* (inferred). Pratyakṣa *Veda* refers to the branches of *Veda* which are available to us now. Anumeya *Veda* refers to those Vedic instructions whose presence is inferred by the instructions present in the smṛtis. Therefore, smṛtis are very much valid as a śabda pramāṇa and enjoy the status of anumeya *Veda*.

Towards the end of the section, Jayanta Bhaṭṭa puts forward another argument for establishing the validity of all sacred texts, and not just smṛtis. He says that the validity of all the sacred texts can be accepted on the grounds that: they are not invalidated from subsequent cognition, they are free from doubt, etcetera and we can assume that the author is reliable in their case, just as in the case of *Veda*, and finally because one sees general agreement with other instruments of knowledge with respect to those parts of teachings which are related to perceptible things. He further notes that contradictions among them, diversity in practice, etcetera cannot be criteria for invalidity. He concludes by saying that all those texts which have reached general consensus among people without any objections, which have been embraced by exemplary people, which may have recent origins, but do not appear unprecedented, which are not based on greed, etcetera, which do not instil fear among people, only those sacred texts can be considered valid (Freschi 2012, 39-48).

Take the case of Manusmṛti for example. The text itself claims that it is valid because Manu is an āpta and that he is well versed in *Veda*. The first chapter provides us with the divine origin of Manu as well as introduces him as being fully versed in the *Veda* and its teachings, thus fulfilling all the reliability criteria defined in Mīmāṁsā and Nyāya Darśanas. Further, we find praise for the authority of Manu as a teacher and authenticity of his teachings from other texts including the *Veda*. *Taittirīya Saṁhitā* 2.2.10.2, for example, says that whatever Manu says is wholesome like medicine.[74] Likewise, Yājñavalkya is a prominent ṛṣi who imparts teachings in *Bṛhadāraṇyaka Upaniṣad*.

From this discussion, we can clearly see that in the Hindu scheme of things, smṛtis and other dharmaśāstras play an important role as śabda pramāṇa which reveal valid knowledge/pramā about dharma, about what actions lead to karmic merit and happiness and what actions lead to demerit and sorrow.

## Conflict Between Śruti and Smṛti

Today, a big issue is being made about the apparent conflict between Śruti and Smṛti. This is a convenient argument used to discredit smṛtis because we find some of its teachings inconvenient to our so-called modern mind.

However, Jayanta Bhaṭṭa notes in his Nyāya-Mañjarī that such contradictions are rarely found, and in case they are found, he suggests three ways to resolve them. These three ways of resolving apparent theological and philosophical contradictions have been arrived at after many centuries of debates and discussions in Mīmāṁsā and Nyāya Darśanas. They are:

1. There is no real contradiction, since the seeming contradictory prescriptions in fact apply to different types or groups of people.
2. One can opt for the one or the other i.e., they are both valid alternatives.
3. The *Veda* overcomes the smṛtis.

In most cases, the so-called contradictions can be easily

resolved using the first and second options mentioned above. Only when both Śruti and Smṛti contradict on a specific issue with respect to a specific context and cannot be alternatives, then and only then, *Veda* is considered to override the Smṛti injunction. This being the case, the modern attitude to jump to option three, without even deliberating upon option one and two, can only be considered a result of preconceived bias.

However, it is important to note that instances where *Veda* is said to overcome the Smṛti, it does not imply that smṛtis have lost their authoritativeness. Instead, it is a case of two alternatives, with one having inherent authority which is directly perceivable, namely the *Veda* which is directly available to us, and the other having inferred authority not directly perceivable, namely the smṛtis whose Vedic basis is inferred, not always directly perceived. This being the case, the alternative whose authority is directly perceived is to be preferred as first best option. That is, the choice of Vedic stipulation over Smṛti stipulation is a matter of preference, and not of setting aside the authoritativeness of Smṛti per se.

Mitramiśra in his magnum opus *Vīramitrodaya* gives a detailed enunciation of the Śruti vs Smṛti debate. In the chapter titled *Paribhāṣā*, pp. 25-29, he writes, 'When there is conflict between a Vedic text and a Smṛti text, preference is to be given to the former as possessed of inherent authority, while the latter owes its authority to an assumed Vedic text.'[75] Then, citing Vyāsa, Mitramiśra notes 'As between Śruti and Smṛti, the conclusion arrived at is thus expressed by Vyāsa:—"That law which is deduced from the *Veda* is the higher, while that declared in the Purāṇa and other smṛtis is the lower"; which means that in cases of conflict, our first duty is to do what is laid down in the *Veda*, and the doing of what is declared in the Smṛti can be justified only as a substitute, i.e., to be adopted only when there is no possibility of the other being adopted. And this for the simple reason that according to Manu (11.30), if one follows the second best course when the best course is possible, his action becomes futile; so that the conclusion indicated by this is that even in cases of conflict, the Smṛti does not entirely lose its authoritative character; all that happens is that the course of action sanctioned by it is rendered fruitless by reason of the superiority of authority attaching to the Vedic text to the contrary.'[76]

Therefore, the so-called conflict between Śruti and Smṛti is one of preference between two courses of action revealed by two distinct authoritative sources, rather than one which implies the non-authoritativeness of smṛtis.

## Function and Purpose of Smṛtis in Hindu Society

As we noted earlier, the primary function of smṛtis is to act as pramāṇa śāstras that reveal knowledge about dharma, a knowledge which cannot be known from any other pramāṇas like pratyakṣa, anumāna, etcetera.

Kullūka Bhaṭṭa in his commentary on Manusmṛti gives two examples to illustrate this:

> Example 1: While everyone indulges in sexual intercourse, only smṛtis reveal in what context and time such sexual intercourse constitutes dharma and imparts *puṇya* (karmic merit) and when it does not constitute dharma and hence leads to *pāpa* (karmic demerit).[77]
>
> Example 2: While everyone practices one or the other job so as to earn a livelihood and maintain families,

it is only dharmaśāstras which reveal what kind of livelihood options are both materially and spiritually beneficial to which group of people.[78]

As pramāṇa śāstra, the smṛtis are concerned only with revealing knowledge about dharma, especially about the connection between karma and karmaphala. They are not law-books or constitutions which were literally and hegemonically imposed upon society in the past, nor are they books of commandments in a biblical sense as it is made out to be in modern scholarship.

The content of dharmaśāstra is broadly divided into three subjects: *ācāra* (practice), *vyavahāra* (jurisprudence), and *prāyaścitta* (expiation). Neither ācāra nor prāyaścitta are related to law and hence smṛtis cannot be law books or constitutions in the strict sense. However, this does not mean they had no relevance in legal matters. They did. Dharmaśāstras formed the ethical and theoretical basis of law. Legal principles were derived from these texts. For example, on the question of inheritance, pre-colonial India largely followed the legal stipulations of *Mitākṣara* of Vijñāneshvara and *Dāyabhāga* of Jīmūtavāhana.

The dharmaśāstras were never imposed in a biblical sense with respect to practices and morals of people. However, they formed the ethical backbone of the society. They provided the material, knowledge and tools to negotiate with reality and handle challenging issues. An example of how dharmaśāstra formed the backbone of society with respect to socio-cultural-ethical issues can be found during the time of Marathas. Dīpāmbā, the wife of Ekoji—the half-brother of Shivaji and the founder of Maratha Empire in Tanjore—commissioned Raghunatha

Pandita to compose texts on *strī*-dharma so that Hindu women who had strayed away from Hindu dharma under Islamic influence could find proper guidance regarding their duties and spiritual practices.

The dharmaśāstras thus constituted the knowledge bank of Hindu society that provided theoretical frameworks like *puruṣārthas*, *varṇāśrama* dharma, *āpad*-dharma, *prāyaścitta*, *raja*-dharma, *vyavahāra*, etcetera. These dharmic principles, derived and contextualised to the needs of society, guided the society, and acted as its socio-religious-cultural-legal backbone.

The tenets of dharma in the form of vidhi (prescribed) and niṣedha (prohibited), enunciated in Manu and other smṛtis are generic and broad guidelines, and are binding only in one sense: that a particular karma or action gives rise to a particular kind of result and that particular result could be favourable leading to *sukha* (happiness) or unfavourable leading to *duḥkha* (sorrow) based on whether they are dharma or adharma. It is for this reason, Bhagavān Kṛṣṇa in Bhagavad Gītā 16.24 says: 'The śāstra is your authority as regards the determination of what is to be done and what is not to be done. After understanding (your) duty as presented by scriptural injunction, you ought to perform (your duty) here (Gambhirananda 1998)'[79]

However, it is important to note that the role of the text itself is limited to imparting this knowledge about action and results for the benefit of mankind. This also implies that smṛtis reveal the first principles of dharma which are eternal and which will always remain valid no matter what socio-political changes occur in society. The latter, i.e. socio-political changes only influence the different applications of dharma in practice and not the first principles of dharma itself.

Whether one chooses to follow it or not, or how much one is able to follow it, or how one would interpret and contextualise the teachings to one's situation is ultimately dependent upon one's own discretion and exertion of free-will. Whether we approach them for knowledge, or for caricaturing them, is up to us. The texts themselves stand tall and unaffected as pramāṇa śāstra.

## Final Words

- Today we are living in a very challenging times wherein the Hindu identity and what it means to be a Hindu are facing immense attacks from within and without.
- The colonial dismantling of Hindu educational institutions and long-term foreign occupation have resulted in Hindus becoming deracinated from their roots.
- We face immense challenges due to the rapid developments in technology as well as the narrative war that is being waged against Hindu civilisation, especially in the field of education, politics, and socio-cultural-religious issues.
- On our part, we are blindly imitating the West and adopting their discourses and frameworks to understand our own society and to negotiate with rising challenges. Obviously, there can be only one end result of this: dismantling and complete destruction of Hindu civilisation.
- The only solution to this is to revive Hindu knowledge traditions, institutions, and discourses. One important area in such a revival has to be the 'dharmaśāstras tradition'.
- The *vidyāsthāna* of dharmaśāstras forms the socio-

cultural backbone of Hindu civilisation. Without it, we will be a value-less society and importantly, we will be analysing and negotiating with socio-cultural issues like abortion, adultery, domestic violence, etcetera using alien frameworks unsuitable to Hindu society.

- A correct understanding of smṛtis and their function in society, followed by the revival of study, discussion, and interpretative tradition of dharmaśāstras will go a long way in resurgence of Hindu civilisation.

Chapter 3

# Decoding Manusmṛti: Some Pointers to Make Sense of Dharmaśāstra Texts[80]

## Introduction

Manusmṛti is among the foremost texts on dharma available in Hindu tradition. While it occupies a preeminent position within the dharmaśāstra tradition as an authentic source for acquiring knowledge about dharma, contemporary engagement with the text has ranged from outright condemnation and at times burning of the text as a political statement to distortion,[81] dismantling,[82] and discarding[83] of the text from the discourse on Hindu philosophy and practice.

The contemporary Hindu society's discomfort with dharmaśāstra tradition in general and with Manusmṛti in particular owes much to the effects of colonialism and the destruction of indigenous educational institutions, as a result of which the society has become deracinated having lost touch with this core aspect of our culture. In particular, people find it exceptionally difficult to relate to the teachings of the smṛti texts owing to their lack of grounding in foundational principles and frameworks of dharmaśāstra tradition as well as the unique language employed in these texts to convey their knowledge about dharma.

This paper attempts to provide some pointers, highlight some foundational frameworks, and clarify few misconceptions about smṛtis as a genre of texts with particular focus on Manusmṛti such that one is better equipped to approach, study, understand and appreciate Manu and other smṛtis.

## Defining Dharma

The term dharma can be variously understood to mean ethics, morality, law, justice, duty, righteousness, etcetera depending upon the context of its usage. But, none of these English terms individually or collectively are able to capture the essence of the term dharma.

Etymologically, the word dharma has been derived from the root *dhṛ* and *dhṛ dhārayati* which means to bear or to support. Hence, dharma can be defined as that which upholds, sustains, nurtures, and provides stability and harmony. As Mahānārāyaṇa Upaniṣad 79.7 states, dharma supports the whole cosmos and removes all karmic demerits.[84] Likewise, Lord Krishna in Mahābhārata Karṇa Parva 49.50 says that dharma is that which upholds all created beings.[85]

However, this definition does not clarify what exactly this 'upholding' implies and how dharma facilitates this upholding and nurturing of individuals. We find clarification on this in the definitions provided by *Vaiśeṣika Sūtra*, *Parāśarasmṛti* and Śrī Mādhavācārya's commentary on it.

Vaiśeṣika Sūtra 1.1.2 defines dharma as that from which (results) the accomplishment of (material) happiness/ wellbeing [called as abhyudaya] and of the supreme good/ mokṣa [called as niḥśreyasa].[86] Parāśarasmṛti 1.2 describes dharma as that which is *hitam* or beneficial for human beings.[87] Śrī Mādhavācārya in his celebrated commentary on the text explains the significance of the use of the phrase hitam thus:

> Dharma is called hitam or beneficial as it is the means to attain our desired fruits. Such desired fruits are of two types: *aihika* (this-worldly) and āmuṣmika (other-worldly). This-worldly fruits refer to prosperity and other fruits that result from performance of *aṣṭaka* and such rituals. The otherworldly fruits are two kinds: abhyudaya (attainment of sukha/happiness and svarga/heaven) and niḥśreyasa (supreme knowledge resulting in liberation). Dharma is the direct means of abhyudaya and dharma by producing *tattvajñāna* (knowledge of reality) is the cause of mokṣa or niḥśreyasa as well.[88]

Thus, dharma upholds, sustains, and nurtures an individual by facilitating him/her to attain worldly happiness (artha/kāma) on the one hand, and otherworldly happiness in the form of svarga[89] on the other hand, as well as absolute bliss or supreme good in the form of mokṣa. That is, dharma is a means for both material and spiritual wellbeing.

A further clarification on the definition of dharma is found in Manusmṛti itself. In verse 1.26, Manu says:[90] 'For the due discrimination of actions, He (Bhagavān) differentiated dharma and adharma; and He connected these creatures/people with such pairs of opposites as happiness-sorrow and the like (such as heaven-hell, attachment-hatred, etc.,).'[91]

In short, the designation of dharma and adharma in the context of individuals is with respect to actions one performs. And such actions could be physical, verbal or mental and they lead to particular results (karmaphala) by the generation of what the Mīmāṃsakas call as *apūrva*. Kumarila Bhatta in his *Tantravārtika* defines apūrva as that potential which was absent before the performance of the act and which is produced after the performance of the said act (U. Jha 2018).[92] To put it differently, every action generates an invisible potency or potential result which endures till such a time it manifests the actual result on the ground.

This apūrva is of two kinds: puṇya and pāpa. Puṇya is the positive and beneficial potency generated by the performance of dharma and it results in karmaphala of svarga (heaven), sukha (happiness), and *cittaśuddhi* (purification of mind) leading to mokṣa or liberation from worldly bondage. Pāpa is the negative and undesirable potency which is generated by performance of adharma and it results in karmaphala of *naraka* (hell), duḥkha (sorrow), and *cittabhrānti* (confusion of mind) leading to further strengthening of *saṃsāra-bandhana* (worldly bondage).

To sum up, irrespective of the context of usage, when an action is designated as dharma, it means that such an action is (and must be) capable of producing puṇya, svarga, sukha and cittaśuddhi. Likewise, an action designated as adharma is (and must be) capable of producing pāpa, naraka, duḥkha, and cittabhrānti.

## Acquiring Authentic Knowledge About Dharma

Once there is clarity on the essential definition of dharma, the next question which naturally follows is how do we acquire authentic knowledge about dharma (and adharma), especially because the actions in themselves do not reveal whether they are beneficial or not, nor can we use any of our sensory or logical faculties to deduce the same.

Hindu epistemology recognises six independent sources of valid knowledge called as pramāṇas. They are pratyakṣa (perception), anumāṇa (inference), upamāṇa (comparison and analogy), arthāpatti (postulation, derivation from circumstances), anupalabdhi (non-perception, negative/cognitive proof) and śabda (word, testimony of past or present reliable experts).

Of these six pramāṇas, none of the first five sources listed above—be it perception, inference, comparison, postulation or non-perception—can impart knowledge about dharma because their field of operation is the empirical world and its objects. Dharma, on the other hand, deals with matters related to karmaphala such as puṇya, pāpa, sukha, duḥkha, svarga, naraka, etcetera which are by nature non-empirical and beyond the grasp of our sensory faculties.

This being the case, our only source of valid knowledge about dharma is śabda or verbal knowledge. It is the knowledge of objects derived from words and sentences. And such knowledge is acquired through the study of trustworthy sacred texts (śāstras) and through instructions from trustworthy teachers (gurus). As Bhagavān Kṛṣṇa instructs in the Gītā 16.24: 'Therefore, the śāstra is your authority as regards the determination of what is to be done and what is not to be done. After understanding (your) duty as presented by scriptural injunction, you ought to perform (your duty) here (Gambhirananda 1998).'[93] Śrī Rāmānujācārya in his commentary on this verse explains that the word śāstras refers to *Veda*s, dharmśāstras (smṛtis), itihāsas, and purāṇas.[94] A similar observation is made by Śrī Madhusūdana Sarasvatī in his commentary on the said verse as well.[95]

Thus, our primary sources of acquiring knowledge about dharma are: *Veda*s, smṛtis, itihāsas and purāṇas. Among them, the *Veda* being apauruṣeya[96] and eternal, it is the most prominent and independent pramāṇa for dharma. All others are dependent upon it. Hence, Jaimini in Mīmāṃsasūtra 1.1.1 defines dharma itself as that which is indicated by injunctions of the *Veda*.[97] After the *Veda*, smṛtis are the most important pramāṇa for dharma as Manu, Yajñavalkya, Parāśara, Narada and other ṛṣis composed their treatises on dharma not only based on their deep knowledge of the entirety of the *Veda*[98] but also based on their complete and direct comprehension of dharma in its entirety through their yogic accomplishments.[99] Hence, Manusmṛti 2.10 says that 'The *Veda* should be known as the Śruti and the dharmaśāstra as the Smṛti; in all matters, these two do not deserve to be criticised, as it is out of these that dharma shone forth.'[100] Itihāsas and purāṇas are in turn based on the *Veda*s and smṛtis and hence they also constitute pramāṇas for dharma. Apart from these primary textual sources, *sadācāra* or good conduct, customs and practices of those who are well versed in śāstras and live their life in accordance to it, and *ātmanastuṣṭi* or what is agreeable to one's own conscience constitute the secondary sources[101] for directly acquiring knowledge about dharma as per Manusmṛti 2.12.[102]

This understanding of the function and role of dharmaśāstras as pramāṇas—authentic sources that impart valid knowledge about dharma—is very significant. A popular misconception prevalent today about Manu and other smṛtis is that they are to be seen either as law-books that stipulated the laws of their times and/or as religious books on the lines of the Bible which provides commandments that were hegemonically imposed on society through religious institutions similar to the church. However, being a pramāṇa-śāstra implies that Manu and other smṛtis are concerned only with revealing knowledge about dharma, especially about the connection between karma and karmaphala; they are neither law-books or constitution documents which were hegemonically imposed upon society in the past, nor are they books of commandments in a biblical sense. The tenets of dharma are actually broad guidelines and are binding only in one sense: that a particular karma or action gives rise to a particular kind of result and that particular result could be favourable leading to sukha (happiness) or unfavourable leading to duḥkha (sorrow) based on whether they are dharma or adharma.

Another implication of the understanding of smṛtis as pramāṇa-śāstra is that they reveal knowledge about the causal relationship that exists between karma and karmaphala in both modes of dharma and adharma, and this causal relationship is eternal, unchanging, and beyond the grasp of the mind and the senses. As Śrī Jnanandanda Bharathi Swami says '…the śāstras are eternal, not because they originated with the beginning of time itself, but because they lay down the eternal relationship between a cause and its effect. If a flame scorches our hand, it is not because the science of physics or chemistry says that it shall so scorch, but because there is an eternal relationship between fire and its effect, scorching (Bharathi 1969, 18).'

Therefore, contrary to popular misconception which posits smṛtis as products of their particular time and context, and hence portrays them as being outdated today, the smṛtis being pramāṇa-śāstras reveal the essential principles of dharma, namely, the eternal causal relationship between different categories of karmas and their karmaphala which are eternal, unchanging, and beyond the socio-political influence of changing conditions. Hence, the smṛtis are as relevant today as they were in the past and they will remain relevant in future as well. What is changing and dependant on situation is not the essential principles of dharma, but the contextualisation of the dharmic teachings to address changing real world situations and thus causing the diversity in the application of dharmic principles.

## Need for Śraddhā in Studying Dharmaśāstra

Since dharma by definition is non-empirical and the dharmaśāstras (Śruti, Smṛti, Itihāsa, Purāṇa, etc.) alone are the means for attaining valid knowledge about dharma, any person who seeks to study these texts and acquire knowledge about dharma must approach them with *śraddhā.*

Śraddhā means 'trust'. Ādi Śaṅkarācārya defines śraddhā as trust in the words of the guru and the śāstras.[103] Without such trust that the text one is studying contains authentic knowledge about a subject, no amount of study will bear any fruit. This is especially so in non-empirical matters as they cannot be verified or falsified through empirical means. Hence, trust in the śāstras and the gurus who teach those śāstras is very vital for unravelling the teachings of these texts. As śraddhā matures, this trust transforms into conviction and finally into actualisation of the truths expounded in the śāstras. It is for this reason Bhagavān Kṛṣṇa says in the Gītā 4.39: 'One who has śraddhā, he alone attains knowledge.'[104]

Contemporary scholarship has largely approached the study of Hindu texts by adopting what is called hermeneutics of suspicion wherein one reads a text with scepticism in order to expose their purported repressed or hidden meanings.

Though the hermeneutics of suspicion has its own importance, in matters of understanding śāstras such as *Veda*, Smṛti, etcetera whose subject is non-empirical, it is completely unsuitable and misleading. Such an approach often leads to rejection of non-empirical elements as superstition or poetic fantasy, filling the vacuum thus created with speculations about ideological, political, and social motives of the texts. It ultimately results in the undermining of the texts and their own self-description of their purposes.

Instead, one should adopt what we may call as 'hermeneutics of śraddhā' to study Hindu texts. In this method, one approaches the text with faith and respect, rather than scepticism, and then attempts to uncover its complete meaning through a contemplative process called as *śravaṇa catuṣṭaya* in Vedānta. In this four-fold process (and hence called catuṣṭaya), one starts with śravaṇa or listening to the enunciation of a particular text from a qualified teacher.[105] This is followed by *manana* or intellectual reflection upon the text and its subject-matter until one arrives at a steady conviction. Then comes *nididhyāsana* or deeper one-pointed contemplation on the essential truths expounded in the text resulting in *sākṣātkāra* or actualisation of those truths. In this way, what starts as śraddhā transforms into sākṣātkāra.[106]

Therefore, it is vital that dharmaśāstras are studied using śraddhā as the method of approach, a point hinted at by Manusmṛti itself when it says in verse 2.10 that 'The *Veda* should be known as the Śruti and the dharmaśāstra as the Smṛti; in all matters, these two do not deserve to be criticised, as it is out of these that dharma shone forth.'[107]

## Locating Dharma: Cosmologically, temporally, teleologically, functionally, and relationally

Manusmṛti is unique among the texts on dharma available in Hindu tradition. Unlike the other texts of this genre, it begins with an account of cosmology. In the very first chapter, it provides a detailed account of cosmogony, which not only recounts the manifestation of Svāyambhuva Brahmā, but also presents a *Vedāntic* (or rather a *Sāṅkhyan*) account of the origination of the universe. It further presents an account of the creation of various objects and beings, including humans.

The first chapter is thus very important to understand how the dharmaśāstra texts conceive of dharma and where they locate dharma cosmologically, temporally, and teleologically.

The first chapter begins with a group of sages approaching Manu and requesting him to enunciate about human duties as applicable to people belonging to different varṇas (verses 1.1-4). In response to this, Manu lays down the foundational framework for approaching the question with a concise account on sṛṣṭi (creation of the world) and laya (dissolution of the world) (verses 1.5-57). Then, he informs the sages that his pupil Bhṛgu who is fully acquainted with the subject will enunciate on the complete treatise (verses 1.58-59). Following this, Bhṛgu begins his response with an account of sṛṣṭi and lays down the foundational framework (verses 1.61-119); he then starts the main discourse on the duties of different varṇas from the second chapter.

While Manu's discourse on sṛṣṭi focusses on the cosmological aspect of creation, Bhṛgu's discourse on sṛṣṭi focusses on the temporal aspect of creation.

Manu gives an account of the manifestation of the Sāṅkhyan categories of *prakṛti*, *mahat*, *tanmatras*, *mahābhūtas*, etcetera (verses 1.8-20) as well as the manifestation of different objects and beings such as *yajña*, *devatās*, *sādhyas*, *Veda*s, dharma-adharma, different varṇas such as brāhmaṇas, etcetera, Manu and other divine sages, different types of non-human beings such as *yakṣas*, *rakṣasas*, *piśācas*, *gandharvas*, *apsaras*, *asuras*, *nāgas*, *sarpas*, *suparṇas*, and the several orders of *pitṛs*, birds, animals, insects etcetera (verses 1.22-53) and locates dharma within this discourse on creation of different beings.

By thus highlighting that humans are merely one among the many beings of the universe, and locating the discourse on *manuṣya*-dharma or the dharma as applicable to humans within the larger cosmological scheme that points to different beings as having their own dharma uniquely applicable to them, Manusmṛti is shifting the focus from a human-centric discourse on dharma to a cosmos-centric discourse. In other words, the text is nudging the readers to withdraw from anthropocentrism[108] and locate themselves in the larger cosmology and then approach the issue of human duties from this cosmological perspective.

Anthropocentrism is problematic as it is a worldview based on a belief in human exceptionalism that feeds on human greed, selfishness, and ego. Hence, it can only speak about human rights and privileges and cannot properly accommodate the notions of dharma, *ṛṇa* (kārmic debt), mokṣa, etcetera which by definition require selflessness. Consequently, this cosmological location of dharma is significant for understanding the teachings of dharmaśāstras as it not only provides an anchorage point to centre our discussions on dharma, but also provides a reference point to cosmologically locate ourselves in these discussions. Prominent examples of such cosmological location of dharma include notions such as manuṣya-dharma, devatā-dharma, ṛṣi-dharma, brāhmaṇa-dharma, kṣatriya-dharma, and so on.

Bhṛgu's discourse on sṛṣṭi focusses on the temporal aspect of creation and locates dharma within this discourse on the different ways in which time functions at different levels and corresponding distinct time durations such as *yuga*, *manvantara*, *kalpa*, etcetera (verses 1.64-73) and how they influence dharma and cause variations in application of dharmic tenets (verses 1.81-86). This temporal location of dharma is also significant as it provides a reference point to locate ourselves temporally and contextualise the teachings of dharmaśāstras as applicable to our temporal location. Prominent examples of such temporal location of dharma include notions such as *yuga*-dharma, *kalivarjya*, āpad-dharma and *anāpad*-dharma.

The first chapter of Manusmṛti also locates dharma teleologically. This it does by making the discourse on dharma a subset of the discourse on cosmogony. Modern scholarship have often found it difficult to make sense of the presence of an account of cosmogony in a text on dharma, so much so that some scholars like George Bühler have designated the whole chapter as a later addition.[109] However, the Sanskrit commentators did not exhibit such discomfort. Consider Medhātithi. In his commentary on Manusmṛti verse 1.5, he remarks:

> What the First Discourse does is to describe the fact of the treatise having an extensive scope; so that what is described here is the whole range of the cosmic process, beginning with Brahman down to the inanimate objects, as forming the basis of dharma and adharma, right and wrong.[110]
>
> (Jha 1920, 21)

That is, for Medhātithi, cosmogony forms the very basis of dharma and any discussion of human duties must be conducted in its context.

Building on this, Kullūka Bhaṭṭa makes an even more comprehensive case for the inclusion of cosmogony in the discourse of dharma. He remarks that the discourse on cosmogony is neither inappropriate nor incoherent because such a discourse which is nothing but an enunciation of *Brahman*, the cause of the world (and which would lead one to ātmajñāna or self-knowledge*)*, is a discourse on dharma itself (*Kauṇḍinyāyana* 2014, 77).[111] Bhatta then cites from a number of textual sources, including the Mahābhārata,[112] Yājñavalkyasmṛti,[113] Brahmasūtra[114] and Taittirīya Upaniṣad[115] to establish that the pursuit of ātmajñāna is in fact the *parama* dharma or the highest duty, and the investigation into cosmogony is an important aspect of this pursuit of ātmajñāna. He then concludes his discussion with a remark that having composed the first chapter to teach about ātmajñāna, which is the parama dharma, Manusmṛti enunciates from the second chapter onwards, the transactional or worldly principles of dharma like saṃskāras which are to be considered as a limb or a subset of parama dharma.[116] In the end, he adds that a careful study of the verses of Manusmṛti will make his exposition on them self-evident.[117]

From Kullūka Bhaṭṭa's exposition, three things become evident (1) exposition on cosmogony is also exposition on dharma, (2) cosmogony is the highest dharma, and (3) worldly human duties of varṇāśrama are a limb or subset of this highest dharma. Bhatta's commentary also reveals how cosmogony forms the basis of both *nivṛtti* dharma and *pravṛtti* dharma. In the case of nivṛtti dharma, the investigation into the origination of the universe leads to dispassion and self-knowledge, leading to final liberation. In the case of pravṛtti dharma, cosmogony provides the context to understand human duties and the place of human beings in the larger scheme of the universe.

Thus, Manusmṛti teleologically locates dharma as a limb or a subset of the spiritual pursuit of mokṣa which also serves as a means to attain mokṣa. A pursuit of pravṛtti-dharma (the dharma of a worldly person) of the nature of varṇāśrama-dharma leads one to purification of the mind (cittaśuddhi) making one competent to pursue nivṛtti-dharma and thereby attain mokṣa. As Śrī Mādhavācārya notes in his commentary on Parāśarasmṛti 1.2: 'Dharma is the direct means of abhyudaya (happiness and heaven) and dharma by producing tattvajñāna (knowledge of reality) is the cause of mokṣa or niḥśreyasa as well.'[118] Consequently practice of dharma is inevitable for all spiritual paths.[119]

Manusmṛti also locates dharma functionally and relationally. Functionally, the text locates dharma under headings such as *varṇa*-dharma, *āśrama*-dharma, *puruṣa*-dharma, *strī*-dharma, *rāja*-dharma, and so on—each of which are related to the function a person performs in society. The function that a *brāhmaṇa* performs in society is for example different from the function that a *kṣatriya*, *vaiśya*, or *śūdra* performs. Therefore, people who belong to different varṇas have distinct varṇa-dharmas which are functional in nature. Manusmṛti summarises such functionally distinguished varṇa duties of the four varṇas in verses 1.87-91. Likewise, the role and function that the students, the householders, the forest-retired, and the renunciates perform in society are distinct from each other. The same is the case with men and women. Owing to difference in their gender and the corresponding physical and psychological differences, men and women play distinct but mutually complementary roles within the family and outside in the larger society. Owing to such functional differences, the dharmas that arise from or are connected to such functions also have differences.

A subset of functionally located dharmas are the relationally located dharmas i.e. duties and obligations towards a person which arise out of the nature of relationship one shares with that person. Relationally, distinct dharmas can be recognised with respect to relational roles such as: father, mother, son, daughter, husband, wife, teacher, student, etcetera.

A comprehensive understanding of dharma is only possible when in any given situation one is able to identify the different strands of dharma located at cosmological, temporal, teleological, functional and relational levels and how their mutual interplay is playing out in the given situation.

## Subject-matter of Dharmaśāstras

One way to look at the subject-matter of dharmaśāstras is to look at it from a thematic perspective. Thematically, the content of dharmaśāstras can be broadly divided into three themes: ācāra (practice), vyavahāra (jurisprudence), and prāyaścitta (expiation).

Ācāra is the most important theme enunciated in the smṛtis. It literally means 'conduct, practice, or custom' and it deals with the karmas of an individual. It covers the various duties, obligations, and activities which constitute dharma and hence lead to overall wellbeing of an individual as well as those activities which constitute adharma causing suffering to an individual and hence must be avoided. Dharmaśāstras primarily conceive of ācāra in terms of *sāmānya*-dharma or dharma that is not tied to a specific function (these are universal ethical principles applicable to everyone) and *viśeṣa*-dharma or context-specific special principles of dharma that apply to individuals based on their varṇa, āśrama, deśa, kāla, gender, relationship, etcetera.

Vyavahāra refers to legal jurisprudence. It covers a broad range of subjects such as civil and criminal laws, duties of a king, court system, judges and witnesses, judicial process, crimes and punishment, etcetera.

Prāyaścitta refers to penance or expiation. It provides guidelines regarding various expiation activities that can be undertaken by an individual to repent for and purify oneself from karmic demerit (pāpa) which accrues as a result of deviation from dharma.

Another way of classifying the content of dharmaśāstras is on the basis of nature of the subject-matter. Accordingly, the content of dharmaśāstras can be divided into five types: *dṛṣṭārtha, adṛṣṭārtha, dṛṣṭādṛṣṭārtha*, *nyāyamūla*, and *anuvāda*.

While dṛṣṭārtha refers to the subject-matter which deals with tangible, seen, and this-worldly purposes such as those relating to wealth (artha) and pleasure (kāma); adṛṣṭārtha refers to the subject-matter which deals with intangible, unseen, and otherworldly purposes such as those relating to punya, svarga, and mokṣa. When the subject-matter has a bearing on both tangible and intangible purposes, then they are called as dṛṣṭādṛṣṭārtha. Nyāyamūla refers to subject-matter based on universal maxims. Anuvāda refers to subject-matter seen by the wise and the knowers of *Veda* (Wadekar 1996, lxxvi).

Of the five, the three, namely dṛṣṭārtha, adṛṣṭārtha, and dṛṣṭādṛṣṭārtha are important as they tell us about the kind of end-result that a particular prescription or guideline when implemented would give rise to. While adṛṣṭārtha and dṛṣṭādṛṣṭārtha have unseen and transcendental results and hence they are absolute, eternal, and always valid and applicable; the dṛṣṭārtha dealing with tangible results are neither absolute nor eternal and are subject to time, location, and context.

This distinction is very important for proper understanding and interpretation of dharmaśāstras. While the ācāra and prayashcitta portions of the smṛtis deal predominantly with adṛṣṭārtha and dṛṣṭādṛṣṭārtha purposes, vyavahāra portion of the smṛtis predominantly deals with dṛṣṭārtha and dṛṣṭādṛṣṭārtha purposes. As a result, while the teachings enunciated in ācāra and prayashcitta are predominantly absolute and not subject to socio-political changes, the teachings of vyavahāra, especially the dṛṣṭārtha portions must be understood as absolute only in their essential spirit and not in external form as they are subject to socio-political changes.

The third way of classifying the content of the smṛtis is by their mode of expression. The Vedic statements can be classified into five types: *vidhi*, *niṣedha*, *arthavāda*, *nāmadheya* and *mantra*.

Vidhi or injunctions are statements that induce one to act. Niṣedha or prohibitions are the opposite of injunctions. They are negative precepts which proscribe actions that are either injurious or disadvantageous. Arthavāda are commendatory and depreciatory texts. Nāmadheya refers to names or appellations of certain yajñas, etcetera. Mantras are sacred formulas to be recited while performing rituals and they do not lay down injunctions.

Among these five, the vidhis[120] and niṣedhas[121] directly indicate about actions, whether they are dharma or adharma. What is prescribed through vidhi is dharma and what is prohibited through niṣedha is adharma. Arthavāda passages serve to supplement the vidhi or niṣedha statements, or in many cases, when they stand alone, vidhi or niṣedha can be inferred from them. All the three—vidhi, niṣedha, and arthavāda—are relevant in the context of smṛtis.

The vidhis can further be classified into: *apūrva-vidhi*, *niyama-vidhi* and *parisaṃkhyā-vidhi*. Apūrva-vidhi is an original injunction. It is an injunction which enjoins something that is not obtained by any other means.[122] Niyama-vidhi is a restrictive injunction. It is an injunction which indicates one among the many available alternatives as a course of action to be adopted.[123] Parisaṅkhya-vidhi is a preclusive injunction. When many alternatives with simultaneity are available, this vidhi excludes all other alternatives except one.[124]

The niṣedhas can also be classified into prohibitions 'regarding the person' (*puruṣārtha*) that are applicable to a person throughout his/her life, and prohibitions 'regarding the sacrifice' (*kratvārtha*) that are applicable only to the specific situation of the sacrifice.[125] A third kind of prohibition is *paryudāsa* which constitutes an exception to the general rule.[126]

A basic familiarity with these different themes, the end-goals, and different modes of expression of the subject-matter of dharmaśāstras is very vital for a proper understanding and interpretation of these texts.

## Decoding the Dharmaśāstra: An illustrative Example from Manusmṛti

There are a number of verses in Manusmṛti regarding women which have become controversial as they are perceived as being anti-women. Two such verses are criticised for stating that women should not have independence and should always be dependent upon menfolk. Let us briefly examine these two verses and what they actually say.

बाल्ये पितुर्वशे तिष्ठेत् पाणिग्राहस्य यौवने ।
पुत्राणां भर्तरि प्रेते न भजेत् स्त्री स्वतन्त्रताम् ॥ *Manu* 5.148 (Kaundinyayana 2014) — **[A]**

*bālye piturvaśe tiṣṭhet pāṇigrāhasya yauvane*
*putrāṇāṃ bhartari prete na bhajet strī svatantratām*

***Translation**: In childhood she should remain under the control of her father, in youth under that of her husband, and on the husband's death under that of her sons; the woman should never have recourse to independence*[127] (G Jha 1920).

पिता रक्षति कौमारे भर्ता रक्षति यौवने ।
रक्षन्ति स्थविरे पुत्रा न स्त्री स्वातन्त्र्यमर्हति ॥ *Manu* 9.3 (Kaundinyayana 2014) — **[B]**

*pitā rakṣati kaumāre bhartā rakṣati yauvane*
*rakṣanti sthavire putrā na strī svātantryamarhati*

***Translation**: The father guards her during virginity, the husband guards her in youth, the sons guard her in old*

*age; the woman is never fit for independence*
(G Jha 1920).

Let us refer to these two verses under examination, namely, verse 5.146 and verse 9.3, as **[A]** and **[B]** respectively.

Both [A] and [B] are very similar in their content, but they appear in two related but distinct contexts. While [A] appears in the context of strī-dharma or duties of women, [B] appears in the context of relational dharma between husband and wife.

## Case [A]:

Cosmologically [A] pertains to manuṣya-dharma, teleologically to pravṛtti-dharma, and functionally to strī-dharma. And we already saw how designation of any action as dharma implies that such an action is capable of giving results of puṇya, sukha, svarga, and cittaśuddhi i.e. overall wellbeing.

Therefore, when [A] says women should remain under the control of i.e. dependent upon father, husband, or son, and should never take recourse to independence, contrary to popular interpretation which takes it as an infringement of women's rights and as impeding women empowerment, it is primarily a statement with respect to pursuit of dharma and not concerned with pursuit of artha or kāma. That it is a statement with respect to dharma and not artha or kāma is explicitly highlighted in *Gautama Dharmasūtras* 18.1 which says 'A wife is not independent with respect to the fulfilment of dharma.'[128]

Consequently, this dependence in dharmic practice does not in any way come in the way of women pursuing what they love or empowering themselves. If anything, it merely prevents such pursuit of artha and kāma from descending into reckless indulgences leading to distress and suffering.

What is unique about [A] is that it defines strī-dharma in terms of the relational dharma that women have with their closest male relationships, namely their father, husband, and son. While puruṣa-dharma or dharma as applicable to men is largely defined in terms of varṇāśrama-dharma, the strī-dharma as illustrated by [A] is largely understood in terms of relational dharma despite the recognition that the whole discourse is a subset of varṇāśrama-dharma itself.

This distinction in dharma discourse regarding men and women is owing to the fact that men and women are distinct from each other in their physical, biological, psychological, social, and spiritual makeup. While men in general are more suited for *karma-yoga* in its aspect of austerity (*tapasyā*) and ritual performance (*karma-anuṣṭhāna*), women in general are more suited for karma-yoga with a stress on devotion (*bhakti*) and service (śuśrūṣu). As a result of this, while puruṣa-dharma is enunciated in terms of varṇāśrama-dharma which stresses on austerity and ritual performance, strī-dharma is enunciated in relational terms where devotion and service play an important role.

However, this does not mean that men's obligations do not involve service or that women are ineligible for all forms of ritual performance.[129] It merely indicates what constitutes the predominant means of pursuing dharma for men and women.

To have further clarity on this, let us examine briefly the Hindu notion of marriage.

In Hindu tradition, marriage or *vivāha* is understood as a saṃskāra—a sacrament and a purificatory ritual that imparts competency and allows a couple to enter the gṛhastha-āśrama or the stage of householder to pursue dharma, artha, kāma, and mokṣa together.

Etymologically, vivāha means a 'special kind of carrying away *(viśiṣṭaḥ vāhaḥ vivāhaḥ)*' of the bride by the bridegroom. The 'carrying away' refers to the process of the bridegroom accepting the bride into his life and family symbolised by the ritual processes of *kanyādāna*, *pāṇigrahaṇa*, and *saptapadī*. It is a special kind of 'carrying away' because the saṃskāra of vivāha on the one hand purifies the bride and makes her competent to enter the householder life and on the other hand it facilitates the groom to embrace her into his life as his half and accept her into his family and *gotra* lineage such that he attains competency to perform householder duties as well (Ananthanarasimhachar 2014, 526).

Further, vivāha is a special relationship, a sacred bond standing on the three pillars of *rati* (desire), dharma (duty), and *prajā* (progeny). It involves the pursuit of both *saha*-dharma and *saha-kāma*, i.e. the pursuit of duties and the experiencing of life-pleasures, accomplished together.

Vivāha as a saṃskāra facilitates the bride and the bridegroom to enter into gṛhastha-āśrama (householder life) thereby facilitating them to practice varṇāśrama dharma in the pursuit of the dharma puruṣārtha. The vows taken during the marriage ceremony show that marriage is a commitment by the bride and bridegroom to pursue all the puruṣārthas of life together and hence, the notion of 'saha-dharma'—pursuing life duties together— is central to Hindu understanding of marriage.

However, though the goal pursued is same, the roles played by the man and the woman in a marriage are different.

While the man plays the role of a husband and a father, the woman plays the role of a wife and a mother. While the husband takes the role of *yajamāna*, the conductor of the rituals and other dharmic duties, the wife takes up the role of *saha-dharmachāriṇī*, one who accompanies the husband in fulfilment of dharmic activities. A virtuous wife is, in fact, identified with the sacred fires of the house itself (Leslie 1995, 141). That is, the role played by the wife is like that of the sacred fire: the role of a facilitator, without whom a gṛhastha man cannot perform any dharmic rituals or actions. That is, the husband is the performer of the dharmic actions like yajñá, etcetera with the support, help and company of his wife. On the other hand, for the wife, facilitating the husband in the accomplishment of the gṛhastha duties is itself the dharmic duty and a means for her overall emancipation. It is for this reason the texts note how half of the dharmic merit of all the actions of the husband automatically gets transferred to the wife. That is, the husband himself becomes the direct means for accomplishing all the puruṣārthas for the wife. This is the true meaning of saha-dharma in the context of Hindu vivāha (Sridhar 2022).

From the above discussion on Hindu view on marriage, it is very clear that though husband and wife pursue life goals together and are dependent upon each other, the role that the wife plays in the relationship is fundamentally different from the role of the husband and hence nature of dependence also differs for both of them. Since the husband constitutes the direct means for accomplishing all puruṣārthas for the wife, Manusmṛti 5.153 says 'There is no separate sacrificing for women, no observances, no fastings; it is by means of serving her husband that she becomes exalted in heaven (G Jha 1920).'[130]

Likewise, when we are children, both men and women are dependent upon their parents. The parents are the first teachers who teach the child what is dharma and what is adharma. Hence, we have famous statements such as '*mātṛdevo bhava, pitṛdevo bhava'*.

Therefore, when [A] says that women in their childhood must remain dependent upon their father, it is merely stating the fact that children are dependent upon their parents for nourishment, love, education, and protection.

In the same way, in old age, parents depend upon their children for multiple reasons, including matters of dharma, wherein the children play the role of facilitator.

Therefore, in recognition of the fact of direct dependence of women on their husbands in dharmic matters (as husbands are the direct means for accomplishing dharma for wives) and secondarily on fathers and sons, the strī-dharma has been enunciated in terms of women's relational dharma towards people who are closest to her.[131]

It is possible that many may take issue with the usage of the phrases: '*vaśe*' which means 'in control of or dependent upon' and '*na bhajet strī svatantratām*' which means 'the woman should never have recourse to independence'.

However, it is important to realise that dependence is a characteristic trait of any group—be it a family, a community, or a professional organisation. Every person is dependent on others in their immediate environment in one way or the other: children are dependent upon their parents while growing up, husband and wife are dependent upon each other in everything they do, parents in their old-age are dependent upon their children, citizens are dependent upon the government, colleagues in a company are dependent upon each other, etcetera.

This being the case, dependence in general should not be seen as a negative trait. Symbiosis is a positive characteristic, be it in the natural world or in our social community. The same is the case in matters of dharma as well. Therefore, there is nothing offensive or demeaning towards women when [A] states that in matters of dharma, women are dependent upon their fathers, husbands, and sons.

As far as not having independence in matters of dharma is concerned, this is equally applicable to both men and women. They are both dependent on the means indicated by śāstras for practicing dharma. Individuals cannot determine on their own what constitutes dharma based on whims and fancies. We must take refuge in our gurus and śāstras for understanding what constitutes dharma and what adharma, and live life accordingly.

## Case [B]:

Cosmologically [B] pertains to manuṣya-dharma, teleologically to pravṛtti-dharma, and relationally to dharma in the context of family, especially as between husband and wife.

While [A] highlights dharma of women especially with respect to important family members such as father, husband, and son, [B] highlights the dharma of menfolk with respect to women of their family. So, functionally, [B] highlights an important aspect of puruṣa-dharma, namely the role and duties of men in the context of family.

Strī-dharma spoken in [A] highlights the centrality of devotion, dedication, service, and the nurturing roles that women play in the family. In contrast to that, the puruṣa-dharma enunciated in [B] highlights the centrality of providing protection to womenfolk. Hence, the repeated use of the phrase *rakṣati*.

Guarding or protection is a broad terminology with many different dimensions. But [B] primarily uses it in the context of dharma i.e. it stipulates that it is the duty of the father, husband, and the son to ensure that women in the family remain protected such that they are able to perform their svadharma without any hindrance.

Such protection has two aspects: One, protecting the womenfolk from all kinds of external threats, interventions, or obstacles that may be inimical to them. Two, ensuring that women themselves do not deviate from dharma due to bad influence by providing proper education and training, encouraging and encouraging to take up healthy and positive activities, etcetera.

One of the implications of this verse is that it is a reminder to menfolk to behave appropriately not only with women of their family, but with women in general. It is a reminder that men should protect women and not oppress them in any way. Another implication is that it stipulates that children, especially sons, should not abandon their aged parents under any pretext. Abandoning aged parents constitutes adharma. Yet another implication is that the husband-wife relationship is not merely that of partnership, but is also that of guru-śiṣya. Hence, it is the duty of the husband to teach dharma to his wife and oversee that she can practice dharma without any hindrance.

The controversial phrase '*na strī svātantryamarhati*' in [B] which means 'women do not deserve independence' does not imply a curtailment of women's freedom, but here the phrase *svātantryam* must be understood as a reference to the 'state of unprotectedness' (Devanathan 2020). That is, women should always be protected and a healthy society be created wherein they are not harassed.

From the above discussion on cases [A] and [B], it is very clear that contrary to popular interpretation of the verses 5.146 and 9.3 which paint them as anti-women, there is nothing inimical towards women in these verses. On the contrary, while [A] highlights the means by which women can attain overall wellbeing, [B] highlights the duty that śāstras enjoin upon men regarding protection of women.

## Conclusion

The contemporary Hindu society's discomfort with Manusmṛti and other dharmaśāstra texts is largely caused due to unfamiliarity and disconnection with the dharma textual tradition as a result of colonialism. However, to truly recover native worldview and express our civilisational thoughts coherently using our own frameworks and categories, it is vital that we reconnect, recover, and revive the study of dharmaśāstras and contextualise its teachings to address contemporary issues. This chapter has presented some pointers that would facilitate such a reconnection with the dharma textual tradition and recovery of its authentic teachings.

Section 02

# Translation and Commentary on the First Four Verses

## Verse One

मनुमेकाग्रमासीनमभिगम्य महर्षयः ।
प्रतिपूज्य यथान्यायमिदं वचनमब्रुवन् ॥ १ ॥
*manumekāgramāsīnamabhigamya maharṣayaḥ* ।
*pratipūjya yathānyāyamidaṃ vacanamabruvan* ॥ *1* ॥

**Word by word translation:** To Manu (मनुम् – *manum*); with one-pointed concentration (एकग्रम् – *ekāgram*); who was seated (आसीनम् – *āsīnam*) in; having approached (अभिगम्य – *abhigamya*); the great sages (महर्षयः – *maharṣayaḥ*); after paying respects (प्रतिपूज्य – *pratipūjya*); in due form (यथान्यायम् – *yathānyāyam*); this (इदम् – *idam*); speech (वचनम् – *vacanam*); (they) uttered (अब्रुवन् – *abruvan*).

**Meaning:** To Manu, who was (calmly) seated in one-pointed concentration, approached the great sages; and after paying (mutual) respects, they addressed (Manu) in a proper way the following words.

**Analysis:** This text on dharma begins in a narrative format with highly accomplished ṛṣis approaching the great

Svāyambhuva-Manu with a request to be taught about the actions pertaining to different sections of human society through which they can attain overall wellbeing.

**मनुम् – *Manum* – To Manu**:

Who is this Manu who was approached by the great sages? Commentator Medhātithi says '"Manu" is the name of a particular person well-known in long-continued Smṛti tradition as having studied several Vedic texts and being endowed with both knowledge and practice of the Vedic precepts (G Jha 1920).'[132] Likewise commentator Kullūka Bhaṭṭa says 'Manu is one who has conceived in his mind the meaning of the entirety of *Veda*.'[133] The text itself notes in verse 1.63 that Manu referred to in the text is Svāyambhuva-Manu, the first of the seven Manus created by Brahmā and whose duty is to create and sustain the world during his time-period (called manvantara).[134]

Further, the word 'Manu' forms the maṅgalācaraṇa of the text. All Hindu texts open with a maṅgalācaraṇa—an auspicious invocation of divinity. Kullūka Bhaṭṭa notes that the term 'Manu' itself performs the function of maṅgalācaraṇa in this text since the omniscient and omnipotent Manu is none other than *Paramātma* himself who has descended to maintain creation.[135]

**एकाग्रमासीनम् – *ekāgramāsīnam* – seated in one-pointed concentration**:

'One-pointed concentration' refers to the state of mind, a mind which has withdrawn itself from worldly objects and is fixed upon a single entity to the exclusion of all others. Here, it refers to Manu being seated in a state of *samādhi* with the mind fully established in *Atman* or innermost

Self. 'Seated' refers to either the posture of sitting or as the commentators note, a state of calm and collectedness.

Medhātithi says:

> The term *ekāgra*, by ordinary usage, connotes 'steadiness of the mind', it being concentrated upon the contemplation of the knowledge of truth, following upon the cessation of all doubts and illusions of the person in whom the contact of all defects of passion and the like is set aside by inhibition. It is only when one has his mind in this condition that he is capable of apprehending sound and other objects that lie within reach of his senses; which is not the case when he is in doubt as to the object being a real entity or otherwise.—Or, etymologically the term *agra* denotes the mind, by reason of the fact that in the act of apprehending things it is the mind that goes before (*agragāmī*) the eye and other sense-organs; and in ordinary parlance that which acts first or goes ahead, is called *agra*;—so that the compound ekāgra is to be expounded as 'he who has his *agra*, or mind, fixed upon one perceptible object'... By this explanation also ekāgra connotes absence of distraction.[136]
>
> (G Jha 1920)

Kullūka Bhaṭṭa, Govindarāja and Sarvajñanārāyaṇa in their commentary on the present verse explain one-pointedness as the mind which exists in a state of non-distraction.[137] Kullūka Bhaṭṭa further adds that being seated in one-pointed concentration denotes that Manu was in a right frame of mind to teach.[138] In *Muṇḍaka Upaniṣad* 1.2.12, it is said that a competent Guru is one who is both *śrotriya* (well learned in the *Veda* and Vedic corpus) and

*Brahmaniṣṭhā* (one who is established in Brahman).[139] In Manu verse 1.3, the sages address Manu as the knower of *Veda* in both its aspect of karma and jñāna.[140] The description of Manu here as being seated in one-pointed concentration shows that Manu was Brahmaniṣṭhā as well, and hence a competent teacher to teach the two-fold dharma of pravṛtti and nivṛtti.

In *Vyāsa Bhāṣya* on *Pātañjala Yoga Sūtra* verse 1.1, ekāgra or one-pointedness is mentioned as one of the five states of *citta* (or mind), the others being *kṣipta* (the wandering state of mind), *mūḍha* (dull or forgetful state), *vikṣipta* (occasionally steady, but otherwise distracted state), and *niruddha* (restrained state).[141] Vyāsa states that it is only in *ekāgra-citta* or one-pointed mind that *samprajñāta samādhi* (i.e. samādhi in which there is consciousness of object) is possible. He defines samprajñāta samādhi as one which 'in the one-pointed mind shows forth fully an object existing as such in its most perfect form, removes the afflictions, loosens the bonds of karma and thus inclines it towards restraint (Prasada 1998, 2).'[142] Vācaspati Miśra in his gloss on Vyāsa Bhāṣya highlights that this knowledge about a real object (as against imagined objects) gained by samprajñāta samādhi in a person with ekāgra-citta is an immediate realisation[143] which reveals the object in full intensity as against indirect knowledge attained through verbal and inferential cognitions which are indirect and hence not competent to remove *avidyā* directly present in the mind (Prasada 1998, 4).[144] In other words, Vyāsa and Vācaspati Miśra define ekāgra-citta or one-pointed state of mind as one which is directed towards one object and has the capacity to illuminate fully and directly the true sense of such an object and is distinct from verbal and inferential cognitions.

Mādhavācārya in his commentary on *Parāśara Smṛti* verses 1.1-2 on a similar reference to ekāgra, cites the Vyāsa Bhāṣya portion above and notes that one-pointedness happens when all the three—*dhāraṇā* (concentration), *dhyāna* (meditation), and *samādhi* (total absorption)—become established in one object. If such one-pointedness happens towards words and meanings, then one will gain knowledge of all words and speeches including the knowledge of speech of birds and animals. Likewise, Mādhavācārya notes, in this case, the ekāgram refers to one-pointedness towards the knowledge of the innumerable branches of *Veda*s.[145] That is, the description of Svāyambhuva-Manu as being seated with 'one-pointed mind' signifies his being seated in a state of samprajñāta samādhi, being absorbed one-pointedly in the knowledge of *Veda*, and directly perceiving such knowledge, and hence being the right teacher of dharma which has its basis in *Veda*.

Mādhavācārya further notes in the context of the phrase *āsīnam* or seated that the one-pointed state of mind is possible only in those who are seated. Such one-pointedness is neither possible in those who are lying down as there is scope for sleep there, nor in those who are standing as that involves concentrating upon one's bodily activities, nor in those who are walking or running as that also involves many distractions.[146]

Notably, Manu being seated in a state of calm and collectedness with his mind and senses under control also implies that he is an āpta or a trustworthy teacher who imparted this teaching about dharma in a condition of calmness, self-restraint, and dispassion and not from a condition of mental turmoil affected by rāga-dveṣa (likes-dislikes) and other *ariṣaḍvargas* (six internal passions) such as lust, anger, pride, attachment, jealousy, and greed. In other words, Manu had no hidden agenda, bias, or prejudice against any person, community, gender, or any other conditions. He imparted his teachings purely for the sake of *loka-saṅgraha* i.e. for the benefit benefit of the entire world.

**अभिगम्य – *abhigamya* – having approached near or stood in front of:**

The great sages approached Manu who was seated in one-pointed concentration. Why did the sages approach Svāyambhuva-Manu to learn about dharma? Since Manu is the originator of the universe, (verse 1.63) and he had learned the tenets of dharma from Brahmā (*Hiraṇyagarbha*) himself (1.58), and he knows the Vedic precepts in entirety (verse 1.3), and he is ever-established in Brahman, and since he had previously taught this treatise on dharma to Marīci and other sages (verse 1.58), he is the best teacher to teach dharma.[147]

We find praise for the authority of Manu as a teacher and authenticity of his teachings in other texts as well. Taittirīya Saṁhitā 2.2.10.2, for example, says that whatever Manu says is wholesome like medicine.[148] Asha Rani Tripathi in her critical study of Manusmṛti notes the widespread reference to Manu in *Ṛgveda*. She writes:

> In many mantras of Ṛgveda, Manu has been mentioned as 'father' (RV 1.80.16, 114.2; VIII.63.1). At another place Manu is addressed as 'our father' *(yāni manur-avrnita pitā nah)*. One may also come across many compounded words like *manu-jāta*, *manu-prītasaḥ* and *manur-hita*. These words are occurring hundreds of

> times throughout Ṛgveda. At another place, the sages pray to gods to show them the ancestral path of Manu (RV VIII.30). Manu is also considered as the light of the people (RV 1.36.19). Manu offers sacrifices to the gods (RV V.35.15. VIII.30.2; X.36.10). Manu is also prayed to along with Indra (VIII.68.6). In Ṛgveda most of the mantras mention Manu as an individual sage. According to another mantra, Manu is a sage who offers prayers to thirty-three gods (VIII.27.4, 30.2). In Ṛgveda there are many stories related to Manu (X.61-63). Manu is also referred to in *Atharvaveda* (XI.33) and in *Sāmaveda* (1.2.33; III.165, 145, 232; IV.123-24; VI.262). Manu has been delineated in Saṃskṛta literature from the early Vedic period onwards. He is regarded as father, as one of the ancient sages, a semi-divine person and a king who received law and regulation from the gods itself. Manusmṛti also mentions that Manu became a king by his own righteous conduct (V11.4).
>
> (Tripathi 2015, 4)

Medhātithi says that the term 'approached' refers to sages intentionally and with special effort approaching Manu by giving up all other endeavours for the sake of instruction about dharma and not by accident.[149] He adds that this shows the authoritative and trustworthy character of Manu as a teacher as only such exceptional teachers would be sought after by sincere seekers.[150] Thus, the authority and trustworthiness of Manu and his teachings are well recognised across Hindu textual tradition.

**महर्षय – *maharṣayaḥ* – The great sages:**

The word ṛṣi refers to a mantradraṣṭā—the seer of Vedic

mantras. Govindarāja notes that ṛṣis are great people as they possess *siddhis* such as *aṇimā*, etcetera and who (presumably on account of the siddhis) have seen *Ṛk*, *Yajus*, and *Sāma* mantras.[151] Skanda Purāṇa 1.2.5.118 lists ṛṣi as one among the eight types of brāhmaṇas and defines him as a brāhmaṇa who has sublimated his sexual urges, who is very excellent, who is moderate in food habits, who is truthful and has no more doubts about reality of Self, and who can curse or bless a person (Tagore 1950).[152] Medhātithi says, 'The word ṛṣi means the *Veda*; and the word ṛṣi is applied also to a person, by virtue of his possessing excellent knowledge of the *Veda* and all that is prescribed therein and acting up to these (G Jha 1920).'[153] The text speaks about 'great sages': great because they excel in their learning, conduct, austerity as well as all the above mentioned qualities. As Ādi Śaṅkarācārya notes in his bhāṣya on Brahmasūtra 3.1.11, those who conduct their life according to the tenets of dharma are well-known in the world as 'Mahatma'.[154] Mādhavācārya explains the usage of the term ṛṣi which appears in a similar context in Parāśara Smṛti verse 1.1, wherein ṛṣis approach Sage Vyāsa with questions about dharma as applicable to *Kaliyuga*. He notes that the phrase ṛṣi is a reference to the perception or knowledge of what is beyond the grasp of the senses (*Atindriya*).

The questioners who approached Vyāsa were called so only in a figurative sense that they would in the future attain the state of ṛṣi (i.e. they would develop the capability to directly perceive what is beyond the grasp of senses) after they have put into practice the dharma which the text would be enunciating upon (in response to their query about dharma). He adds that if this were not the case and if we take the term ṛṣi as a reference to accomplished sages, then it would make no sense for them to ask questions about dharma, since they already perceive dharma (which is beyond the grasp of senses) directly. Alternatively, Mādhavācārya notes, the ṛṣis, despite themselves having complete knowledge about dharma, can be understood as asking for instruction about dharma only for the sake of those who do not have knowledge about dharma (i.e. out of compassion for those who are unaware about dharma).[155]

**प्रतिपूज्य** – ***pratipūjya*** **– after paying (mutual) respects**: The word pūjya refers to paying respects in the form of greetings and salutations. Medhātithi reads pratipūjya along with yathānyāyam and says it refers to paying respects in due form as per the norms laid down in scriptures about how a student must approach a teacher, greet him, and attend upon him with devotion and respect.[156] Another commentator Sarvajñanārāyaṇa takes pratipūjya to mean *pratyekam pūjayitvā* i.e. having honoured them severally. For example, Muṇḍaka Upaniṣad 1.2.12 says, 'For knowing that Reality (Brahman) he should go, with 'sacrificial faggots' in hand, only to a teacher versed in *Veda*s and absorbed in Brahman (Gambhirananda 1958).'[157] Manusmṛti itself mentions in verse 2.71 that 'at the beginning and at the end of the study of the *Veda*, the feet of the teacher should always be clasped; and the *Veda* should be studied with joined palms; this is what has been called the *Brahmāñjali* (G. Jha 1920).'[158] These verses reveal how a student must approach a teacher and pay his respects.

Kullūka Bhaṭṭa, on the other hand, takes the prefix *prati* to mean 'in-turn' and interprets pratipūjya as the devotion and respect the sages offered to Manu the host, after receiving the same from Manu in the form of a respectful welcome.[159]

Therefore, prati-pūjya refers to the greetings and salutations offered by the sages to Svāyambhuva-Manu in the manner that students show reverence to the teacher and this they do after being welcomed by Manu the way a host welcomes a guest.

However, commentator Rāghavānanda Sarasvatī notes that the sages paid only verbal respects and did not perform a full *namaskāra* (which is usually done as sāṣṭāṇga namaskāra) because Manu is a kṣatriya and the sages were brāhmaṇas, and the term yathānyāya (in due form) refers to this convention which is prescribed in the śāstras.[160] We see such verbal salutations in verse 3 where Svāyambhuva-Manu is praised by the sages.

Therefore, the phrase pratipūjya or mutual salutations and show of respect can be understood as an interaction between the teacher and the arriving students as well as that between host and arriving guests.

### यथान्यायमिदं वचनमब्रुवन् – *yathānyāyamidaṃ vacanamabruvan* – in due manner, these words were spoken:

Kullūka Bhaṭṭa reads yathānyāya along with vacanaṁ abruvan and says that the text is noting that the sages who approached Manu and addressed him with questions in verse 1.2-3, did so in a proper manner. What is the proper manner? Kullūka Bhaṭṭa says 'proper manner' is one in which the student approaches the teacher and speaks to him with respect, devotion, trust, and other qualities.[161]

Proper manner also implies that students must approach

and address the teacher in a manner which reveals that they have the relevant qualities that make them competent to receive knowledge. What are these qualities? Bhagavān Kṛṣṇa says in Bhagavad Gītā 18.67 that knowledge should not be given to one who has not undergone austerities in the form of control of mind and the senses, one who is without devotion towards Īśvara and Guru, one who does not serve his Guru with humility, and one who is envious of and cavils against Īśvara.[162] Thus, Kṛṣṇa lists: austerity, devotion, service, and non-enviousness as important qualities of a student. *Kaṭha Upaniṣad* 1.2.24 says, 'One who has not desisted from bad conducts, whose senses are not under control, whose mind is not concentrated, whose mind is not free from anxiety, cannot attain this Self through knowledge (Gambhirananda 1957)'.[163] That is, knowledge should not be given to those who are bereft of these qualities.

According to *Kurma Purāṇa* 1.2.14.37–40[164] quoted in *Parāśara Mādhava* (*ācāra-khaṇḍa*, *prathama adhyāya*) (Tripati, Parasharamadhava: Acharakhandam 2019, 94), there are ten categories of students who are eligible to study the *Veda*, dharmaśāstra, and purāṇas to whom the *Ācārya* must teach. The same list of ten categories of students who should be taught is mentioned in Manu 2.109 itself:[165]

1. *Ācāryaputra*: The son of the teacher.
2. *Śuśrūṣu*: One who does service to the teacher.
3. *Jñānada*: One who teaches something (i.e. one can teach a person in return for learning something else from that person).
4. *Dhārmika*: One who lives by the precepts of dharma.
5. *Śuci*: One who is pure (in body, mind and speech).
6. *Āpta*: One who is a friend or a trustworthy person.

7. *Śakta*: One who is capable and competent (to receive, understand and assimilate knowledge).
8. *Arthada*: One who gives money (i.e. one who pays money in the form of *dakṣiṇā,* etcetera in return for receiving knowledge from the teacher).
9. *Sādhu*: One who is good hearted and well-intentioned.
10. *Sva*: One who is related to the teacher.

The Kurma Purāṇa further notes that the teacher should teach the *Veda*, dharmaśāstra, and purāṇas to only those students who are endowed with good conduct, intelligence, and are not proud and hypocritical.[166] Other qualities listed by the purāṇas for a student include, gratefulness, non-treacherous behaviour, intelligence, performance of auspicious actions, trustworthiness (i.e. one who speaks things as it is), and favourable disposition.[167]

Jagadguru Śaṅkarācārya Śrī Bharati Tirtha Mahaswami in one of his lectures lists the following qualities as being essential for a seeker of shastric knowledge: *sadbuddhi* (one should be endowed with good intentions and good heartedness), *sādhu-sevī* (one should have love, respect, and render service to elders), *sucaritram* (one should be endowed with good conduct), *tattva-bodha-abhilāṣī* (one should have genuine and burning desire to study and understand the truth), *śuśrushū* (one should listen to the teacher with full attention and one-pointed concentration and must lovingly render service to the teacher), *tyakta-manaḥ* (one should give up false prestige which makes one think that one knows everything and prevents one from admitting one's own ignorance about a subject), *praṇipatana-paraḥ* (one should salute the teacher by falling at his feet as a show of respect), *praśna-kāla-*

*pratīkṣā* (one should have patience to wait for the right time to ask questions and get doubts clarified from the teacher), *śāntaḥ* (one should be endowed with restraint over the mind), *dāntaḥ* (one should be endowed with control over the senses), *anasooya* (one must be free from jealousy), śāstra-*vishvāsa-śālī* (one must have complete trust in the *śāstra* being the valid source of correct knowledge), and *śaraṇa-upāgata* (one should take refuge in the teacher with love, humility and devotion) (*Veda*nta 3 of 15: Qualities of a Disciple by the Jagadguru Shankararcharya of Sringeri 2012). The sages have been called *maharṣi* or 'great sages' because they have become endowed with all these qualities, and hence they are competent to approach Manu and learn from him. In the succeeding verses (verse 1.2-3), the sages show these qualities of love, humility, trust, and devotion through the words and the manner in which they address Manu.

Manusmṛti also notes in verse 2.110 that a teacher should not teach unless the student approaches him and asks to be taught out of his own volition. It further says that one should not teach a student who asks in an improper manner.[168] Verse 2.111 says that he who instructs in an unlawful manner, and he who asks in an unlawful manner—of those two, one or the other either untimely dies, or incurs ill-will.[169] That is, knowledge must not be shared unless one is asked about it in a proper manner with humility and devotion. A teacher must never share knowledge with those who demand it as if it is their birthright or who are rude and arrogant towards the teacher.

Thus, the phrase 'in due manner, these words were spoken' shows that the sages approached and asked their question in a proper manner with humility, devotion, and a sincere thirst for knowledge, and not in an improper manner out of ego, prestige, or with an intention to test the teacher. It is because the sages approached Manu, and out of their own volition asked Manu about dharma, and asked these questions in a proper respectful manner, that Manu responds to these questions with an exposition on dharma from verse 1.4.

## Discussion

Manusmṛti presents its teaching on dharma in a narrative format and the first four verses—which narrate how the great sages approached Svāyambhuva-Manu and asked him to teach about dharma as applicable to different sections of the society, and Manu's beginning of his discourse on dharma in response to the request—encapsulate what is known in Hindu textual tradition as anubandha catuṣṭayam.

Anubandha catuṣṭayam literally means four connections and Hindu śāstras often begin with an enunciation of them. The four-fold connections are: *adhikārī* (refers to a qualified student who is eligible to study a śāstra), *viṣaya* (refers to the subject-matter of the text), *sambandha* (refers to inter-relationship between the other three), and *prayojana* (refers to the fruit or the end result of this whole enterprise). In the context of Manusmṛti, Kullūka Bhaṭṭa says viṣaya or subject-matter is dharma, the sambandha or relationship between the subject-matter (i.e. dharma) and the current text is that of *pratipādya-pratipādaka*. Pratipādya refers to the subject which is expounded and pratipādaka refers to that which expounds the subject. The prayojana or the end-result is the attainment of Svarga, mokṣa, and fulfilment of all the puruṣārthas for which dharma acts as the means.[170]

We see the elements of anubandha catuṣṭayam clearly enunciated in these opening four verses of the first chapter. In verse 2, when the great sages request Manu to teach about dharma or duties of the people belonging to all the four varṇas as well as those belonging to mixture of varṇas, the viṣaya or the object of knowledge being dharma is clearly brought out. Further, the adhikārī or those for whom the tenets of dharma have been enunciated has been explicitly stated as the people belonging to the four varṇas as well as those who have mixture of varṇas i.e. the entire humanity. The sambandha or connection between this text and the questions put forth by the sages is also clearly brought out. It further indicates the sambandha between the desire to know and ask questions on one hand and the study of the subject-matter (preferably under a teacher) on the other. Since, dharma by definition is that which leads to material and spiritual wellbeing,[171] the end-result or prayojana of pursuit of dharma is fulfilment of all the four puruṣārthas[172] and the attainment of both Svarga (heaven) and mokṣa (liberation from the cycle of birth and death).[173] In verse 3, when the sages describe Manu as knower of both actions and knowledge, they indicate this two-fold end-result—of worldly happiness that can be attained through performance of actions and final liberation that can be attained through acquisition of knowledge. Likewise, when, in response to the question by the sages, Manu begins his enunciation of dharma with the word 'Listen' in verse 4, it clearly brings out the sambandha between this text and dharma as being that of the propounder and the propounded.

What the narrative structure, and the importance given to the proper manner in which knowledge of dharma should be gained, actually reveals is that Manusmṛti—

which is nothing but an instruction of Manu on dharma in the form of words and sentences—positions itself as *śabda pramāṇa*—the valid source of knowledge about dharma which exists in the form of words, a knowledge which cannot be gained by any other sources of knowledge, be it direct perception, inference, analogy, or other sources. And the proper way to attain this knowledge enunciated in this text is to approach this text as a seeker approaches a Guru with devotion and trust and not with arrogance and scepticism. Only then, would the text reveal itself to the seeker and not otherwise.

Medhātithi says, 'The first four verses describe the fact of the treatise being the work of a highly qualified author, and of its providing instructions bearing upon such ends of man as are not knowable by means of any other source of knowledge (G Jha 1920).'[174] Kullūka Bhaṭṭa provides two examples to illustrate how the text reveals what constitutes dharma even in the context of pursuit of kāma and artha. These two examples show how the knowledge revealed in this text cannot be acquired through any other pramāṇas. In the context of pursuit of kāma, Kullūka notes that though everyone indulges in sexual intercourse, it is only through dharmaśāstra texts like Manu that one can understand one's obligations as well as the ethical practices related to it.[175] Manu, for example, says in verse 3.45: 'One should observe the rule of approaching (one's wife) during the period of her season,—ever attached to his own wife. In consideration of her he may approach her with a desire for sexual intercourse, except on the sacred days (G Jha 1920).'[176] That one should approach one's wife during her season excluding sacred days, and that one should have sexual relationship with his spouse to attain the fruits of gṛhastha-dharma is a knowledge which Manusmṛti and other texts in this genre alone can reveal. Likewise, though every person is involved in one or the other kind of job or business to earn a livelihood, it is only through dharmaśāstras that one can gain knowledge about what kind of work and lifestyle constitutes dharma and could help one to attain overall wellbeing.[177] Manu verses 4.4-4.6, for example, enunciate five methods of earning livelihood that are beneficial for a brāhmaṇa.[178] This knowledge is again something which cannot be acquired through any other pramāṇas like direct perception, inference, etcetera other than the *Veda* and texts like Manusmṛti which constitute śāstra-pramāṇa.

Further, as a pramāṇa śāstra, this text is concerned only with revealing knowledge about dharma, especially about the connection between karma and karmaphala and is not a law-book or a constitution which was hegemonically imposed upon society in the past, nor is it a book of commandments in a biblical sense as it is made out to be in modern scholarship.[179] As Ādi Śaṅkarācārya observes in his commentary on Bṛhadāraṇyaka Upaniṣad verse 1.4.10: 'Knowledge only removes false notion, it does not create anything. Nor can a scriptural statement impart any power to a thing. It is an accepted principle that the scriptures are only informative (i.e. impart knowledge) and not creative (i.e. do not bring about or create anything) (S Madhavananda 1950, 154).'[180] This is as true about dharmaśāstra as it is about *Vedāntaśāstra*. As Medhātithi notes in his commentary on Manu 2.6: 'The *Veda* and Smṛti can be a "cause" (of dharma) only in the sense that they serve to *make known*,—not in that of *producing*, nor in that *helping to stand*, which are the two senses in which the "root" is the cause of the Tree (G Jha 1920).'[181] The tenets of dharma in the form of vidhi (prescribed) and niṣedha (prohibited) enunciated in Manu and other texts in smṛti genre are broad guidelines and are binding only in one sense: that a particular karma or action gives rise to a particular kind of result and that particular result could be favourable leading to sukha (happiness) or unfavourable leading to duḥkha (sorrow) based on whether they are dharma or adharma. It is for this reason, Bhagavān Kṛṣṇa in Bhagavad Gītā 16.24 says: 'The śāstra is your authority as regards the determination of what is to be done and what is not to be done. After understanding (your) duty as presented by scriptural injunction, you ought to perform (your duty) here (Gambhirananda 1998).'[182]

In other words, the dharmaśāstras are revelatory in nature; they impart knowledge about actions and their respective fruits, and this in-turn can inspire a person to take up a particular course of action or avoid some other course of action based on whether they would result in favourable fruits or unfavourable ones. However, beyond this, whether one chooses to follow it or not, or how much one is able to follow it, or how one would interpret and contextualise the teachings to one's situation is ultimately dependent upon one's own capacity, discretion and exertion of free-will.[183] This is again highlighted by Ādi Śaṅkarācārya in his commentary on Bṛhadāraṇyaka Upaniṣad verse 2.1.20:

> The diversity of people's desires, attachments and so forth is another reason. People have innumerable desires and various defects such as attachment. Therefore, they are lured by the attachment etc. to external objects, and the scriptures are powerless to hold them back; nor can they persuade those that are naturally averse

> to external objects to go after them. But the scriptures do this much that they point out what leads to good and what to evil, thereby indicating the particular relations that subsist between the ends and means; just as a lamp, for instance, helps to reveal forms in the dark. But the scriptures neither hinder nor direct a person by force, as if he were a slave. We see how people disobey even the scriptures because of an excess of attachment etc. Therefore, according to the varying tendencies of people, the scriptures variously teach the particular relations subsisting between the ends and means. In this matter people on their own adopt particular means according to their tastes, and the scriptures simply remain neutral, like the sun, for instance, or a lamp.[184]
>
> (S Madhavananda 1950, 313)

This also implies that Manu and other texts in sūtra and smṛti genre that deal with dharma reveal the first principles of dharma which are eternal and which will always remain valid no matter what socio-political changes occur in society. The latter, i.e. socio-political changes only influence the different applications of dharma in practice and not the first principles of dharma itself.

Now, coming to the question of adhikārī or one who is eligible and competent for dharma in general and for this specific text in particular, there are three ways of understanding the notion of adhikāra: First is the fitness to do adhyāyana or shastrically study dharmaśāstras in general and the smṛtis including the present text in particular. Second is the fitness with respect to adhyāpana or shastrically teaching smṛtis (including this text) and other dharmaśāstra texts. Third is the fitness for practicing dharma (i.e. dharma *anuṣṭhāna*) by gaining knowledge about dharma, especially about one's svadharma.

Now, regarding those who are competent to practice dharma, it has been indicated in verse 1.2 wherein the great sages request Svāyambhuva-Manu to teach about dharma of those who belong to four varṇas as well as those who are antarprabhāvas or born from mixture of varṇas, i.e. the entire humanity. Then, regarding the competent seeker who is eligible to study this text of Manusmṛti, it has been indicated by phrases such as maharṣi, pratipūjya and yathānyāyam idam-vacanam abruvan in the present verse.

As we saw before, Skanda Purāṇa defines ṛṣi as a kind of brāhmaṇa who is endowed with certain qualities like control over mind and the senses, truthfulness, and so on. Further, Manusmṛti itself in verse 1.102-104 says, 'It was for the purpose of regulating the actions of the brāhmaṇa—and secondarily of others also—that the wise Manu Svāyambhuva elaborated these institutes. This may be studied with care, and duly taught to pupils, by the learned brāhmaṇa—not by anyone else. The brāhmaṇa studying these institutes, and (thence) discharging all prescribed duties, is never defiled by sins of commission (or omission), proceeding from mind, speech or body (G Jha 1920).'[185] Then, Manu 2.16 says: 'That person alone, and none other, should be regarded as entitled to the scripture, for whom the sacraments beginning with conception and ending with the crematorium, are prescribed as to be done with mantras (G. Jha 1920).'[186] Manu 4.80 says: 'He shall not offer advice to a śūdra, nor the leavings, nor what has been prepared as an offering to the Gods. He shall not expound the dharma to him; nor shall he indicate to him any penance (G Jha 1920).'[187] And Manu 10.1-2 says: 'The three twice-born varṇas, devoted to their duties, shall study; but of these the brāhmaṇa alone shall expound it, not the other two; such is the established law. The brāhmaṇa should know the means of livelihood for all men; he shall duly expound them to the others and himself do accordingly (G Jha 1920).'[188] However, Manu 2.13 also observes that 'The knowledge of dharma is ordained for those who are not addicted to the pursuit of wealth and pleasures; and for those seeking for the knowledge of dharma, the Revealed Word is the highest authority (G Jha 1920).'[189]

A brief explanation of the meaning and context of the above quoted verses from Manusmṛti is necessary. While on the one hand, Manu 2.16 says only *dvijas* are entitled to study this text of Manusmṛti and Manu 4.80 says a brāhmaṇa must not teach dharma to śūdras; on the other hand, Manu 2.13 says all those who are not addicted to pursuit of wealth and pleasure are entitled to the knowledge of dharma. To properly understand these verses and make sense of what appears to be contradictory, we need to distinguish 'studying' from mere 'reading' as well as distinguish 'teaching' from 'imparting of knowledge'.

A proper study in the way of adhyāyana is significantly different from mere reading. A proper in-depth study of a śāstra under a Guru is a study which is accompanied by austerity, reflection and implementation, leading to an accomplishment of the end-results of the text. As Manusmṛti 2.165 says: 'The entire *Veda*, along with the Esoteric Treatises, should be learnt by the twice-born person—by means of various kinds of austerities and observances prescribed by rule (G. Jha 1920).'[190] *Daksha Smṛti* 2.26 says that the study or practice of *Veda*s is five-fold: (1) receiving of the *Veda* through learning up of the text, (2) contemplating upon what is learned, (3) repeatedly practicing what is learned, (4) reciting it, and (5) teaching it (Piovano 2002, 75).[191] In the *ācāra-adhyaya* of Yājñavalkyasmṛti, there is an elaborate discussion on the kind of lifestyle and the austerities that the Brahmachari who does *Veda*-adhyayana must practice. For example, Yājñavalkyasmṛti verses 1.26-29 state:

> Then, he is to bow to the elders, saying – 'I am so and so'; and composing himself, he is to serve the preceptor in order to learn the *Veda*. Being invited (by the preceptor) he ought to study; and whatever may be acquired should be bestowed (on him, the preceptor); and by his mind, speech and body, he should conduct himself so as to benefit him (the preceptor). The grateful, kind, quick of perception and able to retain, pure, strong in body and mind, one who gives out the good acts, but not the faults of others, well-behaved, devoted (to the preceptor's service), one related, one able to give knowledge or money, such (students) should be taught. The staff, the skin (of the black antelope), the sacred thread, and the girdle, let him wear; (and) for his living, let him beg to blameless brāhmaṇas.[192]
>
> (Somayaji 2006, 9)

A similar verse from Viṣṇu Purāṇa 3.9.2–5 is quoted in Parāśara Mādhava (*ācāra khaṇḍa*, *prathama adhyāya*), which says:

> Every day, during morning and evening Sandhya period, a student should worship the Sun and the Fire, and offer salutations to his guru. A student must sit when the teacher sits down and must get up when the teacher gets up. In this manner, a student's activities

> should never be ill-disposed towards the teacher (i.e. a student must always behave favourably towards the teacher). Such a student should, only after receiving the instruction from the teacher to study, study the *Veda* with full concentration and without letting the mind become distracted. Likewise, he must eat the food received in *bhikṣā* only after taking permission from the teacher. By observing fully all *śaucācāra* i.e. activities related to purification, the student must perform śuśrūṣā or service to the teacher. He should then study the *Veda* after properly performing all the austerities and observances that are enjoined upon him and purifying the intellect.[193]

What is said here in the case of *Veda* is also applicable to the case of smṛtis and other dharmaśāstras.[194] When such a śāstra adhyayana or shastric study of the text is done by a competent seeker, then such a study itself leads one to attainment of puṇya or 'karmic merit'.[195] Further, since such a śāstra adhyayana is a stipulated duty (*vihita karma*) of the dvijas, especially brāhmaṇas, not performing them also leads to pāpam or karmic demerit for them. This is especially so because adhyayana is a *nitya karma* for the dvijas, and hence its non-performance leads to pāpa, a point highlighted by Śrī Mādhavācārya in Parāśara Mādhava.[196]

However, a mere reading of the text (either in original or in translation) does not constitute śāstra adhyayana, but instead it is the same as reading any book; it gives intellectual understanding, but it does not lead to any puṇyam. Likewise, learning the text in modern-day school and university settings or through the use of technology such as audio recordings,[197] even when done under a teacher, leads to intellectual understanding, but not the puṇyam involved in śāstra adhyayana because such a learning is not accompanied by the practice of *brahmacarya* (celibacy), *tapas* (austerity), *gurukulavāsa* and *guru-śuśrūṣā* (staying with and serving the teacher), and other observances that come under śāstra adhyayana.[198] This is not to say that reading of the texts or learning them in university settings is without utility. With sincerity, patience, effort, and reflection, intellectual engagement with the texts are very fruitful. However, they do not constitute adhyayanam, and hence do not lead to puṇyam. The fitness criteria that Manu 2.16 cites applies only to shastric study of smṛtis. Only the brāhmaṇas, kṣatriyas, and vaiśyas, who have had all their saṁskāras done with mantras, are entitled to shastrically study smṛtis and attain puṇyam or dharmic merit. It means that there is no prohibition or niṣedha on anyone regarding the reading of the texts by oneself or learning from others in a non-shastric manner out of a desire for information and to satisfy intellectual curiosity, or for getting the doubts clarified from such an effort.

Likewise, what is prohibited in Manu 4.80 is shastric teaching of smṛtis to śūdras and others, and not the sharing of knowledge about dharma, especially duties as relevant to them.[199] Śāstra *upadeśa/adhyāpana* or shastric teaching implies taking someone under tutelage as per the prescribed rules and teaching the text and the meaning of the text as well as the rules of conduct for the student. And since such a shastric teaching to the competent is the svadharma of brāhmaṇas, it gives them puṇyam or karmic merit.[200] However, at the same time, such adhyāpana to those who are prohibited by the śāstras also leads to pāpam or karmic demerit.[201] But, this adhyāpana or shastric teaching is distinct from sharing knowledge about dharma or texts on dharma using modern methods of teaching in schools, universities, etcetera or through online courses, writing books or delivering talks, and so on, wherein there is no guru-śiṣya relationship, nor any adhyāpana of the texts in a shastric manner. As Medhātithi notes on Manu 4.80 that some people opine that, 'The present text contains two injunctions forbidding the teaching of the text of the treatises dealing with dharma, and the expounding of its meaning: one forbids the teaching of the verbal text and the other that of its meaning. But the expounding of dharma, without reference to text, is not forbidden by any (G Jha 1920).'[202] Or, the phrase 'do not teach/expound the dharma' in the verse 4.80 could also refer to not teaching a śūdra about various rituals in the sense of officiating as a priest in a vaidika ritual,[203] as a śūdra is not entitled to *Veda*-adhyayana or vaidika karma.[204] Therefore, the verse 4.80 does not prohibit imparting knowledge about dharma, especially regarding duties which are relevant to śūdras and others. Further, Medhātithi explicitly notes that the prohibition is only for shastric teaching of *Veda*s and this Smṛti, and not for other branches of knowledge, like grammar etcetera.[205] Or as Kullūka Bhaṭṭa notes, the prohibition is merely related to direct instruction, where the śūdra seeks instruction about dharma or about any expiatory rites without the mediation of a brāhmaṇa.[206] Same view is expressed by Aparārka in his commentary on Yājñavalkyasmṛti.[207] Likewise, both *Nṛsiṃhaprasāda* and *Saṃskāramayūkha* say that what is forbidden is 'direct teaching'.

At this juncture, it is pertinent to examine whether the eligibility criteria mentioned in Manu 2.16 that limits the shastric study of smṛtis to only dvijas and the prohibition of shastric teaching of smṛtis to śūdras and others indicated in Manu 4.80 is applicable to study and teaching of all smṛtis or is it only applicable to Manusmṛti. While Manu 2.16 notes that the eligibility criteria regarding limiting the shastric study to dvijas is being mentioned in the particular context of Manusmṛti, dharmaśāstra commentators such as Vijñāneśvara in his Mitākṣarā commentary on Yājñavalkyasmṛti 1.3 cites this verse from Manu to argue that the eligibility criteria is applicable to shastric study of all smṛtis.[208]

Likewise, in *Smṛtimuktāphala*, *Varṇāśrama Khaṇḍa* 9.6, Vaidyanāthadīkṣita quotes Yama as saying that a śūdra is not entitled to *Veda*s and smṛtis.[209] Further, Manu 4.80, which prohibits shastric teaching of smṛtis to śūdras, does not qualify the prohibition as being a reference to only the text of Manusmṛti, though Medhātithi tries to interpret it as such. Therefore, the prohibition can be taken as a general rule applicable to all smṛtis. However, Śrī Mādhavācārya in his commentary on Parāśara Smṛti 1.1-2 observes that the text begins with the phrase '*atha*' indicating that everyone is eligible for the text.[210] Other smṛtis which begin with the phrase 'atha' include *Vasiṣṭha Smṛti*, *Kātyāyana Smṛti*, *Yama Smṛti* and *Auśanasa Smṛti*. Therefore, we can conclude that the prohibition of shastric study and shastric teaching of smṛtis with respect to śūdras and others is, as a general rule, applicable to all smṛtis with the exception of smṛtis such as Parāśara Smṛti, etcetera which begin with the phrase 'atha'.

Further, Appayya Dīkṣita in the third *pariccheda* of his Śāstra *Siddhāntaleśa Saṅgraha* cites Mahābhārata Śānti Parva verse 314.45 which states that one should teach by keeping the brāhmaṇa student in the forefront such that students of all the four varṇas can listen to the teachings[211] and notes that all the four varṇas have eligibility to listen to the shastric teaching of itihāsa-purāṇas (i.e. to shastrically study itihāsa-purāṇas) in the manner prescribed in the Mahābhārata.[212] Same view has been expressed by Smṛtimuktāphala, Varṇāśrama Khaṇḍa 35.11 which says, 'The bar on teaching dharma to śūdra relates to dharma like *Vedic Agnihotra,* etcetera; as it is stated, "with brāhmaṇa in front, itihāsas and purāṇas can be told to all the four varṇas", listening to itihāsas and purāṇas is permissible for a śūdra. Further, it must be stated that there is no bar in teaching śūdra about dharmas of śūdra expounded in Smṛti (Kannan n.d.).'[213] Such shastric study of itihāsa-purāṇas will bring great puṇyam to everyone, including to śūdras and antarprabhāvas.

Therefore, while the śūdras (and others) are ineligible to shastrically study smṛtis in general, they can not only study dharma on their own or seek instruction regarding dharma through non-adhyāpana means; they can also shastrically study those smṛtis which begin with 'atha' as well as itihāsa-purāṇas (which are also dharmaśāstras as they enunciate dharma) through the mediation of a brāhmaṇa in the manner described in the Mahābhārata. The first part of the verse 4.80 which says a brāhmaṇa should not give advice to a śūdra can be taken as merely a reference to not giving advice when unasked for or when asked in an improper manner without humility and respect. Kullūka Bhaṭṭa notes that the prohibition is only about advice related to worldly matters.[214] Or as Medhātithi says, 'This prohibition pertains to being an adviser as a means of livelihood (for the brāhmaṇa); there would be nothing wrong in offering advice in a purely friendly manner; in fact, there may be hereditary friendship between brāhmaṇas and śūdras; and certainly through friendship, advice for welfare is always offered.[215] Further, Manu 10.2, which says, 'The brāhmaṇa should know the means of livelihood for all men; he shall duly expound them to the others and himself do accordingly (G Jha 1920)',[216] points to the fact that it has been obligated upon a brāhmaṇa to 'impart the knowledge about livelihood' to śūdras and others. Though the verse specifically refers to imparting the knowledge about livelihood, it is important to understand that for the śūdras and the others, their means of attaining livelihood itself forms their svadharma which when performed without envy and by adhering to the tenets of sāmānya dharma gives them material and spiritual wellbeing as noted in Manu 10.128[217] and as illustrated in the story of Dharmavyādha in Mahābhārata Vana Parva.[218]

Further, Manu 2.13 explicitly notes that the knowledge of dharma is ordained for all those who are not addicted to the pursuit of wealth and pleasures. Hence, everyone, including śūdras and others who have turned towards dharma and have withdrawn from obsession with artha and kama, is eligible to receive knowledge about dharma in one form or the other. That is, all those who genuinely seek dharma are eligible to receive knowledge about dharma and practice the same. If this were not so, how could these people practice dharma to attain the two fold-goals of abhyudaya and niḥśreyasa.

In this context, Medhātithi makes an important observation in his commentary on Manu 2.16 about why shastrically studying the text of Manu is not necessary to attain knowledge about one's own dharma and for performing them. He first quotes the opponent's objections thus:

> When the śūdra is not entitled to study the scripture and learn its meaning, how can he be entitled to the performance of the acts therein prescribed? Unless the man knows the exact form of the act, he cannot do it; unless he studies the scriptures, he cannot know what is contained in them; and no unlearned person is entitled to the performance of any (religious) act.[219]
>
> (G Jha 1920)

He responds to this objection thus:

> True; but the requisite knowledge can be obtained from the advice of other persons. The śūdra may be dependent upon a brāhmaṇa; or a brāhmaṇa may be doing the work of instructing people for payment; and such a brāhmaṇa might very well instruct the śūdra to 'do this, after having done that' and so forth. So that the mere fact of the śūdra performing the acts does not necessarily indicate that he is entitled to the study and understanding of the scriptures; as performance can be accomplished even on the strength of what is learnt from others; as is done in the case of women; what helps women (in the performance of their duties) is the learning of their husbands, which becomes available to them through companionship.[220]
>
> (G Jha 1920)

That is, none are prohibited from obtaining knowledge about their own duties and performing them to attain material and spiritual wellbeing.

In other words, the primary adhikārī for shastrically

studying (and not merely reading) this text (and by extension other smṛtis with notable exceptions) are brāhmaṇas since it is their special duty to do adhyayana of different śāstras and vidyās and teach them.[221] The secondary adhikārī for shastrically studying smṛtis are kṣatriyas and vaiśyas who undergo *upanayana* and other saṁskāras with mantras and hence become entitled to study. And in a tertiary sense, all others including śūdras and antarprabhāvas are adhikārī to receive knowledge about their own respective duties contained in smṛtis, either through instruction from a brāhmaṇa teacher (approached through the medium of another brāhmaṇa) or through the shastric study of those smṛtis which begin with 'atha'. This knowledge can also be acquired from itihāsa-purāṇas, which have reformulated and contextualised the teachings of Śruti and smṛtis in a narrative, more accessible format, and whose shastric study under a teacher (in the manner mentioned in Mahabharata) is open for everyone. And, in today's context, through reading the texts either in original or in translations all by oneself, or by learning in modern university settings, one can gain intellectual understanding to whatever degree possible. And everyone, people belonging to all the four varṇas, as well as those who are antarprabhāvas, all have adhikāra to practice svadharma anuṣṭhāna, a point which is noted in passing by Medhātithi in his commentary on verse 2.16.[222] If this were not the case, then, the sages' request to Manu to teach about dharma as applicable to all varṇas as well as those applicable to the antarprabhāvas in the next verse would become redundant. The other qualities which the said seeker of knowledge about dharma must possess as indicated by phrases 'prati-pūjya' and 'yathā nyāyam'—the qualities like devotion, respect, thirst for knowledge, etcetera—have already been described in detail.

A discussion on 'adhikārī' for smṛtis and other dharmaśāstras will remain incomplete without discussing the position of women with respect to their eligibility to study smṛtis. On this, two verses from Manusmṛti are of particular relevance. First is verse 2.66, which states that, 'For females, this whole series (of saṁskāras) should be performed at the right time and in the proper order, for the purpose of sanctifying the body; but without the Vedic formulas (G. Jha 1920).'[223] When this verse 2.66 is read along with verse 2.16 quoted before which says, 'That person alone, and none other, should be regarded as entitled to the scripture, for whom the sacraments beginning with conception and ending with the crematorium, are prescribed as to be done with mantras (G. Jha 1920),'[224] it clearly implies that women do not have the eligibility for shastrically studying smṛtis, since their saṁskāras are not accompanied with mantras.

From this, it follows that 'all women', irrespective of their varṇas, do not have the eligibility to shastrically study smṛtis. However, as with the case of śūdras, an exception to this general rule are the smṛtis such as Parāśara Smṛti, etcetera, which begin with the phrase 'atha,' and hence are open for everyone to shastrically study them. Women may also receive knowledge about dharma from others, especially their husbands who are considered as their gurus[225] or through the shastric study of itihāsa-purāṇas and other non-smṛti dharmasastras under a guru, for which they are eligible.

However, the use of the phrase 'all women' requires further explanation. *Hārīta Dharmasūtra* cited by many dharmaśāstra texts like Vīramitrodaya, composed during the last millennium, says that women can be classified into *brahmavādinīs* and *sadyovadhus*. Of them, for the former, there is upanayana and *Veda*-adhyayana; while for the latter, when the time of marriage arrives, upanayana should be performed somehow, which should be followed immediately by marriage.[226] That is, brahmavādinīs have adhikāra for adhyayana of *Veda* and hence for dharmaśāstra as well. We see many examples of brahmavādinīs like Gārgī, Maitreyī, Apālā, and others in itihāsa-purāṇas. However, another text, Yama Smṛti, again cited by dharmaśāstra texts like Vīramitrodaya, says that: 'In former *kalpa*, for girls also there was upanayana, also the teaching of the *Veda* and the pronouncing of the *Sāvitrī*. But she should be taught by her father, uncle or brother, none else. For the girl, alms-begging is to be done in her own home; and she should avoid the skin, the rags and also matted locks.'[227] That is, as per Yama Smṛti, the upanayana and *Veda*-adhyayana for brahmavādinī women was a practice in an older kalpa, and hence not applicable to current times. In the current times, based on other textual authorities like Bhāgavata Purāṇa 1.4.25, which explicitly notes that since for women, *śūdras*, and *dvija-bandhus* (dvijas only in name, being devoid of saṁskāras and Vedic learning), the *Veda*s are beyond reach, for their benefit Vyāsa composed Mahābhārata,[228] and smṛti statements like Manu 9.18 which explicitly notes that for women there is no dealing with (vedic) mantras, we have to conclude that women do not have adhikāra for *Veda*-adhyayana.[229] Then, we have a Śruti statement in *Narasiṁha Pūrva Tāpanī Upaniṣad* 1.3, a minor Upaniṣad attached to Atharva *Veda* and included in *Muktika* cannon of one hundred and eight Upaniṣads, wherein, in the context of enunciation of *Nṛsiṁha-Anuṣṭup* mantra which also consists as its part the *Praṇava mantra* (i.e. *Oṁ*), the eight-syllabled *Sāvitrī mantra* and the *Yajur-Lakshmi mantra*, it explicitly prohibits the imparting of this Vedic mantra along with its parts to women and śūdras.[230] Further, from the smṛti statements such as Manu 5.153, *Śukra Nīti* 4.4.5-6 and *Viṣṇusmṛti* 25.15 which state that there are no separate sacrifices, observances, or fastings for women and they attain heaven through serving the husband,[231] we can see that strī-dharma is the primary dharma for women and that in the current yuga all women are to be taken as sadyovadhus. It is for this reason that Manu 2.67 says that for women, vivāha itself serves the purpose of upanayana, and hence they do not have separate saṁskāra of upanayana (and hence, do not have *Veda-adhyayana*).[232] However, one could argue that there could be exceptions to the above conclusion by interpreting the phrase 'purā kalpa' of Yama Smṛti to merely mean 'olden times' (and not former kalpa) and hence concluding that there could be potential brahmavādinīs even today. Even then, such exceptions only prove the general rule as per the *Kauṇḍinya Nyāya,*[233] and not otherwise.[234]

This change in the nature of dharma for women, limiting it primarily to the dharma of sadyovadhus, must be understood as a result of a change in yuga-dharma caused by the change in the yuga (brought about by the arrival of Kaliyuga) which led to general decrease in the strength and competency of all people. Further, since women undergo biologically significant phases[235] like menstruation, pregnancy, etcetera and since their workload in a traditional household and as part of gṛhastha-dharma involves taking care of the entire family, expecting them to perform daily Vedic performances like *sandhyāvandana* and other rituals would not only be unrealistic, but also unfair to women. It is for this reason, out of compassion towards women, the dharmaśāstra writers restricted the svadharma of women to their duties that come under stri-dharma. Through these they can achieve everything that the men-folk attain through practice of varṇa-āśrama-dharma, a point also highlighted by Vidwan Ranganatha Sharma in his book *Mānava dharmaśāstra Matthu Mahileyaru* (D M Sharma 2004, 102). Therefore, strī-dharma must be understood as the primary dharma for all women in the current yuga, since all women are sadyovadhus. As sadyovadhus, vivāha itself has taken the place of upanayana, with serving the husband and doing the gṛhastha duties taking the place of serving the guru and brahmacarya duties for women as noted by Manu 2.67. Hence, the phrase 'all women' has been used in connection to prohibition of shastric study of smṛtis to women.

However, as noted before, this does not imply a prohibition of reading of the smṛti texts, or learning them in modern school or university settings or learning about dharma from their husbands through companionship.[236] They can very much do these and gain great benefit in the form of knowledge and insights on dharma. They are also entitled to perform the duties prescribed for them by the smṛtis and other dharmaśāstras. There is no prohibition for shastric study of itihāsa-purāṇas and other non-smṛti dharmaśāstras under a guru as well. They are only prohibited from shastrically studying the Śruti and smṛti texts under a guru accompanied by the practice of austerity, etcetera and even here the prohibition is not applicable to smṛti texts like Parāśara Smṛti that begin with the phrase 'atha'.

As an aside, it must be noted that the statement 'all

women are sadyovadhus in Kaliyuga' does not mean that vivāha is the only path available for women. For women with intense *vairāgya*, the path of renunciation is definitely open as noted by Svāmī Vidyāraṇya (Mādhavācārya) in *Jīvanmuktiviveka*. We also have examples of great devotee women like Akkamahadevi, Andal, Meera Bai and others who did not practice the conventional gṛhastha duties, but instead practiced *bhakti-yoga* taking their *iṣṭa* as their husbands. Further, while *kulavadhus* practiced strīdharma, the *nagaravadhus* or *gaṇikās* were considered *varṇa-bāhya* i.e. outside the varṇa-āśrama dharma, and hence, were not bound by strīdharma, nor did they have *Veda-*adhikāra. For them sāmānya dharma and spiritual paths such as bhakti were open.

*Śivarāja Ācārya Kauṇḍinyāyana* (2014) notes in his Hindi translation of Manu 2.16 that 'adhikāra' or eligibility in the context of anubandha catuṣṭayam has a special meaning. He says that when it is said some people are not eligible for practicing a particular action, it means that by the practice of the said action, such people will not gain any puṇya or dharmic merit. That is, while the shastric study and teaching of smṛti texts brings dharmic merit to brāhmaṇas; for kṣatriyas and vaiśyas, the shastric study alone brings dharmic merit; and for śūdras and others, neither the shastric study nor the shastric teaching brings dharmic merit. Therefore, shastric study or *svādhyāya* of smṛtis constitutes svadharma of dvijas and not others. However, the shastric study of itihāsa-purāṇas as well as those smṛtis that begin with the phrase 'atha' does impart dharmic merit to everyone—dvijas, śūdras, women, and antarprabhāvas. In other words, the question of *adhikāratva* with respect to smṛtis is primarily with respect to eligibility regarding shastric study of the text, and not with respect to the performance of dharma. Everyone is entitled to perform their own svadharma and attain overall wellbeing, a point Bhagavān Kṛṣṇa makes in Gītā 3.35: 'One's own duty, though defective, is superior to another's duty well-performed. Death is better while engaged in one's own duty; another's duty is fraught with fear (Gambhirananda 1998).'[237]

Medhātithi further notes that two kinds of students study this śāstra. He says:

> Of enquirers (and students) there are two classes—one following reasoning, and another following tradition. The former of these take up the study of Manu; because they know the importance and greatness of the author and his work from such texts as— 'whatever Manu said is wholesome' (*Kāṭhaka*, 11.5), and 'Manu has said all that has been said in the *ṚgVeda,* the *Yajurveda*, the *Sāmaveda* and the Mantras of the *Atharva*, as also by the Seven Great Sages.' And those of the latter class undertake it merely under the influence of the tradition, the source of which they have carefully investigated—that the treatise has been composed by Prajāpati himself. And for the sake of such persons, the mentioning of the name of the author also is a factor leading to action (towards study).[238]
>
> (G Jha 1920)

Lastly, the first four verses (especially verse 3) highlight the fact that Manu is a highly accomplished and the most-qualified teacher to teach about dharma.

# Verse Two

भगवन् सर्ववर्णानां यथावदनुपूर्वशः ।
अन्तरप्रभवाणां च धर्मान्नो वक्तुमर्हसि ॥ २ ॥

*Bhagavān sarvavarṇānāṃ yathāvadanupūrvaśaḥ |*
*antaraprabhavāṇāṃ ca dharmānno vaktumarhasi || 2 ||*

**Word by word translation:** O one who possesses opulence (भगवन् – *Bhagavān*); of all the varṇas (सर्ववर्णानां – *sarvavarṇānāṃ*); in due form (यथावत् – *yathāvat*); in proper sequence (अनुपूर्वशः– *anupūrvaśaḥ*); those born in between (अन्तरप्रभवाणाम् – *antaraprabhavāṇām*); and (च – *ca*); the dharmas (धर्मान् – *dharmān*);to us (नः– naḥ); you are competent to speak about (वक्तुमर्हसि – *vaktum arhasi*).

**Meaning:** O one who possesses opulence, you (alone) are competent to speak to us about (and hence please give instructions about) the dharmas of all the varṇas as well as those of mixed origins in due form and in proper sequence.

**Analysis:** In this and the next verse, the great sages address Manu.

**भगवन् – *Bhagavān* – O one who possesses opulence:** The term bhaga means opulence and Bhagavān means one who possesses opulence. Viṣṇu Purāṇa 6.5.74 lists six kinds of opulence denoted by the term bhaga: (1) *aiśvarya* (full sovereignty), (2) *dharma* (righteousness), (3) *yaśaḥ* (fame), (4) *śriyaḥ* (glory), (5) *jñāna* (knowledge) and (6) *vairāgya* (freedom from passion) (Wilson 1864-1877).[239] Further in verse 6.5.78, it says that when the phrase Bhagavān is used in reference to a person or an object in a customary or general sense, then it means 'one who knows the origin and end and revolutions of beings (i.e. movement from birth to growth, decay, death, and rebirth), and what is wisdom, what is ignorance (Wilson 1864-1877).'[240] Here Manu is being addressed as Bhagavān by the great sages as a form of praise and adulation of the qualities of Manu, whom they have approached for instruction. This address shows the humility and devotion of the great sages who recognise the superiority of Manu as a competent teacher endowed with opulence, and hence have sought refuge in him.

**सर्ववर्णानां – *sarvavarṇānāṃ* – of all the varṇas:** Varṇa as colour can refer to pre-existing saṃskāras or it can refer to the ritual state of a person. Manusmṛti 10.4 notes that there are only four varṇas; there is no fifth varṇa. These four varṇas are: brāhmaṇa, kṣatriya, vaiśya, and śūdra.[241]

The varṇa classification is based on three factors: *janma* or birth, *guṇa-svabhāva* or inner tendencies, and svadharma karma or one's duties and activities which are in sync with one's *svabhāva*.

In the context of defining a brāhmaṇa, *Atri Saṁhitā* verse 140-141 says: 'By birth, one is known as a brāhmaṇa;

and by purificatory rites (saṁskāra), he becomes a dvija (twice-born). He attains to the dignity of a *vipra* by learning, and by these three, to that of a *śrotriya*. He, who studies the *Veda*-śāstra and follows the import of scriptural injunctions, is called *Vedavid* (one knowing the *Veda*s); his utterance is sanctifying (Dutt 1908, 303).'[242] The same is repeated verbatim in *Padma Purāṇa* 1.46.129-130 (Padma Purana [sanskrit] n.d.). A similar verse is quoted by *Śabdārthacintāmaṇi* which says *tapas* (austerity, self-control), *śruta* (learning), and *yoni* (birth) are the three causes of *brāhmaṇyam*, and one who is devoid of austerity and learning should be known as *jāti-brāhmaṇa* or brāhmaṇa by birth alone.[243] While austerity and learning are acquired qualities that qualify a brāhmaṇa by birth to attain the higher status of dvija, vipra, etcetera, birth itself is posited as the primary criteria for determining varṇa in these verses. Manusmṛti itself states in verse 10.42: 'By the force of austerities and the seed, they attain higher or lower rank among men, through birth, cycle after cycle (G Jha 1920).'[244] In verse 10.5, Manusmṛti further says: 'Among all varṇas, those only who are born of consorts wedded in the natural order, as virgins of equal status, are to be regarded as the same (varṇa as their father) (G Jha 1920).'[245] A similar view is expressed even in the Śruti. *Chāndogya Upaniṣad* verse 5.10.7, for example, states, 'Among them, those who did good work in this world [in their past life] attain a good birth accordingly. They are born as a brāhmana, a kṣatriya, or a vaiśya. But those who did bad work in this world [in their past life] attain a bad birth accordingly, being born as a dog, a pig, or as a casteless person (Lokeswarananda 1998).'[246]

Then, in Bhagavad Gītā 4.13, Bhagavān Kṛṣṇa speaks

about the creation of four varṇas based on guṇa (natural qualities and tendencies) and karma (personal duties); and in verse 18.41, He notes that the duties have been allotted based on the guṇas which have their source in svabhāva (pre-existing impressions which manifest in present life as innate nature).[247] Bhāgavata Purāṇa 11.17.13 stresses that the four varṇas that originated from the Supreme *Puruṣa* are to be recognised/designated by their *ātma-ācāra* (natural activities or personal duties according to inherent nature i.e. svadharma).[248] Ādi *Śa*ṅkarācārya, while commenting on Bhagavad Gītā verse 4.13 says that brāhmaṇa is a designation given to one in whom there is a predominance of *sattva*; kṣatriya is one in whom there is both sattva and *rajas*, but rajas predominates; in vaiśya, both rajas and *tamas* exist, but rajas predominates; and śūdra is one in whom both rajas and tamas exist, but tamas predominates.[249] Thus, through the different combinations of the three guṇas, four varṇas with distinct svabhāvas arise. Manusmṛti 1.87 notes that for the protection of the universe, each of the four varṇas have been given different kinds of dharmas to pursue.[250]

Thus, janma (birth), guṇa, and karma form the three-fold criteria for determining varṇa, with janma constituting the primary criterion for determination, and guṇa and karma constituting secondary factors. And all the three are in-turn dependent upon a person's *prārabdha karma* or the karmas from previous lives which are now ready to fructify in the form of present life and which determine where an individual takes birth, in which family, what kind of saṁskāras one would have, and what kind of life-circumstances one would have to tackle.

*Ṛgveda Puruṣasūkta* depicts this complicated process

through the story of Cosmic Puruṣa from whom emerged the four varṇas from four different parts. The different parts of the Puruṣa represent the different svabhāva and svadharma associated with each of the varṇas, and the fact that they emerge from Puruṣa, shows that these svabhāvas are inherent in a person from birth.

However, neither janma, nor guṇa, nor karma in itself constitute the definition of varṇa.

The term varṇa is derived from the verbal root word '*vr*', which has a number of meanings including to choose, to cover, and colour. Often, the term is interpreted in terms of janma, guṇa, and karma as either a reference to birth in a family, or as a reference to inner temperaments, or as one's duties in life. But, such definitions, though not completely incorrect, mistake the external marks from which the varṇa of an individual can be inferred as constituting varṇa itself.

Varṇa is actually a reference to an individual's ritual state and indicates the presence of the divine essence of particular type of varṇa devatās.[251] Thus, a brāhmaṇa is one who is endowed with the divine essence of brāhmaṇa devata. A kṣatriya is one endowed with the divine essence of kṣatriya devatās. Likewise, with the vaiśya and śūdra. The presence or absence of these varṇa devatās in an individual determine whether he/she can be designated as belonging or not belonging to the said varṇa. And one attains such varṇa devatās primarily through janma which in turn is caused by one's karmas from previous lives. The guṇa and karma of this life act as secondary factors that facilitate the manifestation of these varṇa devatās in a person's current life. (See Appendix I for an elaborate treatment of varṇa with a particular focus on its ritual dimension).

Thus, by saying 'duties of all the varṇas', the sages

are requesting Manu to impart knowledge about different duties and lifestyles in accordance to the ritual condition of each of the four varṇas through which they all can attain overall wellbeing.

**यथावत् – *yathāvat* – in due form:**

Medhātithi says 'The suffix "*vati*" denotes propriety; the meaning being— "in the form in which performance would be proper." This "propriety" also includes such details as— "this is compulsory, that is optional," "this is primary, that is secondary," as also rules relating to substance, place, time, agent and so forth (G Jha 1920).'[252] Kullūka Bhaṭṭa likewise notes, 'in due form' refers to a request for clear enunciation about which dharmas or duties are applicable to which varṇas and to which āśrama, and in what format they must be performed.[253] Since principles of dharma cannot be blindly applied in the same way in all situations and with respect to all persons, the sages are requesting for detailed and tailor-made instructions about dharma, such that each individual can easily understand his or her own current position in the dharmic journey and work their own way towards the ultimate goal of mokṣa.

**अनुपूर्वशः– *anupūrvaśaḥ* – in proper sequence:**

The sages are adding another condition to their request. They are requesting Manu to enunciate the order in which the duties are to be performed. Both Medhātithi[254] and Kullūka Bhaṭṭa[255] give the example of performance of saṁskāras, wherein the sequence is of importance. When a child is born, the very first saṁskāra which is to be performed for it is *Jātakarma* (the ceremony marking the birth), then comes *Nāmakaraṇa* or the naming ceremony, and so on. The sequence in which these are to be performed is very important for them to be beneficial to the child. Likewise, the sequence of duties is important with respect to āśrama-dharma. A child first enters *brahmacarya*, then transitions into *gṛhastha*, then *vānaprastha*, and finally *sannyāsa*.[256] Alternatively, 'in proper sequence' may be a reference to a request for enunciation of the duties of the four varṇas and the antarprabhāvas sequentially one after another and not in a haphazard way. We see that the text follows this sequential format of enunciation of dharma starting with the dharma of brāhmaṇas in Chapter 2 and ending with the dharma of antarprabhāvas in Chapter 10.

**अन्तरप्रभवानां च** – ***antaraprabhavānām ca*** **– and those born in between:**

It refers to those who are born from parents having different varṇas. They are hence endowed with varṇa-svabhāva of mixed nature which is distinct from the svabhāvas of the parents and thus have a ritual state distinct from them.

The phrase sarva-varṇānām or 'of all the varṇas' refers to the duties of those who were born into a particular varṇa owing to both their parents belonging to the same varṇa, and hence inheriting the same varṇa-svabhāva. As Manu 10.5 notes 'Among all varṇas, those only who are born of consorts wedded in the natural order, as virgins of equal status (i.e. of same varṇa), are to be regarded as the same (i.e. same varṇa as their father) (G Jha 1920).'[257]

Therefore, the phrase 'dharmas of all the varṇas' in the current verse does not include those who were born from *anuloma*[258] or *pratiloma*[259] marriages, wherein the children are endowed with a svabhāva, particularly the ritual state, which is distinct from that of their parents, and hence their duties would be distinct from those of the parents. As Medhātithi notes, those born from mixture of varṇas 'could not be classed under the varṇa either of the mother or that of the father; just as the mule born out of the union of the horse and the ass is a distinct species, it is neither the "horse" nor the "ass";—on this ground, these (i.e. antarprabhāvas) would not be included under the "varṇas"; hence they have been mentioned separately (G Jha 1920).'[260]

Thus, it is with an intention to include all these people under the purview of dharma (so as to not exclude anyone) and facilitate their overall wellbeing that the sages explicitly request Manu to enunciate upon the duties of those 'born in between'.

A question may arise here as to why there are only four varṇas as Manu himself declares in verse 10.4, and why the svabhāvas arising from the mixing of four varṇas are not classified as distinct varṇas?

Though innumerable svabhāvas exist and no two individuals have exactly the same svabhāva, the four varṇas refer to four clear-cut svabhāva categories that arise out of the interplay of the guṇas.

Let us reconsider Ādi Śaṅkarācārya's explanation about how four varṇas arise out of the three guṇas. He notes that in the case of the four varṇas, there is clearly one guṇa, which is predominant; one which is influential but secondary; and the third that is negligible. In an ideal brāhmaṇa, there is excess of sattva such that both rajas and tamas are negligible. In an ideal kṣatriya, rajas is predominant, but it is anchored in sattva which is influential but secondary in magnitude, and tamas is negligible. In an ideal vaiśya, rajas predominates, tamas is secondary, and sattva is negligible.

In an ideal śūdra, tamas predominates, rajas is secondary, and sattva is negligible. There is no fifth varṇa as it is not possible to have a situation wherein sattva predominates and is rooted in tamas which acts as secondary or tamas predominates and sattva acts as secondary. These two combinations are not possible because sattva and tamas are contradictory to each other in nature. The combination of sattva and rajas with the former in predominant position and the latter in secondary position gives rise to what the śāstras call 'brahma-kṣatra'. Those who fall under this category are usually classified under brāhmaṇas, unless they take up kṣatriya-dharma.

When people from different varṇas marry, the children inherit different svabhāvas from each of the parents and hence his/her svabhāva would be distinct from his/her parents. Take the case of those born from a kṣatriya father and śūdra mother, they inherit rajas from both parents, but in one, rajas is predominant, and in the other, it is in secondary condition; and they also inherit secondary sattva from the father and predominant tamas from the mother. The guṇa interplay is so complicated and unpredictable here that they cannot be categorised as a distinct varṇa. Instead people with mixed varṇa parentage have been recognised as being endowed with mixed svabhāva, distinct from both the parents, but for practical purposes taking upon some of the duties of either of the parents based on the situation and context.

An analogy using colours for svabhāvas will be helpful here. One of the meanings of varṇa is colour and Mahābhārata Śānti Parva 181.5 assigns a colour to each varṇa that symbolically represents the svabhāva associated with that varṇa, reflecting the three guṇas. Brāhmaṇa varṇa is associated with white, kṣatriya varṇa is associated with red, the vaiśya varṇa with yellow, and the śūdra varṇa with black.[261] Just as when two colours are mixed together, they give rise to a third colour, and based on the proportions of the two colours used in the mixing, different shades of the third colour emerge, so also the case with intermixture of varṇa through anuloma and pratiloma marriages, wherein the child inherits different svabhāvas having guṇas in different magnitudes. As a result, while those born from same varṇa parents are capable of inheriting and fully manifesting the divine essences of their respective types of varṇa devatās, those born from mixed varṇa marriages are unable to do so.

It must be noted that some contemporary commentators like Dr Surendra Kumar have criticised the interpretation of the phrase 'antarprabhava' as a reference to those born with mixed varṇa-svabhāva adopted by all major Saṃskṛta commentators including Bhāruci, Medhātithi, Govindarāja and Kullūka Bhaṭṭa. Dr Kumar in his Hindi commentary on Manusmṛti has instead interpreted the phrase as a reference to āśramas. However, his interpretation is untenable as it is speculative, forced, and with a revisionist agenda (See Appendix II for a critique of his interpretation).

Thus, the great sages by stressing that they want to know not only about the dharmas of all varṇas but also of those born by the mixture of varṇas are including the entirety of humanity under the purview of dharma. It also shows that they have an unselfish interest in posing this question. They are not asking the question for personal benefit, but for the benefit of the whole world.

**धर्मान् – *dharmān* – the dharmas:**

Literally the term 'dharma' is defined as 'that which upholds'. So, naturally the question arises, what is it that dharma is upholding? Anticipating such a question, Bhagavān Kṛṣṇa in Mahābhārata Karna Parva 49.50 says, 'That which upholds is called as dharma. Dharma upholds all beings.'[262] Likewise, Mahānārāyaṇa Upaniṣad 79.7 states: 'Dharma is the support of the whole universe. All people draw near a person who is fully devoted to dharma. Through dharma, a person chases away sin (pāpam/karmic demerit). All are supported by dharma. Therefore, they say that dharma is the supreme means of liberation (Vimalananda 1968).'[263]

What does 'upholding' mean in the context of an individual?

We find an enunciation of this in Vaiṣeśika Sūtra 1.1.2, which says: 'Dharma is that (i.e. those actions) from which (results) the accomplishment of abhyudaya and niḥśreyasa (Sinha 1923).'[264] Abhyudaya means 'wellbeing' and niḥśreyasa means 'spiritual emancipation'. While abhyudaya specially refers to puṇyam or karmic merit that leads to sukha (happiness), svarga (heaven) and better birth, niḥśreyasa refers to the actions which lead to *citta-śuddhi* or purification of the mind which in-turn eventually leads to mokṣa. Therefore, in the context of an individual, all those actions which lead to one's overall wellbeing is dharma and the opposite, those that lead to fall, bondage, and sorrow of the individual is adharma. As Manusmṛti (1.26) says, Bhagavān or Hiraṇyagarbha has created the duality of dharma and adharma so as to distinguish various actions (karmas) and subject various creatures involved in those actions to their respective results of happiness (in case of dharma) and sorrow (in case of adharma) and the like.[265] Ādi Śaṅkarācārya in his introduction to Gītā Bhāṣya summarises the definition of dharma as that which sustains the universe and grants both material and spiritual welfare to all living beings, and is practiced by people of all classes in stages of life who aspire for higher good.[266]

The śāstras broadly divide dharma or actions that lead to overall wellbeing into two categories: sāmānya dharma and vishesha dharma. Sāmānya dharma are common to all. They include ethical practices like non-injury, speaking the truth, non-stealing, purity, control of mind and senses, etcetera. Vishesha or special modes of life are different for different individuals and depend upon multiple factors like time, place, varṇa, āśrama (or stage of life), etcetera, including one's duties and obligations towards family, society, the entire cosmos, and one's own self. Thus, in the context of an individual, dharma includes both ethical practices as well as special duties and modes of life that are beneficial to an individual and at the same time are not harmful to the larger society and do not upset the cosmic balance.

The sages are thus requesting Manu to instruct them about these beneficial actions and modes of life through which all those who are born in different varṇas as well as those born from mixture of varṇas can attain both material and spiritual wellbeing.

The use of the plural 'dharmaan' denotes that there is no single action that leads one to the highest good, but instead each individual must adopt a way of life that is beneficial to him or her based on the guidelines provided in the śāstras. As Bhagavān Kṛṣṇa notes in Bhagavad Gītā 16.24: 'The śāstra is your authority in the matter of determining what (action) is to be done and what is not to be done. After understanding actions as presented by the scriptural injunctions, you ought to perform (your duty) here (in this world) (Gambhirananda 1998).'[267] Likewise, Mīmāṁsā Sūtra 1.1.1 notes, dharma is that which is indicated by injunctions (of *Veda*).[268] Manusmṛti itself in verse 2.6 declares '*Veda*' as the very root of dharma and describes the 'smṛtis' or the recollections of righteous and learned teachers (like Manu) well-versed in *Veda*, the practices of the noble people who practice dharma, and their self-satisfaction as the valid sources for understanding dharma.[269] Yājñavalkya Smṛti 1.3 expands the list and includes purāṇa, nyāya, and mīmāṁsā texts as valid sources for understanding dharma.[270]

Medhātithi says the word 'dharma' in this verse is used in reference to—(1) the injunction of what should be done, (2) the prohibition of what should not be done,—both these bearing upon transcendental purposes,—and also (3) action in accordance with the said injunctions and prohibitions (G Jha 1920).[271] He further adds, 'And when the form of dharma has been duly expounded, that its contrary constitutes "adharma" follows naturally by implication. Thus what is meant is that "dharma" as also "adharma", both form the subject-matter of the scriptural treatise: the performance of the "aṣṭaka" is a duty, as also is the avoidance of brāhmaṇa-murder; the non-performance of "aṣṭaka" is a sin, as also is the performance of brāhmaṇa-murder; such is the distinction (between dharma and adharma as described in the scriptures) (G Jha 1920).'[272] Kullūka Bhaṭṭa expresses the same view as well.[273]

Another aspect to note is that the practice of dharma, be it the performance of ethical, religious, or spiritual duties, is essentially a ritual activity in itself, a point highlighted by Puruṣasūkta verse 16 which identifies yajñá (or fire sacrifice) as the first act of dharma[274]. This implies that living a life of dharma is living a spiritual and ritualised life with happiness, heaven, and liberation being the goal to attain.

**नः– *naḥ* – to us:**
To the sages primarily, but also to all the readers of the text. The sages are requesting Manu to give the instructions about dharma to them and by implication to all humanity.

**वक्तुमर्हसि – *vaktum arhasi* – (you are) competent to speak about:**

> Medhātithi explains thus:
>
> Arhasi indicates ability in the shape of possessing the requisite capacity; and as such expresses the fact of the teacher being a fit and proper person for expounding the duties; the sense being—'in as much as you are fully able to expound the Duties, hence you are a fit and proper person for that work,—as such you are entreated by us to explain to us the said Duties'; it follows by implication that when a man is a fit and proper person for doing a certain act, that act should be done by him. The term of entreaty 'do please explain to us' is supplied from without.[275]
>
> (G Jha 1920)

## Discussion

The sages approached Manu with a request for instructions about beneficial actions that lead to overall wellbeing not only for themselves, or those belonging to their brāhmaṇa varṇa, but for the entire humanity. This shows the inclusive nature of dharma in general and of this text in particular.

An important aspect to note here is, Manusmṛti does not posit an egalitarian socio-political order where everybody is equal, where everyone has equal rights, where there are no gaps between the haves and have-nots, or where everyone is happy. That is a utopian idea which has no basis in human reality. Human reality is that no two persons are same. They are not same in their temperaments, in their life situations, in their competencies, in their ethical compass, and most importantly, they are not same in the karmic burden they are born with. As a result, there is huge diversity in human actions, their ways of life, and their pursuits of life. This diversity is very core to how nature functions.

Hindu philosophy recognises this reality of the world and also recognises the fact that it is not possible to overcome the diversity, differences, and conflict at the socio-political level. These can be transcended only at the ethical and spiritual level by developing *samatvam* (equanimity) and other ethical qualities which would eventually lead to attainment of mokṣa or liberation through the knowledge of oneness and non-duality.

Stated differently, the concept of karma and reincarnation is what differentiates the Hindu worldview from the modern worldview. What is regarded as inequity in the contemporary world influenced by modern western worldview is understood in the dharmic traditions as the workings of karma from past lives which cannot be wished away. For a Hindu, the work of the society is to provide an environment that is conducive to all for practicing their svadharma and pursuing the puruṣārthas undisturbed so that they may quickly progress toward *loka saṅgraha* and mokṣa.

Therefore, Manusmṛti, which is a text in the larger Hindu philosophical tradition, does not posit any utopian ideals. Instead, it accepts the human reality that there is diversity and differences in society; it then provides paradigms and frameworks through which each one of us can better understand life and work out our own individual paths towards our overall wellbeing—both material welfare and spiritual emancipation. The sages' request for instruction about duties of all varṇas and those born in between shows that they recognise human diversity, and the specific request to give instruction regarding all these diverse groups shows the inclusivity of the text.

Manusmṛti and by extension *Sanātana* dharma is universal and inclusive in its teachings. They neither provide a homogenised one-size-fits-all solution to all human problems, nor do they posit a utopian ideal where everything is good and perfect. Instead they take into account human diversity and offer some guidance, some mode of life through which each person can attain material and spiritual wellbeing.

Manusmṛti is not a law-book in the sense of a constitution that was despotically implemented by a ruler. It can be understood as a law-book only in the sense that legal and moral principles were derived from Manu and other texts in the smṛti genre. It is not a biblical commandment in the sense that it needs to be enforced through religious hegemony. It is a pramāṇa-śāstra that reveals knowledge about karma and karmaphala, about what actions lead to happiness and what lead to sorrow, and about what duties apply to whom and who is eligible for what actions. And hence, these texts remain valid today as they did in the past and will remain so even in the future. As Śrī Jnananda Bharathi Svāmī says: 'The Sastras depend for their validity, not on the acceptance of the people professing to follow them nor upon the opinions of persons however sublimely evolved they may seem to be in the eyes of their followers, but solely upon their intrinsic truth which is in the power of nobody to disturb (Bharathi 1969, 18).'

Therefore, whether we approach these texts for knowledge, or for caricaturing them is up to us. What we take from them and how much we take from them, and what we make of that which we take from them is also up to us. But, these smṛtis and other dharmaśāstras stand tall and unaffected as pramāṇa śāstra just as the sun stands unaffected by the happenings on earth.

This is the deeper message of this verse.

# Verse Three

त्वमेको ह्यस्य सर्वस्य विधानस्य स्वयम्भुवः ।
अचिन्त्यस्याप्रमेयस्य कार्यतत्त्वार्थवित् प्रभो ॥ ३ ॥

*tvameko hyasya sarvasya vidhānasya Svāyambhuvaḥ* ।
*acintyasyāprameyasya kāryatattvārthavit prabho* ॥ *3* ॥

**Word by word translation:** You (त्वम् – *tvam*); alone (एक – *ekaḥ*); surely (हि – *hi*); of this (अस्य – *asya*); entire (सर्वस्य – *sarvasya*); ordinance (i.e. *Veda*) (विधानस्य – *vidhānasya*); self-manifest (स्वयम्भुवः – *Svayambhuvaḥ*); inconceivable (अचिन्त्यस्य – *acintyasya*); unknowable (अप्रमेयस्य – *aprameyasya*); the one who knows the import of what ought to be done (and what is) the (highest) reality (कार्यतत्त्वार्थवित् – *kāryatattvārthavit*); Master (प्रभो – *prabho*).

**Meaning:** O Master, you alone surely know the (true and complete) import of what ought to be done (i.e. karma) and (what is) the highest reality (i.e. *tattva*) of this (i.e. as taught in this) entire self-existing inconceivable unknowable *Veda*.

**Analysis:** In this verse, the sages are praising

Svāyambhuvaḥ-Manu as the most competent teacher to teach dharma.

**प्रभो** – ***prabho*** **– O master:**

The term refers to one who is able, capable, mighty, and powerful. It also indicates lordship in the sense that a father has over his children, a teacher over his students, or a king over his subjects. It indicates someone who is powerful and knowledgeable, and yet also approachable and trustworthy. *Prabhu* is someone who holds both immense power and immense responsibility. Like the use of the phrase Bhagavān in verse 1.2, here Manu is being addressed as prabhu by the great sages as a form of praise and adulation of the qualities of Manu, whom they have approached for instruction. Rāghavānanda Sarasvatī notes that prabhu indicates the capability of Manu to teach about both karma and tattva, which are the two-fold import of the *Veda*.[276] Kullūka Bhaṭṭa says that prabhu is used to indicate the capability of Manu to properly establish what is dharma and what is adharma.[277] Medhātithi, likewise, notes that prabhu refers to Manu being possessed of the capacity to expound on dharma on account of him being endowed with a high degree of knowledge of all things.[278]

**त्वमेको हि** – ***tvameko hi*** **– You alone surely:**

The phrase 'you alone' refers to there being no second choice, in the sense there is no one better than you (i.e. Manu) to teach dharma. Further, the use of 'surely' indicates Manu as an āpta—a trustworthy and competent source for knowing dharma. The sages are indicating that if Svāyambhuva-Manu does not know about dharma, surely nobody else does, and hence, he is the best teacher to teach it.

**कार्यतत्त्वार्थवित् – *kāryatattvārthavit* – the one who knows the import of what ought to be done (and what is) the (highest) reality:**

O Manu, you alone know, you alone have complete knowledge about the true import of actions (*kārya*) and reality (*tattva*). In the Muṇḍaka Upaniṣad 1.2.12, it is said that a guru must be both a śrotriya and a Brahmaniṣṭhā i.e. the teacher must be very well versed in the *Veda* and its meaning, as well as be established and absorbed in Brahman.[279] Though, this requirement about the guru was spoken in the context of Vedānta and the pursuit of *brahma-jñāna*, it is equally applicable here as the verse speaks about Manu as having complete knowledge about not only the *karma-kāṇḍa* that teaches about actions, but also about tattva—the highest reality. Therefore, the ṛṣis are praising Manu as not only a knower of *Veda*, but also as one who is established in the highest truth or *brahma-tattva* that the *Veda* reveals.

In the compound phrase kārya-artha-tattva-vit, the term kārya stands for actions that are to be performed, i.e., dharmic actions which one is obligated to perform by the *Veda*[280] and dharmaśāstra,[281] and which leads to abhyudaya (material welfare) and niḥśreyasa (spiritual wellbeing). For example, the ritual actions like *Agnihotra* and *Agniṣṭoma*, which the *Veda* prescribes for a dvija householder, and hence 'ought to be done' by them. Further, it refers to non-performance of those actions which are prohibited by the *Veda* and dharmaśāstras, i.e., non-performance of adharmic actions which lead to suffering and bondage. For example, actions like *brahmahatyā* (killing of a brāhmaṇa) which the *Veda* prohibits, and hence must be avoided. As Medhātithi notes 'Activity is "acting"; so is also "desisting from activity"; and the name "acting" is not restricted to only that which is accomplished by means of instruments and agents set in motion; in fact, when such "acting" is possible, if one desists from it, this desisting also is "acting" (G Jha 1920).'[282] Thus, kārya, implicitly, also includes *akārya* or what ought to be not done, and hence, the verse is referring to both vidhi (prescriptions) and niṣedha (proscriptions) as enunciated in the *Veda*. The ṛṣis are praising Manu as one who is knowledgeable about both dharma and adharma as enunciated in the *pūrva-bhāga* or the karma-kāṇḍa portion of the *Veda*.

The term tattva, on the other hand, refers to the highest reality as expounded in the *uttara-bhāga* or *jñāna-khaṇḍa* portion of the *Veda*. The Upaniṣads expound upon the knowledge of the highest reality, called Brahman or *ātman*, most notably through *Mahavakyas* like *Aham Brahmāsmi* (*Bṛhadāraṇyaka Upaniṣad* 1.4.10), *Tat Tvam Asi* (*Chāndogya Upaniṣad* 6.8.7), *Ayam Ātmā Brahma* (*Māṇḍūkya Upaniṣad* 1.2), *Satyam Jñānam Anantam Brahma* (*Taittirīya Upaniṣad* 2.1.1), etcetera. The ṛṣis are praising Manu saying that he not only has complete knowledge about the kārya-akārya aspect, which is the subject of the *Saṁhitā-brāhmaṇa* portion of the *Veda*, but also has complete knowledge about *parā-tattva* or the highest reality as enunciated in the *Āraṇyaka-Upaniṣad* portion of the *Veda*.

However, Medhātithi interprets the compound phrase kārya-tattva-artha-vit differently, in the sense of Manu being 'conversant with what ought to be done, which forms the true import of this entire *Veda* (G Jha 1920).'[283] He takes tattva-artha to mean the true import of kārya. But, this interpretation has been rightly criticised by other commentators such as Kullūka Bhaṭṭa,[284] and Rāghavānanda Saraṣvatī[285]. *Veda* as a whole is śabda pramāṇa and it imparts two-fold teachings—on dharma and on Brahman. If only the injunctive portions related to dharma are considered as the true import of *Veda*, then it would make the Upaniṣads that enunciate Brahman redundant and a non-pramāṇa. Therefore, Medhātithi's position is unacceptable. Further, the fact that the first chapter of Manusmṛti is dedicated to an enunciation of *Jagat-Utpatti* or cosmogony, and the text locates the teachings of dharma as a limb or a subset of its teachings about cosmogony, shows that the purpose of this text is to not only teach dharma, but also enunciate upon Brahman, the *Jagat-Karanam* or the source of the universe as expounded in the Upaniṣad[286] and Brahmasūtra[287]. Also, the verse describes Manu as the knower of the 'entirety of *Veda*' (*asya sarvasya vidhānasya*), therefore, he is a knower of both kārya and tattva, and not only of kārya.

Hence, the compound phrase kārya-tattva-artha-vit means one who knows the full meaning and true import of kārya and tattva i.e., dharma and Brahman, the very essence of the teachings of the *Veda*. Kullūka Bhaṭṭa says the term artha refers to *pratipādya-bhagah* or the portion propounding the topic. The phrase kārya-tattva-artha-vit will then mean one who knows the portion of the *Veda* that propounds kārya i.e. karma-khanda as well as the portion that propounds tattva i.e. jñāna-khanda.[288]

Alternatively, the term artha refers to prayojana or the purpose or motive to undertake the pursuit of kārya and tattva. This purpose is attainment of abhyudaya and niḥśreyasa, material and spiritual wellbeing. The pursuit of kārya or dharma that constitutes the path of pravṛtti helps one to attain material wellbeing. The pursuit of tattva or Atma-jñāna constitutes the path of nivṛtti and leads one to attain 'self-knowledge' and 'final liberation'. The commentator Nandana while he takes kārya-tattva as a reference to dharma and *Paramartha* (i.e. *Brahman*) respectively, he interprets artha in the sense of prayojana or purpose and posits 'the attainment of abhyudaya as the purpose for such pursuit.'[289] This would mean that Manu is being described by the sages as one who not only knows dharma and Brahman, but also knows the purpose or end-result of the pursuit of dharma and Brahman in the form of overall wellbeing.

**अस्य सर्वस्य विधानस्य – *asya sarvasya vidhānasya* – of this entire ordinance:**

The term *vidhāna* or ordinance refers to that by which actions are enjoined, that which gives knowledge about what ought to be done and what ought to be not done through injunctions (vidhis) and prohibitions (niṣedhas). It refers to *Veda*, because *Veda* alone is the ultimate pramāṇa for knowing kārya-akārya. Therefore, the phrase 'of this entire ordinance' must be understood as 'of this entire *Veda*'. The ṛṣis are addressing Manu as being the knower of the 'entire *Veda*'.

Kullūka Bhaṭṭa notes that the term *sarva* or 'entire' has been used to include both *pratyakṣa śrutiḥ*—the portion which is directly found in extant recensions of *Veda*—and those portions which can be inferred from the existing smṛtis.[290] In a broader sense, even itihāsa-purāṇas can be included under the term smṛti or recollected tradition. Further, Medhātithi says that the term 'entire' includes (a) the directly available verbal texts of the *Veda*, (b) what is only implied by the force of what is directly expressed by the words of the texts.[291] He further adds that the purpose of adding the epithet 'entire' is to indicate that smṛtis have their source in the *Veda* (G Jha 1920).[292] Therefore, the phrase 'entire *Veda*' refers to the *Veda* which is available to us through extant recensions, and Vedic texts whose existence we can infer from the available *Veda*, Smṛti, Itihāsa and Purāṇa texts—in short, the entirety of the *Veda*. As Viśvarūpa notes in his commentary on Yājñavalkyasmṛti 1.2-3 that even though the sages say that dharma is to be known from the *Veda*, it should not be considered in a strictly limited sense of mantra and brāhmaṇa texts, but must be considered as referring to all the fourteen sources of knowledge—the four *Veda*s, their six 'subsidiaries' or 'limbs', Purāṇa, Nyāya, Mīmānsā, and Dharmaśāstra.[293]

Elsewhere under verse 2.6, Medhātithi writes:

> The '*Veda*' is that from which people derive their knowledge of dharma, which cannot be known from any other source of knowledge and this knowledge of dharma is derived from each individual sentence; hence the name is not restricted to the entire collection of *adhyāyas* and *anuvākas* that go under the name 'Ṛgveda'....On the same principle also is the epithet 'whole' found in the injunction that 'the whole *Veda* should be studied', where it serves to indicate the necessity of studying all the sentences contained in the *Veda*; otherwise (if the epithet 'whole' were not there) the learner would be satisfied with the reading of only a few sentences, and would not read the whole *Veda*.[294]
>
> (G Jha 1920)

That is, the phrase 'entire *Veda*' in the present verse can be taken as a reference to Svāyambhuva-Manu being a knower of each and every sentence contained in the *Veda* and what they reveal and not just having a generic knowledge about contents of different adhyāyas and anuvākas.

Alternatively, we find from texts like *Taittirīya brāhmaṇa* 3.10.11.4 that *Veda* is infinite.[295] While it is impossible for humans to master this infinite *Veda*, Svāyambhuva-Manu, being the first of the seven Manus created by Brahmā himself, is a divine being and is perfectly capable of mastering this infinite *Veda* in its entirety. It is this divine omniscience of Manu that is being praised by the ṛṣis who describe him as the knower of the 'entire *Veda*'. This also makes Manu the most trustworthy source or āpta-puruṣa for learning about dharma.

**स्वयम्भुवः – *Svayambhuvaḥ* – self-existent:**

The term Svayambhuvaḥ means that which exists by itself or comes into existence by itself, and is hence without causation or destruction. Here the term is used as an adjective for vidhāna. Therefore, the phrase vidhānasya Svayambhuvaḥ would mean 'of the self-existent *Veda*'. The self-existence implies three things in this context as noted by Medhātithi: that *Veda* is eternal, that *Veda* is not a product created from some other cause, and that it is apauruṣeya i.e., not of human creation.[296] Kullūka Bhaṭṭa, likewise, interprets the term as a reference to the apauruṣeyatva of the *Veda*.[297] This interpretation is in line with Mīmāṁsā Darśana which holds that *Veda* is authoritative because it is eternal and not a product of human imagination or creativity.

However, the term Svayambhuvaḥ can also be taken as a reference to Īśvara, who is self-existent, eternal, and without a beginning or an end. Among the commentators,

Sarvajñanārāyaṇa defines the term as a reference to Prajāpati.[298] In this case, the phrase 'self-existent *Veda*' would refer to *Veda* created by the self-existent Īśvara. This interpretation is in line with Nyāya Darśana which holds that *Veda* is not apauruṣeya, but has been authored by Īśvara, who is the perfected being and the instrumental and intelligent cause of the world.

**अचिन्त्यस्य – *acintyasya* – inconceivable:**

*Veda* is inconceivable because it is infinite as noted by *Taittirīya Brāhmaṇa* 3.10.11.4.[299] The term inconceivable has been used in the sense that we are incapable of fully understanding or defining exactly the extent of the *Veda* owing to it being highly extensive and divided into several recensions, a large number of which have been lost with time. Or it is inconceivable in the sense that it requires great effort to know its meaning.

**अप्रमेयस्य – *aprameyasya* – unknowable:**

*Prameya* is that which is knowable. It refers to the object of knowledge. *Aprameya* therefore refers to that which is unknowable, which is not an object of knowledge. Rāghavānanda Sarasvatī interprets 'aprameya' as the meaning of *Veda* being difficult to understand.[300] Nandana interprets it as being unfathomable owing to it being 'unlimited'.[301]

Medhātithi interprets aprameya as *apratyakṣa* or not available for direct perception. He explains this as 'that which has got to be assumed or inferred, as forming the source of several assertions made in the Smṛti, as a matter of fact, such Vedic texts are not perceived, hence it is called "not directly cognisable" (G Jha 1920).'[302] Kullūka Bhaṭṭa on the other hand interprets aprameya as that which cannot be known using any means other than Mīmāṁsā methods of investigation.[303] Sarvajñanārāyaṇa likewise says, *Veda* is aprameya because what it reveals cannot be known from any of the other pramāṇas or sources of knowledge, be it pratyakṣa (perception), anumāṇa (inference), upamāna (comparison and analogy), arthāpatti (postulation, derivation from circumstances), or anupalabdhi (non-perception, negative/cognitive proof).[304]

Regarding the purpose of including these two adjectives of 'inconceivable' and 'unknowable' to describe *Veda*, Medhātithi says:

> Thus the two epithets serve to indicate that the *Veda* is beyond the reach of the internal as well as the external organs of perception; i.e., it is very extensive; and this mention of the extensiveness of the *Veda* serves as an inducement to the Teacher (i.e. Manu); the meaning being—'it is you alone who have learnt the *Veda* which is so extensive, hence you alone are conversant with what ought to be done', which forms the true import of the said *Veda*.[305]
>
> (G Jha 1920)

The terms *acintya* and aprameya can also be understood as a reference to the fact that though what is dharma and adharma cannot be known through sensory perception and other means as available to humans, Svāyambhuva-Manu being a divine being and a great ṛṣi was able to perceive these directly through his yogic vision. The naiyāyikas like Jayanta Bhaṭṭa put forward this position that smṛtis of Manu, etcetera are valid pramāṇas because their authors have directly perceived dharma and adharma through

Yogic perception, which otherwise cannot be perceived through human faculties. Thus, these descriptions serve the purpose of indicating Manu as an āpta or a trustworthy source on dharma.

## An Alternate Interpretation of the Verse

One of the commentators, Rāmacandra, interprets the phrase 'asya sarvasya vidhānasya' as a reference to the creation of the world consisting of four types of creatures: viviparous beings, oviparous beings, those born of heat, and vegetation.[306] This alternate interpretation of the verse wherein the term vidhāna is taken as a reference to 'creation' (and not to *Veda*) is also mentioned by Medhātithi towards the end of verse 1.11, wherein he provides an alternate interpretation of verses 3-11 by qualifying this as the view of some scholars.

Medhātithi explains the verse thus:

> 'This' refers by direct gesticulation to the world;—the vidhāna, creation, 'of this entire' world i.e., belongs to—the 'self-born.'—It is 'inconceivable' marvellous, wonderful, very extensive;—'not directly cognisable,' *aprame yam*, incapable of being known by all persons. This is what is stated in the *Veda* also—'Who knows it? Who has described it here? Whence have these been born? Whence this creation? (Ṛgveda, 3.54.5).' That is to say,—Does this entire world come into existence through some material cause? Or is it all a mere Idea, as held by the Bauddha? Is it dependent upon the will of a Supreme Being? Or is it dependent only upon the acts of the beings born? Or is it merely a natural process?— All this cannot be rightly ascertained: similarly it cannot be ascertained whether the creation of the world

> proceeds from the '*mahat*' downwards (as held by the *Sāṅkhyas*) or from the Diad downwards (as held by the Vaiśeṣikas).—'Of all this', 'you know (A) the kārya or the product, (B) the tattva or the real character and (C) the artha or the true purpose,'—Kāryatattvārthavit.[307]
>
> (G Jha 1920)

By kārya, Medhātithi refers to evolutes of Sāṅkhya[308] like mahat, ahamkara, manas, indrīyas, tanmātrā, and mahābhūtas, which arise out of prakṛti in a particular order and which constitute this universe.[309] By tattva, Medhātithi refers to the 'real nature' of these evolutes. For example, the real nature of mahat is that it consists of mere materiality being a product of prakṛti which is primordial matter. Likewise, the real nature of ahamkara is the 'notion of I'.[310] Medhātithi explains artha as 'true purpose' or how it would be useful to man (G Jha 1920).[311]

In short, in this alternate interpretation, Medhātithi explains the verse as a praise of Manu wherein he is described as a knower of the entirety of this universe, including its creation process, through the evolution of prakṛti into different evolutes that form the basic building blocks of the universe, the real character of each of these evolutes, and their true purpose with respect to human pursuit.

However, it is possible to interpret the phrase kāryatattvārthavit a bit differently as well. While the term kārya refers to the evolutes of prakṛti that constitute the manifested universe, the term tattva can be understood as a reference to Brahman, which is the *kāraṇa* or the cause of the universe. In Vedānta, Brahman, which is the ultimate reality is also posited as both the material and instrumental cause of the universe. Therefore, tattva in the verse refers to Brahman. And artha can be taken as a reference to prayojana or the purpose or motive to undertake the pursuit of kārya and tattva. In Vedānta, the pursuit of sṛṣti is called pravṛtti-dharma, which involves pursuit and attainment of the three puruṣārthas of dharma, artha, and kāma. The pursuit of Brahman is called nivṛtti-dharma which involves pursuit and attainment of the puruṣārtha of mokṣa, with mokṣa being defined as brahma-jñāna or the 'ultimate knowledge' about Brahman.

Therefore, we can parse the verse thus: 'O master Manu, you alone know this entire universe, which is inconceivable and unknowable, and has been created by self-existing Brahman. You alone know both the sṛṣti which is kārya and brahma-tattva which is kāraṇa, as also the meaning and purpose of pursuing them, which is of the form of attainment of all the four puruṣārthas.'

The reference to Manu as the knower of the entirety of creation, along with all its objects, can be understood as a reference to his same-sightedness and impartiality towards all the objects and beings of the universe, and hence, a fit person to teach dharma about different sections of society.

## Discussion:

The purpose of this verse is to posit beyond doubt that Svāyambhuva-Manu is an āpta or a trustworthy person and this text of Mānavadharmaśastra, which enunciates his teachings that reveal dharma, is a valid source of knowledge of the form of āpta-vākya. In other words, Manu's words constitute śabda pramāṇa for acquiring knowledge about dharma.

Śabda literally means 'verbal knowledge'. It is the knowledge of objects derived from words and sentences. However, all verbal knowledge is not valid. Śabda pramāṇa, however, is the source of valid verbal knowledge i.e., source of knowledge in the form of words and sentences wherein pramā or valid knowledge of objects arises from a correct understanding of the meanings of words and sentences. This is subject to the fulfilment of conditions such as the verbal testimony being uttered by an āpta or trustworthy person, its source being in the *Veda*, being logically sound and relevant, and the listener being competent. Śabda pramāṇa is one of the six major pramāṇas through which valid knowledge can be acquired.

While *Veda* is the ultimate pramāṇa for understanding dharma as enunciated by Mīmāṁsā Sūtra 1.1.1,[312] and has been accepted as so by all the *Āstika* Darśanas, we find smṛti texts positing themselves and other texts as valid sources for understanding dharma as well. Manusmṛti itself in verse 2.6 and again in 2.9-10 posits both Śruti and smṛtis as pramāṇas for gaining correct knowledge or pramā about dharma.[313] Manu 2.10 goes to the extent of saying that when 'dharmaśāstras' or treatises that enunciate about dharma and adharma are mentioned, one must understand it as a reference to the smṛtis. However, the smṛtis are neither apauruṣeya in the sense Mīmāṁsā and Vedānta posit *Veda* to be, nor are they necessarily authored by Īśvara as understood by Nyāya.

How then does Hindu tradition establish the authoritativeness and trustworthiness of these smṛtis with respect to their teachings on dharma?

The Āstika Darśanas put forward two main arguments to establish the authoritativeness and trustworthiness of the smṛtis as a śabda pramāna:

1. Smṛtis are teachings based on *Veda*s and hence they are valid, because *Veda* being apauruṣeya is always valid. This is the argument put forward by the Mīmāṁsākas.

2. Smṛtis are teachings of trustworthy ṛṣis like Manu, Yājñavalkya, and others who can be considered as āptas as they have directly perceived what constitutes dharma and what does not through yogic perception. This is the argument put forward by the naiyāyikas.

We can see that the Manusmṛti fulfils both the criteria mentioned above to be considered as a śabda pramāṇa. In fact, the very purpose of the present verse and the narrative structure in the form of dialogue between the sages and Svāyambhuva-Manu employed in the opening four verses is to posit this text of Manu as an authoritative and trustworthy source or śabda pramāṇa regarding dharma.

The present verse, through the voice of the sages who praise Manu as the knower of *Veda* in its entirety, is illustrating the Vedic base of this text. As we saw above, the Mīmāṁsāka argument for the validity of the smṛtis is that they must have the *Veda* as their basis. The explicit usage of the phrase kārya-tattva-artha-vit (the knower of the meaning of what is dharma and what constitutes the highest tattva) with respect to Manu reinforces the text's self-assertion of its Vedic basis. Then, in Manu 2.7 which says 'Whatever dharma for whatever person has been described by Manu,—all this is declared in the *Veda*; since the *Veda* embodies all knowledge (G Jha 1920),'[314] we have an even more explicit statement of the text's awareness of its own basis in *Veda*. The Mīmāṁsā position that smṛtis function as means for knowing anumeya *Veda* or the inferred *Veda* is noted by Kullūka Bhaṭṭa in his parsing of the phrase 'asya sarvasya vidhānasya'—'this entire *Veda*' in this present verse.[315]

The traditional commentators and other writers in

dharmaśāstra tradition agree with the above assessment that Manu and such smṛtis are authoritative as they have clear Vedic basis.

Medhātithi, for example notes under Manu 2.6:

> As regards the Smṛtis of Manu and others, their relationship to directly perceptible Vedic texts is quite patent; in some cases they are related to the Vedic mantras, in others to the Vedic deities, and in others again with substances and other details.[316]
>
> (G Jha 1920)

He further quotes an author of *Vivaraṇa* as analysing various positions on the question of basis of smṛtis and summarises his conclusion thus:

> The performance of the aṣṭaka and such other acts laid down in the Smṛtis must be regarded as sanctioned by the *Veda*; because they are found to be connected with purely Vedic injunctions, on perceiving which latter the performers undertake the performance. The said connexion we have already shown above;—in some cases what is prescribed in the *Veda* is subservient to what is laid down in the Smṛti, and sometimes it is the contrary; sometimes the *Veda* contains the originative Injunction of the act in question, sometimes its qualifying conditions, and sometimes it lays out a mere arthavāda, a eulogistic description. In this manner all those acts that are prescribed in the Smṛtis are connected with Vedic injunctions.[317]
>
> (G Jha 1920)

Viśvarūpa, the commentator of Yājñavalkya Smṛti, writing under verse 1.7 of the text, remarks:

> How do we know that the Smṛtis are all based upon the *Veda*, from which they derive their authority?... The simple answer to this question is that in the face of the direct assertion of Manu and other Smṛti-writers that their work is 'based on the *Veda*,' we have no justification for thinking otherwise. They being great Vedic scholars, could not have lied on this point. As a matter of fact also we find that every one of the injunctions contained in the Smṛtis has its source in the *Veda*; in some cases the connection is direct, in others indirect; for instance, we have the single Vedic injunction 'one should study the *Veda*'; now studying is not possible without teaching, hence the injunction of teaching is implied by the former—the teaching cannot be done without someone to teach; this implies the receiving and initiating of a pupil; this implies the necessity of having children; this again that of marrying and so on; most of the other injunctions may have their source traced in the single Vedic text.[318]

We find similar views upholding the authoritativeness of Manu and other smṛtis expressed in texts like Nṛsiṃhaprasāda and *Smṛticandrikā* as well.[319] Therefore, there is a consensus across dharmaśāstra tradition that Manu and other smṛtis are authoritative pramāṇa for knowing dharma as they are words of āptas and they are directly or indirectly based on *Veda*s.

The first four verses further indicate the Mīmāṁsā position that smṛtis are not based on deception, doubt, or prejudice. For example, Manu 1.1 notes that Svāyambhuva-Manu was seated with a calm, collected and one-pointed mind when the sages approached him with the request for instructions on dharma. That Manu was seated in a collected manner and that it was the sages who approached him for instruction for the benefit of people and not otherwise, shows that Manu's teachings are not rooted in doubt, confusion, prejudice, etcetera. Further, as noted before, the present verse by its description of Manu as the knower of all *Veda* or alternatively as the knower of the entirety of creation along with all its objects and beings, is positing same-sightedness and impartiality of Manu, as well as the fact that Manu is completely aware of the duties of different objects and beings of the universe, thus precluding doubt, confusion, prejudice, etcetera as the basis of this text.

In recent times, many have argued that Manu and other smṛti writers are prejudiced against certain sections of society, especially śūdras, antarprabhāvas (of mixed origins), and women. There are certainly some verses which appear problematic or at least unsuitable in the contemporary world rooted in a worldview promoted by western modernity. However, what is missing in this narrative is hermeneutics of respect. One cannot understand a text, especially a shastric text, unless it is approached with śraddhā i.e., trust, and an ability and openness to embrace the truth revealed in them.[320] Hermeneutics of suspicion on the other hand is by definition rooted in prejudice and hence prevents one from truly understanding or making sense of the śāstra. Therefore, all interpretations rooted in hermeneutics of suspicion must be discarded.

On the question of Manusmṛti's treatment of certain sections of society like antarprabhāvas, it can be seen that the very second verse of Manusmṛti, wherein the sages request instructions on dharma, explicitly includes both, those belonging to 'four varṇas' and those who are antarprabhāvas and hence do not belong to any varṇa. Further, Manusmṛti in Chapter 10, which discusses the dharma in the context of antarprabhāvas, says in verse 63 that practice of non-injury, truth, non-stealing, restraining of senses, and purity are the tenets of dharma which are applicable to everyone and lead everyone to highest good.[321] If Manusmṛti was prejudiced against people whom it classified as antarprabhāvas, why would sages ask about practices beneficial to them and why would Manu instruct them about practices like non-injury, which would give them overall wellbeing? Similarly we can see from verses like Manu 3.56 which states, 'Where women are honoured, there the gods rejoice; where, on the other hand, they are not honoured, there all rites are fruitless (G Jha 1920)'[322] that the text has utmost concern for the wellbeing of women as well. In the light of these verses, we can only conclude that Manu's teachings are not based on prejudice or deception. Whatever portions appear problematic, must be approached with śraddhā and hermeneutics of respect, so that we arrive at a correct understanding and interpret them in a proper way.

More importantly, as we have seen before, the Mīmāṁsākas show that none of the Smṛti assertions have been invalidated by subsequent cognitions from other pramāṇas like pratyakṣa, etcetera and hence they are valid. This applies to Manusmṛti as well. All the allegations of prejudice, hate, etcetera made against Manusmṛti are just that: allegations based on individual opinions. These cannot invalidate the truth-value of the knowledge revealed by Manu and other smṛtis.

Through the voice of the sages, the present verse also puts forward the Nyāya argument for the validity of smṛtis as pramāṇa śāstra. The description of Manu as the knower of all *Veda*, as the knower of the entirety of creation, as one who is fully versed in dharma and Brahman, and one who is able to perceive (through Yogic perception) that *Veda*, which is otherwise imperceptible to human beings—all these descriptions are aimed at positing Svāyambhuva-Manu as an āpta or a trustworthy person. The Nyāya definition of āpta which we noted before says that an āpta must have direct perception of dharma, he must be able to convey what he perceived exactly as he perceived it, and he must be willing to communicate it. The first four verses illustrate all these criteria of Manu through their narrative structure. The terms 'You alone' and 'knower of dharma and tattva' in the present verse convey Manu's direct perception of dharma as well as his capability to convey exactly what he perceived. In the next verse (i.e. Manu 1.4), the text shows Manu's willingness to teach dharma as well.

The trustworthiness of Svāyambhuva-Manu is further enunciated by positing him as a divine being, a son of Bhagavān Brahmā Himself in Manu 1.33.[323] Manu 1.58 goes a step further and states that it was Bhagavān Brahmā Himself who propounded dharma first to Manu and then Manu taught it to other sages.[324] That is, the verse 1.58 posits Īśvara as the author of Manusmṛti and hence as per the Nyāya view, we can argue that it is not only a valid pramāṇa on dharma, but it also has the same standing as *Veda* in the matters of dharma. This is hinted in Manusmṛti itself when it says in verse 2.10 that, 'The *Veda* should be known as the "revealed word", and the dharmaśāstra as the "recollections"; in all matters, these two do not deserve to be criticised, as it is out of these that dharma shone forth.[325]" Such a view is further reinforced by Vedic assertions like Taittirīya Saṁhitā 2.2.10.2 which says that whatever Manu says is wholesome like medicine.[326] Also, we find praise for Manu as well as quoting of its content in other smṛtis and texts like Mahābhārata, which fulfils one of the Nyāya criteria for the validity of texts, namely 'agreement of exemplary people'.

However one sees it, it is undisputable that Manusmṛti is a valid pramāṇa in the form of śabda or āpta-vakya which reveals true knowledge or pramā about dharma and adharma, a knowledge which can only be gained through the *Veda* and smṛtis (and itihāsa-purāṇas) and not through any other pramāṇas.

# Verse Four

स तैः पृष्टस्तथा सम्यगमितौजा महात्मभिः ।
प्रत्युवाचार्च्य तान् सर्वान् महर्षीञ्छ्रूयतामिति ॥ ४ ॥

*sa taiḥ pṛṣṭasthathā samyagamitaujā mahātmabhiḥ* ।
*pratyuvācārcya tān sarvān maharṣīñchrūyatāmiti* ॥ *4* ॥

**Word by word translation:** He (सः – *saḥ*); by them (तैः – *taiḥ*); being asked (पृष्टः – *pṛṣṭaḥ*); in that manner (तथा – *tathā*); well/in a proper manner (सम्यक् – *samyak*); of immeasurable power (अमितौजाः – *amitaujāḥ*); by the great souls (महात्मभिः – *mahātmabhiḥ*); responded (प्रत्युवाच – *pratyuvāca*); after worshipping (आर्च्य – ārcya); those (तान् – *tān*); all (सर्वान् – *sarvān*); great sages (महर्षीन् – *maharṣīn*); 'Listen' (श्रूयताम् – śrūyatām); thus (इति – *iti*).

**Meaning:** He (i.e. Manu) of immeasurable power, being questioned by those great souled ones (i.e. the sages) in that manner, paid respects to all those great sages and in a proper manner responded to them, saying, 'Listen'.

**Analysis:** In response to the request by the great sages, Svāyambhuva-Manu begins his response from this verse.

**स अमितौजा** – ***sa amitaujā*** **– He of immeasurable power:** 'He' refers to Svāyambhuva-Manu to whom the great sages addressed their questions in the previous two verses. Manu is being described as *amita-ojaḥ*. *Mita* means limited or measurable, and hence *amita* means immeasurable, limitless and infinite. *Ojas* refers to power, strength, vitality, splendour, etcetera. Medhātithi explains the phrase amitaujaḥ as 'with undiminished power of speech; he whose vigour, power, capacity of exposition, is "illimitable", infinite (G Jha 1920).'[327] Likewise, Kullūka Bhaṭṭa also explains amitaujaḥ as the unlimited immeasurable capacity to teach about knowledge, truth, and other such things. He further connects the description with Svāyambhuva-Manu being omniscient and omnipotent.[328] Bhāruci, on the other hand, interprets amita-ojaḥ as 'unimpaired or unobstructed *vijñānam*'. Vijñānam refers to special knowledge. Bhāruci says it is the special knowledge about dharma and its seed by which all things can be accomplished.[329] Another commentator, Sarvajñanārāyaṇa, interprets the phrase as 'infinite strength',[330] while Rāghavānanda Sarasvatī explains it as one who has capacity to know dharma and Brahman i.e. one who knows the two-fold revelations of the *Veda*.[331]

Medhātithi notes a plausible objection to the use of the phrase 'He' i.e., third-person, to refer to Svāyambhuva-Manu, rather than first person.

> Objection: If the whole of this Treatise has been composed by Manu himself, it is not right to attribute it to another person, as is done in the statement—'being questioned by them, he answered'; the proper form would have been—'being questioned by them, I answered'. If, on the other hand, someone else is the author of the Treatise, then why should it be called

> '*Mānava*' (of Manu)[332]
>
> (G Jha 1920)

Medhātithi provides two responses to this objection. He says:

> There is no force in this objection. In the first place, it is a well-known fact that in most cases the authors of Treatises state their own views as if emanating from other persons,—making use of such expressions as—'in this connection they say' or 'they meet this argument thus'; and the form 'being questioned by them, I answered' would not be in keeping with such usage.... Or (another explanation is that) the Treatise is a compilation made and related by Bhṛgu; and since the original Smṛti [which is, in the present Treatise related by Bhṛgu] was compiled (from teachings received directly from Prajāpati) by Manu,—it is styled 'Mānava' (of Manu).[333]
>
> (G Jha 1920)

Kullūka Bhaṭṭa makes a similar observation on the topic. He gives examples from both Jaimini's Mīmāṁsā Sūtra 3.1.4[334] and Bādarāyaṇa's Brahmasūtra 1.3.26[335] wherein the authors refer to themselves in the third person.[336]

However, a third explanation for the usage of 'He' is also possible. The current text is the result of a long line of transmission of Manu's teachings that has gone through multiple redactions. Every redaction is a new presentation of the received knowledge and as such it is not far-fetched to conclude that it is the redactor who has carefully and deliberately used a third-person format to indicate that the views expressed in the text are the teachings of Svāyambhuva-Manu received in the tradition and not the personal views of the redactor pretending to be the voice of Manu. The text is called Mānava-Dharmaśāstra precisely because it represents the teachings of Svāyambhuva-Manu, though the present text is put together by the last redactor, perhaps Sumati Bhargava, who received the teachings of Svāyambhuva-Manu through the Bhṛgu line of transmission.

**पृष्टः तथा तैः महात्मभिः– *pṛṣṭaḥ tathā taiḥ mahātmabhiḥ* – being questioned in that manner by those great-souled ones:**

Svāyambhuva-Manu was questioned by the great sages 'in that manner'. In what manner? Medhātithi notes that the phrase tathā or 'in that manner' denotes the method of questioning, and includes the content as well as the manner of putting forward the question.[337] Kullūka Bhaṭṭa notes that tathā refers to how the sages communicated their question to Svāyambhuva-Manu with praṇati, bhakti, śraddhā and other such qualities, which were flowing in excess.[338]

The three attitudes listed by Kullūka Bhaṭṭa can be understood as the three aspects of the ideal attitude of devotion and dedication expected of a student towards the teacher. Praṇati refers to the attitude of respect and reverence and this implies a recognition of not only one's own ignorance, but also a recognition of the teacher as an abode of knowledge and hence in a higher position than oneself in terms of knowledge and practice—jñāna and ācāra. Such an attitude leads to humility, which in-turn leads to bhakti. Bhakti refers to the attitude of devotion and surrender towards the teacher. However, here surrender does not have the negative connotation present in statements such as 'I will not surrender to my enemy'. Here, surrendering comes from attachment and love. Bhakti has been defined in *Nārada Bhakti Sūtras* 1.2 as *parama-prema-rūpa*—of the form of supreme love.[339] In *Śāṇḍilya Bhakti Sūtra*s 1.2, bhakti is defined as *parā-anuraktiḥ*—supreme unshakable attachment.[340] Therefore, the devotion and surrendering involves deep love and attachment and is a positive quality. This will in-turn lead to śraddhā or trust. Śraddhā is often defined as trust in the guru and śāstra being the authoritative source of knowledge.[341] One will be able to develop complete faith and trust only when one is truly attached and devoted to the teacher. These three aspects reinforce each other.

The phrase mahātmabhiḥ or 'the great souled ones' is a reference to the great sages positing the question to Svāyambhuva-Manu. Medhātithi notes that 'It is the philanthropic person that is called "high-souled", hence the meaning is that though they themselves knew all about duties,—otherwise they would not be "Great Sages",—yet they questioned Manu for the benefit of other people (G Jha 1920).'[342] In his Bhāṣya on Brahmasūtra 3.1.11, Ādi Śaṅkarācārya notes that those who conduct their life according to tenets of dharma are well-known in the world as 'Mahatma'.[343]

**आर्च्य तान् सर्वान् महर्षीन्** – ***ārcya tān sarvān maharṣīn*** – **(He) after worshiping all those great sages:**

Being questioned by the great sages, Svāyambhuva-Manu first paid proper respects to those great sages and then began his discourse in response to their question. Anticipating an objection regarding why a teacher would pay respects to the students who approached him, Medhātithi notes that though the great sages themselves knew all about dharma, yet they approached Svāyambhuva-Manu for instruction for the benefit of other people with the thought that since Manu is a sage whose authoritative character is well-known and well-respected by everyone, and he is one who is always approached with trust and confidence,—hence for the expounding of the treatise, we shall make him our Teacher. He says that it is because of this reason that Manu first paid respects to them before beginning his discourse.[344]

**प्रत्युवाच सम्यक् इति – *pratyuvāca samyak iti* – responded thus in a proper manner:**

After paying respects to the great sages, Svāyambhuva-Manu began his response to the question posed by the sages in a proper manner. The term samyak refers to proper way or proper courtesy. What is the proper way of teaching? What is the proper way of communicating knowledge? Vātsyāyana in his commentary on Nyāyasūtra 1.1.7 notes that an āpta or a trustworthy person is one 'who possesses the direct and right knowledge of things, who is moved by a desire to make known (to others) the thing (in the exact way) as he knows it, and who is fully capable of speaking of it (G Jha 1939, 30).'[345] That is, the proper way of communicating knowledge is to communicate it willingly and communicate it exactly the way it is—accurately and in accordance with truth. While Medhātithi highlights the aspect of willingness when he interprets samyak as 'with proper courtesy' and says it means communicating gladly, and not with anger or any other form of displeasure,[346] Kullūka Bhaṭṭa highlights the aspect of accurate representation when he interprets samyak as being in accordance with truth.[347] Both these aspects are equally important in an āpta.

**श्रूयताम् – *śrūyatām* –'Listen':**
Svāyambhuva-Manu began his response to the question put forth by the great sages with the phrase 'Listen'. It is a motif suggesting *Vedic Vāk* or Śabda Brahman—the primordial speech or word.

## Discussion:

As noted before, the first four verses of Mānava-Dharmaśāstra serve the purpose of indicating certain fundamental principles required for proper understanding of the text. These not only include anubandha catuṣṭaya (adhikārī, viṣaya, prayojana, and sambandha), which has been clearly delineated in these verses, but also include a delineation of tenets such as qualities of the competent and trustworthy teacher, the role of śāstras, and how knowledge was transmitted in the guru-śiṣya paramparā. Significantly, this verse highlights how a teacher must convey knowledge to a sincere disciple—willingly and accurately. This point has been noted by Ādi Śaṅkarācārya in his commentary on Muṇḍaka Upaniṣad verse 3.1.2, wherein he writes that because of some 'very compassionate (*parama-kāruṇikaḥ*)' persons, one learns the path of yoga.[348]

However, the most important aspect of this verse is the use of the phrase śrūyatām or 'Listen' as the opening remark of Svāyambhuva-Manu's response. The phrase śrūyatām has been used five times in the whole text. Other phrases with similar meanings include *śṛṇuta* which has been used six times, and *nibodhata* which has been used as many as twenty-two times in the text. Among the three, śrūyatām is particularly important as both Manu (in the present verse 1.4) and Bhṛgu (in verse 1.60)[349] begin their response to the question put forward by the sages with this phrase, and their discourse begins with an enumeration about sṛṣti or cosmogony.

These phrases are actually motifs suggesting Vedic Vāk or Śabda Brahman—the primordial speech or word. The text uses these recursive phrases to represent cosmogony and to recall to the mind of the reader that the text and its teachings on dharma are to be located within the cosmological discourse. These phrases are, in fact, a part of the text's deeper architecture which imitates the sṛṣti-laya cycle and has been built as a reflection of the cosmic reality.

Moreover, the very narrative structure that we see in the first four verses of Manusmṛti imitates the cosmogonic cycle through its layers of 'telling' and 'retelling'. Patrick Olivelle identifies five such layers, and remarks:

> We have here five layers of 'telling', 'hearing', and 're-telling'. At the most remote level, we have the creator himself soon after his creative activity composing a treatise and reciting it to his son Manu (1.58). Manu is the first 'hearer'. He transmits it to Marīci and the other sages (1.58), who form the second tier of 'hearers'. At Manu's command, one of these sages, Bhṛgu, teaches the seers who had come to Manu with the mission of learning dharma. Bhṛgu's first word (1.60), significantly, is 'Listen' (śrūyatām). This group of seers, still placed *in illo tempore,* constitutes the third tier of 'hearers'. The narrator of the entire text makes only a fleeting and implicit appearance in the very first verse of the text.... Evidently the narrator himself, who at one level can be identified with the historical author of the text, heard the text presumably from the seers....This narrator is the fourth 'hearer'. There is then the implied fifth 'hearer',

that is, all those who listen to or read this text, including modern scholars.

(Olivelle, Manu's Code of Law: A Critical Edition and Translation of the Mānava-Dharmaśāstra 2005, 27)

These five layers of telling and retelling indicate five different narrations of the treatise. This implies that the present text as available to us is not only an account about the earlier narration, but also a narration of the teaching heard at the earlier narration. Thus, there is an imitation of the cosmic cycle, which always begins and ends, with each cycle replicating the earlier cycle.

Manusmṛti thus places the discourse on dharma within a discourse on cosmogony as is evident by the enumeration about sṛṣti in the very first chapter. Then, it places both of them within a text whose very structure embeds literary and narrative motifs that imitate cosmogony. The text does this to draw the attention of the listener or reader away from the anthropocentric approach to human life and actions, which feeds on greed. They are instead enabled to approach dharma and human duties from a cosmological perspective, which is rooted in unselfishness, harmony, order, and a transcendental understanding of the universe.

The opening four verses lay the groundwork for bringing about such a shift in human worldview without which no proper understanding of the tenets of dharma is possible. It nudges the sincere seeker to give-up the obsession with linear history and the associated obsession with human exceptionalism which eventually leads to imbalance and destruction of everything we hold dear to us. In its place, the text encourages the seeker to adopt and embrace the cosmic vision of reality wherein humans are merely one among many beings in the universe. We not only share this universe with them but also share a deeper bond since the same Divinity which pervades us, also pervades the entire universe. Such universal and transcendent wisdom facilitates one to overcome weaknesses like pride, greed, insecurity and a victimhood complex. It encourages approaching life and our role in the universe positively and proactively, from the standpoint of duty, harmony, and order.

This is the full implication of the usage of the phrase 'Listen' in this verse. The text wants us to give up the anthropocentric worldview and instead adopt a dharmic worldview. And only with this perspective would one be able to make sense of the guidance and advice that Manusmṛti and other dharmaśāstras have made available to us.

The purpose of dharmaśāstra is not to teach us how to increase wealth or indulge in mundane pleasures, but to teach us how to attain puṇyam or karmic merit and work towards mokṣa even while pursuing artha and kāma. Since puṇyam or karmic merit is something which cannot be perceived with the mind and the senses, it is beyond the purview of direct perception (pratyakṣa) and other such means of knowledge. Hence it can only be known from śabda pramāṇa in the form of *Veda* and Smṛti. As this text itself notes in verse 2.9-10: 'For the man performing the duty laid down by the Śruti and the Smṛti obtains fame here, and after death, unsurpassed happiness. The *Veda* should be known as the 'revealed word', and the dharmaśāstra as the 'recollections'; in all matters, these two do not deserve to be criticised, as it is out of these that dharma shone forth (G Jha 1920).'[350]

# Appendix I

## Hindu conception of varṇa: Exploring its multifaceted nature

### Introduction

'Varṇa' is a much-misunderstood concept and continues to be controversial. While it is often conflated with categories such as *jāti*, *kula*, caste, etcetera, largely, the concept of varṇa as enunciated in Hindu texts is seen as either a social grouping based on division of labour or as a psychological grouping based on temperaments and character traits.

Both these interpretations anchor themselves on the Bhagavad Gītā which speaks about Bhagavān creating the four varṇas based on *guṇa-karma-vibhāga*. However, these interpretations are simplistic, based on selective reading of texts, and most importantly reduce the varṇa designation to a mere mundane, secular, and transactional categorisation of human society.

To address the gap in contemporary understanding of varṇa, this chapter will examine the multifaceted definition of varṇa with particular focus on its sacred and transcendental dimensions and how they fit in with the larger discourse centred around division of labour and mapping of behavioural traits. The chapter will also explore whether and in what way the definitions of varṇa centred upon birth contribute to the sacred dimensions of varṇa dharma.

## 1. Varṇa as envisioned in Ṛgveda Puruṣasūkta

The *Ṛgveda Puruṣasūkta*[351] provides one of the most explicit descriptions of the conceptual framework of varṇa. It uses the metaphor of human body to represent the universe as a 'Cosmic Puruṣa' with his limbs denoting various aspects, functions, and beings of the universe.[352]

Though many modern scholars tend to dismiss it as a comparatively later composition than other parts of the Ṛgveda,[353] some even designating it as a post-Vedic addition, this would not in any way affect the authenticity of its teachings because there are no time limitations as far as the abilities of ṛṣis to perceive the mantras are concerned. Different mantras of the *Veda* were perceived by the ṛṣis at different points in time, the mantras themselves being eternal. More importantly, similar accounts of Cosmic Puruṣa creating varṇas from different parts of his body are present in other Vedic texts such as Taittirīya Saṃhitā 7.1.1.4-6[354] and Jaiminīya Brāhmaṇa 1.68-69.[355] Therefore, there is no basis to doubt the authenticity of the teachings of Puruṣasūkta irrespective of its historical origins.

The Puruṣasūkta mentions how the brāhmaṇa, kṣatriya, vaiśya, and śūdra manifested out of Cosmic Puruṣa's face, arms, thighs, and feet, respectively.[356] The different limbs of a body, though being inseparable parts of the body, are distinct from each other in their nature and function. For example, the attribute of the head is intelligence and accordingly its function is thinking and decision making. Distinct from this are the feet, which have the attribute of movement and hence a function of carrying the body to different places. The same is the case with other organs.

Further, the entire manifestation is situated in the cosmic yajña—the fire sacrifice performed by the devatās, in which the Puruṣa himself is sacrificed as the *paśu* (the sacrificial animal).[357] And it is from this sacrifice that the four varṇas emerge along with other beings of the universe. On the manner of emergence of the four varṇas, the sūkta says the face of the Puruṣa itself 'became' the brāhmaṇa; the kṣatriya and vaiśya were 'made' from the arms and thighs of the Puruṣa respectively; and the śūdra was 'born' from the feet of the Puruṣa. Thus, the notion of varṇa also has a deep ritualistic significance emphasising the concept of 'birth/emergence' of the varṇa.

From the Puruṣasūkta's poetic exposition, four aspects of varṇa emerge:

- It is a classification of innate individual nature.
- It is a division of human activities.
- It is a function of emergence.
- It has a deep ritualistic significance.

For a comprehensive understanding of varṇa, let us now examine each of these aspects in some detail.

## 2. Varṇa as a classification of individual svabhāva

One of the most popular understandings of varṇa in contemporary discourse is that the term is a reference to individual qualities, temperaments, and behavioural traits—all of which are dependent upon one's innate nature or svabhāva.

While the roots of this dimension of varṇa were already present in the Ṛgveda Puruṣasūkta as we saw in the previous section, we find a more explicit and elaborate enunciation in texts such as the Bhagavad Gītā and Bhāgavata Purāṇa.

> The four varṇas have been created by Me through a classification of the gunas (qualities) and karmas (actions). Even though I am the agent of that (act of classification), still know Me to be a non-creator and changeless.[358] — Bhagavad Gītā 4.13
>
> (Gambhirananda 1998)

> O scorcher of enemies, the duties of the brāhmaṇas, the kṣatriyas and the vaiśyas, as also of the śūdra*s* have been fully classified according to the Gunas (qualities) born from svabhāva (innate nature).[359] — Bhagavad Gītā 18.41
>
> (Gambhirananda 1998)

> The brāhmaṇas, the kṣatriyas, the vaiśyas and the śūdras, each was born respectively from the face, arms, thighs and feet of that mighty form of Puruṣa and are to be recognised from their particular *ātmācāra* (natural activities according to inherent nature).[360] — Bhāgavata Purāṇa 11.17.13

The above verses clearly reveal that the classification of varṇa is a classification based on differences in gunas born from one's innate svabhāva. Ādi Śaṅkarācārya in his commentary on Bhagavad Gītā 18.41 defines svabhāva as a reference to innate nature consisting of individual tendencies of beings, earned in their past lives, which have become manifest in the present life for yielding their own results. He says that the gunas have this svabhāva as their source i.e. the svabhāva constitutes the efficient cause of the gunas.[361]

These gunas are three in number and they determine the natural temperaments and behavioural traits exhibited by the person. They are sattva (goodness, calmness, harmoniousness), rajas (passion, activity, movement), and tamas (ignorance, inertia, laziness).

Ādi Śaṅkarācārya, while commenting on Bhagavad Gītā verses 4.13 and 18.41 says that the brāhmaṇa is a designation given to one in whom there is a predominance of sattva; kṣatriya is one in whom there is both sattva and rajas, but rajas predominates; in vaiśya, both rajas and tamas exist, but rajas predominates; and śūdra is one in whom both rajas and tamas exist, but tamas predominates.[362] Mahābhārata 12.181.5 itself assigns a colour to each varṇa (white, red, yellow and black are assigned to brāhmaṇas, kṣatriyas, vaiśyas and śūdras respectively) which symbolically represents the svabhāva associated with that varṇa, reflecting the three qualities of sattva, rajas, and tamas.[363]

Elaborating on this, Bhagavada Purāṇa 11.17.16-19, lists what temperaments and behavioural traits are likely to be exhibited by which varṇas.[364] The text notes that the natural qualities of the brāhmaṇas include control of the mind and senses, austerity, cleanliness, satisfaction, tolerance, simple straightforwardness, devotion to God, mercy, and truthfulness. Likewise, the natural qualities of the kṣatriyas consist of dynamic power, bodily strength, determination, heroism, forbearance, generosity, great endeavour, steadiness, devotion to the brahmaṇas and leadership. While the vaiśyas exhibit faith in God and the *Veda*, dedication to charity, freedom from hypocrisy, service to the brahmaṇas, and a perpetual desire to accumulate more money; the śūdras are endowed with service without duplicity to others, cows and gods, and complete satisfaction with whatever income is obtained in such service.

These differences in behavioural traits caused by differences in individual svabhāvas have been classified into four svabhāva categories called varṇas.

### 3. Varṇa as division of human activity

From the idea of varṇa as a classification of innate nature of individuals, logically flows the idea of varṇa as a division of human activity. The Bhagavad Gītā 4.13 clearly indicates this when it says, 'The four varṇas have been created by Me through a classification of the gunas (qualities) and karmas (actions) (Gambhirananda 1998).'[365] Ānandagiri in his sub-commentary on Śaṅkarācārya's Gītā commentary on the above verse notes that the classification of the duties is determined by the classification of the gunas.[366] Thus, varṇa in the sense of function is determined by varṇa in the sense of quality. Stated differently, svadharma flows from svabhāva with svadharma referring to actions and duties in sync with one's innate nature (consisting of pre-existing tendencies inherited from past lives).

Explaining the interplay between these principles, R K Sharma notes: 'Within the person, svabhāva is the guiding principle. One who acts on svabhāva acts spontaneously… Thus, following svabhāva results in harmony… And the result is happiness… svadharma means one's duties in society. These duties should not be imposed from outside. In order to be natural, spontaneous and divine, the duties must be based on svabhāva. Thus, svadharma and svabhāva should be identical. Svabhāva should decide svadharma (R K Sharma 2004).'

Based on the above principles, the Bhagavad Gītā 18.42-44 classifies activities into four groups and assigns them to the four varṇas.[367] The brāhmaṇas are assigned activities such as the control of the internal and external organs, austerity, purity, forgiveness, straightforwardness, knowledge (of the śāstras), wisdom (making the scriptural knowledge a matter of one's own experience) and faith. The kṣatriyas are assigned heroism, boldness, fortitude, capability, not retreating from battle, generosity, and lordliness as activities they should strive for. The vaiśyas are assigned agriculture, cattle-rearing and trade, and the śūdras are assigned service as their respective duties.

A similar classification of varṇas based on activities is given in Manusmṛti 1.88-91 as well.[368] Here the brāhmaṇas are assigned studying and teaching (of the *Veda*), conducting yajñas for oneself and for others, giving and accepting (of dāna) as their duties. The kṣatriyas have been stipulated to take up protection of the people, giving charity, offering sacrifices (yajñas), studying (the *Veda*), and abstaining from attaching themselves to sensual pleasures as their duties. To tend cattle, giving charity, to offer sacrifices, to study (the *Veda*), to trade, to lend money, and to cultivate the land are stipulated as the duties of vaiśyas. And the śūdras have been assigned the duty of serving the other varṇas i.e. rest of the society either directly (through service-related activities) or indirectly (through various professions like arts, sculpture making, wood carving, etcetera as has been enunciated in Manu 10.100).[369]

These divisions of activities which naturally flow from the differences in the innate tendencies of individuals constitute the second aspect of varṇa.

## 4. Varṇa as a function of emergence

While the contemporary discourse has often focused upon the quality and functional aspects of varṇa, another key idea which is perhaps more important for a holistic understanding is the notion of varṇa as a function of emergence.

The Puruṣasūkta verse 12 adequately highlights this when it says:

> His (the Puruṣa's) face became the brāhmaṇa.
> The kṣatriyas were made from his arms.
> And the vaiśya from his thighs.
> The śūdra was born from his feet.[370]
>
> (Sreekrishna and Ravikumar 2015)

The above verse highlights two phenomena:

a. That varṇas have emerged.
b. That they have emerged from Cosmic Puruṣa.

### 4.1. Varṇa as a function of emergence of jīvātmā

The idea that varṇa is a function of emergence at the individual level implies that varṇa of a person is determined by the jīvātmā's long journey through the karmic cycle of birth and death, and its emergence or birth in the human world through particular human parents at a particular point in its journey caused by the fruits of past actions.

We find explicit and implicit references to this across Hindu textual landscape. *Chāndogyopaniṣad* 5.10.7, for example, brings this out very clearly:

> Among them, those who did good work[371] in this world [in their past life] attain a good birth accordingly. They are born as a brāhmin, a kṣatriya, or a vaiśya. But those who did bad work in this world [in their past life] attain

> a bad birth accordingly, being born as a dog, a pig, or as a casteless person.[372]
>
> (Lokeswarananda 1998)

The verse explicitly and very graphically notes that a jīvātmā attains a particular varṇa by being born to the parents belonging to that varṇa. The phrases used in the verse such as *brāhmaṇayoniṁ*, *kṣatriyayoniṁ* etcetera literally mean 'being born from the yoni of the brāhmaṇa', 'being born from the yoni of the kṣatriya' etcetera wherein the term 'yoni' could simply mean 'source' (i.e. the parents) or more specifically refer to 'female genitalia'.

In short, the jīvātmā inherits the varṇa from the parents by the act of emerging from them. Further, the Upaniṣad adds that the entire process is caused by the jīvātmā's own conduct in its past life—i.e. the *pūrvajanma-karma* is the cause which makes a person to be born to parents having a particular varṇa, and hence, inherit that varṇa from them in the current life.

Likewise, Gautama Dharmasūtra 11.29 highlights this:

> People belonging to the different classes and orders of life (i.e., varṇas and āśramas) who are steadfastly devoted to the Laws (i.e., duties) proper to them enjoy the fruits of their deeds after death; and then, with the residue of those fruits, take birth again in a prosperous region, a high caste (i.e., jāti), and a distinguished family (i.e., kula), with a handsome body, long life, deep vedic learning, and virtuous conduct, and with great wealth, happiness, and intelligence.[373]
>
> (Olivelle 2000)

And Āpastamba Dharmasūtra 2.11.10-11 says:

> By following the righteous (dharma) path people belonging to a lower class (varṇa) advance in their subsequent birth to the next higher class (varṇa), whereas by following an unrighteous (adharma) path, people belonging to a higher class descend in their subsequent birth to the next lower class.[374]
>
> (Olivelle 2000)

This fact that an individual's own conduct (svakarma)[375] in a particular life determines one's future trajectory post-death—including whether one attains divine abodes or suffers in hells, whether one attains a human body or those of other beings, whether one is born as a brāhmaṇa or as a sudra[376]—is beautifully expressed by Bhagavān Yama in his conversation with Satī Sāvitrī that appears in the *Brahmavaivarta Purāṇa* 2.24.17-36:

> Because one is born as a result of his deeds and also meets with his end because of the same. He achieves pleasure and pain, danger and grief according to his own deeds. By his own deeds he once became Indra and also the son of Brahmā. He also becomes the slave of Lord Viṣṇu getting free from the cycle of birth and death. One becomes eternal and gets all the success because of his own deeds and he also achieves salvation from Lord Viṣṇu because of his own deeds. A man achieves Brāhmaṇahood, salvation, godliness and becomes human or king because of his own deeds. By one's own deeds, one becomes a sage, an ascetic, a *kṣatriya,* a *vaiśya,* a *śūdra,* a *cāṇḍāla* and *mleccha.* There is no doubt about it. By his own deeds a human being moves around and by his own deeds he becomes

> static. By one's own deeds one becomes a mountain, a tree, an animal and a bird. Because of his own deeds one becomes an insignificant creature, an insect, a reptile, a *gandharva,* a *rākṣasa,* a *kinnara,* a *yakṣa* and a *kūṣmāṇḍā,* a *vetāla,* a *preta,* a goblin, a *piśāca* and a *ḍākinī.* He becomes with his own deeds, a *daitya*, a *dānava*, an *asura* and a noble soul or an evil spirit with his own deeds. Because of his own deeds he becomes beautiful, healthy, suffers from the disease and becomes blind, one-eyed and degraded. By his own deeds the creatures go to *indraloka, sūryaloka, candraloka, agniloka, vāyuloka* and *varuṇaloka*. By his own deeds, one reaches the abode of *kubera*, *dhruvaloka*, *śivaloka*, the constellations, *satyaloka*, *janoloka*, *tapoloka* and *maharloka*. By one's own deeds one reaches *brahmāloka* and also takes birth in the land of Bharata which is desired by all. He achieves *vaikuṇṭha* and the sinless *goloka* because of his own deeds. He achieves a long life or a short life because of his own deeds. With his own deeds, he gets life as long as crores of *kalpas* and short life by his own deeds. One gets short life for a moment because of his own deeds and also dies in the mother's womb because of his own deeds.[377]
>
> (Nagar 2005)

Manusmṛti 10.5, on the other hand, elaborates on the aspect of emergence and lucidly defines Varṇa thus:

> Among all varṇas, those only who are born of consorts wedded in the natural order, as virgins of equal status, are to be regarded as the same (as their father).[378]
>
> (G Jha 1920)

Similar definitions focusing on emergence are found in other texts as well.

> When a man has sexual intercourse with his wife during her season, a wife who belongs to same varṇa as he and has not been married before, and whom he has married in the manner prescribed in the scriptures—sons born to him have a claim to follow the occupations of his varṇa.[379] — Āpastamba Dharmasūtra 2.13.1
>
> (Olivelle 2000)

> On women equal in varṇa (to their husbands) sons are begotten, who are equal in varṇa to their fathers.[380] — Viṣṇusmṛti 16.1
>
> (Jolly 1880)

> From women of the same varṇa as their husbands are born sons of the same varṇa.[381] — Yājñavalkyasmṛti 1.90

> Sons of equal varṇa are born from wives of the same varṇa as their husbands.[382] — *Baudhāyana Dharmasūtra* 1.17.2
>
> (Olivelle 2000)

From the above quoted smṛti verses, four conditions can be identified as necessary for classifying a person into the brāhmaṇa, kṣatriya, vaiśya, or śūdra varṇa from the perspective of emergence:

a. The person must be born of marriage and not outside of it.
b. Such marriage should be a dharmically legitimate marriage performed in a manner prescribed in the śāstras.

c. Both the parents must belong to the same varṇa.
d. The mother at the time of marriage should be a virgin, excluding cases such as remarriage, etcetera.

We find implicit references to emergence aspect of varṇa in other texts as well.

> A brāhmaṇa on birth is born with a threefold debt, of pupilship to the ṛṣis, of sacrifice to the gods, of offspring to the *pitṛs.*[383] — *Kṛṣṇayajurveda Taittirīyasaṃhitā* 6.3.10.5
>
> (Keith 1914)

> O *Brahman*, let there be born in the kingdom the brāhmaṇa illustrious for religious knowledge; let there be born the *rājanya*, heroic, skilled archer, piercing with shafts, mighty warrior.[384] — *Śuklayajurveda Vājasaneyisaṃhitā* 22.22
>
> (Griffith 1899)

> The status of a brāhmaṇa is extremely difficult to obtain. One is a brāhmaṇa as a result of creation. It is my view that kṣatriyas, vaiśyas and śūdras are also created.[385] — *Mahābhārata Anuśāsanaparva* 143.6
>
> (Debroy 2015)

> The Brāhmaṇa, by birth alone, is born as verily a great deity[386] — *Mahābhārata Aśvamedhikāparva* 98.82.

> By his very birth the vipra is the abiding symbol of eternal dharma[387] — *Mahābhārata Aśvamedhikāparva* 98.85
>
> (Badrinath 2007, 381)

> The various varṇas and āśramas appeared according to inferior and superior natures manifest in the situation of the individual's birth.[388] — Bhāgavata Purāṇa 11.17.15

From the above discussion, it is clear that at the individual level, varṇa is a function of emergence of jīvātmā in the human world through the parents belonging to the same specific varṇa, As a consequence of this emergence, the individual inherits that varṇa from the parents, with the entire process being determined by one's own conduct and activities in the past life.

However, what the above discussion does not answer are questions such as:

- What exactly does it mean when it is said a jīvātmā inherits the varṇa of the parents, making one eligible for the duties and activities in accordance with that varṇa?
- What does the jīvātmā inherit that is called as varṇa?

Answers to these questions lie in understanding the second aspect of emergence, namely, varṇa as a divine emergence.

### 4.2. Varṇa as divine emergence

This is perhaps the most important but least understood aspect of varṇa.

In contemporary discourse, the birth-based classification of varṇas are often seen as a creation of dominant communities to establish their dominance on society through discriminative and exclusionary practices. However, such a mischaracterisation of varṇa classification is a direct result of the secularisation of the discourse around varṇa, leading to an inability to understand and appreciate the sacred aspect of Hindu institutions and practices.

That varṇa is a function of divine emergence is the central teaching of the Puruṣasūkta which it graphically depicts through the motif of yajña. Through yajña, the Cosmic Puruṣa is sacrificed, transformed, and made to emerge as different beings of the universe, including brāhmaṇas, kṣatriyas, vaiśyas, and śūdras. That is, the four varṇas are obtained through divine emergence and hence, are made of divine essences.

The Taittirīya Brāhmaṇa 3.4.1.1 alludes to this when it says:

> Through *Brahmā* one obtains brāhmaṇa, through Rājanya one obtains *kṣatra*, through *Maruta*, the *vaiśya* among the gods, one attains *vaiśya*, and through *Tapa*, one obtains śūdra.[389]

Sāyaṇācārya in his commentary on the above portion indicates that Brahmā (*Virāja*) is the *abhimānī-devatā* of brāhmaṇas and people who have this brāhmaṇa abhimānī-devatā in them attain brāhmaṇa varṇa characterised by the splendour of Brahma (*brahmatejas*). Likewise, a person who attains kṣatriya abhimānī-devatā obtains kṣatriya-varṇa. Same is the case with vaiśyas and śūdras. While Maruta is the vaiśya abhimānī-devatā, Tapa is the śūdra abhimānī-devatā.[390]

Here, the term 'abhimānī-devatā' refers to deities who identify themselves with particular objects or phenomena. In this case, the verse is referring to deities who identify themselves with the four varṇas. Stated differently, the essence of brāhmaṇa varṇa is divinity in the form of Brahmā (Virāja), who manifests, pervades, and presides over brāhmaṇa varṇa. Likewise, the essence of kṣatriya varṇa is divinity in the form of kṣatra-devatā who pervades and presides over it; the essence of vaiśya varṇa is divinity in the form of Maruta who pervades and presides over it; and essence of śūdra varṇa is divinity in the form of Tapa (austerity) who pervades and presides over it.

To understand and appreciate the full implication of varṇas being devatās (deities), let us now look into Bṛhadāraṇyaka Upaniṣad 1.4.11-15 and excerpts from Ādi Śaṅkarācārya's commentary on it wherein we find an elaborate elucidation on the subject.

> In the beginning this (the kṣatriya and other varṇas) was indeed Brahman, one only. Being one, he did not flourish. He specially projected an excellent form, the kṣatriya—those who are kṣatriyas among the gods: *Indra, Varuṇa, Soma, Rudra, Parjanya, Yama, Mrityu, and Iśāna*. Therefore, there is none higher than the kṣatriya. Hence the brāhmaṇa worships the kṣatriya from a lower position in the *rājasūya* sacrifice. He imparts that glory to the kṣatriya. The brāhmaṇa is the source of the kṣatriya. Therefore, although the king attains supremacy (in the sacrifice), at the end of it he resorts to the brāhmaṇa, his source. He who slights the brāhmaṇa, strikes at his own source. He becomes more wicked, as one is by slighting one's superior.[391] —Bṛhadāraṇyaka Upaniṣad 1.4.11
>
> (Madhavananda 1950)

Ādi Śaṅkarācārya in his commentary on the above verse states, 'In the beginning this, the kṣatriya and other castes, was indeed Brahman, identical with that Brahman (Virāj) who after manifesting Fire (*Agni*) assumed the form of that. He is called Brahman, because he identified himself with the brāhmaṇa varṇa (Madhavananda 1950).'[392] That is, before the manifestation of kṣatriya and other varṇas, the Cosmic Puruṣa, Brahman or Virāj existed as Agni and self-identified himself with the brāhmaṇa varṇa.

However, this Virāj could not perform his brāhmaṇa function properly. He needed a special protector in the form of a kṣatriya. Hence, he specially projected the kṣatriyas among the gods, namely, Indra, Varuṇa, Soma, and the others. Therefore, the Virāj in the form of brāhmaṇa is the source of kṣatriyas among devatās such as Indra, Varuna, Soma, etc. Śaṅkarācārya adds,'It should be understood that after them (i.e. the kṣatriya devatās), the human kṣatriyas, Purūravas and others belonging to the Lunar and Solar dynasties, presided over by the kṣatriya gods, Indra and the rest, were also created. For the creation of the gods is mentioned for this very purpose (Madhavananda 1950).'[393] That is, the kṣatriya varṇa among humans emerged from kṣatriya devatās.

> Yet he did not flourish. He projected the vaiśya—those species of gods who are designated in groups: The *Vasus*, *Rudras*, *Ādityas, Viśvadevas* and *Marutas*. He did not still flourish. He projected the śūdra varṇa—*Pūṣan*. This (earth) is *Pūṣan*. For it nourishes all this that exists.[394] — Bṛhadāraṇyaka Upaniṣad 1.4.12-13
>
> (Madhavananda 1950)

After creating the kṣatriya devatās and the kṣatriya varṇa in the human plane, the Virāj was still incapable of carrying out all his duties. Hence, he created the vaiśya devatās such as Vasus, Rudras, etcetera and śūdra devatā Pūṣan and through these deities their human counterparts, namely the vaiśya and śūdra varṇas among people.

Yet he did not flourish. He specially projected that excellent form, righteousness (dharma). This righteousness is the controller of the kṣatriya. Therefore, there is nothing higher than that. (So) even a weak man hopes (to defeat) a stronger man through righteousness, as (one contending) with the king. That righteousness is verily truth. Therefore, they say about a person speaking of truth, 'He speaks of righteousness,' or about a person speaking of righteousness, 'He speaks of truth,' for both these are but righteousness.[395] — Bṛhadāraṇyaka Upaniṣad 1.4.14

(Madhavananda 1950)

Finally, after creating all the four varṇas, he created dharma to control and provide direction to their activities. To put it differently, Virāj manifested the four varṇas for the sake of performing dharma.

Lastly, the Bṛhadāraṇyaka Upaniṣad says:

(So) these (four varṇas were projected)—the brāhmaṇa, kṣatriya, vaiśya and śūdra. He became a brāhmaṇa among the gods as Fire, and among men as the brāhmaṇa. (He became) a kṣatriya through the (divine) kṣatriyas, a vaiśya through the (divine) vaiśyas and a śūdra through the (divine) śūdra. Therefore, people desire to attain the results of their rites among the gods through fire, and among men as the brāhmaṇa. For Brahman was in these two forms.[396] — Bṛhadāraṇyaka Upaniṣad 1.4.15

(Madhavananda 1950)

Śaṅkarācārya in his commentary elucidates the above verse thus:

He, Brahman, the Projector (Virāj), became a brāhmaṇa

among the gods as Fire, and in no other form, and became a brāhmaṇa among men as the brāhmaṇa, directly. In the other varṇas, he appeared in a changed form: (He became) a kṣatriya through the (divine) kṣatriyas, i.e., being presided over by Indra and other gods; a vaiśya through the (divine) vaiśyas (i.e., presided over by the *Vasus*) and a śūdra through the (divine) śūdra (presided over by Pūṣan). Because Brahman, the Projector, was changed in the kṣatriya and other varṇas, and was unchanged in Fire and the brāhmaṇa, therefore people desire to attain the results of their rites among the gods through fire, i.e. by performing rites connected with it. It is for this purpose that Brahman abides in the form of fire, which is the receptacle in which sacrificial rites are performed. Therefore, it stands to reason that people wish to attain results by performing those rites in the fire. And among men as the brāhmaṇa: If they want human results, there is no need for rites depending on fire etc., but simply by being born as a brāhmaṇa they attain their life's ends.[397]—Śaṅkarācārya's commentary on Bṛhadāraṇyaka Upaniṣad 1.4.15

(Madhavananda 1950)

That is, while Virāj, the Cosmic Puruṣa, exists as himself in the brāhmaṇas, the kṣatriyas became kṣatriyas through the manifestation of kṣatriya devatās (such as Indra, Varuṇa, Soma etcetera) in them, the vaiśyas are likewise inhabited by vaiśya devatās such as Vasus, Rudras, Marutas, etcetera, and the śūdras contain within them the śūdra devatā, Pūṣan.

Stated differently, the four varṇas are reference to the emergence of the four types of devatās from Cosmic

Puruṣa, Virāj. These varṇa-devatās exist in the *ādhidaivika* plane; and as the abhimānī-devatās of their respective varṇas, they manifest in the human physical plane as divine essences in the people belonging to those varṇas, presiding over their activities. It is the manifestation of the divine essence of a varṇa devatā in a person's body that causes the person to be considered as belonging to that varṇa.

Interesting, Sri Aurobindo alludes to varṇas as a reference to emergence of divine principles in his discussion on *śakti-catuṣṭayam* in his work 'Records of Yoga'. While explaining the phrase *'vīrya'* he writes:

> "By vīrya is meant the fundamental *svabhāvaśakti* or the energy of the divine temperament expressing itself in the fourfold type of the cāturvarṇya—in *brāhmaṇyam, brahmaśakti, brahmatejas,* in *kṣātram, kṣātraśakti, kṣātratejas,* in *vaiśyasvabhāva, śakti* and *tejas,* in *śūdrasvabhāva, śakti* and *tejas.* We must realise that the ancient Aryan Rishis meant by the cāturvarṇya not a mere social division, but a recognition of God manifesting Himself in fundamental *svabhāva*...".
>
> (Ghose 2001,7)

He further notes that the *brāhmaṇa* is the *Śivaśakti,* the *kṣatriya* is the *Rudraśakti,* the *vaiśya* is the *Viṣṇuśakti,* and the *śūdra* is the *Śūdraśakti* (Ghose 2001,10) However, Sri Aurobindo seems to dismiss the connection between human birth and varṇa as divine essence perhaps owing to his unfamiliarity or disbelief regarding Smriti Pramana.

## 4.3. Varṇa is jīvātmā attaining divine essence through emergence

The connection between varṇa and a jīvātmā's long karmic journey through many lives to attain it, is not often appreciated in contemporary discourse. In this context, there is an insightful account of Ṛṣi Mātaṇga that Bhīṣma narrates to Yudhiṣṭhira in Mahābhārata Anuśāsanaparva, chapters 28-30. The section opens with Yudhiṣṭhira's question to Bhīṣma:

> O supreme among kings! If a person is a kṣatriya, vaiśya or a śūdra, you should tell me how he can become a brāhmaṇa. O grandfather! Does one become a brāhmaṇa through austerities, great deeds or learning? Tell me that.[398]
>
> (Debroy 2015)

In response to this question, Bhīṣma says:

> O son! O Yudhiṣṭhira! For a kṣatriya and the others, the three varṇas, becoming a brāhmaṇa is extremely difficult. For all beings, that is the best state. O son! If one is repeatedly and progressively cooked in the cycle of life, one can then be born as a brāhmaṇa.[399]
>
> (Debroy 2015)

Then, Bhīṣma narrates the story of Mātaṇga, who, though was a cāṇḍāla by birth (i.e. born from śūdra father and brāhmaṇa mother), wanted to attain, through austerity, the brāhmaṇa varṇa in that body itself. However, when Mātaṇga failed to secure his goal despite thousands of years of austerity, Indra counsels him thus:

> O Mātaṇga! The supreme state (i.e. the state of brāhmaṇa) that you desire is extremely difficult to obtain. O son!

Do not exhibit this futile rashness. This isn't the path of dharma. You cannot obtain what you wish for and will soon be destroyed. O Mātaṇga! I have sought to restrain you from aspiring to obtain that supreme state. If you still desire to perform these austerities, you will be destroyed in every possible way. Among all the men who are born as inferior species, only a few are reborn as *pukkasa* or cāṇḍāla. O Mātaṇga! Anyone on earth who is seen to have been born as wicked species, will have to whirl around in that state for a long period of time. After having spent one thousand births in this way, one obtains the status of a śūdra. One is whirled around in the state of a śūdra for a long period of time. After three thousand births in this way, one obtains the status of a vaiśya. One is whirled around in the state of a vaiśya for a long period of time. After six thousand births in this way, one obtains the status of a king. One is whirled around in the state of a king (i.e., kṣatriya) for a long period of time. After six thousand births in this way, one obtains the status of being a friend of a brāhmaṇa. One is whirled around in the state of being a friend of a brāhmaṇa for a long period of time. After two thousand births in this way, one obtains the status of a brāhmaṇa who earns a living by selling weapons. One is whirled around in the status of a brāhmaṇa who earns a living by selling weapons for a long period of time. After three thousand births in this way, one obtains the status of an ordinary brāhmaṇa. Having obtained this status, one is whirled around for a long period of time. After four thousand births in this way, one is born as a learned brāhmaṇa. One is whirled around in the state of a learned brāhmaṇa for a long period of time. O son!

> In that state, anger, delight, desire, hatred, insolence and argumentation penetrate him and try to make him the worst among brāhmaṇas. When he abandons these enemies, he obtains a virtuous end. However, if they defeat him, he falls down, as if from the top of a palm tree. O Mātaṇga! That is the reason I have spoken to you, restraining you and asking you to ask for some other boon. The status of a brāhmaṇa is something that is extremely difficult to obtain (by you)![400]
>
> (Debroy, The Mahabharata, Volume 9 2015)

After being thus counselled, Mātaṇga requested for a different boon. Indra readily granted it, blessing him to be celebrated as the deity of metre (*chandodeva*) and to receive worship from women.[401] After receiving these boons, Ṛṣi Mātaṇga discarded his body and attained the exalted place (i.e. the state of chandodeva).[402]

The essential message from the account of Ṛṣi Mātaṇga is that one can primarily attain a particular varṇa through birth. While austerity, good conduct, etcetera will help one to get birth in a higher varṇa in the next life, they cannot grant one a different varṇa in the current life itself, which was what Mātaṇga had desired, but failed to obtain. The account further shows how a jīvātmā gradually makes a transition from animal life to human life, from life as a cāṇḍāla to that of a śūdra, vaiśya, kṣatriya, and finally to that of a brāhmaṇa over thousands of lives, i.e. obtaining a particular varṇa is a result of a long spiritual journey of a jīvātmā over thousands of lives.

A similar teaching is given in a conversation between Umā and Maheśvara found in Mahābhārata Anuśāsanaparva chapter 131 wherein Maheśvara narrates how people born in each varṇa should perform their respective varṇaāśrama dharma in order to attain a higher varṇa in the next birth. Likewise, those who forsake their svadharma fall from their varṇa and are born in a lower varṇa in their next life.[403]

Why is attaining a particular varṇa so difficult, a point repeatedly asserted by Indra? The reason is: varṇa is not a social construct, nor is it merely a function of qualities and conduct. Instead, as seen in the previous section, varṇa refers to the emergence of varṇa abhimānī-devatās in the human body, thereby making the attainment as well as sustaining of these divine essences a very difficult task.

Vallabhācārya in his *Subodhinī* commentary on Bhāgavata Purāṇa 2.1.37 writes:

> Brāhmaṇa is a devatā and when it manifests in the human body, then such a person will be known as brāhmaṇa. It is for this reason that someone could become a śūdra or a cāṇḍāla after being cursed or become a brāhmaṇa through receiving a boon. The brāhmaṇa devatā resides in the body through upanayana saṃskāra.[404]

This is briefly indicated in Mahābhārata Anuśāsanaparva 131.51-52 itself, where Maheśvara says:

> O Goddess, wherever pure Brahman devoid of qualities exists, such a person is a brāhmaṇa with the fruits of birth serving the purpose of classification.[405]

What Mahābhārata and Vallabhācārya say in the context of brāhmaṇas holds true for other varṇas as well. A person is said to belong to a particular varṇa only when there is a manifestation of the divine essence of the respective varṇa devatā in them, and not otherwise. It is this divine essence one seeks to protect and harness through the performance of various duties and sacraments in accordance with respective varṇas, and it is this divine essence one could lose through non-performance of respective varṇa duties or through performance of adharmic actions.

However, the question remains how and when does a jīvātmā become infused with the divine essence of a varṇa devatā? The quote from Śrī Subodhinī seems to suggest that one attains the varṇa devatā through upanayana saṃskāra. But, this cannot be the case since it would make all the pre-upanayana saṃskāra that a child is given redundant. Further, it would then be difficult to explain the definition of varṇa propounded in the Chāndogyopaniṣad as well as in a number of smṛtis which define it in terms of birth from parents who belong to same varṇa.

Therefore, it is only proper to consider that a jīvātmā becomes infused with the divine essence of the varṇa devatā at birth itself. In fact, the jīvātmā receives the divine essence from the parents through the very act of conception. Therefore, a child becomes a brāhmaṇa by inheriting the brāhmaṇya—the essence of brāhmaṇa devatā—from its brāhmaṇa parents by the virtue of taking birth through them. Same is the case with kṣatriyas, vaiśyas, and śūdras.

That a jīvātmā inherits the divine essence of a varṇa devatā from its parents is implied in the Vedic idea that the father, through his wife, is born again as progeny. *Aitareyopaniṣad* 2.1.1-4, for example, gives the following account:

> In man indeed is the soul first conceived. That which is the semen is extracted from all the limbs as their vigour. He holds that self of his in his own self. When he sheds it into his wife, then he procreates it. That is its first birth. That becomes non-different from the

> wife, just as much as her own limb is. Therefore (the foetus) does not hurt her. She nourishes this self of his that has entered here (in her womb). She, the nourisher, becomes fit to be nourished. The wife bears that embryo (before the birth). He (the father) protects the son at the very start, soon after his birth. That he protects the son at the very beginning, just after birth, thereby he protects his own self for the sake of the continuance of these worlds. For thus is the continuance of these worlds ensured. That is his second birth. This self of his (viz. the son) is substituted (by the father) for the performance of virtuous deeds. Then this other self of his (that is the father of the son), having got his duties ended and having advanced in age, departs. As soon as he departs, he takes birth again. That is his (i.e. the son's) third birth.[406]
>
> (Gambhirananda 1958)

Manusmṛti 9.8 expresses the same idea in a more concise manner thus:

> The husband, entering the womb of his wife, becomes the embryo and is then born; the wife-hood of the 'wife' consists in this that the husband is re-born of her.[407]
>
> (G Jha 1920)

The idea is that the son becomes eligible for the father's varṇa dharma because it is the father himself who, through his wife, is born again as son. That is, the father (and the mother) transmit the divine essence of the varṇa devatā to their progeny through the act of conception and subsequently through pregnancy and birth, which is what makes the progeny eligible for the varṇa duties of the parents.

This idea is hinted at in the Puruṣasūkta wherein it is the Cosmic Puruṣa who is born again in the form of the four varṇas and other beings through the process of yajña. Bṛhadāraṇyaka Upaniṣad 6.4.3 further notes how sexual intercourse is a form of yajña:

> Her lap is the [sacrificial] altar, her hair the [sacrificial] grass, her skin [within the organ] the lighted fire; the two labia of the vulva are the two stones of the soma-press. He who, knowing this, practises sexual intercourse wins as great a world as is won through the *Vājapeya* sacrifice.[408]
>
> (Nikhilananda 1956)

Therefore, just as the Cosmic Puruṣa is reborn as the four varṇas by the act of the cosmic yajña, the human father through the yajña called sexual intercourse is reborn through the wife as progeny. Through such a yajña of sexual intercourse, the parents transmit the divine essence of the varṇa devatās to their children.

However, this divine varṇa essence inherited at birth is in an *avyakta* or unmanifest condition. It then becomes *vyakta* or manifest through saṃskāras (religious sacraments), especially through upanayana, hence giving rise to the notion of dvija or twice born. This is clearly brought out by Pārāśarasmṛti, which says:

> Just as a painting becomes manifest gradually through mixing of (layers) of colours, (in the same way) the brāhmaṇya (the divine essence of a brāhmaṇa) becomes manifest through (successive) performance of saṃskāras in the stipulated manner and accompanied by proper mantras.[409]— Pārāśarasmṛti 8.26
>
> (Dutt 1908)

Śrī Mādhavācārya in his commentary on the above verse cites a verse from *Aṅgirā* which reiterates the same:

> The state of brāhmaṇa (*brāhmaṇatvaṃ*) is established by birth, body, knowledge, conduct, vedic learning, and practice of dharma as stipulated (in the śāstras). Just as a painting becomes manifest gradually through mixing of (layers) of colours, (in the same way) the brāhmaṇya (the divine essence of a brāhmaṇa) becomes manifest through (successive) performance of saṃskāras in the stipulated manner and accompanied by proper *mantras*.[410]

Likewise, Manusmṛti 2.28 indicates:

> This body is made godly,—by a thorough study of the three *Veda*s, by Observances, by libations, by offerings, by children, by the Great Sacrifices and by the Sacrifices.[411]
>
> (G Jha 1920)

The above quoted verses are very instructive for they not only show how the varṇa, which is primarily attained through birth (and hence listed first in the verse from Aṅgirā), is gradually made manifest through successive performance of saṃskāras; they also show that the body is the vessel in which varṇa is established. Further, the other factors listed in Aṅgirā such as knowledge, conduct, vedic learning, and practice of svadharma, though they are listed as causal factors for establishing varṇa, they are causal only in the sense that they together determine whether one is able to strengthen and reinforce the varṇa essence already established in one's body through birth or one ends weakening and completely losing the varṇa essence. This is indicated by the usage of terms such as dvija, vipra, śrotriya, etcetera across the texts to refer to those brāhmaṇas who have strengthened and reinforced their brāhmaṇya through saṃskāras, conduct and vedic learning.[412] Likewise, the texts use terms such as *brahmabaṃdhu*, *vrātya*, and *patita* to indicate those brāhmaṇas who have either weakened or completely lost their brāhmaṇya through either non-performance of proper saṃskāras, forsaking of their svadharma, or indulging in criminal conduct contrary to dharma.[413]

In any case, what is important here is that the divine varṇa essence inherited at birth is in an unmanifest condition, which then becomes manifest through saṃskāras, especially through upanayana. This holds true not only for the brāhmaṇas, but also for kṣatriyas and vaiśyas. For the śūdras, however, the śūdra devatā is manifest at birth itself and hence, does not need a ritualistic second birth.[414]

However, this idea is not unique to Smṛtis, but can be traced back to the *Veda* itself. Jaiminīya Brāhmaṇa, for example, provides this insightful perspective on varṇa in the context of *Agniṣṭoma yajña*:[415]

> Two of its Services (Pressings) have also a correspondence with the *bṛhati.* The Third Service is equal to what is before the Third Service. The Morning Service has 69 (24-syllabic *gāyatrī)* verses. These are equal to 46 (36-syllabic) bṛhati verses. For two bṛhatīs are three gāyatrīs. These (separate verses) are not equal to 46 bṛhati verses. It is the Morning Service (itself) which during its course becomes equal to the bṛhati. Because the Morning becomes equal to the bṛhati during its course, therefore the brāhmaṇa obtains his position by birth, but makes this (position) more or

less important by his course of life (or conduct).[416] — Jaiminīya Brāhmaṇa 1.244

(Bodewitz 1990, 136)

Agniṣṭoma yajña is a sacrificial ritual performed over several days during the spring season. It belongs to a class of yajñas called *Somayajñas* wherein soma juice is offered to various Devatās in the fire. The soma-pressing ritual consisting of the pressing of soma plant for its juice and then offering the juice to the Devatās is performed thrice a day: in the morning, afternoon and evening. The morning soma-pressing is accompanied by the chanting of *sāmans* in gāyatrī metre. In the afternoon service, sāmans in four metres, namely gāyatrī, bṛhati, *kakup,* and *triṣṭup* are used; whereas in the evening service, sāmans in six metres, namely gāyatrī, *uṣṇik,* kakup, *anuṣṭup, jagatī,* and bṛhati are used.

The Jaiminīya Brāhmaṇa quotation above informs us that during the morning pressing, 69 verses of gāyatrī metre are chanted and these 69 gāyatrī verses are equal to 46 verses of bṛhati metre. The equality mentioned here is with respect to the total number of syllables. The gāyatrī metre has 24 syllables whereas the bṛhati has 36 syllables. As a result, 69 gāyatrī verses would contain a total of 1656 syllables (69 X 24 = 1656), which is the same number of syllables as is present in the 46 bṛhati (46 X 36 = 1656).

The Jaiminīya Brāhmaṇa indicates that though gāyatrī verses are exalted in themselves, they do not individually become equal to bṛhati (which also means 'great'). Instead, it is the morning service as a whole, consisting of adding gāyatrī verses upon gāyatrī verses until 69 gāyatrī verses are chanted in full, which becomes equal to bṛhati. Likewise, the text says that a brāhmaṇa is born as a brāhmaṇa (i.e. attains brāhmaṇya through birth) and thus is exalted from birth. However, depending upon his conduct, he could become either a greater brāhmaṇa (through accumulaton of more and more brāhmaṇya by performance of actions in accordance to brāhmaṇa-dharma including performance of relevant saṃskāras) or a lesser brāhmaṇa (through dissipation of brāhmaṇya as a result of actions which deviate from brāhmaṇa-dharma).[417]

What the Śruti states in the context of a brāhmaṇa, is true with respect to other varṇas as well. Be it a kṣatriya, a vaiśya or a śūdra, one attains varṇa through birth. However, one's conduct determines whether one is able to strengthen and fully realise the varṇa-devatā that one has inherited, or one causes dissipation of the varṇa-devatā essence present in him/her.

This makes birth the most important visible indicator for the purpose of designation and classification of society based on varṇa category—a point indicated by the Mahābhārata Anuśāsanaparva 131.51-52 cited before.[418]

However, it is interesting to note that while the attainment of varṇa through emergence from parents is considered as the primary mode of attainment across the Hindu textual landscape, the itihāsa-purāṇas also notably mention at least two cases of exceptional exceptions to this: The first is the account of the kṣatriya king Vītahavya, who became a brāhmaṇa through the blessings of Ṛṣi Bhṛgu and the second is Ṛṣi Viśvāmitra who was also originally a kṣatriya king who became a brāhmaṇa through austerity.

Mahābhārata Anuśāsanaparva Chapter 31 (Debroy 2015) narrates the story of King Vītahavya, about how he attained the state of brāhmaṇa and gained mastery over

*Veda* purely through the words of blessings from Ṛṣi Bhṛgu. This account illustrates the greatness of ṛṣis and how they could use the power of their austerity, gained through years of spiritual effort, to bestow the divine essence of varṇa devatas upon an individual. Even today there are many brāhmaṇa families who trace their lineage to ṛṣis such as Āṅgīrasa or Bhṛgu but who are not direct descendants of the said ṛṣis; instead were blessed by the ṛṣis to attain the state of brāhmaṇa. However, this is an exceptional case, a rarest of the rare case, because only a high calibre ṛṣi is capable of accomplishing it and in Kaliyuga there are hardly any ṛṣis in the physical plane.

The case of Ṛṣi Viśvāmitra is more well-known and is often posited as an example to illustrate that anybody can attain any varṇa through austerity. However, we have to examine Ṛṣi Viśvāmitra's life account in the light of what we already saw in the case of Ṛṣi Mātaṇga. While both Ṛṣi Mātaṇga and Ṛṣi Viśvāmitra performed intense austerities in order to attain the brāhmaṇa varṇa, why did Ṛṣi Mātaṇga fail to achieve this objective, whereas Ṛṣi Viśvāmitra succeeded? The answer to this question is found in Mahābhārata Anuśāsanaparva itself as well as a shorter version in *Harivaṃśa Purāṇa,* the *khila* or appendix to Mahābhārata.

In chapter 3-4 of Mahābhārata Anuśāsanaparva (Debroy 2015), the unique circumstances leading to the birth of Ṛṣi Viśvāmitra is narrated. Ṛṣi Viśvāmitra's father was King Gādhi whose daughter Satyavatī was married to Ṛṣi Ṛcīka, son of Ṛṣi Bhṛgu. Being pleased with the conduct of Satyavatī, Ṛṣi Ṛcīka desired to grant her a son. When Satyavatī's mother (Gādhi's wife) came to know about this, she also requested to be given a boon by the great ṛṣi to bear a son. Due to his love for his wife, Ṛṣi Ṛcīka agreed and prepared two cups of *caru* (a sweet porridge-like foodstuff offered in the yajña) ritualised with mantras, one for his wife meant to facilitate the birth of a glorious brāhmaṇa child and one for his mother-in-law meant to facilitate the birth of an illustrious kṣatriya child. He then instructed his wife that after her monthly periods were complete, Satyavatī should embrace a *uḍumbara* tree and then consume the caru given to her, while her mother should likewise embrace a *aśvattha* tree (after the bath at the completion of her periods) and consume the caru prepared for her. However, Satyavatī's mother coaxed her to exchange the caru cups as well as the trees they were supposed to embrace. Thus, Satyavatī ended up eating the caru and embracing the tree meant for her mother and vice versa. As a result of this, while Satyavatī's child though born a brāhmaṇa, became endowed with kṣatriya essence as well and Satyavatī's brother Viśvāmitra, though born a kṣatriya, became endowed with brāhmaṇa essence as well. Upon the birth of his son, Ṛṣi Ṛcīka explicitly says to his wife:

> It will soon be apparent that you have not done well in exchanging the caru. O beautiful one! It is clear that you have exchanged the trees too. I had placed all the brāhmaṇa energy in the universe in your caru. I had placed all the kṣatriya valour in her caru. You would have given birth to a brāhmaṇa who would have been famous in the three worlds because of his qualities. She would have given birth to an excellent kṣatriya. That is what I had arranged for. However, you and your mother have effected an exchange. Therefore, your mother will give birth to the best among brāhmaṇas. O fortunate one! You will give birth to a kṣatriya who will be terrible

in his deeds. O beautiful one! Thanks to your affection for your mother, you have not done a good deed.[419] — Mahābhārata Anuśāsanaparva 4.35-40

(Debroy 2015)

The above account clearly indicates that while Viśvāmitra had inherited the divine essence of the kṣatriya varṇa devata from his parents, he had also become endowed with the divine essence of the brāhmaṇa varṇa devata due to his mother consuming ritualised caru which was meant to facilitate the birth of a brāhmaṇa son. That is, Viśvāmitra embodied the divine essences of both the brāhmaṇa and kṣatriya varṇa devatas since birth. However, the former was weak and unmanifest initially as a result of being overshadowed by the kṣatriya nature. Through intense austerities performed for many thousand years, Viśvāmitra was able to free himself of his kṣatriya nature, such that the divine essence of the brāhmaṇa devata which was already present in him was able to manifest fully without any obstruction. This was the reason why Viśvāmitra succeeded where Mātaṇga had failed. Another factor which perhaps contributed to the success of Viśvāmitra and the failure of Mātaṇga was the fact that Viśvāmitra being a kṣatriya was a dvija (had ritualistic second birth) and hence his body was capable of holding the brāhmaṇa devata, whereas in the case of Mātaṇga, because he was born from pratilōmavivāha,[420] and did not have eligibility for dvijatva, his body was incapable of holding the brāhmaṇa devata, as a result of which Indra denied his request of brāhmaṇya, though he granted Mātaṇga his other requests.

Even if we were to disregard the circumstances surrounding the birth of Viśvāmitra and hold that it is possible to change varṇa purely through austerity, even then it must be kept in mind that it took Viśvāmitra many thousands of years of austerity to change his varṇa from kṣatriya to brāhmaṇa. To change varṇa from other varṇas into brāhmaṇa varṇa would take a much longer duration. This makes the case of Viśvāmitra a rarest of the rare case as well. And in Kaliyuga, it is almost impossible to replicate.

## 5. Varṇa as a designation signifying ritual state

The Puruṣasūkta verse 16 says:

> Devas performed yajña offering the yajña to yajña.
> That was the first act of dharma.
> Thus, they attained heaven just as the sādhyas and devas of old.[421]
>
> (Sreekrishna and Ravikumar 2015)

By terming the cosmic yajña that resulted in the emergence of the four varṇas as the first act of dharma through which the devas attained heaven, the Puruṣasūkta sets out clearly the spiritual and ritualistic significance of the varṇas. The yajña is not only the primordial ritual through which the devas attained heaven, it is also the ritualistic path through which the humans can attain heaven and much more. By designating such yajña as the first act of dharma, the Puruṣasūkta unambiguously posits practice of dharma itself as a ritualistic performance and the emergence of varṇas as having a ritualistic meaning and purpose.

As noted in the previous section, the Bṛhadāraṇyaka Upaniṣad 1.4.11-15 also highlights the ritual significance of the varṇas. After noting how Virāj, the Cosmic Puruṣa himself, manifested as the four varṇas for the sake of flourishing, in verse 1.4.14, the Upaniṣad says that even after the emergence of the four varṇas, the Virāj still did not flourish and therefore he specially projected the excellent form of dharma, which is the controller of kṣatriyas (and of other varṇas) and there is nothing higher than dharma.[422] That is, the Upaniṣad posits dharma and its performance as the means for flourishing of the four varṇas, so much so that the very emergence of varṇas was for the sake of performing dharma without which they were incomplete.

In his commentary on this verse (i.e. Bṛhadāraṇyaka Upaniṣad 1.4.14), Ādi Śaṅkarācārya writes:

> Hence, an ignorant man (i.e., a jīvātmā who is yet to attain self-realisation) identified with dharma, in order to practice its particular forms, identifies himself with one or other of the varṇas, brāhmaṇa, kṣatriya, vaiśya or śūdra, which is the pre-condition of that practice; and these are naturally (i.e. designated by nature) the means that qualify one for the performance of rites (karma).[423]
>
> (Madhavananda 1950)

Again, in his commentary on the next verse (i.e. Bṛhadāraṇyaka Upaniṣad 1.4.15), Śaṅkarācārya quotes an opponent who in the course of a discussion about attainment of the Supreme Self, writes about the relationship between varṇas and ritualistic work which is not disputed by Śaṅkarācārya:

> Brahman projected the four varṇas for the sake of ritualistic work. And that work, called dharma, being obligatory on all, controls all and helps them to achieve their life's ends.[424]
>
> (Madhavananda 1950)

Both these excerpts clearly bring out the fact that varṇa designation signifies ritual state which acts as a pre-condition, a marker which constitutes the eligibility criteria for the ritualistic performance of a particular form of dharma. Simply stated, the varṇa designation brāhmaṇa signifies the ritual state of a person who is competent and eligible for performing brāhmaṇa dharma, such as adhyayana (studying) and adhyāpana (teaching) of *Veda*, etcetera as enunciated in Manusmṛti 1.88.[425] Likewise, the varṇa designations for kṣatriya, vaiśya, and śūdra signify their respective ritual states and mark the respective varṇa dharmas which they are qualified to perform.

Moreover, the notion that dharma itself is a ritual and the performance of dharma constitutes a ritualistic performance is clearly brought out by the fact that the primary purpose and end-goal of the performance of dharma is not the acquisition of wealth or the fulfilment of worldly pleasures. Rather, it is the acquisition of puṇya or karmic merit through which one can attain sukha, svarga, cittaśuddhi, and eventually mokṣa—a point highlighted in the stipulation of Manusmṛti 2.13 which states that 'the knowledge of dharma is ordained for those who are not addicted to the pursuit of wealth and pleasures (G Jha 1920).'[426] In other words, the practice of dharma is a ritualistic action whose nature is teleological having a religious, spiritual, and transcendental end-goal.

However, this understanding of varṇa as a designation signifying ritual state does not exist in vacuum. It directly flows from the understanding of varṇa as a function of emergence.

In the previous section, it was extensively discussed how a jīvātmā attains a particular varṇa through the inheritance of the divine essences of the varṇa devatās from parents belonging to the same varṇas. It is the presence of this divine essence of a particular varṇa (inherited from parents) in an individual that is designated as the varṇa of the individual which in-turn constitutes the ritual state of the individual. That is, an individual who is born to brāhmaṇa parents, both of whom are practicing brāhmaṇas (i.e. those who retain their brāhmaṇya—the divine essence—through proper conduct), inherits the brāhmaṇya from the parents, thereby becoming a brāhmaṇa who is now eligible for performing brāhmaṇa dharma. Same is the case with the other varṇas. The second birth through the upanayana saṃskāra of the dvijas—namely, the brāhmaṇas, the kṣatriyas, and the vaiśyas—causes the divine essences, which lie hidden at birth, to manifest, thereby making them eligible for ritual actions in accordance with their respective varṇas.

We find many explicit and implicit references to varṇa being a designation signifying ritual state across the textual landscape of dharmaśāstra tradition. Let us examine some relevant verses from Manusmṛti. Towards the end of the first chapter, Manusmṛti clearly brings out the ritual significance of the brāhmaṇa varṇa, when it says:

> Him (i.e., the brāhmaṇa) the self-existent one, after performing austerities, created, in the beginning, out of his own mouth, for the conveying of offerings (to the gods) and of oblations (to the pitṛs), and for the preservation of this entire creation. What being is superior to him through whose mouth the gods always eat the offerings and the Pitṛs the oblations.[427] — Manusmṛti 1.94-95
>
> (G Jha 1920)

That the very emergence and existence of brāhmaṇa varṇa is for the sake of conveying the offerings to the devatās and the oblations to the pitṛs and through such ritualistic acts facilitating the preservation of this entire universe clearly brings out the ritual status, purpose, and function of the brāhmaṇa varṇa. Regarding how the brāhmaṇas by their ritual performance facilitate preservation of the universe, Medhātithi in his commentary on Manusmṛti 1.94 writes:

> By the said act (of conveying the oblations and offerings) is accomplished 'the preservation,'—nourishment—of this whole Trio of Worlds: the gods live upon offerings made from this world (by men),—the Gods again nourish plants and herbs and make them ripe by means of cold, heat and rains; this mutual benefit leads to 'preservation'.[428]
>
> (G Jha 1920)

In short, the very purpose of the brāhmaṇa varṇa's emergence and existence is for the sake of performing this ritual function and they alone are empowered to perform this function because they emerged from the face of Cosmic Puruṣa and have thus received the divine essence of the brāhmaṇa devatā.

Therefore, brāhmaṇa is a designation signifying ritual state. This is reiterated in the below verse:

> The very genesis of the brāhmaṇa is the eternal incarnation of dharma; for he is born for the sake of dharma; and this (birth) leads to the state of Brahman.[429]
> — Manusmṛti 1.98
>
> (G Jha 1920)

Then, in the second chapter, Manusmṛti provides the most explicit account of how varṇa is a designation signifying ritual state:

> Bereft of this verse (i.e., sāvitrī mantra), and of the timely performance of his own duty, a person of brāhmaṇa, kṣatriya or vaiśya birth incurs the odium of good men.[430] — Manusmṛti 2.80
>
> (G Jha 1920)

Commenting on the above verse, Medhātithi notes that the person who is bereft of the sāvitrī becomes a *vrātya* i.e. one who has fallen from his varṇa duty. This verse clearly brings out the fact that not just in the case of brāhmaṇas, but even in the case of kṣatriyas and vaiśyas, the varṇa is a designation of their ritual state. All the three of them are considered 'dvijas'—a ritual designation implying one having a second ritualistic emergence through the saṃskāra of upanayana that makes one eligible for the practice of *Veda* adhyayana as well as *sandhyopāsana* (twilight worship) through *japa* of sāvitrī mantra. The verse says that such a person, be he a brāhmaṇa, kṣatriya, or vaiśya, if he does not perform the mandatory japa of sāvitrī mantra, then he loses his ritual state and hence, becomes blameworthy. If varṇa is not a designation of ritual state, why would one become a vrātya for merely not performing the sāvitrī mantra japa regularly?

Likewise, Manusmṛti 2.103 states:

> But he who does not stand during the morning-twilight, and who does not sit through the evening-twilight, should be excluded, like the śūdra, from all that is due to twice-born persons.[431]
>
> (G Jha 1920)

We have similar quotations from other texts as well:

When Brahmins do not worship the morning twilight before the sun rises and the evening twilight before the sun sets, how can they be considered Brahmins. When Brahmins never worship the morning or the evening twilight, a righteous king may freely employ them to do the work of südras.[432] — Baudhāyana Dharmasūtra 2.7.15

(Olivelle 2000)

Brāhmaṇas, who are ignorant of the *Veda*s, and Gāyatrī and *Sandhya*, and those who do not cast any oblation in the sacrificial fire and live by agriculture, are only Brāhmaṇas in name.[433] — Pārāśarasmṛti 8.11

(Dutt 1908)

The *Veda* itself indicates that varṇa is a ritual state:

Prajāpati (and nothing else) existed here in the beginning. Now Prajāpati was the (vital) power mind. He desired: 'May I become manifold. May I procreate. May I become abundant'. He created from his top, from his head, the Trivṛt laud, the gāyatri metre, the rathamtara melody, the deity Agni, the human being brāhmaṇa, the animal goat. Therefore the brāhmaṇa has the gāyatri as his metre and Agni as his deity. And therefore also he is the head of the creatures. For he (Prajāpati) created him from the head. He desired: 'May I procreate'. He created from both his arms and from his breast the Fifteenfold laud, the triṣṭup metre, the bṛhat melody, the deity Indra, the human being kṣatriya, the animal horse. Therefore the kṣatriya has the triṣṭup as his metre and Indra as his deity. And therefore also he displays his force with his arms. For he (P.) created him from his two arms, from his breast, from his force. He desired: 'May I procreate'. He created from his belly, from his middle, the Seventeenfold laud, the Jagatī metre, the vāmadevya melody, the deity All-gods (Viśvedevā), the human being vaiśya and the animal cow. Therefore the vaisya has the jagatī as his metre and the All-gods as his deity. And therefore he is always intent on producing (procreating). For he (P.) created him from his belly, from his generative organ. He desired: 'May I procreate'. He created from his two feet, from his support, the Twenty-onefold laud, the anuṣṭup metre, the yajñāyajñīya melody, no deity at all, the human being śūdra and the animal sheep. Therefore the śūdra has the anuṣṭup as his metre and the landlord as his deity.[434]—Jaiminīya Brāhmaṇa 1.68-69

(Bodewitz 1990)

The above verses clearly bring out the fact that varṇa is a ritual state which one could lose as a result of non-performance of ritual acts enjoined upon them. This is especially so for the brāhmaṇas, kṣatriyas, and vaiśyas.

As far as the status of śūdra varṇa with respect to ritual is considered, while they are not eligible for dvija dharma, they are eligible for other ritual practices, and their own śūdra dharma is a ritualistic and spiritual practice in itself. As Manusmṛti 10.127-128 notes:

If those who, knowing their duty, and wishing to acquire merit, imitate the practices of righteous men, with the exception of reciting the sacred texts, they incur no guilt; they obtain praise. As the Śūdra, free from envy, maintains the right course of conduct, so does he, free from blame, gain this world and the next.[435]

(G Jha 1920)

Regarding the ritual practices of śūdra varṇa, Yajñavalkyasmṛti 1.121, for example says:

He should be attached to his wife, should be pure (internally and externally), maintain those who depend on him for support, and perform Śrāddha ceremonies. He should not neglect (the performance of) the five sacrifices, making use of the mantra '*Namah*'.[436]

(Somayaji 2006)

We have an entire class of dharmaśāstra texts popularly called śūdra-dharma texts[437] devoted specifically to enunciate in detail the various duties and ritual practices applicable to the śūdra varṇa.

From above, it is clear that not just the dvijas, but even śūdra varṇa is a designation referring to ritual state of the individual. It is for this reason Manusmṛti 10.130 states that people belonging to any of the four varṇas will attain the highest state i.e. mokṣa through the practice of their respective varṇa dharma:

The duties of the four varṇas in times of distress have thus been expounded; by properly carrying out which they attain the highest state.[438]

(G Jha 1920)

Likewise, Ādi Śaṅkarācārya in his Gītābhāṣya notes:

When rightly pursued, the natural result of these duties enjoined for the castes is the attainment of heaven.[439]

— Gītābhāṣya of Śaṅkarācārya on Bhagavad Gītā 18.44

(Gambhirananda 2018)

However, the Ācārya does not stop there. Instead, right in the beginning of his Gītābhāṣya, he answers a very pertinent question, namely: apart from providng a means for individual pursuit of svarga and mokṣa, what purpose does the practice of varṇa dharma serve in the larger scheme of the universe? He says:

> After projecting this world, and desiring to ensure its stability, He, the Bhagavān, first created the Prajāpatis, namely Marīci and others, and made them follow the dharma (virtuous path) characterized by action (rites and duties) as revealed in the *Veda*s. And then, having created others, namely, Sanaka, Sanandana, etc., He made them espouse the dharma characterized by renunciation and distinguished by Knowledge and detachment. For, the dharma revealed in the *Veda*s is of two kinds—one characterized by action, and the other by renunciation. That dharma, which is meant for the stability of the world and is the direct means to both secular and spiritual welfare of living beings, continues to be followed by brāhmaṇas and others belonging to different castes and stages of life, who aspire after the highest.[440]—Introductory section, Gītābhāṣya of Śaṅkarācārya
>
> (Gambhirananda 2018)

That is, the larger purpose served by the practice of the ritualistic social function of varṇa dharma is cosmological—maintainance of the stability and order of the entire universe.

Chittaranjan Naik in his essay 'Varṇa and Birth' beautifully brings out this cosmological orientation of varṇas when he writes:

The brāhmaṇa, the kṣatriya, the vaiśya and the śūdra, are not just people; they are people that have specific roles in the Government of the Universe. The yajñas for performance by the brāhmaṇa are not for him alone but for the governance of the Universe. This governance is the way of *Sanātana* Dharma, and it maintains Order in this Universe. We live in this universe in a relationship of mutual welfare with the gods.

When a brāhmaṇa is about to be born, the gods in heaven rejoice, for they await his arrival in joy. The brāhmaṇa is he who shall give to them their desire, the subtle elements from the yajña that he is to perform, for these subtle elements from the yajña are their food. The gods need people as much as people need the gods. Nurturing one another, they bring happiness to the world. When they stop nurturing one another, there is darkness and sorrow in the world. That is why the gods need the brāhmaṇa, for the brāhmaṇa is their connection to the world of men and to the food that they are to receive from *bhūlōka*.

When a kṣatriya is about to be born, the gods in heaven rejoice, for they await his arrival in joy. The kṣatriya is he who shall protect the brāhmaṇa and the Eternal Dharma so that the gods and humans may live nurturing one another. The kṣatriya is the protector of the Order. It is he who ensures that the brāhmaṇa may continue to provide the gods with food.

When the vaiśya is about to be born, the gods in heaven rejoice, for they await his arrival in joy. The vaiśya is he who shall cater to the needs of the Order so that the brāhmaṇas and kṣatriyas may devote themselves to the Order of exchange between the gods and the people. For without the actions of the Vedic vaiśya, there will be starvation of Vedic dharma and its accessories.

When the śūdra is about to be born, the gods in heaven rejoice, for they await his arrival in joy. The śūdra is he who shall till the soil, who shall toil to bring forth the produce of the earth, and who shall serve so that the Kingdom of the Universe may prosper. He is the true servant of the Lord.

People born into *Vaidika* Dharma are part of the executive body of the Government of the Universe. Their actions in adhering to their dharma are not meant for their own welfare but for the welfare of the whole Universe.

(Naik and Gopal 2023)

He further adds:

Just as every citizen of a nation cannot be a member of the Government, it is not for every person in the world to be a member of the Government of the Universe. It is for the people of Vaidika Dharma alone. The *Veda*s belong to the whole universe, but the people of Bhāratavarṣa are its custodians. They shall be failing the gods by failing in their duty; they shall be failing their brothers and sisters of the world by failing in their duty; they shall be failing all the creatures of the world by failing in their duty. This is the dark age of *kaliyuga*, when desire and darkness, instead of dharma, decide our actions. But the Eternal Dharma does not change.

(Naik and Gopal 2023)

## Conclusion

Contemporary approaches to understanding the Hindu conception of varṇa largely limit its examination to secular dimensions of social order and/or behavioural traits, thereby failing to consider the ritual dimension of varṇa and its full implication. This approach is faulty and has resulted in serious gaps and distortion in our understanding of varṇa.

In this chapter, we have attempted to fill this gap by an examination into the ritual dimension of varṇa. The above discussion clearly demonstrates that varṇa is essentially a designation signifying one's ritual state which indicates the type of varṇa devatā and its divine essence that is present in an individual which in turn determines the specific form of varṇa-dharma that an individual is eligible to practice and through which they can attain happiness, heaven, and final liberation.

Further, it was shown that the ritual state of varṇa is primarily a function of emergence or birth with other factors such as *guṇa-karma* largely playing the role of facilitating principles. In fact, the *guṇa-svabhāva* a person becomes endowed with in a particular life is a result of pre-existing saṃskāras accumulated in the past lives which are now ready to manifest results in the current life. They facilitate the unfolding of the divine essence of the varṇa-devatā when a person undertakes the performance of varṇa dharma as indicated by the śāstras.

In short, *janma* (birth) is the *upadāna-karaṇa* (material cause) for the attainment of varṇa, and karma or actions performed in the previous life is the upadāna-karaṇa for the kind of janma one attains in this life. Thus, with attaining the divine essence of the varṇa devatā from the parents during the process of conception and birth itself constitutes the attainment of varṇa.

Stated differently, while janma is the immediate material cause which acts as the mechanism through which one attains the varṇa, the karma performed in previous lives is the remote material cause. Karma facilitates a jīvātmā in attaining a particular varṇa by causing it to take janma from particular parents and endows such a jīvātmā with the guṇa-svabhāva needed for the unfoldment of the divine essence of the varṇa devatā through the ritualistic performance of varṇa dharma in the current life.

A corollary to understanding varṇa as a ritual state is that any discourse that discounts this and reduces varṇa to a purely socio-secular or psychological category (be it in a positive or a negative sense) does not reflect the view of the Hindu Śāstra tradition.

# Appendix II

## 'Antarprabhāva' in Surendra Kumar's 'Viśuddha Manusmṛti': A critical examination in the view of its professed revisionist interpretation.[441]

Dr Surendra Kumar, a Saṃskṛta scholar with affiliation to Ārya Samaj, is one of the contemporary commentators on Manusmṛti. He has brought out what can be called as a revisionist edition of the text which he calls as the Viśuddha Manusmṛti' (Kumar, *Vishuddha* Manusmṛti, 1996). Thie edition professes to be a 'purified' version of the Manusmṛti, created after identifying and omitting what Dr Kumar considers to be later-day interpolations from the available text. He has also brought out *The* Manusmṛti *(Sampuran Edition)* (Kumar 2018) [along with a Hindi commentary titled *Anuśīlan*] which includes the entire text of Manu including what Dr Kumar designates as interpolations. For the purpose of this essay, we will use The Manusmṛti (Sampuran Edition) (Kumar 2018).[442]

In his Anuśīlan commentary, Dr Kumar has often differed with the interpretations of Manusmṛti by traditional Saṃskṛta commentators. Instead, he has provided revisionist interpretations, especially with respect to controversial topics such as meat-eating, caste, etcetera.

In this appendix chapter, we will examine only one such instance of revisionist interpretation: the interpretation of the phrase antarprabhāva in verse 1.2:

भगवन् सर्ववर्णानां यथावदनुपूर्वशः ।
अन्तरप्रभवाणां च धर्मान्नो वक्तुमर्हसि ॥
*Bhagavān sarvavarṇānāṃ yathāvadanupūrvaśaḥ* ।
*antaraprabhavāṇāṃ ca dharmānno vaktumarhasi* ॥
*May Thou, O blessed One, explain to us, in due form and in proper order, the duties of all castes (varṇa-s) and intermediate castes (antarprabhāvas)*
(G Jha 1920) !

The context of the verse is that Manusmṛti opens with a group of sages approaching Svāyambhuva-Manu, requesting for an instruction regarding dharma (duties) as applicable to different categories of people. In this regard, the sages explicitly request for duties 'of all the (four) varṇas' (sarvavarṇānāṃ) and 'of antarprabhāvas'. While all the major Saṃskṛta commentators starting from Bhāruci[443] and Medhātithi[444] to Govindarāja[445] and Kullūka-Bhaṭṭa[446] have interpreted the phrase antarprabhāva as a reference to those born from a mixture of varṇas (and hence, have a mixed varṇa-svabhāva), i.e. the *varṇasaṅkara-jātis* or *saṅkīrṇa-jātis*, Dr Kumar (2018, 2-5) indicates that this interpretation is born out of prejudice and the correct meaning to be adopted is that it is a reference to āśramas or stages in life.

Dr Kumar lists six arguments to justify his position (2018, 2-4). We will examine each of them in detail below.

a. **Argument 1:** A phrase similar to antarprabhāva

namely *sāntarālānāṃ* appears in verse 2.18 wherein it refers to āśramas, and hence, antarprabhāva must also refer to āśramas (Kumar 2018, 2-3).

According to Manu 2.18, 'That practice, which has come down through an unbroken line of tradition (*paramparā*) among the several castes (varṇas) and subcastes (sāntarālānāṃ) in that country (i.e. *Brahmāvarta*), is called the sadācāra or the practice of good men (G Jha 1920).'[447] While all traditional commentators including Medhātithi and Kullūka-Bhaṭṭa have taken sāntarāla as a reference to those belonging to mixed varṇas, Dr Kumar argues that sāntarāla instead refers to āśrama. The reason he gives for his reading is that the practices of saṅkīrṇa-jātis i.e. those with mixed varṇa-svabhāva cannot be designated as sadācāra or practices of good people because in Chapter 10, Manu has described those belonging to saṅkīrṇa-jātis in a negative way. The examples he cites include descriptions such as 'tainted by defect of the mothers[448] in the context of those begotten by twice-born men on wives of the next lower castes in verse 10.6; 'cruel in his deeds and dealings[449] in the context of *Ugras* who are born from kṣatriya fathers and śūdra mothers in verse 10.9; 'lowest of men[450] with reference to Caṇḍālas born from śūdra fathers and brāhmaṇa mothers in verse 10.16; 'Vrātya[451] as designation for dvijas who have fallen from their duties in verse 10.20; 'evil-natured[452] in the context of *Bhṛjjakaṇṭaka* who are born from *Vrātya-dvija* parents in verse 10.21; and 'greatly tainted and despised[453] in the context of those born from inter-mixing of *Āyogava,* etcetera who were themselves born from intermixing of four varṇas in pratiloma or inverse order in verse 10.29. Dr Kumar writes that due to negative descriptions such as above with respect to people of mixed varṇas, the hereditary ācāras or practices done by such families cannot be designated as sadācāra (good practices) and hence, the phrase sāntarāla in verse 2.18 cannot refer to those belonging to mixed varṇas.

While a detailed examination of Chapter 10 is beyond the scope of exposition here, it should be noted that the objection raised by Dr Kumar is untenable. The negative descriptions given in the above-cited verses are neither a reference to ethical values nor a commentary on the ability of mixed-varṇa people to live an ethical life. That is, it is not a moral judgement per se. Instead, the descriptions are part of an analysis of the svabhāva of those belonging to different mixed-varṇa categories and their respective svadharma. It is in this context that Manusmṛti undertakes a detailed examination of how, when there is varṇasaṅkara, the different kinds of varṇa-svabhāvas of parents become mixed and integrated into the children born of them, giving rise to such children having a svabhāva distinct from those of their fathers and mothers. As a result of this, such children become ineligible to perform fully the varṇa-dharma of the parents i.e., the svadharma of the children deviates from the svadharma of the parents and hence, a separate exposition is taken up regarding the svadharma of such mixed-varṇa people. This is clearly brought out in verse 10.41, which lists who among the mixed-varṇa people can be designated as dvija and can perform svadharma as applicable to dvijas, and who among them is eligible to take up the duties of śūdras.[454] Further, in verse 10.63, Manu speaks about ethical tenets such as non-injury, truth, abstention from unlawful appropriation, purity, and control of the sense-organs as dharma common to everyone and hence, must be practiced by everyone.[455] Though the verse uses the phrase 'dharma common to four varṇas', it is a reference to the entire humanity, including those belonging to mixed-varṇa categories, since it appears in the context of the discussion related to duties of mixed-varṇa people, a point noted by Medhātithi, Kullūka-Bhaṭṭa and other traditional commentators.[456] Therefore, the negative descriptions must be seen not as moral judgements upon inability of certain people or communities to perform sadācāra as taken by Dr Kumar, but instead as a reference to the alienation of the mixed-varṇa people from the svadharma of their respective parents as a consequence of their having mixed-varṇa svabhāva. If mixed-varṇa people are incapable of performing sadācāra, or if none of the practices of such people (be it hereditary or not) can be considered as sadācāra, then why would Manu consider some of them as being eligible to practice dvija dharma and some others as being eligible for śūdra dharma and all of them as being eligible for the practice of sāmānya dharma, such as ahiṁsā, etcetera? Would the performance of such practices as sāmānya dharma, which can be understood as 'good' practices in the context of the four varṇas, become 'bad' when practiced by those of mixed-varṇas?

More importantly, the sadācāra mentioned in verses 2.6 and 2.18 refers to various customs and practices, often hereditary, practiced in different families and communities, with great diversity from location to location. Medhātithi in his commentary on verse 2.6 gives the following examples of sadācāra:

> To this category belong such acts as the following—(a) the tying of the bracelet and such other auspicious rites performed during marriage, etc., (b) the worshipping of famous trees, *yakṣas*, road-crossings and such things, varying in various countries, done by the girl on her day of marriage, (c) the number of hair-locks kept on the head, varying with different countries; (d) the exact manner of attending on guests, teachers and other respectable persons, consisting in the addressing of sweet and agreeable words, saluting, rising to receive and so forth; for instance, it is customary with some people to recite the *Pṛṣṇi-sūkta* with grass in hand, when handing over the horse consecrated for the *Aśvamedha* sacrifice.[457]
>
> (G Jha 1920)

What distinguishes these customary practices from ritualistic practices is that ritualistic practices have their basis in *Veda* and smṛtis, whereas these customs are inherited in one's family or are specific to one's community. As long as they do not contradict dharma as enunciated in *Veda* and smṛtis, these practices are also considered auspicious and constitute dharma. Therefore, to restrict sadācāra to only the four varṇas and consider the rest of the society as being incapable of leading a good, healthy, and auspicious life goes against the teachings of śāstras, which uphold that everyone is eligible to puṇya and mokṣa, though their paths could be different. Hence, the correct reading of the verse 2.18 would be sadācāra as good practices inherited by tradition among people belonging to both—varṇa and mixed-varṇa—categories.

Therefore, in the light of the above discussion, we must reject Dr Kumar's argument that the phrase sāntarāla in verse 2.18 and by extension the phrase antarprabhāva in the present verse (i.e. verse 1.2) cannot be a reference to mixed-varṇa people as none of their practices can be called sadācāra.

b. **Argument 2:** Since, along with the description of varṇa-dharma, Manusmṛti gives a detailed description of āśrama-dharma and not of the dharma of varṇasaṅkara people, the phrase antarprabhāva must refer to āśramas and not saṅkīrṇa-jātis (Kumar 2018, 3).

This second argument put forward by Dr Kumar is with respect to the structure of the text of Manusmṛti. He notes that just as dharma of different varṇas and of antarprabhāvas are given together in the present verse, in the same order, varṇa and āśramas have been discussed side by side in Chapters 2-6. He asks that: 'If antarprabhāvas were to mean varṇasaṅkara and not antarprabhāvas then how come while in the present verse no question has been raised about āśramas, Manu discusses about āśrama dharma at such length and detail? Also, if the question is about varṇasaṅkara, then why is it that a discussion of varṇasaṅkara not found side-by-side with the discussion on varṇas in all the chapters? (Kumar 2018, 3)'. Dr Kumar concludes that since varṇa and āśrama have been discussed together and āśrama dharma has been given a prominent place in the discussion, the phrase antarprabhāva in the present verse must refer to āśramas and not varṇasaṅkara.

However, this argument is again flawed because it is based on a faulty understanding of the structure of the text of Manusmṛti.

Firstly, the assertion that the discussion about varṇas and antarprabhāvas must necessarily happen side-by-side because they have been mentioned together in the present verse is unreasonable because there is no causal connection between their appearance together in the verse 1.2 and their enunciation in the rest of the text. If there was such a causal connection, then why is the discourse on dharma of the four varṇas not appearing side-by-side in all the chapters but instead they appear sequentially? The Chapters 2-6 discuss dharma of brāhmaṇas, the Chapters 7-9 discuss the duties of kṣatriyas, and after the conclusion of duties of kṣatriyas, Chapter 9 discusses sequentially duties of vaiśyas and śūdras, and finally Chapter 10 discusses the duties of different categories of varṇasaṅkara. If Dr Kumar's argument is to be accepted, then all the duties of all groups of people should have been clubbed together side by side in one mammoth chapter perhaps, but thankfully that is not the case. More importantly, in the present verse, the ṛṣis explicitly request Manu that the duties of all the varṇas and antarprabhāvas must be expounded in due form and proper sequence. And the structure of the text reflects this sequential and ordered exposition.

Secondly, regarding the question, 'If antarprabhāvas

were to mean varṇasaṅkara and not āśrama, then how how is it that even though no question has been raised about āśramas in the present verse, Manu discusses āśrama dharma at such length and detail?', the answer is found within the text itself. In verse 2.25, Manu says 'Learn now the dharmas of different varṇas[458] (G Jha 1920)' and from verse 2.27 begins the description of the duties of the brāhmaṇa varṇa starting from saṃskāras. This then is followed by a description of brahmachārya, grihasta-āśrama, vanaprastha and sannyasa-āśrama which concludes in Chapter 6. The concluding verse 6.97 says, 'Thus has the four-fold duty of the brāhmaṇa been expounded to you, which is conducive to imperishable rewards after death[459] (G Jha 1920).' This shows that for Manu, the four āśrama-dharmas constitute the 'four-fold dharmas of brāhmaṇa varṇa' and hence the āśrama-dharma is integral to varṇa dharma. Further, while commenting on verse 2.15 of Parāśarasmṛti in Parāśara Mādhava (Ācāra khaṇḍa), Śrī Mādhavācārya (Svāmī Vidyāraṇya) quotes *Yogī-Yājñavalkya* 1.29 and *Vāmana Purāṇa* 15.61-63 which says that for brāhmaṇas there are four āśramas, for kṣatriyas only three āśramas, for Vaiśyas only two āśramas, and for śūdras only one āśrama[460] (Tripati, Parasharamadhava: Acharakhandam 2019, 511-512), i.e. āśrama-dharmas are considered as integral and embedded aspects of varṇa-dharma itself across Hindu textual tradition. Hence, it is neither out of place nor inconsistent in any way that when asked by the ṛṣis about dharma of all varṇas, Manu enunciates in great depth about different āśrama dharmas as well.

Therefore, in the light of the above discussion, we

must reject this argument of Dr Kumar as well on the grounds of it being untenable and based on a faulty understanding of the textual structure.

c. **Argument 3:** The compositional style of the text is such that varṇa and āśrama are always mentioned together. Hence, antarprabhāvas mentioned along with varṇas in the present verse must also refer to āśramas (Kumar 2018, 3-4).

Dr Kumar provides two examples to substantiate his claim that āśramas are always mentioned together with varṇas: verses 12.97 and 7.35. We can straightaway discard 12.97 from our consideration as the verse does not mention varṇa and āśrama in a way which could show their inter-connectedness. Instead, it merely states, 'The four varṇas, the three worlds, the four āśramas, the past, the present and the future are each learnt from the *Veda* (G Jha 1920).'[461] In the case of verse 7.35,[462] while it does use varṇa and āśrama in an inter-connected manner, and this inter-connectedness as noted before is due to the fact that āśrama dharma is integral and embedded within varṇa dharma, this in itself cannot serve as a necessary and sufficient evidence to conclude that the phrases varṇa and āśrama must necessarily always appear together. We have plenty of instances (as in verses 1.91, 1.107, 2.25, 2.132, 2.210, 9.336, etcetera) where the phrase varṇa appears alone in a verse without any reference to āśrama. Thus, the statement of Dr Kumar that the compositional style of Manusmṛti is such that the phrase varṇa is always accompanied by the phrase āśrama is incorrect.

However, even if we were to accept the contention that the phrases varṇa and āśrama have been used together in several instances, even then it cannot be used as an evidence to conclude that the phrase varṇa has to be necessarily used only in conjunction with the phrase āśrama and it cannot be used in conjunction with any other phrases because such a contention is not only speculative in nature, it is simply logically untenable. What authors or teachers choose to use in their expositions primarily depends upon the matter they want to convey, rather than merely compositional elements. Therefore, compositional styles and patterns cannot override the content of the exposition.

Therefore, in the light of the above evidence, we must reject this third argument of Dr Kumar as well.

d. **Argument 4:** The antarprabhāva in the present verse cannot refer to varṇasaṅkara since the only place a discussion on varṇasaṅkara happens in the text is in Chapter 10 and this discussion is a later-day interpolation, which goes against the context of the overall text (Kumar 2018, 4).

It is beyond the scope of this work to analyse in detail the arguments that Dr Kumar puts forward to establish that the verses enunciating varṇasaṅkara in Chapter 10 are all later-day interpolations, and will be taken up in future in an appropriate place and format. For the present purpose, it would be enough to review what Dr Kumar writes in his comments on the present verse under discussion.

He makes a three-fold argument to substantiate his position:

I. First, the only place where there is a discussion on varṇasaṅkara in the entire text of Manu is in Chapter 10. Except for this chapter, there is absolutely no discussion of varṇasaṅkara either independently or in conjunction with some other topic such as nāmakaraṇa (naming sacrament), vivāha (marriage sacrament), punishments, etcetera.

II. Second, the way the discussion on varṇasaṅkara has been embedded in Chapter 10, it goes against the larger context of the text, and hence, can be considered as a later-day addition. The discussion on dharma starts at verse 2.25 wherein it mentions, 'learn now the duties of the several varṇas,[463] and this discussion finally concludes in verse 10.131 where it mentions, 'thus has the entire law relating to the duties of the four varṇas been described.[464] In both places, there is only a mention of the duties of varṇas and not of varṇasaṅkara and hence, the inclusion of a discussion on varṇasaṅkara in Chapter 10 is neither according to the larger context (as established by verses 2.25 and 10.131) nor is it desirable. Hence, the verses with respect to varṇasaṅkara must have been interpolated at a later day when society had accepted the notion of varṇasaṅkara due to casteism.

III. Third, Manu himself notes in verse 10.4 that there are only four varṇas and there is no fifth varṇa[465] and then again in 10.45 that all those who are other than the four varṇas are called *Dasyus* be they be speaking *Mleccha* language or Ārya language.[466] Even here there is no mention of varṇasaṅkara. Therefore, verses 10.5-73 which contain description of varṇasaṅkara must be considered inauthentic.

Let us first take up argument (I). For a particular topic to be authentic, it is not necessary that the topic has to be mentioned in every context and every chapter. For example, the discussion on prāyaścitta is taken up for detailed treatment only in Chapter 11. Likewise, treatment of civil and criminal law is taken up mainly in Chapter 8. Does it mean they are also interpolations? The fact is, presence of a discussion about a particular topic at only one place and its absence elsewhere does not imply that it is an interpolation. In Chapters 2-6 where a discussion of various saṃskāras including nāmakaraṇa and vivāha are taken up, they are specifically mentioned in the context of dvijas who alone are entitled for these saṃskāras which are conducted with mantras. And it is only in Chapter 10, verse 127 that we find an explicit mention in the context of śūdras:'If those who, knowing their duty, and wishing to acquire merit, imitate the practices of righteous men, with the exception of reciting the sacred texts, they incur no guilt; they obtain praise[467] (G. Jha 1920).' That is, śūdras can perform saṃskāras but without using mantras. Though mentioned in the context of śūdras, it is equally applicable to all non-dvijas including saṅkīrṇa-jātis. As long as any ritual or activity is not explicitly prohibited for a particular non-dvija group and the activity in itself is not mandated to be done only with mantras (as in yajñas), then, such activities can be undertaken by non-dvijas, and they can attain overall wellbeing by such practice. Further, one of the purposes behind Manu taking up the discussion on varṇasaṅkara in Chapter 10 is to enunciate upon and provide clarity about what tenets of dharma and ācāra (for example, verses 10.6-7, 10.41-42), and what forms of livelihood options (verses 10.46-56) are available for which category of saṅkīrṇa-jātis. Therefore, the argument put forward by Dr Kumar that varṇasaṅkara is discussed only in Chapter 10 and hence must be interpolated is untenable.

Now, let us take up argument (II). We can straightaway reject his claim that the verses on varṇasaṅkara were interpolated at a later time because the society was afflicted with casteism, as a mere speculation without basis as he offers no evidence to substantiate the same. Further, his argument that since verses 2.25 and 10.131, which mark the beginning and conclusion of the discussion on varṇa, mention only varṇa and not varṇasaṅkara, embedding a discussion on varṇasaṅkara in Chapter 10 is beyond the context of the text and hence interpolated, is also untenable. First, there is no compulsion that an introductory half verse and a concluding half verse of a section must necessarily and explicitly list every topic that particular section expounds upon. Such an expectation is laughable. Second, if this were to be the case, then the said verses do not mention āśrama as well, so does it mean the discussion regarding āśramas found in Chapters 2-6 are interpolated as well? Third, the statement that there is no context for Manu to discuss about varṇasaṅkara under the heading of varṇa is incorrect as the text itself provides context. Verse 9.336 says: 'Thus has the excellent law for the conduct of the varṇas in normal times (anāpad) been expounded; now listen in due order to what forms their duty in abnormal times (āpad)[468] (G Jha 1920).' That is, the enunciation of the duties of the four varṇas taken up from 2.25 till 9.335 were in the context of anāpad' i.e. normal or ideal times. From verse 10.1 onwards till verse 10.130, the discussion is about duties of varṇas in āpad or abnormal times or times of calamity. Verse 10.130 says, 'The duties of the four varṇas in times of distress have thus been expounded; by properly carrying out which, they attain the highest state[469] (G Jha 1920).' Therefore, the discussion of varṇasaṅkara is taken up in the context of a society which is abnormal, in distress, and great disharmony as a result of varṇasaṅkara. It is to provide clarity on how to perform one's dharma during such confusing and challenging conditions that Manu includes a detailed discussion about the genesis and causes of varṇasaṅkara, what categories of varṇasaṅkaras are eligible for what dharmas, what could be their means of livelihood, what ethical tenets they have to practice, and how they can attain material and spiritual wellbeing. Āpad-dharma or the way of life to be adopted during emergency and/or abnormal times is an important aspect of dharmaśāstra and one which is most helpful in practically wading through challenges of everyday life.

The description of varṇasaṅkara as a great calamity is found in other texts as well. For example, in Bhagavad Gītā 1.40-43, Arjuna describes how varṇasaṅkara causes the ruin of families and a complete destruction of *kula*-dharma and *jāti*-dharma.[470] Further, in verse 3.24, Bhagavān Kṛṣṇa himself says: 'These worlds will be ruined if I do not perform action. And I shall become the agent of intermingling (i.e. varṇasaṅkara) and shall be destroying these beings (Gambhirananda

1998).'[471] In Mahābhārata Vanaparva Chapter 177, Yudhiṣṭhira indicates how due to varṇasaṅkara in the form of intermingling of various varṇas, it has become difficult to correctly identify varṇa of a person (Debroy 2012). In *Bṛhaddharma Purāṇa*, a minor Purāṇa, the entire Chapter 57 is dedicated to genesis of varṇasaṅkara and describes how varṇasaṅkara leads to destruction (Banerji 1915). It is to address concerns like the above, namely, confusion regarding the practice of dharma and ācāra that arises from varṇasaṅkara that Manusmṛti takes up a detailed discussion of the same in Chapter 10 under the heading 'dharma for abnormal times'. Therefore, to term such an important discussion as being 'without context', 'a later-day interpolation', 'having casteist motives', etcetera on the part of Dr Kumar is unfortunate and is a result of preconceived bias and a misreading of the structure and purpose of Manusmṛti.

Now let us take up argument (III). It is difficult to understand what Dr Kumar is trying to establish here. According to him, verses 10.4[472] and 10.45[473] are connected and all the verses in between them i.e. verses 10.5-10.44 are interpolated; and further, majority of the verses that appear between 10.45 and 10.73 are interpolated. He designates all the verses that discuss varṇasaṅkara as interpolated and then states that verses 10.4 and 10.45, which as per him do not mention varṇasaṅkara, are connected and are original verses. While it is beyond the scope here to carefully examine his arguments for designating only a few verses as authentic and branding the rest as interpolations, it must be stated that to the present writer, prima facie, it appears that Dr Kumar has a tendency to discard any verse that does not confirm to his revisionist objective as an interpolation. The study of verses 10.4-10.45 using traditional commentators shows how all of them are connected and are an intrinsic part of the same discourse about varṇasaṅkara. Further, under verse 10.45, Dr Kumar himself notes that dasyus are those who have fallen from the duties of the four varṇas due to non-practice or those who are uninitiated into the duties of the four varṇas. What Dr Kumar ignores is that this is precisely one of the definitions or causes of varṇasaṅkara as noted in verse 10.24 which says 'Varṇasaṅkaras are produced by infidelity among the varṇas, by the marrying of women unfit for marriage, and by the neglect of one's duties[474] (G Jha 1920).' This last criterion causing varṇasaṅkara is how Dr Kumar defines dasyus but designates the said verse i.e. 10.24 as an interpolation! Moreover, when 10.45 is taken along with the previous two verses, then the context of the verse becomes very clear. Verses 10.43-44 say: 'But by the omission of the sacred rites, and also by their neglect of brāhmaṇas, the following kṣatriya castes have gradually sunk to the position of the low-born. The *Puṇḍrakas*, the *Coḍas*, the *Draviḍas*, the *Kāmbojas*, the *Yavanas*, the *Śākas,* the *Pāradas*, the *Pahlavas*, the *Cīnas*, the *Kirātas*, the *Daradas* and the *Khaśas*[475] (G Jha 1920).' This provides the context regarding who Manu is designating as dasyus in 10.45. Further, the verse 10.44 which mentions different communities like yavanas, śakas, cīnas, etcetera which are present outside the geographical boundaries of *Āryāvarta* also provides the context for the use of the phrase 'be one a speaker of Mleccha language or Ārya language'. If verses 10.4 and 10.45 were really directly connected with the verses in-between being interpolations, why would 10.45 suddenly bring up the issue of those who speak 'mleccha language'? From all these, we must conclude that the designation of dasyu in verse 10.45 is with respect to varṇasaṅkara itself and not otherwise, though it specifically refers to the aspect of giving up one's svadharma. Therefore, merely stating that verses 10.4 and 10.45 do not mention varṇasaṅkara and hence, varṇasaṅkara is not part of authentic Manusmṛti, is an untenable position.

e. **Argument 5:** In the concise introduction provided in Chapter 1, Manu mentions only four varṇas and their duties in verses 1.87-91. From this we can know that Manu accepts the presence of only four varṇas. Hence, enunciation of dharma of only these four varṇas in the text are authentic and not those portions that mention varṇasaṅkara. Hence, antarprabhāva cannot mean varṇasaṅkara and must be taken as āśrama (Kumar 2018, 4).

This is again another speculative argument. If it is the case that since verses 1.87-91[476] speak about dharma of only the four varṇas in concise form and not of varṇasaṅkara categories and hence, antarprabhāva cannot refer to varṇasaṅkara, then we have to accept that antarprabhava cannot be āśrama as well since the said verses do not mention the four-fold āśramas or āśrama dharma as well. This argument is of course untenable. More importantly, towards the end of Chapter 1 itself, Manusmṛti provides a detailed overview of all the major themes that the text will be dealing with. In verse 1.116, it explicitly states genesis of varṇasaṅkara and the duties of varṇas during abnormal (āpad) times as one of the topics the text will be dealing with.[477] Therefore, in the light of the above discussion, we must reject the fifth argument as well.

f. **Argument 6:** Various purāṇas describe Manu as a teacher of varṇāśrama dharma and not as an enunciator of dharma of varṇasaṅkara. Hence, antarprabhāva cannot mean varṇasaṅkara, but should mean āśrama (Kumar 2018, 4).

This argument constitutes neither a necessary condition nor a sufficient condition to designate the discussion of varṇasaṅkara in Manusmṛti as inauthentic. If this argument were to be accepted, then we would have to designate the chapters dealing with cosmogony, prāyaścitta (expiation), and vyavahāra (civil and criminal laws) as inauthentic as well, since, in the said purāṇas cited by Dr Kumar, Manu has not been described as an enunciator of cosmogony, expiation, civil and criminal laws, etcetera. An absence of evidence does not constitute evidence of its absence. Therefore, absence of explicit mention of Manu as expounder of varṇasaṅkara dharma does not constitute evidence for the discussion on varṇasaṅkara in Manusmṛti being inauthentic and a later addition.

We will therefore have to reject the sixth argument as inadmissible and untenable.

From the above discussion, it is very clear that Dr Kumar's interpretation of the phrase antarprabhāva is not only based on speculation, but it also suffers from the fallacy of *petitio principii* i.e., presuming as true the conclusion that needs to be demonstrated without demonstrating it. Therefore, his interpretation is untenable as it is speculative, forced, and with a revisionist agenda.

On the other hand, the interpretation of antarprabhāva in the present verse as a reference to varṇasaṅkara is meaningful in the light of the following elements from the text:

a. In the present verse, the ṛṣis explicitly requesting for enunciation of dharma of antarprabhāvas in addition to the dharmas of the four varṇas, distinguishes the duties of antarprabhāvas from those of the four varṇas. Therefore, āśramas cannot be the meaning of antarprabhāva as āśrama-dharma (as shown before) has been described in verse 6.97 as being an integral aspect of varṇa-dharma itself. Hence, antarprabhāvas must be a reference to varṇasaṅkara groups whose dharma would be distinct from those of the four varṇas (though with considerable areas of overlapping).
b. The Chapter 1 explicitly lists varṇasaṅkara as one of the topics the text will enunciate upon in verse 116.[478]
c. The entire discussion of varṇasaṅkara is placed within the discussion of duties of varṇa in abnormal or emergency times and hence, without it, the discussion of varṇa-dharma would be incomplete.
d. The notion of varṇasaṅkara as a condition of emergency and danger, a sign of Kaliyuga, is well known from itihāsa-purāṇas as well, and hence, a concept well-established in Hindu worldview.

e. The structure of the text places the discussion of varṇa-dharma first followed by a discussion of dharma of varṇasaṅkara groups. This sequence follows the sequence provided in the current verse (i.e. verse 1.2) wherein sages explicitly request an enunciation of dharma of all varṇas and antarprabhāvas in 'due form and proper sequence'.
f. There is a consensus among all traditional commentators regarding antarprabhāva being a reference to varṇasaṅkara and hence, this interpretation has the stamp of authenticity of the dharmaśāstra tradition and its achāryas spanning more than 1200 years at the least.
g. The great sages by stressing that they want to know not only about the dharmas of all varṇas but also of those born by the mixture of varṇas are including the entirety of humanity under the purview of dharma. It also shows that they have an unselfish interest in posing this question. They are not asking the question for personal benefit, but for the benefit of the whole world.

# Appendix III

## Stutiḥ dedicated to Svāyambhuva-Manu

*vedopadeśamadhigamya purā vidhātur*
*yo'sthāpayat svakulajeṣu paramparāyāḥ |*
*rājarṣaye nigamadharmavivardhanāya*
*tasmai subhadravacase manave namo'stu ||1*

*yadbheṣajopamagiraṃ samupāśrayante,*
*ācārasaṃśayasamudbhavamohamagnāḥ |*
*ārṣāḥ suśiṣṭamatayo bhuvi laukikāśca*
*tasmai praśastavacase manave namo'stu ||2*

*yenopadiṣṭavacanāśrayamālalambe*
*kaṇvātmajā sabharatā vibhayā sabhāyām |*
*bhāryādhikāravinikṛtpururājapatnī*
*tasmai suśarmavacase manave namo'stu ||3*

*yatrādṛtā hi mahilā mahitāśca vṛddhās*
*tatrāniśaṃ sumanasaḥ saguṇā ramante |*
*ityājñayā manujadharmapathapradāya*
*tasmai viśuddhavacase manave namo'stu ||4*

*āmnāyatattvaviduṣe vidhimarmavettre*
*pūrvarṣideśikavarāya jagaddhitāya |*
*varṇāśrameṣu nihitākhilakarmagoptre*
*tasmai sudharmyavacase manave namo'stu ||5*

This stutiḥ was kindly composed and translated into English by Śrī Kushagra Aniket at the request of the author for the purpose of paying homage to Svāyambhuva Manu, the great teacher of dharma.

**Translation of the Stutiḥ:**

1. Obeisance to that Manu of beneficial speech, who having obtained the teaching of the *Veda*s from the Creator in the past, established it in his descendants by tradition; who is a royal sage; and who augmented the Vedic Dharma.
2. Obeisance to that Manu of commendable speech, whose medicine-like words are sought by those who are immersed in the delusion originating from confusion regarding duties—be they the well-disciplined descendants of the sages or other worldly people.
3. Obeisance to that Manu of pleasing speech, whose instructions were sought as refuge by the daughter of Kaṇva (Śakuntalā), when she stood fearlessly in the assembly along with Bharata, and emerged as the wife of the Puru king (Duṣyanta), humbled by the rights of a wife.
4. Obeisance to that Manu of pure speech, who ordained the path of Dharma for humanity through his commandment that 'where women are respected and elders are worshipped, there reside the Devas, along with their (divine) attributes.'

5. Obeisance to that Manu of righteous (Dharmic) speech, scholar of the essence of the *Veda*s, knower of the core of law, foremost teacher to the ancient sages, benefactor to the world, and protector of all actions enshrined in the system of Varṇāśramas.

# Bibliography

Adluri, Vishwa & Bagchee, Joydeep, ed. 2011. *Reading the Fifth Veda: Studies on the Mahābhārata— Essays by Alf Hiltebeitel, Volume 1.* Leiden/ Boston: Brill.

n.d. 'Aitereyoupanishad-bhashyam.' *Advaita Sharada.* Accessed 08 17, 2023. https://advaitasharada.sringeri.net/display/bhashya/Aitareya.

Aiyer, R. K. (1956). *Dialogues with the Guru*. Bombay: Chetana.

n.d. "Anandagiri Tika on Gita Bhashya." *Advaita Sharada*. Accessed 08 20, 2024. https://advaitasharada.sringeri.net/display/bhashyaVyakhya/Gita?vyakhya=AG.

Ananthanarasimhachar, Dr. A. 2014. *Samskara Mahodadhi.* Bengaluru: Anantha Prakashana.

Apate, Hari Narayana, ed. 1904. *Yajnavalkyasmriti with Aparaditya's commentary Apararka Part II*. Pune: Anandasrama Mudranalaya. https://archive.org/details/yajnavalkya-smriti-with-aparadityas-tippani-anandasram-edition/Yajnavalkya%20Smriti%20with%20Aparaditya%27s%20Tippani%20Part%201-%20Anandasram%201903/.

Apte, Vinayak Ganesh & Anandashrama Pandits, ed. 1929. *Nrsimhapurvottaratapaniyopanisat: With Bhashya of Shankaracharya on Purva Tapani and Dipika of Vidyaranya on Uttara Tapani.* Pune: Anandashrama Mudranalaya. https://archive.org/details/bhashyadipikaofvidyaranyavinayakganeshapteanandashram_881_X.

Badrinath, Chaturvedi. 2007. *The Mahābhārata: An Inquiry in the Human Condition*. New Delhi: Orient BlackSwan.

Balasubramanian, R & Revathy, S, trans. 2012. *Vedanta Sangraha of Ramaraya Kavi: Essentials of Vedanta.* Ernakulam: Chinmaya International Foundation Shodha Sansthan.

Banerji, Syama Charan, trans. 1915. *The Brihaddharma Purana.* Lucknow: "n.p". https://www.wisdomlib.org/hinduism/book/brihaddharma-purana-abridged.

Benke, Theodore. 2010. 'The Śūdrācāraśiromani of Krsna Śesa: A 16Th Century Manual of *Dharma* for Śūdras.' http://repository.upenn.edu/edissertations/159.

Bharathi, Swami Jnanananda. 1969. *Stray Thoughts on Dharma.* Chennai: Sri Jnanananda Grantha Prakasana Samiti.

Bodewitz, H. W. 1990. *The Jyotiṣṭoma ritual : Jaiminīya Brāhmaṇa I, 66-364, Introduction, Translation and Commentary.* Leiden: E.J. Brill.

n.d. 'Brahmasutra-bhashya.' *Advaita Sharada.* Accessed December 01, 2022. https://advaitasharada.sringeri.net/display/bhashya/BS.

n.d. 'Brahmasutra-bhashya Bhamati-vyakkya.' *Advaita Sharada.* Accessed December 06, 2022. https://advaitasharada.sringeri.net/

display/bhashyaVyakhya/BS?vyakhya=BM.

n.d. 'Brihadaranyakopanishad-bhashyam.' *Advaita Sharada.* Accessed December 06, 2022. https://advaitasharada.sringeri.net/display/bhashya/Brha.

Bodas, Rajaram Shastri, ed. 1917. *The Yogasutras of Patanjali With the Scholium of Vyasa and the Commentary of Vachaspatimisra.* Bombay: Government Central Press.

Bühler, George. 1886. *The Laws of Manu.* Oxford: Clarendon Press. Accessed December 25, 2018. http://www.sacred-texts.com/hin/manu.htm.

Chaitanya, Svarupa, trans. 1997. *Tattva Bodha of Sankaracharya.* Mumbai: Central Chinmaya Mission Trust. Accessed August 04, 2022. https://ia903401.us.archive.org/11/items/Acc.No.13056TattvaBodha1997/Acc.No.13056-Tattva%20Bodha-1997.pdf.

Chatterjee, Satischandra. 2015. *The Nyaya Theory of Knowledge.* New Delhi: Rupa Publications.

Colebrooke, H T. 1837. "Miscellaneous Essays Volume 1." Chap. Footnotes at page 309. London: WH Allen & Co. https://archive.org/details/miscellaneouses00unkngoog/page/n8/mode/2up?view=theater.

Danielou, Alain. 1994. *The Complete Kāma Sūtra:The First Unabridged Modern Translation Of The Classic Indian Text.* Rochester, Vermont: Inner Traditions India.

Datta, Sreejit. 2022. *Interpreting Sacred Hindu texts: Case for a Hindu Hermeneutic.* 25 September. https://www.youtube.com/watch?v=s6DAMK0ljWA&t=2919s.

Dave, Jayantakrishna Harikrishna, ed. 1972. *Manu-smrti : with nine commentaries by Medhatithi, Sarvajñanarayana, Kulluka, Raghvananda, Nandana, Ramacandra, Manirama, Govindaraja and Bharuci.* Vol. 1. Bombay: Bharatiya Vidya Bhavan.

Debroy, Bibek, trans. 2015. *The Mahabharata, Volume 10.* New Delhi: Penguin Books.

Debroy, Bibek, trans. 2012. *The Mahabharata, Volume 3.* New Delhi: Penguin Books.

Debroy, Bibek, trans. 2013. *The Mahabharata, Volume 8.* New Delhi: Penguin Books.

Debroy, Bibek, trans. 2015. *The Mahabharata, Volume 9.* New Delhi: Penguin Books.

Devanathan, Ramanuja. 2020. 'Understanding Manu Smriti Part I: Women and Freedom.' *Indica Today.* 27 October. Accessed August 04, 2022. https://www.indica.today/quick-reads/understanding-manu-smriti-part-i-women-freedom/.

Devi, V Yamuna. 2017. *Amarakosodghatana of Ksirasvamin: A Socio-Cultural Study.* Dharwad: Karnatak Historical Research Society. Accessed 08 23, 2023. https://www.wisdomlib.org/hinduism/essay/amarakoshodghatana-of-kshirasvamin-study.

Doniger, Wendy (tr.). 1991. *The Laws of Manu.* London: Penguin Books.

Doniger, Wendy. 1991. *The Laws of Manu.* Penguin Books.

Dutt, Manmatha Nath, trans. 1897. *A Prose English Translation of Harivamsha Purana.* Calcutta: Elysium Press.

Dutt, Manmatha Nath, trans. 1908. *The Dharma Sastra or The Hindu Law Codes Vol I.* Calcutta: Elysium Press.

Dutt, Manmatha Nath, trans. 1908. *The Dharma Sastra or The Hindu Law Codes, Vol II.* Calcutta: Elysium Press.

Eliade, Mircea. 1959. *The Sacred and The Profane: The Nature of Religion.* Translated by Willard R. Trask. New York: Harcourt.

2004. *Exalting Elucidations.* Chennai: Sri Vidyatheertha Foundation.

Fitzgerald, James L. 2003. 'The Many Voices of the Mahābhārata.' *Journal of the American Oriental Society* (American Oriental Society) 123 (4): 803-818.

Frawley, David. 2014. *Universal Hinduism: Towards a New Vision of Sanatana Dharma.* New Delhi: Voice of India.

Freschi, E., & Kataoka, K. 2012. 'Jayanta on the Validity of Sacred Texts (other than the *Veda*).' *South Asian Classical Studies* 7: 1-55.

Gambhirananda, Swami, trans. 1998. *Bhagavad Gita with the annotation Gudhartha-Dipika by Madhusudana Sarasvati.* Mayavati: Advaita Ashrama.

Gambhirananda, Swami, trans. 2018. *Bhagavad Gita: With the commentary of Shankaracharya.* Mayavati: Advaita Ashrama.

—. 1957. *Eight Upanisads: With the Commentary of Sankaracarya Vol 01.* Mayavati: Advaita Ashram.

—. 1958. *Eight Upanishds: With the Commentary of Sankaracarya Vol 02.* Mayavati: Advaita Ashram.

Ganguli, K M (tr.). 1883-1896. *The Mahabharata of Krishna-Dwaipayana Vyasa Translated into English Prose from Original Sanskrit Text.* Calcutta: Pratap Chandra Roy. Accessed December 18, 2018. http://www.sacred-texts.com/hin/maha/index.htm.

n.d. 'Gautama *Dharma* Sutra.' *Reading the Vedic Literature in Sanskrit.* Maharshi University of Management, Department of Maharshi Vedic Science. Accessed August 04, 2022. http://vedicreserve.miu.edu/kalpa/*dharma*/gautama_*dharma*_sutra.pdf.

Gharpure, J R, ed. 1937. *Sri Vaidyanatha Dixita's Smrtimuktaphalam, Part I, Varnasramadharma Kanda.* Bombay: The Office of the Collection of Hindu Law Texts. https://sulkurl.com/cyX

n.d. *Gita Supersite.* IIT Kanpur. Accessed August 04, 2022. https://www.gitasupersite.iitk.ac.in/.

Ghose, Aurobindo. 2001. *Records Of Yoga.* Pondicherry: Sri Aurobindo Ashram.

Griffith, Ralph T.H., trans. 1899. *The texts of the White Yajurveda / translated with a popular commentary.* Benares: E.J. Lazarus and Co. https://sacred-texts.com/hin/wyv/wyvtp.htm.

Gupt, Dr. Bharat. 2016. 'Shastra, What is it? (Video Talk).' Youtube, 23 October. Accessed January 10, 2022. https://youtu.be/EPcFkGQB5VU.

Gupta, Anand Swarup, Satyamsu Mohan Mukhopadhyaya, Ahibhushen Bhattacharya, N. C. Nath, and V. K. Verma, . 1968. *The Vamana Purana with English Translation.* Varanasi: All India Kashiraj Trust.

GV, Shivakumar. 2020. 'Mahabharata Metaphors: Dharmavyadha imparts the Essence of the *Veda*s to Kaushika Part II.' *Indica Today*, 24 July. https://www.indictoday.com/quick-reads/mahabharata-metaphors-dharmavyadha-vedas-kaushika/.

Hiltebeitel, Alf. 2001. *Rethinking the Mahabharata: A Reader's Guide to the Education of the Dharma King.* Chicago: University of Chicago Press.

Hopkins, E W. 1885. 'On the Professed Quotations from Manu Found in the Mahäbhärata.' *Journal of the American Oriental Society 11* 239-75.

Indirāramaṇa. 1942 (Vikram Samvatsar 1999). Mānavārṣa Bhāṣya on Mānava-Dharmaśāstra (Manusmṛti) Volume 01. Kashi: Kashi Vidyapeetha.

n.d. 'Jatibrahmana.' *Wisdom Library.* Accessed December 08, 2022. https://www.wisdomlib.org/definition/jatibrahmana.

Jha, Durgadhar, trans. 1979. *Mimamsa Shloka Vartika of Kumaril Bhatta with Hindi Translation.* Darbhanga: Kameshwar Singh Darbhanga Sanskrit University.

Jha, Ganganath, trans. 1923. *The Chhandogya Upanishad Second Part.* Madras: The India Printing Press.

Jha, Ganganath, trans. 1939. *Gautama's Nyayasutras With Vatsyayana Bhashya.* Poona: Oriental Book Agency.

Jha, Ganganath, trans. 1920. *Manusmriti with the 'Manubhashya' of Medatithi.* Delhi: Motilal Banarsidass Publishers Private Limited. https://www.wisdomlib.org/hinduism/book/manusmriti-with-the-commentary-of-medhatithi.

Jha, Ganganath, trans. 1900. *Slokavartika.* Calcutta: Sri Satguru Publications.

Jha, Ganganath, trans. 1903-24. *Tantravartika: A Commentary on Sabara's Bhashya on Purva Mimamsa Sutras of Jaimini.* Vol. 1. Calcutta: Sri Satguru Publications.

Jha, Ujjwala. 2018. "Mimamsa Theory of Apurva." *Journal of East-West Thought* 8 (1). Accessed 2024. https://journals.calstate.edu/jet/article/view/2318.

Jolly, Julius, trans. 1880. *The Institutes of Vishnu.* Oxford: The Clarendon Press. Accessed 08 11, 2023. https://sacred-texts.com/hin/sbe07/index.htm.

—. 1889. *The Minor Law-Books Part 1.* Oxford: The Clarendon Press. Accessed December 19, 2018. http://www.sacred-texts.com/hin/sbe33/index.htm.

Jolly, Julius, ed. 1881. *Vishnusmrti: The Institutes of Vishnu.* The Asiatic Society: Calcutta.

—., ed. 1885. *The Institutes of Narada*. Calcutta: The Asiatic Society.

Kane, P. V. 1930. *History of Dharmasastra Vol 1.* Poona: Bhandarkar Oriental Research Institute.

Kannan, P R, trans. n.d. *Smritimuktaphalam - Varnashrama Dharma Kandam Of Sri Vaidhyanatha Dikshitar.* Giri Trading Agency Private Limited. Accessed 08 13, 2024. https://www.celextel.org/mantras-and-rituals/smriti-mukta-phalam/.

Kaundinyayan Shivraj Acharya, trans. 2014. *Manusmriti.* Varanasi: Chowkhamba Vidyabhawan.

Keith, Arthur Berriedale, trans. 1914. *The Veda of the Black Yajus School Entitled Taittiriya Sanhita*. Cambridge, Massachusetts: Harvard University Press. https://sacred-texts.com/hin/yv/yv00.htm.

Krishnacharya, T R, and T R Vyasacharya, . 1910. *Sriman Mahabharatam; a New edition; mainly based on the South Indian Texts, with footnotes and Readings, Ashvamedhikaparva XIV*. Bombay: Nirnaya-Sagar Press. https://archive.org/details/mahAbhArata-kumbhakoNam/9014/page/n3/mode/2up?view=theater.

Kumar, Surendra. 2018. *The Manusmriti.* Eighth Edition. Delhi: Arsh Sahitya Prachar Trust.

—. 1996. *The Vishuddha Manusmriti.* Fourth Edition. Delhi: Arsh Sahitya Prachar Trust.

Laine, James W. 1981. 'The Creation Account In Manusmṛti.' *Annals of the Bhandarkar Oriental Research Institute* (Bhandarkar Oriental

Research Institute) 62 (1/4): 157-168.

Leslie, Julie (tr.). 1995. *The Perfect Wife (Stridharmapaddhati).* New Delhi: Penguin Books India.

Lokeswarananda, Swami, trans. 1998. *Chandogya Upanisad - Translated with notes based on Shankara's commentary.* Golpark: Ramakrishna Math. Accessed 08 05, 2023. https://www.wisdomlib.org/hinduism/book/chandogya-upanishad-english.

Madhavananda, Swami, trans. 1950. *The Brhadaraṇnyaka Upanisad With the Commentary of Sankaracharya.* Mayavati, Almora: Advaita Ashrama.

Madhavananda, Swami, trans. 1921. *Vivekachudamani of Sri Sankaracharya.* Mayavati: The Advaita Ashrama. https://www.wisdomlib.org/hinduism/book/vivekachudamani.

n.d. 'Mahabharata: Critical Edition Prepared by Scholars at Bhandarkar Oriental Research Institute BORI.' *Sanskrit Documents.* Accessed August 03, 2022. https://sanskritdocuments.org/mirrors/mahabharata/mahabharata-bori.html.

Mandlik, Rao Saheb V. N. 1880. *The Vyavahara Mayukha Or Hindu-law.* New Delhi: Asian Publication Services. Accessed December 19, 2018. https://archive.org/details/in.ernet.dli.2015.93083/page/n5.

Mandlik, Vishvanath Narayan, ed. 1886. *Manava Dharma-Sastra with the Commentaries of Medhatithi, Sarvajnanarayana, Kulluka, Raghavananda, Nandana, and Ramachandra.* Bombay: Ganpat Krishnaji's Press,. Accessed December 29, 2018. https://archive.org/details/manusmriti/page/n3.

Misra, Pandit Brahmasankar, ed. 1968. *Sukraniti of Sri Maharshi Sukracarya.* Varanasi: The Chowkhamba Sanskrit Series Office.

n.d. 'Mundakopanishadbhashyam.' *Advaita Sharada.* Accessed December 10, 2022. https://advaitasharada.sringeri.net/display/bhashya/Mundaka.

Nagar, Shanti Lal, trans. 2005. *Brahmavaivarta Purana.* 2 vols. Delhi: Parimal Publications.

Naik, Chittaranjan. 2022. 'Apaurusheyatva of the *Veda*s.' 21 March. Accessed September 2022. https://pingaligopi.wordpress.com/2022/03/21/apaurusheyatva-of-the-vedas-by-chittaranjan-naik/.

—. and Pingali Gopal. 2023. "Varna And Birth." Pragyata. 11 12. Accessed 12 11, 2023. https://pragyata.com/varna-and-birth/.

Neelakandan, Aravindan. 2015. 'How Ashok Singhal Fought The Caste Orthodoxy.' *Swarajya Mag.* 19 November. Accessed August 08, 2022. https://swarajyamag.com/politics/how-ashok-singhal-fought-the-caste-orthodoxy.

Nikhilananda, Swami. 1956. *The Upanishads: Aitereya and Brihadaranyaka.* Vol. 3. New York: Harper & Brothers Publishers.

Olivelle, Patrick, trans. 2000. *Dharmasutras: The Law Codes of Āpastamba, Gautama, Baudhāyana, and Vasistha.* Delhi: Motilal Banarsidass Publishers Private Limited.

—. 2005. *Manu's Code of Law: A Critical Edition and Translation of the Mānava-Dharmaśāstra.* New York: Oxford University Press.

n.d. 'Padma Purana [sanskrit].' *Wisdom Library.* Accessed December 08, 2022. https://www.wisdomlib.org/hinduism/book/padma-purana-sanskrit.

Pansikar, Wasudev Laxman Sastri, ed. 1936. *Yajnavalkyasmrti, with the Commentary Mitaksara of Vijnanesvara.* Bombay: Nirnaya Sagar Press. Accessed December 06, 2022. https://sites.utexas.edu/sanskrit/resources/dharmasastra/mitak%e1%b9%a3ara/.

Piovano, Irma, ed. 2002. *The Daksa-smrti: Introduction, Critical edition, Translation and Appendices.* Torino: Comitato Promotore per la Pubblicazione del Corpus Juris Sanscriticum.

Prasada, Rama, trans. 1998. *Patanjali's Yoga Sutras with the Commentary of Vyasa and the Gloss of Vachaspati Misra.* New Delhi: Munshiram Manoharlal Publishers Pvt. Ltd.

n.d. 'Purusha Suktam.' *Slokam.* Accessed 08 02, 2023. https://shlokam.org/purushasuktam/.

Rao, Anusha Sudindra. 2020. 'Women and Adhikāra in Dvaita Vedānta.' *The Indian Philosophy Blog.* 23 June. Accessed December 08, 2022. https://indianphilosophyblog.org/2020/06/23/women-and-adhikara-in-dvaita-vedanta/.

Rao, S K Ramachandra. 2004. *Ṛgveda Darśana: Sāyaṇa's Ṛgabhāṣya-Bhūmikā.* Bangalore: Kalpatharu Research Academy.

Rau, S Subba, ed. 1904. *The Vedanta-Sutras with the Commentary by Sri Madhwacharya.* Madras: Minerva Press. https://archive.org/details/BrahmasutraMadhvaEnglish/mode/2up.

Sandal, Pandit Mohan Lal (tr.),. 1923. *The Mimamsa Sutras of Jaimini: Chapters I-III.* Allahabad: The Panini Office.

2018. 'Sanjay Dixit.' *Twitter.* 10 January. Accessed January 10, 2022. https://twitter.com/Sanjay_Dixit/status/951024133042618368?s=20.

n.d. 'Sanskrit Maxims and Proverbs Nyayavali.' *Sanskrit Documents.* Accessed December 08, 2022. https://sanskritdocuments.org/doc_z_misc_major_works/nyaayaavalii.html.

Sarma, Subramania, ed. 2004-2005. *Taittiriya Brahmana.* Chennai: Sanskrit Web. Accessed December 10, 2022. http://www.sanskritweb.net/yajurveda/.

Sastri, T. Ganapati, ed. 1922–1924. *The Yājñavalkyasmṛti with the Commentary Bālakrīda of Visvarūpāchārya. Two Parts.* Trivandrum: Government Press. https://sites.utexas.edu/sanskrit/resources/dharmasastra/balakri%e1%b8%8da/.

Sayanacharya. 1863. *The Taittiriya Brahmana of the Black Yajur Veda.* Edited by Rajendralal Mitra. Vol. 03. 03 vols. Calcutta: Baptist Mission. Accessed 08 12, 2023. https://archive.org/details/in.ernet.dli.2015.345087/page/n1/mode/2up.

Sharma, Dr. Mahamahopadhyaya N Ranganath. 2004. *Manava Dharmashastra Mattu Mahileyaru.* Sirsi: Shri Bhagavatpada Prakashana. https://vidwannrs.in/listing/toc/028.

Sharma, Ramanand, ed. 2016. *Kāmasūtram of Sri Vātsyāyana Muni with the Jayamangala Sanskrit Commentary of Sri Yasodhara.* Varanasi: Chowkhamba Krishnadas Academy.

Sharma, R K. 2004. *Indian Society, Institutions and Change.* New Delhi: Atlantic Publishers and Distributors.

n.d. 'Shastra Siddantalesha Sangraha by Appayya Dikshita.' *Advaita Sharada.* Accessed December 07, 2022. https://advaitasharada.sringeri.net/display/prakarana/shastra-siddanthalesha-sangraha.

Shivarajappa, S & Jagannath, S, ed. 2020. *Manushastra Vivaranam of Bharuci.* Mysuru: Prachyavidya Samshodhanalaya.

n.d. 'Shri Yoga Yajnyavalkya.' *Sanskrit Documents.* Accessed 10 04, 2023. https://sanskritdocuments.org/doc_yoga/yogayAjnyavalkya.pdf.

Sinha, Nandalal (tr.). 1923. *The Vaisesika Sutras of Kanada.* Allahabad: The Panini Office. Accessed August 03, 2022. https://www.wisdomlib.org/hinduism/book/vaisheshika-sutra-commentary.

Sivananda, Swami. 1957. *Narada Bhakti Sutras: Text, Transliteration, Translation & Commentary.* Rishikesh: The Yoga-*Veda*nta Forest University. https://ia903405.us.archive.org/9/items/narada-bhakti-sutras/narada-bhakti-sutras.pdf.

n.d. 'Skanda Purana [sanskrit].' *Wisdom Library.* Accessed December 01, 2022. https://www.wisdomlib.org/hinduism/book/skanda-purana-sanskrit.

Somayaji, Daivajna K N, ed. 2006. *Yajnavalkya Smriti Volume-I.* Bangalore: Kalpatharu Research Academy.

Sreekrishna, Dr. Koti, and Hari Ravikumar. 2015. *Srishti: Songs of Creation from the Veda*s. Change this to: Mason, OH: W.I.S.E. Words Inc.

Sridhar, Nithin. 2022 '"Antaraprabhava" in Surendra Kumar's "Viśuddha Manusmṛti": A critical assessment in light of its avowedly revisionist interpretation.' *Pragyata.* 16 January. Accessed August 03, 2022. https://pragyata.com/antaraprabhava-in-surendra-kumars-visuddha-manusm%E1%B9%9Bti-a-critical-assessment-in-light-of-its-avowedly-revisionist-interpretation/.

—.2021. 'Abortion, a Dharmic Perspective- I: Who is a Jiva?' *Indica Today.* https://www.indica.today/long-reads/abortion-*dharma*-i-jiva/.

—. 'Abortion, a Dharmic Perspective- II: Giving Birth as a Noble Act.' *Indica Today.* https://www.indica.today/long-reads/abortion-*dharma*-ptii-birth/.

—. 'Abortion, a Dharmic Perspective- III: When does the Jiva enter fetus?' *Indica Today.* https://www.indica.today/long-reads/abortion-dharmic-perspective-iii-jiva-enter-fetus/.

—.2 021. 'Abortion, a Dharmic Perspective– IV: Is Abortion murder?' *Indica Today.* https://www.indica.today/long-reads/abortion-dharmic-perspective-iv-abortion-murder/.

—. 2020. 'Homosexuality and Marriage: A Hindu Perspective.' *Indica Today.* https://www.indica.today/research/homosexuality-marriage-hindu-perspective/.

—. 2018. *Menstruation Across Cultures: A Historical Perspective.* New Delhi: Vitasta Publishing Private Limited.

—. 2022. 'Revisiting Sati.' *Indica Today.* 17 November. Accessed August 04, 2022. https://www.indica.today/research/sati-understanding-practice-dharmic-perspective/.

—. 2020. 'Revisiting Sati.' *Indica Today.* https://www.indica.today/research/sati-understanding-practice-dharmic-perspective/.

—. 2019. *Samanya Dharma: Ethical duties common to all.* Hubli: Subbu Publication.

—. 2018. 'Saṅgrahaṇa: An Indic View on Adultery.' *IndiaFacts.* https://www.indiafacts.org.in/sa%E1%B9%85graha%E1%B9%87a-an-indic-view-on-adultery/.

n.d. 'Srimad-Bhagavadgita-bhashya.' *Advaita Sharada.* Accessed 08 02, 2023. https://advaitasharada.sringeri.net/display/bhashya/Gita.

n.d. 'Śrīmad-Bhāgavatam (Bhāgavata Purāṇa).' *Bhaktivedanta Vedabase.* Accessed December 08, 2022. https://vedabase.io/en/library/sb/.

Tagare, G V, trans. 1950. *The Skanda Purana.* Vol. 2. Delhi: Motilal Banarsidass Publishers. https://www.wisdomlib.org/hinduism/book/the-skanda-purana.

Tailanga, Gangadhara Sastri, ed. 1896. *The Nyayasutras with Vatsyayana's Bhashya and Extracts from the Nyayavarttika and the Tatparyatika.* Benaras: E. J. Lazarus & Co.

n.d. 'Taittiriya Samhita- Searchable Text .' *Sanskrit Web.* http://www.sanskritweb.net/yajurveda/ts-find.pdf.

1952. *The Smriti Sandarbha: Collection of the Ten Dharmashastric Texts by Maharshis Vol I.* Calcutta: The Bangla Printing Works.

Tripathi, Asha Rani. 2015. *Manu-Smriti: A Critical Study and Its Relevance in the Modern Times.* New Delhi: D.K. Printworld.

Tripati, Kamalakantha, ed. 2019. *Parasharamadhava: Acharakhandam.* Varanasi: Chowkhamba Vidyabhawan.

Tripati, Kamalakantha, ed. 2019. *Parasharamadhava: Prayashchittakhandam.* Varanasi: Chowkhamba Vidyabhawan.

Upreti, Pandit Thaneshchandra, ed. 2003. *Visnumahapuranam of Maharsi Vedavyasa with Sanskrit Commentary 'Atmaprakasha' of Sridharacharya Vol I.* Delhi: Parimal Publications. https://archive.org/details/vp_vol1/page/n1/mode/2up.

Upreti, Pandit Thaneshchandra, ed. 2011. *Visnumahapuranam of Maharsi Vedavyasa with Sanskrit Commentary 'Atmaprakasha' of Sridharacharya Vol II.* Delhi: Parimal Publications. https://archive.org/details/vp_vol2/page/n1/mode/2up.

Vallabhacharya. 1986. *Subodhini.* Vol. 01. Mumbai: Gowswami Shyam Manohar.

n.d. *Valmiki Ramayana.* https://www.valmikiramayan.net/index.html.

2012. '*Veda*nta 3 of 15: Qualities of a Disciple by the Jagadguru Shankararcharya of Sringeri.' Sharada Peetham, 27 August. Accessed December 01, 2022. https://youtu.be/vT4xzoCfRZk.

Vimalananda, Swami (tr.). 1968. *Mahanarayanopanisad: Introduction, Translation, Interpretation in Sanskrit, and Critical and Explanatory Notes.* Mylapore: Sri Ramakrishna Math.

Vira, Raghu, and Lokesh Chandra,. 1986. *Jaiminiya Brāhmaṇa of the Samaveda*. New Delhi: Motilal Banarsidass Publishing House. https://archive.org/details/in.ernet.dli.2015.226836/mode/2up.

n.d. 'Viramitrodaya Vol 01 & Vol 02 .' *Internet Archieve.* Accessed December 08, 2022. https://archive.org/details/viramitrodayavol01vol021117paribhasha117586sanskaraprakashamitramisrachowkambham_202003_14_Y/page/n1/mode/2up.

Weber, Albrecht, ed. 1852. *The Vajasaneyi-sanhita : in the Madhyandina and the Kanva-Sakha with the commentary of Mahidhara.* Berlin: F. Dümmler. https://archive.org/details/in.ernet.dli.2015.486971/page/n3/mode/2up.

Wadekar, Dr. Mukund Lalji. 1996. *Devalasmriti: Reconstructed and Critical Study.* New Delhi: Koshal Book Depot.

Wilson, H H. 1864-1877. *The Vishnu Purana: a system of Hindu mythology and tradition.* Edited by Fitzedward Hall. London: Trübner & co. https://www.wisdomlib.org/hinduism/book/vishnu-purana-wilson.

Yati, Tridandi Sri Bhakti Prajnan, trans. 1991. *Sri Shandilya Bhakti Sutras.* Madras: Sree Gaudiya Math. https://archive.org/

# Endnotes

1 This śloka dedicated to Svāyambhuva-Manu is taken from *Maṅgalācaraṇa* included by *Indirāramaṇa* in his *Mānavārṣa Bhāṣya* on *Manusmṛti*.

2 This stutiḥ was composed by Śrī Kushagra Aniket at the request of present author for the purpose of using in this book. See Appendix III for a translation of the stutiḥ.

3 My work on abortion was originally published as a series of four articles in 2017 by *IndiaFacts* and was later republished by *Indica Today* in 2021:

1. Abortion, a Dharmic Perspective-I: Who is a Jiva? (Sridhar 2021)
2. Abortion, a Dharmic Perspective-II: Giving Birth as a Noble Act (Sridhar 2021)
3. Abortion, a Dharmic Perspective-III: When does the Jiva enter fetus? (Sridhar 2021)
4. Abortion, a Dharmic Perspective-IV: Is Abortion murder? (Sridhar 2021)

4 My work on sati titled 'Revisiting Sati (Sridhar 2020)' was originally published in 2017 by *IndiaFacts* and was later republished by *Indica Today* in 2020.

5 My work on adultery titled 'Saṅgrahaṇa: An Indic View on Adultery (Sridhar 2018)' was published in 2018 by *IndiaFacts*.

6 My work on homosexuality titled 'Homosexuality and Marriage: A Hindu Perspective (Sridhar 2020)' was published in 2020 by *Indica Today*.

7 This paper was presented at the International Conference on 'Dispassionate Churning of Indology' organised by Bharatiya Vidvat Parishad (BVP) and the Tattvasamshodhana Samsat, with support from Indian Council for Philosophical Research (ICPR), New Delhi and Indic Academy, Hyderabad in Udupi, Karnataka in January 2019. This was later published online in *Indic Today* on 19 November 2020 – https://www.indica.today/research/manusmṛti-patchwork-careful-construction/

8 'The repeated themes and lists are inherited pieces of the bricolage of ancient Indian culture, scraps that can be woven into a patchwork, but that patchwork is, in the end, a whole blanket, a security blanket for the civilization (W Doniger 1991).'

9 इदं शास्त्रं तु कृत्वासौ मामेव स्वयमादितः ।
वधिविद् ग्राहयामास मरीच्यादींस्त्वहं मुनीन् ॥ *Manusmṛti* 1.58 (Kaundinyayana 2014)
*idaṁ śāstraṁ tu kṛtvāsau māmeva svayamāditaḥ|*
*vidhivad grāhayāmāsa marīcyādīṃstvahaṃ munīn||*

10 All translations of *Manusmṛti* in this chapter are taken from Patrick Olivelle's translation of the Critical Edition.

11 मरीचिमत्र्यङ्गिरसौ पुलस्त्यं पुलहं क्रतुम् ।
प्रचेतसं वसष्ठिं च भृगुं नारदमेव च ॥ *Manusmṛti* 1.35
(Kaundinyayana 2014)
*marīcimatryaṅgirasau pulastyaṃ pulahaṃ kratum* ।
*pracetasaṃ vasiṣṭhaṃ ca bhṛguṃ nāradameva ca* ॥

12 एतद् वोऽयं भृगुः शास्त्रं श्रावयिष्यत्यशेषतः ।
एतद्धि मत्तोऽधिजगे सर्वमेषोऽखिलं मुनिः ॥ *Manusmṛti* 1.59
(Kaundinyayana 2014)
*etad vo'yaṃ bhṛguḥ śāstraṃ śrāvayiṣyatyaśeṣataḥ* ।
*etaddhi matto'dhijage sarvameṣo'khilaṃ muniḥ* ॥

13 Medhātithi on *Manusmṛti* 1.58: इह शास्त्रशब्देन स्मार्तोविधिप्रतिषेधसमूहउच्यते नतु ग्रन्थस्तस्य मनुना कृतत्वात् । तथा हि मानवइति व्यपदेशोऽस्येतरथा हि हैरण्यगर्भइति व्यपदिश्येत । केचित्तु हिरण्यगर्भेनापि कृते ग्रन्थे मनुना बहूनां प्रकाशितत्वात्तेन व्यपदेशोयुज्यतएव यथा हिमवति प्रथममुपलभ्यमाना गङ्गाऽन्यतोप्युत्पन्ना हैमवतीति व्यपदिश्यते यथा च नित्यदर्शनात्काठकंप्रवचनंकठेन व्यपदिश्यते । सत्स्वप्यन्येष्वध्येतृष्वध् यापयितृषु च प्रवचनप्रकर्षात्कठेनव्यपदेशः । (V. N. Mandlik 1886)
*iha śāśtraśabdena smārtovidhipratiṣedhasamūhaucyate natu granthaśtasya manunā kṛtatvāt* ।
*tathā hi mānavaiti vyapadeśo'syetarathā hi hairaṇyagarbhaiti vyapadiśyeta* ।
*kecittu hiraṇyagarbhenāpi kṛte granthe manunā bahūnāṃ prakāśitatvāttena vyapadeśoyujyataeva yathā himavati prathamamupalabhyamānā gaṅgā'nyatopyutpannā haimavatīti vyapadiśyate yathā ca nityadarśanātkāṭhakaṃpravacanaṃkaṭhena vyapadiśyate* ।
*satsvapyanyeṣvadhyetṛṣvadhyāpayitṛṣu ca pravacanaprakarṣātkaṭhenavyapadeśaḥ* ।

14 A good illustration of this interplay between apauruṣeya origination and the pauruṣeya composition of a text is present in *Mahābhārata Śānti Parva*, Chapter 322, which notes about the composition of a treatise of *dharma* thus: 'Marīci, Atri, Aṅgiras, Pulastya, Pulaha, Kratu, and Vasiṣṭha—these seven extremely energetic sages were known as the *Citraśikhaṇḍins*. The *Citraśikhaṇḍins* came together and prepared an excellent sacred text. They were like seven Prakṛtis and Svayambhū was the eighth. The sacred text that emerged from their mouths is studied by all the worlds.... Together, all those *ṛṣis* performed austerities and worshipped the lord god, Hari Nārāyaṇa, for one thousand celestial years. For the welfare of the worlds, instructed by Nārāyaṇa, the goddess Sarasvatī entered all those rishis. That is the reason those brāhmaṇas could engage so well in the composition of that first creation—full of words, meanings and reasons. Right at the beginning, the sacred text was ornamented with the syllable *Oṃ*. The rishis first recited it at the spot where the compassionate one was (Debroy, *The Mahabharata*, Volume 9 2015).'

15 भार्गवी नारदीया च बार्हस्पत्याङ्गिरस्यापि।
स्वायम्भुवस्य शास्त्रस्य चतस्त्रः संहिता मताः ।।
*bhārgavī nāradīyā ca bārhaspatyāṅgirasyāpi* |
*svāyambhuvasya śāstrasya catasraḥ saṃhitā matāḥ* ||

16 In his introduction to *Bṛhaspati smṛti*, Jolly notes the intimate connection between the extant texts of *Bṛhaspati smṛti* and *Manusmṛti*. He says: 'The connexion between the *Manu* and *Brihaspati smṛtis* appears first from the way in which Brihaspati refers to, and quotes from, the *Code of Manu*.... Secondly, in a number of other instances, the *Code of Manu*, though not appealed to by name, is nevertheless distinctly

referred to by Bṛhaspati.... Thirdly, Bṛhaspati, even when not expressly referring to Manu, presupposes throughout an acquaintance with his Code, and a very large portion of his Smṛti is devoted to the interpretation of technical terms or to the elucidation or amplification of the somewhat laconic enunciations of Manu.... Fourthly, Bṛhaspati declares emphatically that any Smṛti text opposed to the teaching of Manu has no validity (Jolly 1889, 270 274).' We can similarly see the intimate connection between *Nāradasmṛti* and *Manusmṛti*, with the former explicitly stating that it is an elaboration and enumeration of a particular section of the original śāstra of Svāyambhuva-Manu. Jolly, who recognised this intimate connection rightly notes: 'Under these circumstances the tradition preserved in the *Skanda-purāna* that there are four versions of the *Code of Manu*, by Bhrigu, Nārada, Bṛhaspati, and Aṅgiras, acquires a peculiar significance (Jolly 1889, 274)'. It is clear that the presence of such an intimate connection between these texts cannot have been coincidental. Therefore, we must take the *purānic* account seriously and consider it as narrating a factual account about the presence of different recensions of *Manusmṛti*.

17 Even Jolly appears to have come to a similar conclusion. In his introduction to *Bṛhaspati smṛti*, he says: 'Taking the version attributed to Bhṛgu to be identical with the *Code of Manu*, the soi-disant composition of Bhṛgu, it is impossible to doubt its connexion with the *Nārada* and *Bṛhaspati Smṛti*s (Jolly 1889, 274).'

18 मानवे धर्मशास्त्रे भृगुप्रोक्तायाम् सम्हितायाम् or मानवे धर्मशास्त्रे भृगुप्रोक्ते
*mānave dharmaśāstre bhṛguproktāyām samhitāyām or mānave dharmaśāstre bhṛguprokte*

19 तदेतदत्र श्लोकशतसहस्रेण साशीतिनाध्यायसहस्रेण च भगवान्मनुरूपनिबध्य देवर्षये नारदाय प्रायच्छत् । स च तस्मादधीत्य महत्त्वान्नायं ग्रन्थः सुकरो मनुष्यैरेव धारयितुमिति द्वादशभिः सहस्रैः संचिक्षेप तं च महर्षये मार्कण्डेयाय प्रायच्छत् २

स च तस्मादधीत्य तथैवायुःशक्तिमपेक्ष्य मनुष्याणामष्टभिः सहस्रैः संचिक्षेप तं च सुमतये भार्गवाय प्रायच्छत् ३
सुमतिरपि भार्गवस्तस्मादधीत्य तथैवायुर्ह्रासादल्पीयसी शक्तिर्मनुष्याणामिति चतुर्भिः सहस्रैः संचिक्षेप ४
तदेतत्पितृमनुष्या ह्यधीयन्ते विस्तरेण शतसहस्रं देवगन्धर्वादयः
|| *Nāradasmṛti Preface* verses 2-5 (Jolly, The Institutes of Narada 1885)

*tadetadatra ślokaśatasahasreṇa sāśītinādhyāyasahasreṇa ca bhagavānmanurūpanibadhya devarṣaye nāradāya prāyacchat | sa ca tasmādadhītya mahattvānnāyaṃ granthaḥ sukaro manuṣyaireva dhārayitumiti dvādaśabhiḥ sahasraiḥ saṃcikṣepa taṃ ca maharṣaye mārkaṇḍeyāya prāyacchat 2*
*sa ca tasmādadhītya tathaivāyuḥśaktimapekṣya manuṣyāṇāmaṣṭabhiḥ sahasraiḥ saṃcikṣepa taṃ ca sumataye bhārgavāya prāyacchat 3*
*sumatirapi bhārgavastasmādadhītya tathaivāyurhrāsādalpīyasī śaktirmanuṣyāṇāmiti caturbhiḥ sahasraiḥ saṃcikṣepa 4*
*tadetatpitṛmanuṣyā hyadhīyante vistareṇa śatasahasraṃ devagandharvādayaḥ* ||

20 All translations of *Nāradasmṛti* are taken from Julius Jolly's translation.

21 In the Critical Edition prepared by Patrick Olivelle, the total number of verses is 2680.

22 Julius Jolly writes thus in his footnote to verse 1 of the preface of *Nāradasmṛti*: 'The table of contents, which is here given for the original *Code of Manu*, corresponds in the main to the contents of the now extant version of that work. Thus the creation of the world is treated of, *Manu* I, 5-57; the various kinds of living beings, I, 34-50; the virtuous countries, II, 17-23; the constitution of a judicial assembly, XII, 108-114; the performance of offerings, III, 69-286; IV, 21-28, &c.; established usage (*ākāra*), passim, all the multifarious rules of private morals and social economy falling under this head; forensic law, chapters VIII and IX; the extirpation of offenders, IX, 252-293; the mode of life of a king, chapter VII; the system of the four castes and four orders, I, 87-101; IX, 325-336, &c.; marriage laws, III, 1-62; the mutual relations between husband and wife, IX, 1-103; the order of succession, IX, 103-220; the performance of obsequies, III, 122-286; rules of purification, V, 57-146; rules of diet, V, 1-56; saleable commodities, and those which may not be sold, X, 85-94; the classification of offences, XI, 55-71; the twenty-one hells, IV, 88-90; penances, XI, 72-266. The *Upaniṣads* are frequently referred to, e.g. II, 165; VI, 29. Secret or mysterious doctrines are e.g. those taught in the twelfth chapter of the *Code of Manu*. A somewhat analogous table of contents of the *Code of Manu* is given in that work itself, I, 111-118 (Jolly 1889).'

23 तचायमाद्यः श्लोकः आसीदिदं तमोभूतं न प्राज्ञायत किं च न ततः
स्वयंभूर्भगवान् प्रादुरासीच्चतुर्मुखः ५
*tacāyamādyaḥ ślokaḥ āsīdidaṃ tamobhūtaṃ na prājñāyata kiṃ ca na tataḥ svayaṃbhūrbhagavān prādurāsīccaturmukhaḥ 5, Nāradasmṛti Preface verse 5 (Jolly, 1885)*

24 आसीदिदं तमोभूतमप्रज्ञातमलक्षणम् ।
अप्रतर्क्यमविज्ञेयं प्रसुप्तमिव सर्वतः ॥ ५ ॥
ततः स्वयम्भूर्भगवानव्यक्तो व्यञ्जयन्निदम् ।
महाभूतादि वृत्तोजाः प्रादुरासीत् तमोनुदः ॥ ६ ॥
*āsīdidaṃ tamobhūtamaprajñātamalakṣaṇam* ।
*apratarkyamavijñeyaṃ prasuptamiva sarvataḥ* ॥ *5* ॥
*tataḥ svayambhūrbhagavānavyakto vyañjayannidam* ।
*mahābhūtādi vṛttojāḥ prādurāsīt tamonudaḥ* ॥ *6* ॥ Manusmṛti 1.5-6 (Kaundinyayana 2014)

25 Paramparā denotes a succession of teachers and disciples. In Indic knowledge traditions, the transmission of knowledge is accomplished through such teacher-disciple paramparās.

26 Jolly writes thus in his introduction to *Nāradasmṛti*: 'the now extant *Code of Manu*, is not posterior, but decidedly anterior, in date to the *Nāradasmṛti*, as may be gathered easily from a comparison of both works. Thus e.g. Nārada mentions twenty-one modes of acquiring property, fifteen sorts of slaves, fourteen species of impotency, three kinds of women twice married, and four kinds of wanton women, twenty women whom a man must not approach, thirty-two divisions of the law of gift, eleven sorts of witnesses, five or seven ordeals, four or five losers of their suit, two kinds of proof and two kinds of documents, seven advantages resulting from a just decision, eight members of a lawsuit, one hundred and thirty-two divisions of the eighteen principal titles of law. The first germs of some of these theories may be traced to the *Code of Manu*, and it is interesting to note how these germs have been developed by Nārada. As a rule, his judicial theories show an infinitely advanced stage of development as compared to Manu's, and his treatment of the law of procedure, in particular, abounding as it does in

technical terms and nice distinctions, and exhibiting a decided preference for documentary evidence and written records over oral testimony and verbal procedure, exhibits manifest signs of recent composition (Jolly 1889, xiii).'

27 Noting the role of traditional commentaries in fixing the text in its transmission, Olivelle (2005, 51) notes: 'I agree with Lariviere's (1989, xii) hypothesis that the dharmaśāstra continued to expand with the addition of new materials "until a commentary on the collection was composed. A commentary would have served to fix the text, and the expansion of the text would have been more difficult after that." Because I consider the MDh to have a single author, I take these emendations as produced by redactors working on the original text. Such activities were made more difficult after the text was "fixed" by early commentators such as Bhāruci and Medhātithi, but they did not cease completely. Changes after that period, however, were limited to the addition of individual verses and minor changes in the wording of verses detectable through "lower criticism".'

28 प्रजापतिर् हि प्रजाः सृष्ट्वा तासां स्थिति-निबन्धनं त्रिवर्गस्य साधनम् अध्यायानां शतसहस्रेणाग्रे प्रोवाच || १.१.५
*prajāpatir hi prajāḥ sṛṣṭvā tāsāṃ sthiti-nibandhanaṃ trivargasya sādhanam adhyāyānāṃ śatasahasreṇāgre provāca* || *Kāmasūtra* 1.1.5 (R. Sharma 2016)

29 तस्यैकदेशिकं मनुः स्वायंभुवो धर्माधिकारिकं पृथक् चकार || १.१.६
बृहस्पतिर् अर्थाधिकारिकम् || १.१.७
महादेवानुचरश् च नन्दी सहस्रेणाध्यायानां पृथक् काम-सूत्रं प्रोवाच || १.१.८, Kāmasūtra 1.1.6-8 (R. Sharma 2016)

*tasyaikadeśikaṃ manuḥ svāyaṃbhuvo dharmādhikārikaṃ pṛthak cakāra || 1.1.6*
*bṛhaspatir arthādhikārikam || 1.1.7*
*mahādevānucaraś ca nandī sahasreṇādhyāyānāṃ pṛthak kāma-sūtraṃ provāca || 1.1.8*

30 तद् एव तु पञ्चभिर् अध्याय-शतैर् औद्दालकिः श्वेतकेतुः संचिक्षेप || १.१.९
*tad eva tu pañcabhir adhyāya-śatair auddālakiḥ śvetaketuḥ saṃcikṣepa || Kāmasūtra 1.1.9 (R. Sharma 2016)*

31 Alain Daniélou takes Bābhravyaḥ as a reference to 'sons of Babhru' (Danielou 1994).

32 तद् एव तु पुनरध्यर्धेनाध्यायशतेन [१]साधारण-[२]सांप्रयोगिक-[३]कन्या-संप्रयुक्तक-[ ४]भार्याधिकारिक-[५]पारदारिक-[६]वैशिक-[७]औपनिषदिकैः सप्तभिर् अधिकरणैर् बाभ्रव्यः पाञ्चालः संचिक्षेप || १.१.१०
*tad eva tu punaradhyardhenādhyāyaśatena [1] sādhāraṇa-[2]sāṃprayogika-[3]kanyā-saṃprayuktaka-[ 4] bhāryādhikārika-[5]pāradārika-[6]vaiśika-[7]aupaniṣadikaiḥ saptabhir adhikaraṇair bābhravyaḥ pāñcālaḥ saṃcikṣepa ||* Kāmasūtra 1.1.10 (R. Sharma 2016)

33 तस्य षष्टं वैशिकम् अधिकरणं पाटलिपुत्रकाणां गणिकानां नियोगाद् दत्तकः पृथक् चकार || १.१.११
तत्-प्रसङ्गात् चारायणः साधारणम् अधिकरणं पृथक् प्रोवाच सुवर्णनाभः सांप्रयोगिकम्. घोटकमुखः कन्या-संप्रयुक्तकम्. गोनर्दीयो भार्याधिकारिकम्. गोणिकापुत्रः पारदारिकम्. कुचुमार औपनिषदिकम् इति || १.१.१२, Kāmasūtra 1.1.11-12 (R. Sharma 2016)

*tasya ṣaṣṭaṃ vaiśikam adhikaraṇaṃ pāṭaliputrakāṇāṃ gaṇikānāṃ niyogād dattakaḥ pṛthak cakāra || 1.1.11*
*tat-prasaṅgāt cārāyaṇaḥ sādhāraṇam adhikaraṇaṃ pṛthak provāca suvarṇanābhaḥ sāṃprayogikam. ghoṭakamukhaḥ kanyā-saṃprayuktakam. gonardīyo bhāryādhikārikam. goṇikāputraḥ pāradārikam. kucumāra aupaniṣadikam iti || 1.1.12*

34 एवं बहुभिर् आचार्यैस् तच् छास्त्रं खण्डशः प्रणीतम् उत्सन्न-कल्पम् अभूत् || १.१.१३
तत्र दत्तकादिभिः प्रणीतानां शास्त्रावयवानाम् एकदेशत्वात् महद् इति च बाभ्रवीयस्य दुरध्येयत्वात् संक्षिप्य सर्वम् अर्थम् अल्पेन ग्रन्थेन कामसूत्रम् इदं प्रणीतम् || १.१.१४, Kāmasūtra 1.1.13-14 (R. Sharma 2016)

*evaṃ bahubhir ācāryais tac chāstraṃ khaṇḍaśaḥ praṇītam utsanna-kalpam abhūt || 1.1.13*
*tatra dattakādibhiḥ praṇītānāṃ śāstrāvayavānām ekadeśatvāt mahad iti ca bābhravīyasya duradhyeyatvāt saṃkṣipya sarvam artham alpena granthena kāmasūtram idaṃ praṇītam || 1.1.14*

35 Consider *Kāmaśāstra*, we see a condensation phase (Nandī till Bābhravyaḥ), followed by an expansion phase (Cārāyaṇaḥ and others), which again was followed by a condensation phase (Vātsyāyana) and an expansion phase (post-Vātsyāyana). While the condensation in Vātsyāyana and Pre-Vātsyāyana period was in the form of abridgement, the expansion carried out by Cārāyaṇaḥ and others were elaborations on particular aspects of the treatise as well as the knowledge field. In post-Vātsyāyana period, except for the commentary on *Kāmasūtra*, other expansions have been in the form of newer treatises. In parallel, there have been certain texts summarising the knowledge field as well. In the case of *Vedānta*-śāstra, while

condensation has been in the form of summarised presentation of the knowledge field, expansion has been in the form of both robust commentary tradition as well as independent works, both flourishing together.

36 See endnote 32

37 In the case of dharmaśāstras, post-Manu independent works could be considered a commentary upon or an exploration and expansion of the subject matter of *Manusmṛti*. Olivelle (2005, 69) comments: 'In some sense, we can extend what Lingat (1973,104) says about Brhaspati to all the authors of dharmaśāstras subsequent to Manu—they are all commentators on the MDh, which is their exemplar and model. They are certainly not commentators in the traditional sense; but their works can be viewed as commentaries in the sense that they are drawing inspiration from and responding to the work of Manu. It is certainly at the back of their minds and perhaps in front of their eyes as they tried to both emulate it and to surpass it. Brhaspati, however, was prescient in his observation that no other smrti will ever measure up to, much less surpass, the sastra of Manu. This is demonstrated by the influence of Manu on the medieval production of texts on *dharma*.'

38 *Manusmṛti* verse 1.32-35: 'Dividing his body into two, he became a man with one half and a woman with the other. By that woman the Lord brought forth Viraj. By heating himself with ascetic toil, that man, Virāj, brought forth a being by himself—know, you best of the twiceborn, that I am that being, the creator of this whole world. Desiring to bring forth creatures, I heated myself with the most arduous ascetic toil and brought forth in the beginning the ten great seers, the lords

of creatures: Marīci, Atri, Añgiras, Pulastya, Pulaha, Kratu, Pracetas, Vasiṣṭha, Bhṛgu, and Nārada.'

39 George Bühler writes: 'No *dharma-sūtra* begins with a description of its own origin, much less with an account of creation. The former, which would be absurd in a *dharma*-sutra, has been added in order to give authority to a remodelled version… (Bühler 1886, lxvi).' James W Laine writes: 'Only verses 32-36 seem to pose a problem. Here Manu proclaims himself as a demiurge creator, one of the seven Manus born from the mind of the Svayambhū. This disrupts the flow of the text and can only be seen as an insertion from a separate tradition which is worked in here only for the apologetic purpose of establishing the divine origin of this dharmaśāstra (Laine 1981, 166).'

40 'The myth relates a sacred history, that is, a primordial event that took place at the beginning of time, ab initio. But to relate a sacred history is equivalent to revealing a mystery. For the persons of the myth are not human beings; they are gods or culture heroes, and for this reason their gesta constitute mysteries; man could not know their acts if they were not revealed to him. The myth, then, is the history of what took place in illo tempore, the recital of what the gods or the semidivine beings did at the beginning of time. To tell a myth is to proclaim what happened ab origine. Once told, that is, revealed, the myth becomes apodictic truth; it establishes a truth that is absolute. "It is so because it is said that it is so," the Netsilik Eskimos declare to justify the validity of their sacred history and religious traditions. The myth proclaims the appearance of a new cosmic situation or of a primordial event. Hence it is always the recital of a creation; it tells how

something was accomplished, began to *be*. It is for this reason that myth is bound up with ontology; it speaks only of *realities*, of what *really* happened, of what was fully manifested (Eliade 1959, 95).'

41 'Hiltebeitel argues for seeing the Brahminic Vyāsa as a "narrative fiction", just as the references to orality are "literary tropes" (Adluri 2011, xxiv).'

42 'According to Hiltebeitel, the composing committee cloaked its ultimate authorial voice in the persona of a shadowy seer, *Veda*-Vyāsa, whose "thought entire" the epic portrays being unfolded to the sattra-sitting brahmins of the Naimisa Forest (Fitzgerald 2003, 816).'

43 'Thus, rather than reducing Yudhisṭhira or Vyāsa to historical personages anḍ interpreting their interaction as evidence of a historical conflict between the Ksatriya and Brahmin castes, Hiltebeitel argues for a completẹ shift in perspective: the epic, he suggests, is from the very beginning the product of Brahmins, who make use of tropes such as orality and bardic transmission (in the many references to the *sūta*), in order to articulate a comprehensive view of the proper *dharma* and of the way a righteous king (such as the fictional Yudhisṭhira) might be instructeḍ in maintaining this *dharma* (Adluri 2011, xxiv).'

44 'And Hiltebeitel sees in the fictional author's extraordinary boy Suka an evocative representation of the text and story of the MBh itself (p. 289). The boy, a dazzling gift to Vyāsa from the great god, Siva, emblem of the written composition of the MBh, goes on to outshine his more world-bound father by

gaining moksa as a mere boy, leaving his forlorn father with only a shadow (Fitzgerald 2003, 816-817).'

45 'The dharmasūtras are not only written in prose but are also presented as nothing more than scholarly works. There is no literary introduction; the author gets right down to business. He presents his material in a straightforward manner, and on points of controversy and debate, he presents opposing viewpoints. All this is eliminated by Manu *(Olivelle, Manu's Code of Law: A Critical Edition and Translation of the Mānava-Dharmaśāstra* 2005, 26).'

46 श्रुत्वैतान् ऋषयो धर्मान् स्नातकस्य यथोदितान् ।
इदमूचुर्महात्मानमनलप्रभवं भृगुम् ॥ १ ॥
एवं यथोक्तं विप्राणां स्वधर्ममनुतिष्ठताम् ।
कथं मृत्युः प्रभवति वेदशास्त्रविदां प्रभो ॥ २ ॥ *Manusmṛti* 2-5.1 (Kaundinyayana 2014)
*śrutvaitān ṛṣayo dharmān snātakasya yathoditān* ।
*idamūcurmahātmānamanalaprabhavaṃ bhṛgum* ॥ *1* ॥
*evaṃ yathoktaṃ viprāṇāṃ svadharmamanutiṣṭhatām* ।
*kathaṃ mṛtyuḥ prabhavati vedaśāstravidāṃ prabho* ॥ *2* ॥

47 चातुर्वर्ण्यस्य कृत्स्नोऽयमुक्तो धर्मस्त्वयाऽनघः ।
कर्मणां फलनिर्वृत्तिं शंस नस्तत्त्वतः परम् ॥ १ ॥
*Manusmṛti* 12.1 (Kaundinyayana 2014)
*cāturvarṇyasya kṛtsno'yamukto dharmastvayānaghaḥ* ।
*karmaṇāṃ phalanirvṛttiṃ śaṃsa nastattvataḥ parām* ॥ *1* ॥

48 See verses 3.150, 4.103, 8.168, 9.182

49 See verses 3.222, 5.41, 8.204, 10.63

50 See verses 6.54, 8.124

51 See verses 8.139, 8.279

52 See verse 9.183

53 I have elaborately dealt with the subject of mimetic architecture of Manusmṛti in my paper ''Mimetic Cosmogony In Manusmṛti's Structure" presented at the 51st All India Oriental Conference held on October 24-26, 2024 at Udupi.

54 A version of this chapter was first published as a standalone essay in *Indic Today*, 1 July 2021- https://www.indica.today/long-reads/place-of-dharmashastras-in-hindu-worldview/

55 Sanjay Dixit posted on Twitter on 10 January 2018 thus: 'Intrigued by Dalit narratives, I had a survey done in 1000 Hindu households to check what religious books they kept at home. Results: *Gita*: 993, *Ramayana/Ramacharitmanas*: 955, *Mahabharata*: 253, *Hanuman Chalisa*: 999, *Durga Saptashati*: 844, any *Veda*: 251, an *Upanishad*: 651, *Manusmriti*: 4. Those who base their counter-narrative on *Manusmriti* fail to realise that it is not a holy scripture or even a shāstra (Sanjay Dixit 2018).'

56 धर्मो विश्वस्य जगतः प्रतिष्ठा... धर्मेण पापमपनुदन्ति...
*dharmo viśvasya jagataḥ pratiṣṭhā...dharmeṇa pāpamapanudati...| Mahānārāyaṇa Upaniṣad 79.7* (Vimalananda 1968)

57 धारणाद्धर्ममित्याहुः धर्मो धारयति प्रजाः ।
*dhāraṇāddharmamityāhuḥ dharmo dhārayati prajāḥ* ।
*Mahābhārata Karṇa Parva 49.50* (Mahabharata: Critical Edition Prepared by Scholars at Bhandarkar Oriental Research Institute BORI n.d.)

58 यतोऽभ्युदयनिःश्रेयससिद्धिः स धर्मः ॥ *Vaiśeṣika Sūtra* 1.1.2 (Sinha 1923)
*yato'bhyudayaniḥśreyasasiddhiḥ sa dharmaḥ* ॥

59 तस्माच्छास्त्रं प्रमाणं ते कार्याकार्यव्यवस्थितौ ।
ज्ञात्वा शास्त्रविधानोक्तं कर्म कर्तुमिहार्हसि॥
*tasmācchāstraṃ pramāṇaṃ te kāryākāryavyavasthitau |*
*jñātvā śāstravidhānoktaṃ karma kartumihārhasi || Bhagavad Gita 16.24* (Gambhirananda 1998)

60 प्रवृत्तिनिवृत्तिपराणां च सन्दर्भाणां शास्त्रत्वम् । यथाहुः - "प्रवृत्तिर्वा निवृत्तिर्वा नित्येन कृतकेन वा । (Brahmasutra-bhashya Bhamati-vyakkya n.d.)
pravṛttinivṛttiparāṇāṃ ca sandarbhāṇāṃ śāstratvam । yathāhuḥ - "pravṛttirvā nivṛttirvā nityena kṛtakena vā ।

61 वेदोऽखिलो धर्ममूलं स्मृतिशीले च तद्विदाम् ।
आचारश्चैव साधूनामात्मनस्तुष्टिरेव च ॥ Manusmṛti 2.6 (Kaundinyayana 2014)
*vedo'khilo dharmamūlaṃ smṛtiśīle ca tadvidām ।*
*ācāraścaiva sādhūnāmātmanastuṣṭireva ca ॥*

62 पुराणन्यायमीमांसाधर्मशास्त्राङ्गमिश्रिताः । वेदाः स्थानानि विद्यानां धर्मस्य च चतुर्दश ॥ *Yājñavalkya Smṛti* 1.3 (Pansikar 1936)
*purāṇanyāyamīmāṃsādharmaśāstrāṅgamiśritāḥ । vedāḥ sthānāni vidyānāṃ dharmasya ca caturdaśa ॥*

63 For the sections on Hindu epistemology and Śabda Pramāṇa, apart from primary sources, I have also relied upon Satischandra Chatterjee's *The Nyaya Theory of Knowledge* (2015).

64 आप्तोपदेशः शब्दः । *āptopadeśaḥ śabdaḥ* । *Nyāyasūtras* 1.1.7 (Tailanga 1896)

65 आप्तः खलु साक्षात्कृतधर्मा यथादृष्टस्यार्थस्य चिख्यापयिषया प्रयुक्त उपदेष्टा । *āptaḥ khalu sākṣātkṛtadharmā yathādṛṣṭasyārthasya cikhyāpayiṣayā prayukta upadeṣṭā* । *Vātsyāyana-Bhāṣya* on *Nyāyasutra* 1.1.7 (Tailanga 1896)

66 शाब्द-प्रमा-करणम् आप्तवाक्यम् । तच्च आकाङ्क्षा-योग्यता-आसत्तयः तात्पर्यञ्च इति चतुष्टयात्मकम्। उपपाद्य- ज्ञानेन उपपादक- कल्पनम् अर्थापत्तिः। (Balasubramanian 2012, 46)
*śābda-pramā-karaṇam āptavākyam* । *tacca ākāṅkṣā-yogyatā-āsattayaḥ tātparyañca iti catuṣṭayātmakam* । *upapādya-jñānena upapādaka- kalpanam arthāpattiḥ* ।

67 स द्विविधो दृष्टादृष्टार्थत्वात् । *sa dvividho dṛṣṭādṛṣṭārthatvāt* । *Nyāyasutra* 1.1.8 (Tailanga 1896)

68 वैदिकाश्च विधिपराः निषेधपराः ब्रह्मपराश्च इति त्रिविधाः। तत्र विधि-निषेधपराणां पूर्ववेदस्थानां न अत्र उपयोगः। परिशेषात् वेदान्त-वाक्यानामेव इह उपयोगः। (Balasubramanian 2012, 52)
vaidikāśca vidhiparāḥ niṣedhaparāḥ brahmaparāśca iti trividhāḥ। tatra vidhi-niṣedhaparāṇāṃ pūrvavedasthānāṃ na atra upayogaḥ। pariśeṣāt vedānta-vākyānāmeva iha upayogaḥ।

69 चोदनालक्षणार्थो धर्मः । *codanālakṣaṇo artho dharmaḥ* । *Mīmāṁsā Sūtra* 1.1.1 (Sandal 1923)

70 वेदोऽखिलो धर्ममूलं स्मृतिशीले च तद्विदाम् ।
आचारश्चैव साधूनामात्मनस्तुष्टिरेव च ॥ *Manusmṛti* 2.6 (Kaundinyayana 2014)
*vedo'khilo dharmamūlaṃ smṛtiśīle ca tadvidām* ।
*ācāraścaiva sādhūnāmātmanastuṣṭireva ca* ॥

श्रुतिस्मृत्युदितं धर्ममनुतिष्ठन् हि मानवः ।
इह कीर्तिमवाप्नोति चाऽनुत्तमं सुखम् ॥
श्रुतिस्तु वेदो विज्ञेयो धर्मशास्त्रं तु वै स्मृतिः ।
ते सर्वार्थेष्वमीमांस्ये ताभ्यां धर्मो हि निर्बभौ ॥ ॥ *Manusmṛti* 2.9-10
(Kaundinyayana 2014)

*śrutismṛtyuditaṃ dharmamanutiṣthan hi mānavaḥ* ।
*iha kīrtimavāpnoti pretya cā'nuttamaṃ sukham* ॥
*śrutistu vedo vijñeyo dharmaśāstraṃ tu vai smṛtiḥ* ।
*te sarvārtheṣvamīmāṃsye tābhyāṃ dharmo hi nirbabhau* ॥

71 पुराणन्यायमीमांसाधर्मशास्त्राङ्गमिश्रिताः । वेदाः स्थानानि विद्यानां धर्मस्य च चतुर्दश ॥ *Yājñavalkya Smṛti* 1.3 (Pansikar 1936)
*purāṇanyāyamīmāṃsādharmaśāstrāṅgamiśritāḥ* । *vedāḥ sthānāni vidyānāṃ dharmasya ca caturdaśa* ॥

72 श्रुतिस्तु वेदो विज्ञेयो धर्मशास्त्रं तु वै स्मृतिः ।
ते सर्वार्थेष्वमीमांस्ये ताभ्यां धर्मो हि निर्बभौ ॥ ॥ *Manusmṛti* 2.10
(Kaundinyayana 2014)
*śrutistu vedo vijñeyo dharmaśāstraṃ tu vai smṛtiḥ* ।
*te sarvārtheṣvamīmāṃsye tābhyāṃ dharmo hi nirbabhau* ॥

73 All the arguments put forward by Jayanta Bhaṭṭa are taken from "Jayanta on the validity of sacred texts (other than the *Veda*)" (2012) by Elisa Freschi and Kei Kataoka. This is a translation of the *Sarvāgamaprāmāṇya* section of book four of *Nyāya-Mañjarī* of Jayanta Bhaṭṭa.

74 यद्वै किञ्च मनुरवदत्तद्भेषजम् *Taittirīya Saṁhitā* 2.2.10.2
(Taittiriya Samhita- Searchable Text n.d.)
*yadvai kiñca manuravadattadbheṣajam*

75 The translation has been taken from Ganganath Jha's entry "Comparative notes by various authors" under *Manusmṛti* verse 2.6 which cites passages from Mitramiśra's Vīramitrodaya-Paribhāṣā. [https://www.wisdomlib.org/hinduism/book/manusmriti-with-the-commentary-of-medhatithi/d/doc145579.html]

श्रुतिस्मृत्योर्विरोधे तु श्रुतिर्बलीयसी निरपेक्षत्वात् ।
स्मृतेस्तु मूलभूतवेदानुमानसापेक्षत्वेन विलम्बितत्वाद् दुर्बलत्वम् ।
śrutismṛtyorvirodhe tu śrutirbalīyasī nirapekṣatvāt ।
*smṛtestu mūlabhūtavedānumānasāpekṣatvena vilambitatvād* durbalatvam । (Viramitrodaya Vol 01 & Vol 02 n.d., 25)

76 The translation has been taken from Ganganath Jha's entry 'Comparative notes by various authors' under *Manusmṛti* verse 2.6 which cites passages from Mitramiśra's Vīramitrodaya-Paribhāṣā. [https://www.wisdomlib.org/hinduism/book/manusmriti-with-the-commentary-of-medhatithi/d/doc145579.html]

अतः स परमो धर्मो यो वेदादवगम्यते ।
अवरः स तु विज्ञेयो यः पुराणादिषु स्मृतः ॥

इति व्यासवचनाद्वेदस्मृत्यवबोधितयोर्द्धर्मयोरुत्कर्षापकर्षावगम्येते । तथाच वैदिको धर्मो मुख्य उत्कृष्टत्वात् । स्मार्त्तोऽनुकल्पः अपकृष्टत्वात्। मुख्या संभवे चानुकल्पानुष्ठानात्फलं भवति न तत्संभवे ।

प्रभुः प्रथमकल्पस्य योऽनुकल्पेन वर्त्तते ।
न सांपरायिकं तस्य दुर्मतेर्विद्यते फलम् ॥

इति मनूक्तेः । तथाच श्रुतिविरुद्धार्थाननुष्ठाने फलाभाव एव बीजं न तु अप्रामाण्यसंदेहादि । अविरोधे तु स्मृत्यर्थानुष्ठानादेव फलं तस्या अपि धर्मे प्रमाणत्वात् इति सर्व सुस्थम् । (Viramitrodaya Vol 01 & Vol 02 n.d., 29)

*ataḥ sa paramo dharmo yo vedādavagamyate* ।
*avaraḥ sa tu vijñeyo yaḥ purāṇādiṣu smṛtaḥ* ॥

*iti vyāsavacanādvedasmṛtyavabodhitayorddharmayorut-karṣāpakarṣāṣavagamyete* ।
*tathāca vaidiko dharmo mukhya utkṛṣṭatvāt* ।
*smārtto'nukalpaḥ apakṛṣṭatvāt* ।
*mukhyā saṃbhave cānukalpānuṣṭhānātphalaṃ bhavati na tatsaṃbhave* ।

*prabhuḥ prathamakalpasya yo'nukalpena varttate* ।
*na sāṃparāyikaṃ tasya durmatervidyate phalam* ॥

*iti manūkteḥ* । *tathāca śrutiviruddhārthānanuṣṭhāne phalābhāva eva bījaṃ na tu aprāmāṇyasaṃdehādi* ।
*avirodhe tu smṛtyarthānuṣṭhānādeva phalaṃ tasyā api dharme pramāṇatvāt iti sarva sustham* ।

77 ऋतुकालाभिगामी स्यात् स्वदारनिरतः सदा इत्यृतुकालादिनियमेन सोऽपि धर्म एव । Kullūka Bhaṭṭa on *Manu* 1.1 (Kaundinyayana 2014)
*ṛtukālābhigāmī syāt svadāraniratah sadā ityṛtukālādiniyamena so'pi dharma eva* ।

78 एवं चार्थार्जनमपि ऋताऽमृताभ्यां जीवेदित्यादिनियमेन धर्मएवेत्यवगन्तव्यम् । Kullūka Bhaṭṭa on *Manu* 1.1 (Kaundinyayana 2014)
*evaṃ cārthārjanamapi ṛtā'mṛtābhyāṃ jīvedityādiniyamena dharmaevetyavagantavyam* ।

79 तस्माच्छास्त्रं प्रमाणं ते कार्याकार्यव्यवस्थितौ । ज्ञात्वा शास्त्रविधानोक्तं कर्म कर्तुमिहार्हसि॥

*tasmācchāstraṃ pramāṇaṃ te kāryākāryavyavasthitau | jñātvā śāstravidhānoktaṃ karma kartumihārhasi || Bhagavad Gita 16.24* (Gambhirananda 1998)

80 A longer version of this chapter was presented as a paper at Nirvighnam, a two-day conference on 'Texts and Traditions of India' organised by Saptaparni and The Thinking Cap Series at Hyderabad on 20-21 August 2022.

81 Dr Surendra Kumar, a Sanskrit scholar affiliated with the Arya Samaj, in his revisionist commentary (The Manusmriti 2018) has indulged in many instances of distortion and misinterpretation of key verses. See one such instance highlighted in 'Antarprabhāva in Surendra Kumar's Viśuddha *Manusmṛti*: A critical assessment in light of its avowedly revisionist interpretation' (Sridhar, 2022). This is included in the book as Appendix II.

82 Wendy Doniger (1991) writes: 'The *Laws of Manu* encompasses contradictions that may indeed be ultimately "insoluble", but not necessarily irreconcilable, nor are its attempts to reconcile them necessarily "frenzied". Given the historical background, it is not surprising that Manu expresses a number of different views on many basic points. Different parts of the text were added at different periods (the portions dealing with legal cases are generally regarded as the latest) and, in the recension that we have, some topics are split up and treated in several different places, or in what seem to us to be the wrong places.'

83 Ashok Singhal of VHP has stated: 'The VHP totally rejects the Manu Smriti as it has no place in a civilized & cultured society (Neelakandan 2015).'

84 धर्मो विश्वस्य जगतः प्रतिष्ठा... धर्मेण पापमपनुदति... (महानारायण उपनिषद् ७९: ७)
*dharmo viśvasya jagataḥ pratiṣṭhā...dharmeṇa pāpamapanudati...| Mahānārāyaṇa Upaniṣad 79.7* (Vimalananda 1968)

85 धारणाद्धर्ममित्याहुः धर्मो धारयति प्रजाः ।
*dhāraṇāddharmamityāhuḥ dharmo dhārayati prajāḥ* | *Mahābhārata Karṇa Parva 49.50* (Mahabharata: Critical Edition Prepared by Scholars at Bhandarkar Oriental Research Institute BORI n.d.)

86 यतोऽभ्युदयनिःश्रेयससिद्धिः स धर्मः॥ (वैशेषिक सूत्राणि १:१:२)
*yato'bhyudayaniḥśreyasasiddhiḥ sa dharmaḥ || Vaiśeṣika Sūtra 1.1.2* (Sinha 1923)

87 मानुषाणां हितं धर्मम्...। (पराशरस्मृतिः १:२)
*mānuṣāṇām hitaṃ dharmmaṃ...| Parāśarasmṛti 1.2* (Tripati, Parasharamadhava: Acharakhandam 2019)

88 अभिमतफलसाधनत्वं हि धर्मस्य हितत्वम् ।तच्च फलं द्वेधा-ऐहिकमामुष्मिकञ्च इति।अष्टकादिसाध्यं पृष्ट्यादिकमैहिकम्।आमुष्मिकं द्वेधा अभ्युदयो निःश्रेयसञ्च । तत्राभ्युदयस्य साक्षात् साधनं धर्मः। निःश्रेयसस्य तु तत्त्वज्ञानोत्पादनद्वारेण। (पराशरमाधवः, आचारखण्डः, प्रथमः अध्यायः)
*abhimataphalasādhanatvaṃ hi dharmasya hitatvam |tacca phalaṃ dvedhā-aihikamāmuṣmikañca iti |aṣṭakādisādhyaṃ pṛṣṭyādikamaihikam |āmuṣmikaṃ dvedhā abhyudayo niḥśreyasañca | tatrābhyudayasya sākṣāt sādhanaṃ dharmaḥ | niḥśreyasasya tu tattvajñānotpādanadvāreṇa | Parāśaramādhava, Acharakhanda, Prathama Adhyaya* (Tripati, Parasharamadhava: Acharakhandam 2019)

89 Svarga can be roughly translated as heaven though unlike Abrahamic notion of heaven, *svarga* is not a permanent abode. Instead svarga is a realm to experience fruits of one's punya karma. Likewise, naraka loosely translated as hell is not a permanent abode. There is no concept of eternal hell in Hindu *dharma*. Naraka is a realm where one experiences the fruits of one's pāpa karma.

90 All translations from *Manusmṛti* are adopted with minor modifications from (G. Jha, Manusmriti with the 'Manubhashya' of Medatithi 1920).

91 कर्मणां च विवेकार्थं धर्माधर्मौ व्यवेचयत् ।
द्वन्द्वैरयोजयच्चेमाः सुखदुःखादिभिः प्रजाः ॥ मनुस्मृति १.२६
*karmaṇāṃ ca vivekārthaṃ dharmādharmau vyavecayat |*
*dvandvairayojayaccemāḥ sukhaduḥkhādibhiḥ prajāḥ ||*
*Manusmṛti 1.26* (Kaundinyayana 2014)

92 कर्मभ्यः प्रागयोग्यस्य कर्मणः पुरुषस्य वा योग्यता शास्त्रागम्य य पर सापूर्वमिष्यते।
*karmabhyaḥ prāgayogyasya karmaṇaḥ puruṣasya vā yogyatā śāstrāgamya ya para sāpūrvamiṣyate* | *Tantravārtika of Kumārila, on Bhāṣya of Sābara, on Mīmāṃsa Sutra 2.1.5* (U. Jha 2018)

93 तस्माच्छास्त्रं प्रमाणं ते कार्याकार्यव्यवस्थितौ । ज्ञात्वा शास्त्रविधानोक्तं कर्म कर्तुमिहार्हसि॥
*tasmācchāstraṃ pramāṇaṃ te kāryākāryavyavasthitau | jñātvā śāstravidhānoktaṃ karma kartumihārhasi ||* *Bhagavad Gita 16.24* (Gambhirananda 1998).

94 धर्मशास्त्रेतिहासपुराणाद्युपबृंहिता वेदा यद् एव...।
*dharmaśāstretihāsapurāṇādyupabṛṃhitā vedā yad eva...|*
Sri Rāmānujācārya's *Bhagavad Gita Bhashya on verse 16.24* (Gita Supersite n.d.).

95 शास्त्रं वेदतदुपजीविस्मृतिपुराणादिकमेव...।
śāstraṃ vedatadupajīvismṛtipurāṇādikameva...| Śrī Madhusūdana Sarasvatī's *Gudartha Dipika on Gita verse 16.24* (Gita Supersite n.d.).

96 *Apauruṣeya* means 'not authored by a being, either human or divine'. The *Mīmāṃsakas* hold that any text or composition that is authored will have some flaws, even those created by perfected beings. It is *apauruṣeyatva* or non-authorship of *Veda* which makes *Veda* flawless and this is the reason why it is the ultimate source of knowledge. For a more elaborate enunciation on this, see: (Naik 2022)

97 चोदनालक्षणार्थो धर्मः ।
codanālakṣaṇo artho dharmaḥ | *Mīmāṃsa Sutra* 1.1.1 (Sandal 1923)

98 *Manusmṛti* 1.3 describes Manu as the knower of the entirety of *Veda*.

99 *Manusmṛti* 1.1 describes Manu as being seated in ekāgra one-pointedness—when sages approached him with a request for instruction on *dharma*. Likewise, *Parāśara Smṛti* 1.1 makes a similar reference to Vyasa as being seated in ekāgra. Madhavacharya in his commentary on said verse from *Parāśara Smṛti* notes that one-pointedness happens when all the three—*Dhāraṇā* (concentration), *Dhyāna* (meditation), and Samadhi

(total absorption)—become established in one object. If such one-pointedness happens towards words and meanings, then one will gain the knowledge of all words and speeches including the knowledge of speech of birds and animals. He adds that in this case, the ekāgra refers to one-pointedness towards the knowledge of the innumerable branches of *Veda*s (and hence of *dharma*).

100 श्रुतिस्तु वेदो विज्ञेयो धर्मशास्त्रं तु वै स्मृतिः |
ते सर्वार्थेष्वमीमांस्ये ताभ्यां धर्मो हि निर्बभौ ||
śrutistu vedo vijñeyo dharmaśāstraṃ tu vai smṛtiḥ |
*te sarvārtheṣvamīmāṃsye tābhyāṃ dharmo hi nirbabhau* ||
*Manusmṛti 2.10* (Kaundinyayana 2014)

101 Sadācāra and ātmanastuṣṭi are not independent pramāṇas. They are secondary sources dependent upon śabda pramāṇa. For example, one learns sadācāra from the lives of Bhagavān Rāma and Bhagavān Kṛṣṇa, which can be known from studying the Rāmāyaṇa and Mahābhārata, respectively. Likewise, one is able to implement ātmanastuṣṭi only on the basis of one's learning in Śāstras.

102 वेदः स्मृतिः सदाचारः स्वस्य च प्रियमात्मनः |
एतच्चतुर्विधं प्राहुः साक्षाद् धर्मस्य लक्षणम् ||
*vedaḥ smṛtiḥ sadācāraḥ svasya ca priyamātmanaḥ* |
*etaccaturvidhaṃ prāhuḥ sākṣād dharmasya lakṣaṇam* ||
*Manusmṛti 2.12* (Kaundinyayana 2014)

103 गुरुवेदान्तवाक्यादिषु विश्वासः श्रद्धा । *guruvedāntavākyādiṣu viśvāsaḥ śraddhā* । *Tattvabodha* 1.3.5 (Chaitanya 1997)

104 श्रद्धावाँल्लभते ज्ञानं ...| śraddhāvā~llabhatee jñānaṃ ...|
*Bhagavad Gita 4.39* (Gambhirananda 1998)

105 A qualified teacher is one who is both well versed in a branch of knowledge and has also actualised the essential truths of that field. In Vedānta, such a teacher is called *śrotriya-brahmaniṣṭha*.

106 Also watch this talk by Prof Sreejit Datta titled "Interpreting Sacred Hindu texts: Case for a Hindu Hermeneutic (2022)".

107 श्रुतिस्तु वेदो विज्ञेयो धर्मशास्त्रं तु वै स्मृतिः |

ते सर्वार्थेष्वमीमांस्ये ताभ्यां धर्मो हि निर्बभौ ||
*śrutistu vedo vijñeyo dharmaśāstraṃ tu vai smṛtiḥ* |
*te sarvārtheṣvamīmāṃsye tābhyāṃ dharmo hi nirbabhau* ||
*Manusmṛti 2.10* (Kaundinyayana 2014)

108 Anthropocentrism or the belief in human centrality and exceptionalism, in its essence, is very part of human nature as it has ego and selfishness at the very heart of it. When ego, selfishness, and other internal passions that afflict the mind are not kept in check and instead are allowed to manifest, then it directly results in an ideology based on anthropocentrism. We see such tendencies depicted in various accounts given in the Purāṇas, most notably that of Hiraṇyakaśipu who forced his subjects including his own son, Prahlāda, to worship him instead of Bhagavān Viṣṇu.

109 George Bühler remarks: 'The whole first chapter must be considered as a later addition. No *Dharmasūtra* begins with a description of its own origin, much less with an

account of creation. The former, which would be absurd in a *Dharmasūtra*, has been added in order to give authority to a remodelled version (Bühler 1886, lxvi).'

110 Medhätithi *on Manusmṛti 1.5:* शास्त्रस्य महाप्रयोजनत्वमनेन सर्वेण प्रतिपाद्यते । ब्रह्माद्याः स्थावरपर्यन्ताः संसारगतयो धर्माधर्मनिमित्ता अत्र प्रतिपाद्यन्ते ।
*śāstrasya mahāprayojanatvamanena sarveṇa pratipādyate* । *brahmādyāh sthāvaraparyantāḥ saṃsāragatayo dharmādharmanimittā atra pratipādyante* । (Harikrishna Dave 1972-85)

111 Kullūka Bhaṭṭa *on Manusmṛti 1.5:* इदंतु वदामः मुनीनां धर्मविषये प्रश्ने जगत्कारणतया ब्रह्मप्रतिपादनंधर्मकथनमेवेति नाप्रस्तुताऽभिधानम् ।
*idaṃtu vadāmaḥ munīnāṃ dharmaviṣaye praśne jagatkāraṇatayā brahmapratipādanaṃdharmakathanameveti nāprastutā'bhidhānam* । (Harikrishna Dave 1972-85)

112 आत्मज्ञानंतितिक्षा च धर्मःसाधारणो नृपे |
ātmajñānaṃtitikṣā ca dharmaḥsādhāraṇo nṛpe | Mahābhārata 12.285.24 (Harikrishna Dave 1972-85)

113 इज्याचारदमाहिंसादानस्वाध्यायकर्मणाम् |अयं तु परमोधर्मोयद्योगेन आत्मदर्शनम् || *ijyācāradamāhiṃsādānasvādhyāyakarmaṇām | ayaṃ tu paramodharmoyadyogena ātmadarśanam || Yājñavalkya smṛti 1.8* (Harikrishna Dave 1972-85)

114 जन्माद्यस्य यतः| *janmādyasya yataḥ | Brahmasūtra 1.1.2* (Harikrishna Dave 1972-85)

115 यतो वा इमानि भूतानि जायन्ते | येनजातानिजीवन्ति | यत्प्रयन्त्यभिसंविशन्ति | तद्विजिज्ञासस्व | तद्ब्रह्मेति ||

*yato vā imāni bhūtāni jāyante | yenajātānijīvanti | yatprayantyabhisaṃviśanti | tadvijijñāsasva | tadbrahmeti || (Taittirīya Upaniṣad 3.1)* (Harikrishna Dave 1972-85)

116 Kullūka Bhaṭṭa *on Manusmṛti 1.5:* आत्मज्ञानरूपपरमधर्मावगमाय प्रथमाध्यायं कृत्वा संस्कारादिरूपं धर्मं तदङ्गतया द्वितीयाध्यायादिक्रमेण वक्ष्यतीति न कश्चिद्विरोधः| *ātmajñānarūpaparamadharmāvagamāya prathamādhyāyaṃ kṛtvā saṃskārādirūpaṃ dharmaṃ tadaṅgatayā dvitīyādhyāyādikrameṇa vakṣyatīti na kaścidvirodhaḥ |* (Harikrishna Dave 1972-85)

117 Kullūka Bhaṭṭa *on Manusmṛti 1.5:* किंच प्रश्नोत्तरवाक्यानामेव स्वरसादयं मदुक्तोऽर्थो लभ्यते । *kiṃca praśnottaravākyānāmeva svarasādayaṃ madukto'rtho labhyate* । (Harikrishna Dave 1972-85)

118 तत्राभ्युदयस्य साक्षात् साधनं धर्मः। निःश्रेयसस्य तु तत्त्वज्ञानोत्पादनद्वारेण। *tatrābhyudayasya sākṣāt sādhanaṃ dharmaḥ* । *niḥśreyasasya tu tattvajñānotpādanadvāreṇa* । *Parāśara Madhava, Acharakhanda, Prathama Adhyaya.* (Tripati, Parasharamadhava: Acharakhandam 2019)

119 See (Sridhar 2019)

120 Examples of *vidhi* statement: *svargakāmo yajeta* (Those who desire heaven must perform sacrifice); *satyaṃ vada* (Speak truth).

121 Example for *niṣedha* statement: *na kalañjaṃ bhakṣayet* (Do not eat *kalañja*, i.e. fermented food).

122 Example of *apūrva-vidhi*: *svargakāmo yajeta* – One who desires heaven must perform yajña. It is imparting an original revelation, something which cannot be known from elsewhere, namely, that performance of yajña directly results in attainment of heaven. All such injunctions which are original revelations about karma and karmaphala are called as apūrva-vidhi.

123 Example for *niyama-vidhi*: If 'A' is to be done, and there are many ways of doing it like 'B', 'C', and 'D'; the niyama-vidhi restricts that 'A' is to be done only by way of 'B' and not by other means.

124 Example for *parisaṅkhya-vidhi*: *Rāmāyaṇa* 4.17.39 says: *pañca pañcanakhā bhakṣyāḥ* [Five animals each having five nails may be consumed as food (Valmiki Ramayana n.d.)]. It is not prescribing that everyone must eat five animals each having five nails. It is merely saying that if one desires to eat meat, then one should not consume meat of any animals, except the five animals having five nails (namely rabbit, porcupine, iguana, rhinoceros, and tortoise) mentioned in the verse. That is, by this vidhi, while eating meat is not compulsory, if one were to eat meat, then for such a person, meat of animals except those allowed are prohibited.

125 While the statement, 'One should not threaten a Brāhmaṇa or strike him', is a prohibition regarding the person which is applicable in all contexts and situations and hence is a *puruṣārtha niṣedha*; the statement, 'The yajamāna of a sacrifice should abstain from sexual intimacy', is a prohibition with respect to sacrifice and is applicable only in the context of and during the duration of that particular sacrifice and hence is a *kratvārtha niṣedha*.

126 Example for paryudāsa: When there is an injunction like 'perform śrāddha ceremony during full moon' and a prohibition like 'śrāddha not to be performed in the night'; this prohibition is not niṣedha but is paryudāsa. It is an exception to the general rule. The person is to perform the śrāddha ceremony during full moon, except during the night.

127 The verse appears as 5.146 in Ganganath Jha edition.

128 अस्वतन्त्रा धर्मे स्त्री | *asvatantrā dharme strī* | *Gautama Dharmasūtras* 18.1 (Gautama *Dharma* Sutra n.d.)

129 In *Manusmṛti* 2.228-2.237, a man is told to always act in accordance with his mother, father and ācārya.

To serve these three is told to be the highest austerity. This service to parents and teachers is an integral part of varṇāśrama-*dharma*. Likewise, when *Manusmṛti* 5.153 says that there is no separate sacrificing, observations or fastings for women, other than serving her husband, it does not mean total exclusion, but only that all other religious activities are secondary and a limb of serving the husband which is primary *dharma* and hence, her ritual practice must be done either together with the husband or with the permission of the husband, a point noted by Medhātithi in his commentary on the verse (G Jha 1920).

130 The verse appears as 5.153 in Ganganath Jha edition and as 5.155 in Kaundinyayana edition.

नाऽस्ति स्त्रीणां पृथग् यज्ञो न व्रतं नाऽप्युपोषणम् ।
पतिं शुश्रूषते येन तेन स्वर्गे महीयते ॥

*Manusmṛti* 5.155 (Kaundinyayana 2014)
*nā'sti strīṇāṃ pṛthag yajño na vrataṃ nā'pyupoṣaṇam* ।
*patiṃ śuśrūṣate yena tena svarge mahīyate* ॥

131 While strī-*dharma* has been defined in terms of women's relational *dharma* towards parents, husband, and children, one could ask, what about *dharma* for women who neither have parents nor are they married and hence without children? Or for women in professions such as prostitution, or women who are divorced and hence cannot practice pativratā *dharma*? The answer to this is that while they may be ineligible to practice strī-*dharma* as enunciated in Manu 5.146, which is a viśeṣa-*dharma*, they could still practice sāmānya-*dharma*, which is available for everyone. This is similar to cases of those menfolk who remain unmarried or have become widowers and are hence ineligible to perform gṛhastha-āśrama-*dharma*, but are nevertheless eligible to perform sāmānya-*dharma*. Thus, no one is excluded from *dharma*.

132 मनुर्नाम कश्चित्पुरुष विशेषोऽनेकवेदशाखाध्ययनविज्ञानानुष्ठानसम्पन्नः स्मृतिपरम्पराप्रसिद्धः । Medhātithi on Manu 1.1 (Dave 1972)
*manurnāma kaścitpuruṣa viśeṣo'nekavedaśākhādhyayanavijñānānuṣṭhānasampannaḥ smṛtiparamparāprasiddhaḥ* ।

133 सकलवेदार्थादिमननान्मनुः Kullūka Bhaṭṭa on *Manu* 1.1 (Kaundinyayana 2014)
*sakalavedārthādimananānmanuḥ*

134 स्वायम्भुवाद्याः सप्तैते मनवो भूरितेजसः ।
स्वे स्वेऽन्तरे सर्वमिदमुत्पाद्यापुश्चराचरम् ॥ *Manusmṛti* 1.63 (Kaundinyayana 2014)

*svāyambhuvādyāḥ saptaite manavo bhūritejasaḥ* ǀ
*sve sve'ntare sarvamidamutpādyāpuścarācaram* ǁ

135 श्लोकस्याऽऽदौ मनुनिर्देशो मङ्गलार्थः परमात्मन एव संसारस्थितये सार्वज्ञैश्वर्यादिसंपन्नमनुरूपेण प्रादुर्भूतत्वात् तदभिधानस्य मङ्गलातिशयत्वात् । Kullūka Bhaṭṭa on *Manu* 1.1 (Kaundinyayana 2014)
*svāyambhuvādyāḥ saptaite manavo bhūritejasaḥ* ǀ
*sve sve'ntare sarvamidamutpādyāpuścarācaram* ǁ

136 एकाग्रशब्दो रूढ्या निश्चलतामाह। प्रत्याहारेण परिहृतरागादिदोषसंसर्गस्य विकल्पनिवृत्तौ तत्त्वावबोधचिन्तायां मनसः स्थैर्यमेकाग्रता । तथाभूत एव च संनिहितरूपशब्दादिविषयावधारणे योग्यो भवति, न सदसद्विकल्पयुक्तः। अथवा योगतोऽग्रशब्दो मनसि वर्तते, अर्थग्रहणे चक्षुरादिभ्योऽग्रगामित्वात् । प्रथमप्रवृत्तियुक्तः पुरःसरो लोकेऽग्र उच्यते। एकस्मिन् ध्येये ग्राहये वाऽग्रमस्येति विग्रहः, व्यधिकरणानामपि वहुव्रीहिर्गमकत्वात् । अत्रापि व्याक्षेपनिवृत्तिरेवैकाग्रता। Medhātithi on *Manu* 1.1 (Dave 1972)
*ekāgraśabdo rūḍhyā niścalatāmāha* ǀ *pratyāhāreṇa parihṛtarāgādidoṣasaṃsargasya vikalpanivṛttau tattvāvabodhacintāyāṃ manasaḥ sthairyamekāgratā* ǀ *tathābhūta eva ca saṃnihitarūpaśabdādiviṣayāvadhāraṇe yogyo bhavati, na sadasadvikalpayuktaḥ* ǀ *athavā yogato'graśabdo manasi vartate, arthagrahaṇe cakṣurādibhyo'gragāmitvāt* ǀ *prathamapravṛttiyuktaḥ puraḥsaro loke'gra ucyate* ǀ *ekasmin dhyeye grāhaye vā'gramasyeti vigrahaḥ, vyadhikaraṇānāmapi vahuvrīhirgamakatvāt* ǀ *atrāpi vyākṣepanivṛttirevaikāgratā* ǀ

137 एकाग्रं विषयान्तराव्याक्षिप्तचित्तम्। *(ekāgraṃ viṣayāntarāvyākṣiptacittam* ǀ*)* Kullūka Bhaṭṭa on *Manu* 1.1 (Dave 1972); एकाग्रमासीनं अविक्षिप्तचित्तं स्थितं *(ekāgramāsīnaṃ*

*avikṣiptacittaṃ sthitaṃ)* Govindarāja on *Manu* 1.1 (Dave 1972); एकाग्रमविक्षिप्तमनस्कम् *(ekāgramavikṣiptamanaskam)* Sarvajñanārāyaṇa on *Manu* 1.1 (Dave 1972).

138 आसीनं सुखोपविष्टमीदृशस्यैव महर्षिप्रश्नोत्तरदानयोग्यत्वात् । Kullūka Bhaṭṭa on *Manu* 1.1 (Kaundinyayana 2014)
*āsīnaṃ sukhopaviṣṭamīdṛśasyaiva maharṣipraśnottaradānayogyatvāt* ।

139 परीक्ष्य लोकान् कर्मचितान् ब्राह्मणो
निर्वेदमायान्नास्त्यकृतः कृतेन ।
तद्विज्ञानार्थं स गुरुमेवाभिगच्छेत्
समित्पाणिः श्रोत्रियं ब्रह्मनिष्ठम् ॥ १२ ॥ *Muṇḍaka Upaniṣad* 1.2.12 (Gambhirananda 1958)
*parīkṣya lokān karmacitān brāhmaṇo*
*nirvedamāyānnāstyakṛtaḥ kṛtena* ।
*tadvijñānārthaṃ sa gurumevābhigacchet*
*samitpāṇiḥ śrotriyaṃ brahmaniṣṭham* ॥*12*॥

140 त्वमेको ह्यस्य सर्वस्य विधानस्य स्वयम्भुवः ।
अचिन्त्यस्याप्रमेयस्य कार्यतत्त्वार्थवित् प्रभो ॥ *Manu* 1.3 (Kaundinyayana 2014)
*tvameko hyasya sarvasya vidhānasya svayambhuvaḥ* ।
*acintyasyāprameyasya kāryatattvārthavit prabho* ॥

141 क्षिप्तं मूढं विक्षिप्तमेकाग्रं निरुद्धमिति चित्तभूमयः। *Vyāsa-Bhāṣya* on *Pātañjala Yoga Sūtra* 1.1 (Prasada 1998)
*kṣiptaṃ mūḍhaṃ vikṣiptamekāgraṃ niruddhamiti cittabhūmayaḥ* ।

142 यस्त्वेकाग्रे चेतसि सद्भूतमर्थं प्रद्योतयति क्षिणोति च क्लेशान्कर्मबन्धनानि श्लथयति निरोधमभिमुखं करोति स संप्रज्ञातो

योग इत्याख्यायते। *Vyāsa-Bhāṣya* on *Pātañjala Yoga Sūtra* 1.1 (Prasada 1998)
*yastvekāgre cetasi sadbhūtamarthaṃ pradyotayati kṣiṇoti ca kleśānkarmabandhanāni ślathayati nirodhamabhimukhaṃ karoti sa saṃprajñāto yoga ityākhyāyate* |

143 This immediate realisation (sākṣātkāra) is a direct perceptual knowledge but must be distinguished from pratyakṣa or perception, which stands for knowledge derived from our senses.

144 द्योतनं हि तत्त्वज्ञानमागमाद्वाऽनुमानाद्वा भवदपि परोक्षरूपतया न साक्षात्कारवतीमविद्यामुच्छिनत्ति द्विचन्द्रदिङ्गोहादिष्वनुच्छेदकत्वा दत आह – प्रेति । प्रशब्दो हि प्रकर्षं द्योतयन्साक्षात्कारं सूचयति ।
Vācaspati Miśra's *Tattvavaiśāradī - Ṭīkā* on *Vyāsa-Bhāṣya* on *Pātañjala Yoga Sūtra* 1.1 (Bodas 1917)
*dyotanaṃ hi tattvajñānamāgamādvā'numānādvā bhavadapi parokṣarūpatayā na sākṣātkāravatīmavidyāmucchinatti dvicandradiṅmohādiṣvanucchedakatvādata āha – preti* | *praśabdo hi prakarṣaṃ dyotayansākṣātkāraṃ sūcayati* |

145 तत्र संयमविशेषात् नानाविधयोगैश्वर्यम् आविर् भवति | धारणा-ध्यान-समाधित्रयम् एकविषयं संयम इत् उच्यते | "शब्दार्थप्रत्ययेष्व् अन्योन्यविभक्तेषु यः संयमः तेनाशेषशब्दादिसाक्षात्कारे सति पक्ष्यादिभाषा ज्ञायन्ते" इति पतञ्जलिनोक्तम् | तेनैव न्यायेनानेकविधवेदशाखाज्ञानम् अभिप्रेत्य "एकाग्रम्" इत् उक्तम् | *Parāśara Mādhava* on *Parāśara Smṛti* 1.1-2 (Tripati, Parasharamadhava: Acharakhandam 2019)
*tatra saṃyamaviśeṣāt nānāvidhayogaiśvaryam āvir bhavati* | *dhāraṇā-dhyāna-samādhitrayam ekaviṣayaṃ saṃyama ity ucyate* | *"śabdārthapratyayeṣv anyonyavibhakteṣu yaḥ saṃyamaḥ tenāśeṣaśabdādisākṣātkāre sati pakṣyādibhāṣā jñāyante" iti*

*patañjalinoktam | tenaiva nyāyenānekavidhavedaśākhājñānam abhipretya "ekāgram" ity uktam |*

146 एकाग्रतामासीनस्य मन्वानः "आसीनम्" इत्याह | ....
शयानस्याकस्मादेव निद्राभिभवात्, उत्थितस्य देहधारणोचितव्यापारात्, गच्छतो धावतो वा विक्षेपबाहुल्यात्, परिशेषेणासीनस्यैवैकाग्रतासम्भवात् आसीनो योगमभ्यस्यन्नुपासीतेत्यर्थः | Parāśara Mādhava on *Parāśara Smṛti* 1.1-2 (Tripati, Parasharamadhava: Acharakhandam 2019)

*ekāgratāmāsīnasya manvānaḥ 'āsīnam' ityāha | .... śayānasyākasmādeva nidrābhibhavāt, utthitasya dehadhāraṇocitavyāpārāt, gacchato dhāvato vā vikṣepabāhulyāt, pariśeṣeṇāsīnasyaivaikāgratāsambhavāt āsīno yogamabhyasyannupāsītetyarthaḥ |*

147 स्वायम्भुवाद्याः सप्तैते मनवो भूरितेजसः ।
स्वे स्वेऽन्तरे सर्वमिदमुत्पाद्याऽपुश्चराचरम् ॥

*Manu* 1.63 (Kaundinyayana 2014)

*svāyambhuvādyāḥ saptaite manavo bhūritejasaḥ* |
*sve sve'ntare sarvamidamutpādyā'puścarācaram* ||

इदं शास्त्रं तु कृत्वाऽसौ मामेव स्वयमादितः ।
विधिवद् ग्राहयामास मरीच्यादींस्त्वहं मुनीन् ॥

*Manu* 1.58 (Kaundinyayana 2014)

*idaṃ śāstraṃ tu kṛtvā'sau māmeva svayamāditaḥ* |
*vidhivad grāhayāmāsa marīcyādīṃstvahaṃ munīn* ||

त्वमेको ह्यस्य सर्वस्य विधानस्य स्वयम्भुवः ।
अचिन्त्यस्याऽप्रमेयस्य कार्यतत्त्वार्थवित् प्रभो ॥

*Manu* 1.3 (Kaundinyayana 2014)

*tvameko hyasya sarvasya vidhānasya svayambhuvaḥ* |
*acintyasyā'prameyasya kāryatattvārthavit prabho* ||

148 यद्वै किञ्च मनुरवदत्तद्भेषजम् *Taittirīya Saṁhitā* 2.2.10.2 (Taittiriya Samhita- Searchable Text n.d.)
*yadvai kiñca manuravadattadbheṣajam*

149 तमभिगम्याभिमुख्येन तत्समीपं गत्वा, व्यापारान्तरत्यागेन, न यदृच्छया, संगम्य । Medhātithi on *Manu* 1.1 (Dave 1972)
*tamabhigamyābhimukhyena tatsamīpaṃ gatvā, vyāpārāntaratyāgena, na yadṛcchayā, saṃgamya* ।

150 अनेन चाभिगमनप्रयत्नेन पृच्छ्यमानवस्तुगौरवं वक्तुश्च प्रामाण्यं ख्याप्यते। न ह्यकुशलः प्रतिवचने यत्नेन पृच्छयते आगत्य । Medhātithi on *Manu* 1.1 (Dave 1972)
*anena cābhigamanaprayatnena pṛchyamānavastugauravaṃ vaktuśca prāmāṇyaṃ khyāpyate*। *na hyakuśala: prativacane yatnena pṛcchayate āgatya* ।

151 अणिमादिगुणयोगान्महान्तः ऋग्यजुस्सामदर्शनान्महर्षयः । Govindarāja on *Manu* 1.1 (Dave 1972)
*aṇimādiguṇayogānmahāntaḥ ṛgyajussāmadarśanānmaharṣayaḥ*

152 ऊर्ध्वरिता भवत्यग्र्यो नियताशी नसंश यी ।
शापानुग्रहयोः शक्तः सत्यसंधो भवेदृषिः ॥ *Skanda Purāṇa* 1.2.5.118 (Skanda Purana [sanskrit] n.d.)
*ūrdhvaretā bhavatyagryo niyatāśī nasaṃśa yī* ।
*śāpānugrahayoḥ śaktaḥ satyasaṃdho bhavedṛṣiḥ* ॥

153 ऋषिर् वेदः,तदध्ययनविज्ञानतदर्थानुष्ठानातिशययोगात् पुरुषे ऽप्य् ऋषिशब्दः। Medhātithi on *Manu* 1.1 (Dave 1972)
*ṛṣir vedaḥ,tadadhyayanavijñānatadarthānuṣṭhānātiśayayogāt puruṣe 'py ṛṣiśabdaḥ*|

154 धर्मं चरत्येष महात्मेति । *dharmaṃ caratyeṣa mahātmeti* । *Śaṅkara Bhāṣya* on *Brahmasūtra* 3.1.11 (Brahmasutra-bhashya n.d.)

155 ऋषिशब्दोऽतीन्द्रियार्थदर्शनम् आचष्टे | ज्ञास्यमानधर्मानुष्ठानोत्तरकालीकमृषित्वम्....अन्यथा अतीन्द्रियार्थं पश्यतां तेषाम् अबुभुत्सुतया प्रश्नो न सङ्गच्छेत | अथ वा स्वयम् अबुभुत्सूनाम् अपि मन्दबुद्ध्यनुग्रहार्थम् आचारशिक्षार्थं वा प्रश्नोऽस्तु | Parāśara Mādhava on *Parāśara Smṛti* 1.1-2 (Tripati, Parasharamadhava: Acharakhandam 2019)
*ṛṣiśabdo'tīndriyārthadarśanam ācaṣṭe* | *jñāsyamānadharmānuṣṭhānottarakālīkamṛṣitvam anyathā atīndriyārthaṃ paśyatāṃ teṣām abubhutsutayā praśno na saṅgaccheta* | *atha vā svayam abubhutsūnām api mandabuddhyanugrahārtham ācāraśikṣārthaṃ vā praśno'stu* |

156 प्रतिपूज्य यथान्यायम्| न्यायः शास्त्रविहिता मर्यादा| ताम् अनतिक्रम्य यादृशी शास्त्रेणाभिवादनोपासनादिका गुरोः प्रथमोपसर्पणे पूजा विहिता तथा पूजयित्वा भक्त्यादरौ दर्शयित्वा| Medhātithi on *Manu* 1.1 (Dave 1972)
*pratipūjya yathānyāyam| nyāyaḥ śāstravihitā maryādā| tām anatikramya yādṛśī śāstreṇābhivādanopāsanādikā guroḥ prathamopasarpaṇe pūjā vihitā tathā pūjayitvā bhaktyādarau darśayitvā|*

157 तद्विज्ञानार्थं स गुरुमेवाभिगच्छेत्समित्पाणिः श्रोत्रियं ब्रह्मनिष्ठम् ॥ *Muṇḍaka Upaniṣad* 1.2.12 (Gambhirananda 1958)
*tadvijñānārthaṃ sa gurumevābhigacchetsamitpāṇiḥ śrotriyaṃ brahmaniṣṭham* ॥

158 ब्रह्मारम्भेऽवसाने च पादौ ग्राह्यौ गुरोः सदा । संहत्य हस्तावध्येयं स हि ब्रह्माञ्जलिः स्मृतः ॥ *Manusmṛti* 2.71 (Kaundinyayana 2014)

*brahmārambhe 'vasāne ca pādau grāhyau guroḥ sadā* ।
*saṃhatya hastāvadhyeyaṃ sa hi brahmāñjaliḥ smṛtaḥ* ॥

159 यद्वा मनुना पूर्वं स्वागतासनदानादिना पूजितास्तस्य पूजां कृत्वेति प्रतिशब्दादुन्नीयते। Kullūka Bhaṭṭa on *Manu* 1.1 (Kaundinyayana 2014)
*yadvā manunā pūrvaṃ svāgatāsanadānādinā pūjitāstasya pūjāṃ kṛtveti pratiśabdādunnīyate* ।

160 न्यायोऽत्र क्षत्रियेषु ब्राह्मणादीनां न नमस्कारः किंतु वाक्पूजा तमनतिक्रम्य पृष्टवन्त इत्यर्थः ॥ Rāghavānanda Sarasvatī on *Manu* 1.1 (Dave 1972)
Rāghavānanda Sarasvatī's view that the sages paid only verbal respects because Manu was a kṣatriya presumes that varṇa conventions in the context of devatas and divine beings (such as Svāyambhuva-Manu) will be same as the varṇa conventions that exist in the case of humans. This could lead to a possible objection that Manu's teaching of *dharma* to brāhmaṇa sages can imply a kṣatriya doing adhyāpana to a brāhmaṇa which violates the śāstra stipulation that adhyāpana is the special duty of brāhmaṇas and not others. This objection could be answered in the following ways: First, just like the non-traivarṇika Sūta of Bhāgavata Purāṇa answered queries of ṛṣis, or the kṣatriya king Janaka taught a brāhmaṇa when requested by him, etcetera, so did Svāyambhuva-Manu. Second, *Manusmṛti* 2.238 itself says that the knowledge of Paradharma should be taken even from an antya, and as Paradharma (mokṣa) is connected with Aparadharma (abhyudaya), where the latter constitutes the limb of the former and paves the way for the former, there's no problem in Manu expounding on *dharma* to ṛṣis. In fact, Manu explicitly locates the teachings of *dharma* within the larger

context of Paradharma through his discourse on cosmogony in the first chapter itself. We have the example of Dharmavyadha giving upadesha on *dharma* in Mahābhārata as well. Third, Manu did not take the ṛṣis as his formal śiṣyas (via upanayana etc.) to teach them *dharma*. So the issue of adhyāpana by a non-brāhmaṇa doesn't exist in this case. It is a case of *dharma* Upadesha and not *dharma* adhyāpana. However, it is important to note that the underlying assumption which guides Rāghavānanda Sarasvatī's view, namely the varṇa conventions will be exactly same in both human context and in context of divine beings has not been substantiated by him. There is no basis to assume that they will be exactly same in all respects. In fact, while the śāstras enunciate human duties interms of varṇa-*dharma*, they do not enunciate similar duties to devatas who are also classified into different *varṇas*. Moreover, even in the ritualistic context where varṇa discourse originates for both human and divine context, there is a difference in the way they are conceptualized for the two groups (See Appendix I). Therefore, while there is definitely some basis within the text that sages indeed paid verbal respects as we see from verse 1.3 and this could well point towards brāhmaṇa-kṣatriya interaction as put forth by Rāghavānanda Sarasvatī, this author believes that there is an ambiguity associated with this interpretation and thus, this instance should not be taken as evidence for equating in toto the varṇa conventions in human context with the varṇa conventions in the context of divine beings.

*nyāyo'tra kṣatriyeṣu brāhmaṇādīnāṃ na namaskāraḥ kiṃtu vākpūjā tamanatikramya pṛṣṭavanta ityarthaḥ* ||

161 यथान्यायं येन न्यायेन विधानेन प्रश्नः कर्तुंयुज्यते प्रणतिभक्तिश्रद्धाऽतिशयादिना। Kullūka Bhaṭṭa on *Manu* 1.1 (Kaundinyayana 2014)

*yathānyāyaṃ yena nyāyena vidhānena praśnaḥ kartuṃyujyate praṇatibhaktiśraddhā'tiśayādinā* |

162 इदं ते नातपस्काय नाभक्ताय कदाचन।
न चाशुश्रूषवे वाच्यं न च मां योऽभ्यसूयति॥ *Bhagavad Gītā* 18.67 (Gambhirananda 1998)
*idaṃ te nātapaskāya nābhaktāya kadācana* |
*na cāśuśrūṣave vācyaṃ na ca māṃ yo'bhyasūyati* ||

163 नाविरतो दुश्चरितान्नाशान्तो नासमाहितः ।
नाशान्तमानसो वापि प्रज्ञानेनैनमाप्नुयात् ॥ *Kaṭha Upaniṣad* 1.2.24 (Gambhirananda 1957)
*nāvirato duścaritānnāśānto nāsamāhitaḥ* |
*nāśāntamānaso vāpi prajñānenainamāpnuyāt* ||

164 आचार्यपुत्रः शुश्रूषुर्ज्ञानदो धार्मिकः शुचिः ।
आप्तः शक्तोऽर्थदः साधुः स्वोऽध्याप्या दश धर्मतः॥ *Kurma Purāṇa* 1.2.14.39 cited in *Parāśara Mādhava Ācāra Khaṇḍa* (Tripati, Parasharamadhava: Acharakhandam 2019)
*ācāryaputraḥ śuśrūṣuḥ karniṣṭho dhārmikaḥ śuciḥ* |
*āptaḥ śakto'rthadaḥ sādhuḥ svo'dhyāpyā daśa dharmataḥ* ||

165 आचार्यपुत्रः शुश्रूषुर्ज्ञानदो धार्मिकः शुचिः ।
आप्तः शक्तोऽर्थदः साधुः स्वोऽध्याप्या दश धर्मतः ॥ *Manusmṛti* 2.109 (Kaundinyayana 2014)
*ācāryaputraḥ śuśrūṣurjñānado dhārmikaḥ śuciḥ* |
*āptaḥ śakto›rthadaḥ sādhuḥ svo'dhyāpyā daśa dharmataḥ* ||

166 एवम् आचारसंपन्नम् आत्मवन्तम् अदाम्भिकम् ।
वेदम् अध्यापयेद् धर्म पुराणाङ्गानि नित्यशः॥ *Kurma Purāṇa* 1.2.14.37 cited in *Parāśara Mādhava Ācāra Khaṇḍa* (Tripati, Parasharamadhava: Acharakhandam 2019)

*evam ācārasampannam ātmavantam adāmbhikam |*
*vedam adhyāpayed dharma purāṇāṅgāni nityaśaḥ ||*

167 कृतज्ञश् च तथाद्रोही मेधावी शुभकृत्तरः |
आप्तः प्रियोऽथ विधिवत् षड् अध्याप्या द्विजोत्तमैः|| *Kurma Purāṇa* 1.2.14.40 cited in *Parāśara Mādhava Ācāra Khaṇḍa* (Tripati, Parasharamadhava: Acharakhandam 2019)
*kṛtajñaś ca tathādrohī medhāvī śubhakṛttaraḥ |*
*āptaḥ priyo'tha vidhivat ṣaḍ adhyāpyā dvijottamaiḥ ||*

168 नाऽपृष्टः कस्य चिद् ब्रूयान्न चान्यायेन पृच्छतः ।
जानन्नपि हि मेधावी जडवल्लोक आचरेत् ॥ *Manusmṛti* 2.110 (Kaundinyayana 2014)
*nā'pṛṣṭaḥ kasya cid brūyānna cānyāyena pṛcchataḥ* ।
*jānannapi hi medhāvī jaḍavalloka ācaret* ॥

169 अधर्मेण च यः प्राह यश्चाऽधर्मेण पृच्छति ।
तयोरन्यतरः प्रैति विद्वेषं वाऽधिगच्छति ॥ *Manusmṛti* 2.111 (Kaundinyayana 2014)
*adharmeṇa ca yaḥ prāha yaścā'dharmeṇa pṛcchati* ।
*tayoranyataraḥ praiti vidveṣaṃ vā'dhigacchati* ॥

170 तेन सह वचनसंदर्भरूपस्य मानवशास्त्रस्य प्रतिपाद्यप्रतिपादकलक्षणःसंवन्धः, प्रमाणान्तराऽसन्निकृष्टस्य स्वर्गापवर्गादिसाधनस्य धर्मस्य शास्त्रैकगम्यत्वात्। प्रयोजनं तु स्वर्गापवर्गादि तस्य धर्माधीनत्वात्। Kullūka Bhaṭṭa on *Manu* 1.1 (Kaundinyayana 2014)
*tena saha vacanasaṃdarbharūpasya mānavaśāstrasya pratipādyapratipādakalakṣaṇaḥ saṃvandhaḥ, pramāṇāntarā'sannikṛṣṭasya svargāpavargādisādhanasya dharmasya śāstraikagamyatvāt। prayojanaṃ tu svargāpavargādi tasya dharmādhīnatvāt।*

171 *Vaiśeṣika Sūtra* 1.1.2 defines *dharma* as those actions which yield material and spiritual attainments.

172 Puruṣārtha refers to four goals of life. They are *dharma* (righteous duties), artha (wealth, power, and prosperity), kāma (worldly desires), and mokṣa (final liberation).

173 In *Parāśara Smṛti* 1.1.2, 'hitam' or well-being is indicated as the prayojana of the smṛti text. Śrī Mādhavācārya in his commentary notes that *dharma* is the means to attain the desired fruits. Such attainment itself constitutes the 'well-beingness' of *dharma*. He further notes that desired fruits can be classified into two kinds: '*aihika*' or 'this-worldly' (i.e. fruits enjoyed in this world) and '*āmuṣmika*' or 'other-worldly' (i.e. fruits enjoyed after death in other worlds). The otherworldly fruits are two types: abhyudaya and niḥśreyasa. While abhyudaya refers to attainment of puṇyam (karmic merit) which is directly caused by practice of *dharma*, niḥśreyasa refers to attainment of ultimate knowledge of reality (i.e., mokṣa) which is indirectly accomplished by practice of *dharma*. This is equally applicable to Manu and other texts in the Smṛti genre.

174 चतुर्भिः पदश्लोकैर् विशिष्टकर्तृत्वम् अनन्यप्रमाणवेद्यपुरुषार्थोपदेशकत्वं Medhātithi on *Manu* 1.1 (Dave 1972)
*caturbhiḥ padaślokair viśiṣṭakartṛtvam ananyapramāṇavedyapuruṣārthopadeśakatvaṃ*

175 ऋतुकालाभिगामी स्यात् स्वदारनिरतः सदेत्यृतुकालादिनियमेन सोऽपि धर्म एव । Kullūka Bhaṭṭa on *Manu* 1.1 (Kaundinyayana 2014)
*ṛtukālābhigāmī syāt svadāraniratah sadetyṛtukālādiniyamena so'pi dharma eva* ।

176 ऋतुकालाऽभिगामी स्यात् स्वदारनिरतः सदा ।
पर्ववर्जं व्रजेच्चैनां तद्व्रतो रतिकाम्यया ॥ *Manusmṛti* 3.45
(Kaundinyayana 2014)
*ṛtukālā'bhigāmī syāt svadāraniratah̩ sadā* ।
*parvavarjaṃ vrajeccaināṃ tadvrato ratikāmyayā* ॥

177 एवं चार्थार्जनमपि ऋताऽमृताभ्यां जीवेदित्यादिनियमेन
धर्मएवेत्यवगन्तव्यम् । Kullūka Bhaṭṭa on *Manu* 1.1
(Kaundinyayana 2014)
*evaṃ cārthārjanamapi ṛtā'mṛtābhyāṃ jīvedityādiniyamena*
*dharmaevetyavagantavyam* ।

178 ऋताऽमृताभ्यां जीवेत् तु मृतेन प्रमृतेन वा ।
सत्याऽनृताभ्यामपि वा न श्ववृत्त्या कदा चन ॥
ऋतमुञ्छशिलं ज्ञेयममृतं स्यादयाचितम् ।
मृतं तु याचितं भैक्षं प्रमृतं कर्षणं स्मृतम् ॥
सत्याऽनृतं तु वाणिज्यं तेन चैवापि जीव्यते ।
सेवा श्ववृत्तिराख्याता तस्मात् तां परिवर्जयेत् ॥ *Manusmṛti* 4.4-6
(Kaundinyayana 2014)
*ṛtā'mṛtābhyāṃ jīvet tu mṛtena pramṛtena vā* ।
*satyā'nṛtābhyāmapi vā na śvavṛttyā kadā cana* ॥
*ṛtamuñchaśilaṃ jñeyamamṛtaṃ syādayācitam* ।
*mṛtaṃ tu yācitaṃ bhaikṣaṃ pramṛtaṃ karṣaṇaṃ smṛtam* ॥
*satyā'nṛtaṃ tu vāṇijyaṃ tena caivāpi jīvyate* ।
*sevā śvavṛttirākhyātā tasmāt tāṃ parivarjayet* ॥

The five ways are called as the: *Ruta* (truth), *Amrta* (nectar), *Mrta* (death), *Pramrta* (super-death), and *Satya-anruta* (truth and falsehood). Gleaning and picking is known as 'Truth'; and what is obtained unasked, 'Nectar'; alms obtained by begging is 'Death'; and cultivation is declared to be 'Super-death'. Trade is 'Truth and Falsehood'. A brāhmaṇa can obtain livelihood in any of the five modes, however, 'Truth' and 'Nectar' are more superior means for gaining livelihood than the other three, with 'Truth and Falsehood' being the most inferior of the five paths.

179 Śrī Jnanandanda Bharathi says, 'The (Vedic) sentence does not command or compel anybody to do anything but only says that Svarga is an object that can be secured by the performance of the Jyotishtoma sacrifice…therefore, the Sastras are eternal, not because they originated with the beginning of time itself, but because they lay down the eternal relationship between a cause and its effect. If a flame scorches our hand, it is not because the science of physics or chemistry says that it shall so scorch, but because there is an eternal relationship between fire and its effect, scorching (Bharathi 1969, 18).'

180 मिथ्याज्ञाननिवर्तकत्वव्यतिरेकेणाकारकत्वमित्यवोचाम । न च वचनं वस्तुनः सामर्थ्यजनकम् । ज्ञापकं हि शास्त्रं न कारकमिति स्थितिः । *Śaṅkara-Bhāṣya* on *Bṛhadāraṇyaka Upaniṣad* 1.4.10 (S Madhavananda 1950)
*mithyājñānanivartakatvavyatirekeṇākārakatvamityavocāma । na ca vacanaṃ vastunaḥ sāmarthyajanakam । jñāpakaṃ hi śāstraṃ na kārakamiti sthitiḥ ।*

181 तच्च वेदस्मृत्योर् धर्मं प्रति ज्ञापकतयैव,न निर्वर्तकतया,न च स्थितिहेतुतया,वृक्षस्येव| *Medhātithi* on *Manu* 2.6 (Dave 1972)
*tacca vedasmṛtyor dharmaṃ prati jñāpakatayaiva,na nirvartakatayā,na ca sthitihetutayā,vṛkṣasyeva|*

182 तस्माच्छास्त्रं प्रमाणं ते कार्याकार्यव्यवस्थितौ। ज्ञात्वा शास्त्रविधानोक्तं कर्म कर्तुमिहार्हसि।। *Bhagavad Gītā* 16.24 (Gambhirananda 1998)

*tasmācchāstraṃ pramāṇaṃ te kāryākāryavyavasthitau | jñātvā śāstravidhānoktaṃ karma kartumihārhasi* | |

183 Śrī Chandrashekara Bharati, the *Śaṅkarācārya* of Śrīngeri, in one of his conversations with a disciple notes: 'Religion does not fetter man's free-will. It leaves him quite free to act, but tells him at the same time what is good for him and what is not. The responsibility is entirely and solely his. He cannot escape it by blaming fate, for fate is of his own making, nor by blaming God, for he is but the dispenser of fruits in accordance with the merits of actions. You are the master of your own destiny. It is for you to make it, to better it or to mar it. This is your privilege. This is your responsibility.' (Aiyer 1956, 53)

184 पुरुषेच्छारागादिवैचित्र्याच्च — अनेका हि पुरुषाणामिच्छा ; रागादयश्च दोषा विचित्राः ; ततश्च बाह्यविषयरागाद्यपहृतचेतसो न शास्त्रं निवर्तयितुं शक्तम् ; नापि स्वभावतो बाह्यविषयविरक्तचेतसो विषयेषु प्रवर्तयितुं शक्तम् ; किन्तु शास्त्रात् एतावदेव भवति — इदमिष्टसाधनम् इदमनिष्टसाधनमिति साध्यसाधनसम्बन्धविशेषा भिव्यक्तिः — प्रदीपादिवत् तमसि रूपादिज्ञानम् ; न तु शास्त्रं भृत्यानिव बलात् निवर्तयति नियोजयति वा ; दृश्यन्ते हि पुरुषा रागादिगौरवात् शास्त्रमप्यतिक्रामन्तः । तस्मात् पुरुषमतिवैचित्र्यमपेक्ष्य साध्यसाधनसम्बन्धविशेषान् अनेकधा उपदिशति । तत्र पुरुषाः स्वयमेव यथारुचि साधनविशेषेषु प्रवर्तन्ते; शास्त्रं तु सवितृप्रदीपादिवत् उदास्त एव । *Śaṅkara-Bhāṣya* on *Bṛhadāraṇyaka Upaniṣad* verse 2.1.20 (Brihadaranyakopanishad-bhashyam n.d.) *puruṣecchārāgādivaicitryācca — anekā hi puruṣāṇāmicchā ; rāgādayaśca doṣā vicitrāḥ ; tataśca bāhyaviṣayarāgādyapahṛtacetaso na śāstraṃ nivartayituṃ śaktam ; nāpi svabhāvato bāhyaviṣayaviraktacetaso viṣayeṣu pravartayituṃ śaktam ; kintu śāstrāt etāvadeva bhavati — idamiṣṭasādhanam idamaniṣṭasādhanamiti*

*sādhyasādhanasambandhaviśeṣābhivyaktiḥ — pradīpādivat tamasi rūpādijñānam ; na tu śāstraṃ bhṛtyāniva balāt nivartayati niyojayati vā ; dṛśyante hi puruṣā rāgādigauravāt śāstramapyatikrāmantaḥ* । *tasmāt puruṣamativaicitryamapekṣya sādhyasādhanasambandhaviśeṣān anekadhā upadiśati* । *tatra puruṣāḥ svayameva yathāruci sādhanaviśeṣeṣu pravartante ; śāstraṃ tu savitṛpradīpādivat udāsta eva* ।

185 तस्य कर्मविवेकार्थं शेषाणामनुपूर्वशः ।
स्वायम्भुवो मनुर्धीमानिदं शास्त्रमकल्पयत् ॥
विदुषा ब्राह्मणेनेदमध्येतव्यं प्रयत्नतः ।
शिष्येभ्यश्च प्रवक्तव्यं सम्यङ् नाऽन्येन केन चित् ॥
इदं शास्त्रमधीयानो ब्राह्मणः शंसितव्रतः ।
मनोवाग्देहजैर्नित्यं कर्मदोषैर्न लिप्यते ॥ *Manusmṛti* 1.102-104 (Kaundinyayana 2014)
*tasya karmavivekārthaṃ śeṣāṇāmanupūrvaśaḥ* ।
*svāyambhuvo manurdhīmānidaṃ śāstramakalpayat* ॥
*viduṣā brāhmaṇenedamadhyetavyaṃ prayatnataḥ* ।
*śiṣyebhyaśca pravaktavyaṃ samyaṅ nā'nyena kena cit* ॥
*idaṃ śāstramadhīyāno brāhmaṇaḥ śaṃsitavrataḥ* ।
*manovāgdehajairnityaṃ karmadoṣairna lipyate* ॥

186 निषेकादिश्मशानान्तो मन्त्रैर्यस्योदितो विधिः ।
तस्य शास्त्रेऽधिकारोऽस्मिन् ज्ञेयो नाऽन्यस्य कस्य चित् ॥ *Manusmṛti* 2.16 (Kaundinyayana 2014)
*niṣekādiśmaśānānto mantrairyasyodito vidhiḥ* ।
*tasya śāstre'dhikāro'smin jñeyo nā'nyasya kasya cit* ॥

187 न शूद्राय मतिं दद्यान्नोच्छिष्टं न हविष्कृतम् ।
न चाऽस्योपदिशेद् धर्मं न चाऽस्य व्रतमादिशेत् ॥ *Manusmṛti* 4.80 (Kaundinyayana 2014)

*na śūdrāya matiṃ dadyānnocchiṣṭaṃ na haviṣkṛtam* ।
*na cā'syopadiśed dharmaṃ na cā'sya vratamādiśet* ॥

188 अधीयीरंस्त्रयो वर्णाः स्वकर्मस्था द्विजातयः ।
प्रब्रूयाद् ब्राह्मणस्त्वेषां नेत्राविति निश्चयः ॥
सर्वेषां ब्राह्मणो विद्याद् वृत्त्युपायान् यथाविधि ।
प्रब्रूयादितरेभ्यश्च स्वयं चैव तथा भवेत् ॥ *Manusmṛti* 10.1-2
(Kaundinyayana 2014)
*adhīyīraṃstrayo varṇāḥ svakarmasthā dvijātayaḥ* ।
*prabrūyād brāhmaṇas teṣāṃ netarāviti niścayaḥ* ॥
*sarveṣāṃ brāhmaṇo vidyād vṛttyupāyān yathāvidhi* ।
*prabrūyāditarebhyaśca svayaṃ caiva tathā bhavet* ॥

189 अर्थकामेष्वसक्तानां धर्मज्ञानं विधीयते ।
धर्मं जिज्ञासमानानां प्रमाणं परमं श्रुतिः ॥ *Manusmṛti* 2.13
(Kaundinyayana 2014)
*arthakāmeṣvasaktānāṃ dharmajñānaṃ vidhīyate* ।
*dharmaṃ jijñāsamānānāṃ pramāṇaṃ paramaṃ śrutiḥ* ॥

190 तपोविशेषैर्विविधैर्व्रतैश्च विधिचोदितैः ।
वेदः कृत्स्नोऽधिगन्तव्यः सरहस्यो द्विजन्मना ॥ *Manusmṛti* 2.165
(Kaundinyayana 2014)
*tapoviśeṣairvividhairvrataiśca vidhicoditaiḥ* ।
*vedaḥ kṛtsno'dhigantavyaḥ sarahasyo dvijanmanā* ॥

191 वेदस्वीकरणं पूर्वं विचारोऽभ्यसनं जपः |
ततो दानञ् च शिष्येभ्यो वेदाभ्यासो हि पञ्चधा || *Dakṣa Smṛti* 2.26
(Piovano 2002)
*vedasvīkaraṇaṃ pūrvaṃ vicāro'bhyasanaṃ japaḥ* |
*tato dānañ ca śiṣyebhyo vedābhyāso hi pañcadhā* ||

192 ततोऽभिवादयेद्वृद्धानसावहमिति ब्रुवन् ।
गुरुं चैवाप्युपासीत स्वाध्यायार्थं समाहितः ॥
आहूतश्चाप्यधीयीत लब्धं चास्मै निवेदयेत् ।
हितं तस्याचरेन्नित्यं मनोवाक्कायकर्मभिः ॥

कृतज्ञाद्रोहिमेधाविशुचिकल्पानसूयकाः ।
अध्याप्या धर्मतः साधुशक्ताप्तज्ञानवित्तदाः ॥
दण्डाजिनोपवीतानि मेखलां चैव धारयेत् ।
ब्राह्मणेषु चरेद्भैक्षमनिन्द्येष्वात्मवृत्तये ॥ *Yājñavalkya Smṛti* 1.26-29 (Pansikar 1936)
*tato'bhivādayedvruddhānasāvahamiti bruvan* |
*guruṃ caivāpyupāsīta svādhyāyārthaṃ samāhitaḥ* ||
*āhūtaścāpyadhīyīta labdhaṃ cāsmai nivedayet* |
*hitaṃ tasyācarennityaṃ manovākkāyakarmabhiḥ* ||
*kṛtajñādrohimedhāviśucikalpānasūyakāḥ* |
*adhyāpyā dharmataḥ sādhuśaktāptajñānavittadāḥ* ||
*daṇḍājinopavītāni mekhalāṃ caiva dhārayet* |
*brāhmaṇeṣu caredbhaikṣamanindyeṣvātmavṛttaye* ||

193 उभे संध्ये रविं भूप तथैवाग्निं समाहितः |
उपतिष्ठेत् तथा कुर्याद् गुरोरप्यभिवादनम् ||
स्थिते तिष्ठेद् व्रजेत् याते नीचैरासीत चासने |
शिष्यो गुरोर् नरश्रेष्ठ प्रतिकूलं न संचरेत् ||
तेनैवोक्तः पठेद् वेदं नान्यचित्तः पुरःस्थितः |
अनुज्ञातश् च भिक्षान्नम् अश्नीयात् गुरुणा ततः ||
व्रतानि चरता ग्राह्यो वेदश् च कृतबुद्धिना || *Viṣṇu Purāṇa* 3.9.2–5 cited in *Parāśara Mādhava Ācāra Khaṇḍa* (Tripati, Parasharamadhava: Acharakhandam 2019, 99)
*ubhe saṃdhye raviṃ bhūpa tathaivāgniṃ samāhitaḥ* |
*upatiṣṭhet tathā kuryād gurorapyabhivādanam* ||
*sthite tiṣṭhed vrajet yāte nīcairāsīta cāsane* |
*śiṣyo guror naraśreṣṭha pratikūlaṃ na saṃcaret* ||

*tenaivoktaḥ paṭhed vedaṃ nānyacittaḥ puraḥsthitaḥ* |
*anujñātaś ca bhikṣānnam aśnīyāt guruṇā tataḥ* ||
*vratāni caratā grāhyo vedaś ca kṛtabuddhinā* ||

194 Śrī Mādhavācārya (Vidyāraṇya Svāmī) in his *Parāśara Mādhava* (*Ācāra Khaṇḍa*, *Prathama Adhyāya*) (Tripati, Parasharamadhava: Acharakhandam 2019, 100), while commenting on the verse 1.36 of *Parāśara Smṛti* quotes a verse from *Bṛhaspati* which says that a father should, after properly performing the Saṃskāra (i.e., upanayana) of his son, engage the son in the study of the *Veda* and then in the study of Shastras like *Manu*, etc. Since a brāhmaṇa has *Veda* as his foundation, the Śruti, smṛti, and sadācāra—all the three are always situated in him.

195 As per the *Mīmāṁsā* principles, the verses *Manu* 2.165 constitute a niyama vidhi or restrictive injunction which stipulates that a particular action must be done in a particular way and not in other ways. In this case, the niyama vidhi restricts the method of study of *Veda*, etcetera by the dvijas to one which involves practice of various austerities and observances and not otherwise. This niyama vidhi when implemented generates what *Mīmāṁsā* calls as niyama-apūrva or the 'invisible result arising from implementation of restrictive injunction'. This apūrva or invisible result is positive and beneficial to the practitioner and hence can be designated as puṇyam. In this case, complete understanding and competency to practice constitutes puṇyam. The violation of niyama-apūrva leads to non-arising of this puṇyam resulting in non-generation of competency for practice and non-perfection of knowledge. For a discussion about whether the vidhi stipulating adhyayana in *Veda,* etcetera constitute niyama vidhi and whether such adhyayana generates niyama-apūrva,

see *Jaiminiya Nyāyamālā* of Mādhavācārya on '*athāto dharma jijñāsā*' *Sūtra* of *Jaimini*.

196 अध्ययनन्तु नित्यम् | अकरणे प्रत्यवायस्य मनुना स्मृतत्वात् | *Parāśara Mādhava*, *Ācāra Khaṇḍa*, *Prathama Adhyāya* (Tripati, Parasharamadhava: Acharakhandam 2019, 97) *adhyayanantu nityam | akaraṇe pratyavāyasya manunā smṛtatvāt*

197 '*Vedādhyayana* is characterised by a śiṣya listening to his Guru reciting the *Veda* and then repeating the same. It is not learning with the aid of recorded sound.'- Śrīmad Abhinava Vidyātīrtha Svāmī, the erstwhile pontiff of the Śriṅgeri Pīṭha (Exalting Elucidations 2004, 191).

198 This distinction between adhyayana type of study and non-adhyayana type of study is indicated by Vācaspati Miśra in his *Bhāmatī* subcommentary on *Brahmasūtraśāṅkarabhāṣya* on *Brahmasūtra* verse 1.3.34 wherein he says that although a Śūdra may learn the meaning of *Veda*s by studying books, it won't provide him the phala (puṇyam) of that study, and hence he doesn't have adhikāra in *Brahmavidyā* (Brahmasutra-bhashya Bhamati-vyakkya n.d.). Similar views are expressed by other commentators like Rāmānanda Sarasvatī on *Brahmasūtraśāṅkarabhāṣya* on the said verse.

199 *Smṛtimuktāphala*, *varṇa-āśrama Khaṇḍa* 35.11 says, 'The bar on teaching *dharma* to śūdra relates to *dharma* like *Vedic Agnihotra* etcetera; as it is stated, "with brāhmaṇa in front, Itihāsas and Purāṇas can be told to all the four *varṇas*", listening to Itihāsas and Purāṇas is permissible for śūdra. Further, it must be stated that there is no bar in teaching śūdra about dharmas of śūdra expounded in smṛti (Kannan n.d.).'

200 *Manu* 10.75 clearly enunciates adhyāpana or Shastric teaching as one of the six duties of brāhmaṇas, the others being: studying, sacrificing for oneself, sacrificing for others, giving and receiving gifts. However, in 10.76, *Manu* notes that 'From among these six functions, three are his means of livelihood: viz., sacrificing for others, teaching, and receiving gifts from pure men (G Jha 1920).' Here, Medhātithi notes that 'The division of the functions into groups of three is for a distinct purpose. One group of three has been put forward as serving (temporal) ends, while the other is conducive to invisible (spiritual) ends (G Jha 1920).' Likewise, *Mitākṣarā*, (1.118) quotes this verse to the effect that three out of the six functions are conducive to merit and these are to be practised as means of livelihood; so that while the former are obligatory, the latter are not so (Pansikar 1936). But, we find that adhyāpana has been given as a niyama vidhi in *Taittirīya Upaniṣad* 1.11.1 itself. Therefore, apart from acting as a means of livelihood, adhyāpana generates niyama-apūrva or puṇyam when practiced by a brāhmaṇa.

201 Just as practice of niyama vidhi leads to niyama-apūrva of the form of puṇyam, the violation of niṣedha vidhi or prohibition leads to apūrva called as pāpam or karmic demerit.

202 धर्मशास्त्रोपदेशस् तदर्थव्याख्यानं वाऽनेन निषिध्यते शास्त्रद्वयेन "न चाऽस्योपदिशेत्" इति। एकेन शास्त्राध्ययनम् अपेरणार्थव्याख्यानम्। अग्रन्थकस् तूपदेशो न केनचिन् निषिद्धः। Medhātithi on *Manu* 4.80 (Dave 1972)

*dharmaśāstropadeśas tadarthavyākhyānaṃ vā'nena niṣidhyate śāstradvayena "na cā'syopadiśet" iti | ekena śāstrādhyayanam aperaṇārthavyākhyānam | agranthakas tūpadeśo na kenacin niṣiddhaḥ |*

203 अन्ये तु पार्वणश्राद्धपाकयज्ञादिष्वितिकर्तव्यतां न शिक्षयेत् याजकत्वादिरूपेणेत्याहुः | Medhātithi on *Manu* 4.80 (Dave 1972)
*anye tu pārvaṇaśrāddhapākayajñādiṣvitikartavyatāṃ na śikṣayet yājakatvādirūpeṇetyāhuḥ* |

204 A śūdra however is entitled to perform saṁskāras without mantras as noted in *Manu* 10.127 and other rituals that are prescribed in Purāṇas or perform rituals using *paurāṇika* mantras.

205 युक्तम् एतत्, यदि कश्चिन् न ब्रूयात् प्रधानेऽनधिकृतस्य कुतोऽङ्गेषु प्राप्तिरिति | वेदः स्मृतिशास्त्रे च प्रधानम् | न च तत्र शूद्रस्याधिकारः| Medhātithi on *Manu* 4.80 (Dave 1972)
*yuktam etat, yadi kaścin na brūyāt pradhāne 'nadhikṛtasya kuto 'ṅgeṣu prāptiriti* | *vedaḥ smṛtiśāstre ca pradhānam* | *na ca tatra śūdrasyādhikāraḥ* |

206 धर्मोपदेशो न शूद्रस्य कर्तव्यः व्रतंचाऽस्य प्रायश्चित्तरूपंसाक्षान्नोपदिशेत् किंतु ब्राह्मणंमध्ये कृत्वा तदुपदेशव्यवधानात् । यथाऽऽहाऽङ्गिराः तथा शूद्रंसमासाद्य सदा धर्मपुरःसरम् । अन्तरा ब्राह्मणं कृत्वा प्रायश्चित्तंसमादिशेत् ॥ Kullūka Bhaṭṭa on *Manu* 4.80 (Kaundinyayana 2014)
*dharmopadeśo na śūdrasya kartavyaḥ vrataṃcā'sya prāyaścittarūpaṃsākṣānnopadiśet kiṃtu brāhmaṇaṃmadhye kṛtvā tadupadeśavyavadhānāt* । *yathā"hā'ṅgirāḥ tathā śūdraṃsamāsādya sadā dharmapuraḥsaram* । *antarā brāhmaṇaṃ kṛtvā prāyaścittaṃsamādiśet* ॥

207 तद् अन्तरा ब्राह्मणम् अकुर्वतां प्रायश्चित्तात्मकव्रतातिदेशनिषेधपरम् | Aparārka on *Yājñavalkya Smṛti* 3.262 (H. N. Apate 1903)
*tad antarā brāhmaṇam akurvatāṃ prāyaścittātmakavratātideśaniṣedhaparam* ॥

208 मनुरपि द्विजातीनां धर्मशास्त्राध्यायनेऽधिकारो ब्राह्मणस्य प्रवचने नान्यस्येति दर्शयति | *Mitākṣarā* on *Yājñavalkya Smṛti* 1.3 (Pansikar 1936)
*manurapi dvijātīnāṃ dharmaśāstrādhyāyane'dhikāro brāhmaṇasya pravacane nānyasyeti darśayati* |

209 शूद्रं प्रकृत्य यमः-"तस्मादस्याधिकारोऽस्ति न वेदेषु न तु स्मृतौ" इति।
*śūdraṃ prakṛtya yamaḥ-"tasmādasyādhikāro›sti na vedeṣu na tu smṛtau" iti* | *Smṛtimuktāphala, Varṇāśrama Khaṇḍa 9.6* (Gharpure 1937)

210 अधिकारिपर्यालोचनेनापि ॐकाराथशब्दयोरुक्तविषयव्यवस्था सिध्यति।...अथशब्दस्य पौरुषेयग्रन्थानाञ्च सर्ववर्णविषयत्वात् स एव तेषु योग्यः।
*adhikāriparyālocanenāpi oṃkārāthaśabdayoruktaviṣayavyavasthā sidhyati* |.
*athaśabdasya pauruṣeyagranthānāñca sarvavarṇaviṣayatvāt sa eva teṣu yogyaḥ* |

*Parāśara Mādhava, Ācāra Khaṇḍa, Prathama Adhyāya* (Tripati, Parasharamadhava: Acharakhandam 2019, 21)

211 श्रावयेच्चतुरो वर्णान्कृत्वा ब्राह्मणमग्रतः*Mahābhārata Śānti Parva* 314.45 (Mahabharata: Critical Edition Prepared by Scholars at Bhandarkar Oriental Research Institute BORI n.d.)
*śrāvayeccaturo varṇānkṛtvā brāhmaṇamagrataḥ*

212 'श्रावयेच्चतुरो वर्णान् कृत्वा ब्राह्मणमग्रतः।' इति इतिहासपुराणश्रवणे चातुर्वर्ण्याधिकारस्मरणेन पुराणाद्यवगतविद्यामाहात्म्यस्य तस्यापि तदर्थित्वसम्भवात् । *Śāstrasiddhāntaleśa Saṅgraha*, Third *Paricchedha, Vidyārthakarmasu Adhikārivicāraḥ* (Shastra

Siddantalesha Sangraha by Appayya Dikshita n.d.)
*śrāvayeccaturo varṇān kṛtvā brāhmaṇamagrataḥ* | ' *iti itihāsapurāṇaśravaṇe cāturvarṇyādhikārasmaraṇena purāṇādyavagatavidyāmāhātmyasya tasyāpi tadarthitvasambhavāt* |

213 'न शूद्राय मतिं दद्यात्, न चास्योपदिशेद्धर्ममित्यादि धर्मनिषेधः शूद्रानुपयोगि वैदिकाग्निहोत्रादिधर्मज्ञानविषयः । 'श्रावयेच्चतुरो वर्णान् कृत्वा ब्राह्मणमग्रत' इतीतिहासपुराणादि श्रवणस्य ब्राह्मणमुखेन शूद्रस्यापि विहितत्वात् । किञ्च स्मृत्युक्ते शूद्राणामप्युपदेशे प्रतिषेधाभावो वाच्यः।
*'na śūdrāya matiṃ dadyāt, na cāsyopadiśeddharma' mityādi dharmaniṣedhaḥ śūdrānupayogi vaidikāgnihotrādidharmajñānaviṣayaḥ* | *‹śrāvayeccaturo varṇān kṛtvā brāhmaṇamagrata› itītihāsapurāṇādi śravaṇasya brāhmaṇamukhena śūdrasyāpi vihitatvāt* | *kiñca smṛtyukte śūdrāṇāmapyupadeśe pratiṣedhābhāvo vācyaḥ* |
*Smṛtimuktāphala, Varṇāśrama Khaṇḍa 35.11* (Gharpure 1937)

214 शूद्राय मतिंदृष्टार्थोपदेशं न दद्यात् Kullūka Bhaṭṭa *on Manu 4.80* (Kaundinyayana 2014)
*śūdrāya matiṃdṛṣṭārthopadeśaṃ na dadyāt*

215 वृत्त्यर्थश् चायं निषेधः | सौहार्दादिना तु न दोषः | भवन्ति हि शूद्राः कुलमित्राणि | मैत्र्या चावश्यं हितम् उपदिश्यते | Medhātithi on *Manu* 4.80 (Dave 1972)
*vṛttyarthaś cāyaṃ niṣedhaḥ | sauhārdādinā tu na doṣaḥ | bhavanti hi śūdrāḥ kulamitrāṇi | maitryā cāvaśyaṃ hitam upadiśyate |*

216 सर्वेषां ब्राह्मणो विद्याद् वृत्त्युपायान् यथाविधि ।
प्रब्रूयादितरेभ्यश्च स्वयं चैव तथा भवेत् ॥ *Manusmṛti* 10.2

(Kaundinyayana 2014)
*sarveṣāṃ brāhmaṇo vidyād vṛttyupāyān yathāvidhi* |
*prabrūyāditarebhyaśca svayaṃ caiva tathā bhavet* ||

217 यथा यथा हि सद्वृत्तमातिष्ठत्यनसूयकः ।
तथा तथेमं चाऽमुं च लोकं प्राप्नोत्यनिन्दितः ॥ *Manusmṛti* 10.128
(Kaundinyayana 2014)
*yathā yathā hi sadvṛttamātiṣṭhatyanasūyakaḥ* |
*tathā tathemaṃ cā'muṃ ca lokaṃ prāpnotyaninditaḥ* ||

218 A summary of the story of Vyadha is given in Shivakumar GV's essay "Mahabharata Metaphors: Dharmavyadha imparts the Essence of the *Veda*s to Kaushika Part II (2020)."

219 ननु कथम् अध्ययनावबोधाधकिारनषिधे कर्माधकिारः| न ह्यवदितिकर्मरूपस्य तदनुष्ठानसंभव; न चाध्ययनम् अन्तरेण तदर्थावबोधसंभव; न चावैद्योऽधक्रियिते | Medhātithi on *Manu* 2.16 (Dave 1972)
*nanu katham adhyayanāvabodhādhikāraniṣedhe karmādhikāraḥ | na hyaviditakarmarūpasya tadanuṣṭhānasaṃbhavaḥ, na cādhyayanam antareṇa tadarthāvabodhasaṃbhavaḥ, na cāvaidyo 'dhikriyate |*

220 सत्यम् | परोपदेशादपि यावत्तावत्सिद्ध्यति परिज्ञानम् | यं ब्राह्मणमाश्रितः शूद्रो, यो वाऽर्थतः प्रवृत्तः स एनं शिक्षयिष्यतीदं कृत्वेदं कुर्विति | अतो न कर्मानुष्ठानप्रयुक्ते शूद्रस्याध्ययनवेदने, स्त्रीवत्परप्रत्ययादप्यनुष्ठानसिद्धेः | यथा स्त्रीणां भर्तृविद्यैव प्रसङ्गादुपकरोति न कर्मश्रुतयो विद्यां प्रयुञ्जते | Medhātithi on *Manu* 2.16 (Dave 1972)
*satyam | paropadeśādapi yāvattāvatsiddhyati parijñānam | yaṃ brāhmaṇamāśritaḥ śūdro, yo vā'rthataḥ pravṛttaḥ sa enaṃ śikṣayiṣyatīdaṃ kṛtvedaṃ kurviti | ato na karmānuṣṭhānaprayukte śūdrasyādhyayanavedane,*

*strīvatparapratyayādapyanuṣṭhānasiddheḥ | yathā strīṇāṃ bhartṛvidyaiva prasaṅgādupakaroti na karmaśrutayo vidyāṃ prayuñjate |*

221 That studying and teaching is a special duty of brāhmaṇas has been indicated in *Manusmṛti* in many places including verse 1.88 which says, 'To *brāhmaṇas* he assigned teaching and studying (the *Veda*) (G. Jha 1920).'

222 अर्थानुष्ठानं तु शास्त्रविषयः | तत्र चातुर्वर्णस्याधिकारः| Medhātithi on *Manu* 2.16 (Dave 1972)
*arthānuṣṭhānaṃ tu śāstraviṣayaḥ | tatra cāturvarṇasyādhikāraḥ |*

223 अमन्त्रिका तु कार्येयं स्त्रीणामावृदशेषतः ।
संस्कारार्थं शरीरस्य यथाकालं यथाक्रमम् ॥ *Manusmṛti* 2.66 (Kaundinyayana 2014)
*amantrikā tu kāryeyaṃ strīṇāmāvṛdaśeṣataḥ* ।
*saṃskārārthaṃ śarīrasya yathākālaṃ yathākramam* ॥

224 निषेकादिश्मशानान्तो मन्त्रैर्यस्योदितो विधिः ।
तस्य शास्त्रेऽधिकारोऽस्मिन् ज्ञेयो नाऽन्यस्य कस्यचित् ॥ *Manusmṛti* 2.16 (Kaundinyayana 2014)
*niṣekādiśmaśānānto mantrairyasyodito vidhiḥ* ।
*tasya śāstre'dhikāro'smin jñeyo nā'nyasya kasyacit* ॥

225 *Padma Purāṇa Svarga Khaṇḍa* 51.51-52 says *Agni* is *guru* of *dvijas*, *brāhmaṇa* is *guru* of all *varṇas*, the husband is the *guru* of women, and *atithi guru* of all. (Padma Purana [sanskrit] n.d.). Also see *Cāṇakya Nīti* 5.1.

226 द्विविधाः स्त्रियो ब्रह्मवादिन्यः सद्योवध्वश्च । तत्र ब्रह्मवादिनीनामग्नीन्धनं

वेदाध्ययनं स्वगृहे भिक्षाचर्येति । सद्योवधूनां तूपस्थिते विवाहे कथचिदुपनयनमात्रं कृत्वा विवाहः कार्य इति । *Hārīta Dharmasūtra* cited in *Vīramitrodaya, Saṁskāraprakāśa* (Viramitrodaya Vol 01 & Vol 02 n.d., 402)
*dvividhāḥ striyo brahmavādinyaḥ sadyovadhvaśca* । *tatra brahmavādinīnāmagnīndhanaṃ vedādhyayanaṃ svagṛhe bhikṣācaryeti* । *sadyovadhūnāṃ tūpasthite vivāhe kathacidupanayanamātraṃ kṛtvā vivāhaḥ kārya iti* ।

227 पुराकल्पे कुमारीणां मौञ्जीबन्धनमिष्यते । अध्यापनं च वेदानां सावित्रीवाचनं तथा ॥ पिता पितृव्यो भ्राता वा नैनामध्यापयेत्परः। स्वगृहे चैव कन्याया भैक्षचर्या विधीयते ॥ वर्जयेदजिनं चीरं जटाधारणमेवच ॥ *Yama Smṛti* cited in *Vīramitrodaya, Saṁskāraprakāśa* (Viramitrodaya Vol 01 & Vol 02 n.d., 402-403)
*purākalpe kumārīṇāṃ mauñjībandhanamiṣyate* । *adhyāpanaṃ ca vedānāṃ sāvitrīvācanaṃ tathā* ॥ *pitā pitṛvyo bhrātā vā naināmadhyāpayetparaḥ* । *svagṛhe caiva kanyāyā bhaikṣacaryā vidhīyate* ॥ *varjayedajinaṃ cīraṃ jaṭādhāraṇamevaca* ॥

228 स्त्रीशूद्रद्विजबन्धूनां त्रयी न श्रुतिगोचरा ।
कर्मश्रेयसि मूढानां श्रेय एवं भवेदिह ।
इति भारतमाख्यानं कृपया मुनिना कृतम् ॥ *Bhāgavata Purāṇa* 1.4.25 (Śrīmad-Bhāgavatam (Bhāgavata Purāṇa) n.d.)
*strīśūdradvijabandhūnāṃ trayī na śrutigocarā* ।
*karmaśreyasi mūḍhānāṃ śreya evaṃ bhavediha* ।
*iti bhāratamākhyānaṃ kṛpayā muninā kṛtam* ॥

229 नास्ति स्त्रीणां क्रिया मन्त्रैरिति धर्मे व्यवस्थितिः ।
निरिन्द्रिया ह्यमन्त्राश्च स्त्रीयोऽनृतमिति स्थितिः ॥ *Manusmṛti* 9.18 (Kaundinyayana 2014)
*nāsti strīṇāṃ kriyā mantrairiti dharme vyavasthitiḥ* ।

*nirindriyā hyamantrāśca strīyo'nṛtamiti sthitiḥ* ||

230 सावित्रीं प्रणवं यजुर्लक्ष्मीं स्त्रीशूद्राय नेच्छन्ति द्वात्रिंशदक्षरं साम जानीयाद्यो जानीते सोऽमृतत्वं च गच्छति सावित्रीं लक्ष्मीं यजुः प्रणवं यदि जानीयात्स्त्रीशूद्रः स मृतोऽधो गच्छति *Narasimha Purva Tapani Upaniṣad* 1.3 (V. G. Apate 1929)

*sāvitrīṃ praṇavaṃ yajurlakṣmīṃ strīśūdrāya necchanti dvātriṃśadakṣaraṃ sāma jānīyādyo jānīte so'mṛtatvaṃ ca gacchati sāvitrīṃ lakṣmīṃ yajuḥ praṇavaṃ yadi jānīyātstrīśūdraḥ sa mṛto'dho gacchati*

231 नास्ति स्त्रीणां पृथग् यज्ञो न व्रतं नाप्युपोषणम् ।
पतिं शुश्रूषते येन तेन स्वर्गे महीयते ॥ *Manusmṛti* 5.155 (Kaundinyayana 2014)

This verse appears as 5.153 in Ganganath Jha edition and as 5.155 in Kaundinyayana edition.

*nāsti strīṇāṃ pṛthag yajño na vrataṃ nāpyupoṣaṇam* |
*patiṃ śuśrūṣate yena tena svarge mahīyate* ||

देवपूजां नैव कुर्यात् स्त्री शूद्रस्तु पतिं विना ।
जपस्तपस्तीर्थसेवा प्रव्रज्यां मन्त्रसाधनम् ॥
न विद्यते पृथक् स्त्रीणां त्रिवर्गविधिसाधनम् । *Śukra Nīti* 4.4.5-6 (Misra 1968)

*devapūjāṃ naiva kuryāt strī śūdrastu patiṃ vinā* |
*japastapastīrthasevā pravrajyāṃ mantrasādhanam* ||
*na vidyate pṛthak strīṇāṃ trivargavidhisādhanam* |

नास्ति स्त्रीणां पृथग्यज्ञो न व्रतं नाप्युपोषितम् ।
पतिं शुश्रूषते यत्तु तेन स्वर्गे महीयते ॥ *Viṣṇu Smṛti* 25.15 (Jolly 1881)

*nāsti strīṇāṃ pṛthagyajño na vrataṃ nāpyupoṣitam* |
*patiṃ śuśrūṣate yattu tena svarge mahīyate* ||

232 वैवाहिको विधिः स्त्रीणां संस्कारो वैदिकः स्मृतः ।
पतिसेवा गुरौ वासो गृहार्थोऽग्निपरिक्रिया ॥ *Manusmṛti* 2.67
(Kaundinyayana 2014)
*vaivāhiko vidhiḥ strīṇāṃ saṃskāro vaidikaḥ smṛtaḥ* ।
*patisevā gurau vāso gṛhārtho'gniparikriyā* ॥

233 *Kauṇḍinya Nyāya* refers to the maxim of Kauṇḍinya. This maxim has its origin in the following story. There was a brāhmaṇa named Kauṇḍinya. On the occasion of a feast in which many brāhmaṇa*s* were invited, curdled milk was served to all except Kauṇḍinya for whom ghol (a variety of that milk) was provided. It is used to denote that exception proves the rule. See (Sanskrit Maxims and Proverbs Nyayavali n.d.).

234 See for example, *Vyoma Saṁhitā* quoted by Śrī Madhvācārya (*Ananda Tirtha*) in his commentary to *Brahmasūtra* 1.1.1 (Rau 1904). The said text notes that apart from dvija men only *uttama-strīs* are eligible for *Veda*-adhyayana, while women in general are eligible only for acquiring knowledge of Bhagavān's name, and for acquiring the knowledge of *Tantra* (acquired indirectly when they are in the same place where others who are independently qualified are being instructed, and not directly from the sacred text). With respect to the uttama-strīs or women of superior qualities, for the purpose of illustration with examples, *Vyoma Saṁhitā* notes 'such as Ūrvaśī, Yamī, Śacī, etc., and the rest.' Jayatīrtha in his *Tattva-Prakāśikā* sub-commentary on Madhvācārya's commentary on *Brahmasūtra*, glosses the phrase, 'and the rest' as 'the wives of the sages and women born in human and other kulas' indicating that these are exceptions (A S Rao 2020).

235 It is often not realised how significant the biological changes

that women experience due to menstruation and pregnancy are in the context of spiritual practice. The *upanayana*, for example, is a ritual of giving *mantra- dīkṣa* into *Gāyatrī-mantra*, which is to be practiced daily as part of one's *nitya karma*. This means one must practice *sandhyāvandana* and chant *Gāyatrī-mantra* as part of it by following all conditions of *śauca* (purity) each and every day without any break. However, women enter a state of *aśauca* or ritual impurity during monthly periods resulting in a break of all spiritual practices during that period. Likewise, there would be a long break during pregnancy, childbirth, and post-childbirth. These breaks imply that women cannot successfully practice *sandhyāvandana* as a *nitya-karma* without any breaks, thus diminishing the effectiveness of the *mantra-dīkṣā* given through upanayana. This is a practical difficulty that cannot be overcome due to the unique biological condition of women. It is for this reason that *Veda-adhyayana* and *Veda mantra* are prohibited for women. Instead, they are adviced to adopt those spiritual paths such as *pati-vrata-dharma* and *bhakti* in which these significant biological conditions do not act as obstacles, but they are actually conducive to women's spiritual pursuit. More details about how menstruation results in a temporary state of *aśauca* and what it implies, and how menstruation itself can be perceived as a process of austerity are available in Sridhar, *Menstruation Across Cultures: A Historical Perspective* (2018).

236 Medhātithi notes in his commentary to 2.16 that what helps women, is the learning of their husbands, which becomes available to them through companionship (G Jha 1920).

237 श्रेयान्स्वधर्मो विगुणः परधर्मात्स्वनुष्ठितात्।
स्वधर्मे निधनं श्रेयः परधर्मो भयावहः।। *Bhagavad Gītā* 3.35 (Gambhirananda 1998)
*śreyānsvadharmo viguṇaḥ paradharmātsvanuṣṭhitāt*।
*svadharme nidhanaṃ śreyaḥ paradharmo bhayāvahaḥ*।।

238 द्वये च प्रतिपत्तारः – न्यायप्रतिसरणाः प्रसिद्धिप्रतिसरणाश्च | तत्र मनुः "मनुर्वै यत्किंचावदत्तद्भेषज" मिति – "ऋचो यजूंषि सामानि मन्त्रा आथर्वणाश्च ये |सप्तर्षिभिस्तु यत्प्रोक्तं तत्सर्वं मनुरब्रवीदि" त्याद्यर्थवादेतिहासपुराणादिभ्यः प्रख्यातप्रभावः लोके तत्प्रसिद्ध्यैव वा निरूपितमूलजातेन प्रजापतिनैतत्प्रणीतमित्येतावतैव श्रोत्रियाः प्रवर्तन्त इति | तान्प्रति कर्तृविशेषसंबन्धोऽपि प्रवृत्त्यङ्गम् | Medhātithi on *Manu* 1.1 (Dave 1972)
*dvaye ca pratipattāraḥ – nyāyapratisaraṇāḥ prasiddhipratisaraṇāśca | tatra manuḥ "manurvai yatkiṃcāvadattadbheṣaja"miti – "ṛco yajūṃṣi sāmāni mantrā ātharvaṇāśca ye | saptarṣibhistu yatproktaṃ tatsarvaṃ manurabravīdi"tyādyarthavādetihāsapurāṇādibhyaḥ prakhyātaprabhāvaḥ loke tatprasiddhyaiva vā nirūpitamūlajātena prajāpatinaitatpraṇītamityetāvataiva śrotriyāḥ pravartanta iti | tānprati kartṛviśeṣasaṃbandho'pi pravṛttyaṅgam |*

239 ऐश्वर्यस्य समग्रस्य धर्मस्य यशसः श्रियः। ज्ञानवैराग्ययोश्चैव षण्णां भग इतीङ्गना ।। *Viṣṇu Purāṇa* 6.5.74 (Upreti, Visnumahapuranam of Maharsi *Veda*vyasa with Sanskrit Commentary "Atmaprakasha" of Sridharacharya Vol II 2011)
*aiśvaryasya samagrasya dharmasya yaśasaḥ śriyaḥ*।
*jñānavairāgyayoścaiva ṣaṇṇāṃ bhaga itīṅganā* ।।

240 उत्पत्तिं प्रलयं चैव भूतानामगतिं गतिम् । वेत्ति विद्यामविद्यां च स वाच्यो भगवानिति ।। *Viṣṇu Purāṇa* 6.5.78 (Upreti, Visnumahapuranam

of Maharsi *Veda*vyasa with Sanskrit Commentary "Atmaprakasha" of Sridharacharya Vol II 2011)
*utpattiṃ pralayaṃ caiva bhūtānāmagatiṃ gatim* | *vetti vidyāmavidyāṃ ca sa vācyo bhagavāniti* ||

241 ब्राह्मणः क्षत्रियो वैश्यस्त्रयो वर्णा द्विजातयः ।
चतुर्थ एकजातिस्तु शूद्रो नाऽस्ति तु पञ्चमः ॥ *Manusmṛti* 10.4 (Kaundinyayana 2014)
*brāhmaṇaḥ kṣatriyo vaiśyastrayo varṇā dvijātayaḥ* |
*caturtha ekajātistu śūdro nā'sti tu pañcamaḥ* ||

242 जन्मना ब्राह्मणो ज्ञेयः संस्कारैर्द्विज उच्यते ॥ विद्यया याति विप्रत्वं श्रोत्रियस्त्रिभिरेव च । वेदशास्त्राण्यधीते यः शास्त्रार्थञ्च निषेवते ।। *Atri Saṁhitā verse 140-141.* (The Smriti Sandarbha: Collection of the Ten Dharmashaśtric Texts by Maharshis Vol I 1952, 365)
*janmanā brāhmaṇo jñeyaḥ saṃskārairdvija ucyate* || *vidyayā yāti vipratvaṃ śrotriyastribhireva ca* | *vedaśāstrāṇyadhīte yaḥ śāstrārthañca niṣevate* ||

243 तपः श्रुतं च योनिश्च त्रयं ब्राह्मण्यकारणम्। तपःश्रुताभ्यां यो हीनो जातिब्राह्मण एव सः॥ *Śabdārthacintāmaṇi* cited in (Jatibrahmana n.d.)
*tapaḥ śrutaṃ ca yoniśca trayaṃ brāhmaṇyakāraṇam* |
*tapaḥśrutābhyāṃ yo hīno jātibrāhmaṇa eva saḥ* ||

244 तपोबीजप्रभावैस्तु ते गच्छन्ति युगे युगे ।
उत्कर्षं चाऽपकर्षं च मनुष्येष्विह जन्मतः ॥ *Manusmṛti* 10.42 (Kaundinyayana 2014)
*tapobījaprabhāvaistu te gacchanti yuge yuge* |
*utkarṣaṃ cā'pakarṣaṃ ca manuṣyeṣviha janmataḥ* ||

245 सर्ववर्णेषु तुल्यासु पत्नीष्वक्षतयोनिषु ।
आनुलोम्येन सम्भूता जात्या ज्ञेयास्त एव ते ॥ *Manusmṛti* 10.5
(Kaundinyayana 2014)
*sarvavarṇeṣu tulyāsu patnīṣvakṣatayoniṣu* ।
*ānulomyena sambhūtā jātyā jñeyāsta eva te* ॥

246 तद्य इह रमणीयचरणा अभ्याशो ह यत्ते रमणीयां योनिमापद्येरन्ब्राह्मणयोनिं वा क्षत्रिययोनिं वा वैश्ययोनिं वाथ य इह कपूयचरणा अभ्याशो ह यत्ते कपूयां योनिमापद्येरञ्श्वयोनिं वा सूकरयोनिं वा चण्डालयोनिं वा ॥ *Chāndogya Upaniṣad* verse 5.10.7 (Lokeswarananda 1998)
*tadya iha ramaṇīyacaraṇā abhyāśo ha yatte ramaṇīyāṃ yonimāpadyeranbrāhmaṇayoniṃ vā kṣatriyayoniṃ vā vaiśyayoniṃ vātha ya iha kapūyacaraṇā abhyāśo ha yatte kapūyāṃ yonimāpadyerañśvayoniṃ vā sūkarayoniṃ vā caṇḍālayoniṃ vā* ॥

247 चातुर्वर्ण्यं मया सृष्टं गुणकर्मविभागशः।
तस्य कर्तारमपि मां विद्ध्यकर्तारमव्ययम्।। *Bhagavad Gītā* 4.13
(Gambhirananda 1998)
*cāturvarṇyaṃ mayā sṛṣṭaṃ guṇakarmavibhāgaśaḥ*।
*tasya kartāramapi māṃ viddhyakartāramavyayam*।।

ब्राह्मणक्षत्रियविशां शूद्राणां च परंतप।
कर्माणि प्रविभक्तानि स्वभावप्रभवैर्गुणैः।। *Bhagavad Gītā* 18.41
(Gambhirananda 1998)
*brāhmaṇakṣatriyaviśāṃ śūdrāṇāṃ ca paraṃtapa*।
*karmāṇi pravibhaktāni svabhāvaprabhavairguṇaiḥ*।।

248 विप्रक्षत्रियविट्शूद्रा मुखबाहूरुपादजा: ।
वैराजात् पुरुषाज्जाता य आत्माचारलक्षणा: ॥ *Bhāgavata Purāṇa* 11.17.13 (Śrīmad-Bhāgavatam (Bhāgavata Purāṇa) n.d.)

*viprakṣatriyaviṭśūdrā mukhabāhūrupādajā:* ।
*vairājāt puruṣājjātā ya ātmācāralakṣaṇā:* ॥

249 तत्र सात्त्विकस्य सत्त्वप्रधानस्य ब्राह्मणस्य 'शमो दमस्तपः' इत्यादीनि कर्माणि, सत्त्वोपसर्जनरजःप्रधानस्य क्षत्रियस्य शौर्यतेजःप्रभृतीनि कर्माणि, तमउपसर्जनरजःप्रधानस्य वैश्यस्य कृष्यादीनि कर्माणि, रजउपसर्जनतमःप्रधानस्य शूद्रस्य शुश्रूषैव कर्म इत्येवं गुणकर्मविभागशः चातुर्वर्ण्यं मया सृष्टम् इत्यर्थः । *Śaṅkara-Bhāṣya* on *Bhagavad Gītā* 4.13 (Srimad-Bhagavadgita-bhashya n.d.)
*tatra sāttvikasya sattvapradhānasya brāhmaṇasya 'śamo damastapaḥ› ityādīni karmāṇi, sattvopasarjanarajaḥpradhānasya kṣatriyasya śauryatejaḥprabhṛtīni karmāṇi, tamaupasarjanarajaḥpradhānasya vaiśyasya kṛṣyādīni karmāṇi, rajaupasarjanatamaḥpradhānasya śūdrasya śuśrūṣaiva karma ityevaṃ guṇakarmavibhāgaśaḥ cāturvarṇyaṃ mayā sṛṣṭam ityarthaḥ* ।

250 सर्वस्याऽस्य तु सर्गस्य गुप्त्यर्थं स महाद्युतिः ।
मुखबाहूरुपज्जानां पृथक्कर्माण्यकल्पयत् ॥ *Manusmṛti* 1.87 (Kaundinyayana 2014)
*sarvasyā'sya tu sargasya guptyarthaṃ sa mahādyutiḥ* ।
*mukhabāhūrupajjānāṃ pṛthakkarmāṇyakalpayat* ॥

251 *Mahābhārata Anuśāsanaparva* 131.51-52 for example states: "O Goddess, wherever pure *Brahman* devoid of qualities exists, such a person is a *brāhmaṇa* with the fruits of birth serving the purpose of classification" See *Bṛhadāraṇyaka Upaniṣad* 1.4.11-15 for a detailed treatment. All these have been elaborated in Appendix I.

252 "अर्हत्यर्थे वतिः" येन प्रकारेणानुष्ठानम् अर्हति । इदं नित्यम् इदं काम्यम्

इदम् अङ्गम् इदं प्रधानं द्रव्यदेशकालकर्त्रादिनियमश् च प्रकारोऽर्हतेर् विषयः| Medhātithi on *Manu* 1.2 (Dave 1972)
*"arhatyarthe vatiḥ" yena prakāreṇānuṣṭhānam arhati |*
*idaṃ nityam idaṃ kāmyam idam aṅgam idaṃ pradhānaṃ dravyadeśakālakartrādiniyamaś ca prakāro 'rhater viṣayaḥ |*

253 यथावत् यो धर्मो यस्य वर्णस्य येन प्रकारेणाऽर्हतीत्यनेनाऽऽश्रमधर्मादीनामपि प्रश्नः। Kullūka Bhaṭṭa on *Manu* 1.2 (Kaundinyayana 2014)
*yathāvat yo dharmo yasya varṇasya yena prakāreṇā'rhatītyanenā"śramadharmādīnāmapi praśnaḥ* |

254 "जातकर्मानन्तरं चौडमौञ्जीनिबन्धनेत्यादि"| Medhātithi on *Manu* 1.2 (Dave 1972)
*"jātakarmānantaraṃ cauḍamauñjīnibandhanetyādi"* |

255 अनपूर्वशः क्रमेण, जातकर्म तदनु नामधेयमित्यादिना । Kullūka Bhaṭṭa on *Manu* 1.2 (Kaundinyayana 2014)
*anapūrvaśa: krameṇa, jātakarma tadanu nāmadheyamityādinā* ।

256 There is an exception to the sequence mentioned with respect to āśrama-dharma. One can enter sannyāsa-āśrama from any of the other three āśramas only criteria being one must have intense dispassion and internal renunciation.

257 सर्ववर्णेषु तुल्यासु पत्नीष्वक्षतयोनिषु ।
आनुलोम्येन सम्भूता जात्या ज्ञेयास्त एव ते ॥ *Manusmṛti* 10.5 (Kaundinyayana 2014)
*sarvavarṇeṣu tulyāsu patnīṣvakṣatayoniṣu* ।
*ānulomyena sambhūtā jātyā jñeyāsta eva te* ॥

258 Anuloma marriages refer to natural order of marriages in which the husband is of a higher varṇa than the wife. Ex. A brāhmaṇa marrying a kṣatriya wife, a kṣatriya marrying a vaiśya wife, etc. The notion of higher or lower in this context is only with reference to ritual state of the person which the Varna designation denotes. It is not a reference to social, political, or any other worldly hierarchies.

259 Pratiloma marriages refer to reverse order of marriages wherein the wife is of a higher varṇa than her husband. Ex. A brāhmaṇa woman marrying a kṣatriya husband, a kṣatriya woman marrying a vaiśya husband, etc.

260 Here it should be noted that Medhātithi is merely trying to explain a dharmic principle using a well-known example from the external world as analogy. It is not used in an offensive or degrading sense. A contemporary reader may find the analogy unpleasant or outright offensive due to one's contemporary socio-political experience. However, it would be incorrect to superimpose such attitudes to writings of a commentator who lived many centuries ago in a different socio-political setup.

न हि ते मातापित्रोरन्यतरयाऽपि जात्या व्यपदेष्टु युज्यन्ते | यथा रासभाश्वसंयोगतः खरो न रासभो नाश्वो जात्यन्तरम् एव | अतः वर्णग्रहणेनाग्रहणात् पृथग् उपादीयन्ते | Medhātithi on *Manu* 1.2 (Dave 1972)

*na hi te mātāpitroranyatarayā'pi jātyā vyapadeṣṭuṃ yujyante | yathā rāsabhāśvasaṃyogataḥ kharo na rāsabho nāśvo jātyantaram eva | ataḥ varṇagrahaṇenāgrahaṇāt pṛthag upādīyante |*

261 ब्राह्मणानां सितो वर्णः क्षत्रियाणां तु लोहितः
वैश्यानां पीतको वर्णः शूद्राणामसितस्तथा || *Mahābhārata Śānti Parva* 181.5 (Mahabharata: Critical Edition Prepared by Scholars at Bhandarkar Oriental Research Institute BORI n.d.)
*brāhmaṇānāṃ sito varṇaḥ kṣatriyāṇāṃ tu lohitaḥ*
*vaiśyānāṃ pītako varṇaḥ śūdrāṇāmasitastathā* ||

262 धारणाद्धर्ममित्याहुर्धर्मो धारयति प्रजाः| *Mahābhārata Karna Parva* 49.50 (Mahabharata: Critical Edition Prepared by Scholars at Bhandarkar Oriental Research Institute BORI n.d.)
*dhāraṇāddharmamityāhurdharmo dhārayati prajāḥ* |

263 धर्मो विश्वस्य जगतः प्रतिष्ठा लोके धर्मिष्ठ प्रजा उपसर्पन्ति धर्मेण पापमपनुदति धर्मे सर्वं प्रतिष्ठितं तस्माद्धर्मं परमं वदन्ति || *Mahānārāyaṇa Upaniṣad* 79.7 (Vimalananda 1968)
*dharmo viśvasya jagataḥ pratiṣṭhā loke dharmiṣṭha prajā upasarpanti dharmeṇa pāpamapanudati dharme sarvaṃ pratiṣṭhitaṃ tasmāddharmaṃ paramaṃ vadanti* ||

264 यतोऽभ्युदयनिःश्रेयससिद्धिः स धर्मः ॥ *Vaiśeṣika Sūtra* 1.1.2 (Sinha 1923)
*yato 'bhyudayaniḥśreyasasiddhiḥ sa dharmaḥ* ॥

265 कर्मणां च विवेकार्थं धर्माधर्मौ व्यवेचयत् ।
द्वन्द्वैरयोजयच्चेमाः सुखदुःखादिभिः प्रजाः ॥ *Manusmṛti* 1.26 (Kaundinyayana 2014)
*karmaṇāṃ ca vivekārthaṃ dharmādharmau vyavecayat* ।
*dvandvairayojayaccemāḥ sukhaduḥkhādibhiḥ prajāḥ* ॥

266 द्विविधो हि वेदोक्तो धर्मः, प्रवृत्तिलक्षणो निवृत्तिलक्षणश्च, जगतः स्थितिकारणम् । प्राणिनां साक्षादभ्युदयनिःश्रेयसहेतुर्यः स धर्मो ब्राह्मणाद्यैर्वर्णिभिराश्रमिभिश्च श्रेयोर्थिभिः अनुष्ठीयमानो दीर्घेण कालेन

। *Śaṅkara-Bhāṣya* introduction to *Bhagavad Gītā* (Srimad-Bhagavadgita-bhashya n.d.)
*dvividho hi vedokto dharmaḥ, pravṛttilakṣaṇo nivṛttilakṣaṇaśca, jagataḥ sthitikāraṇam* । *prāṇināṃ sākṣādabhyudayaniḥśreyasaheturyaḥ sa dharmo brāhmaṇādyairvarṇibhirāśramibhiśca śreyorthibhiḥ anuṣṭhīyamāno dīrgheṇa kālena* ।

267 तस्माच्छास्त्रं प्रमाणं ते कार्याकार्यव्यवस्थितौ ।
ज्ञात्वा शास्त्रविधानोक्तं कर्म कर्तुमिहार्हसि ॥ *Bhagavad Gītā* 16.24 (Gambhirananda 1998)
*tasmācchāstraṃ pramāṇaṃ te kāryākāryavyavasthitau* |
*jñātvā śāstravidhānoktaṃ karma kartumihārhasi* ||

268 चोदनालक्षणार्थो धर्मः । *codanālakṣaṇo artho dharmaḥ* । *Mīmāṁsā Sūtra* 1.1.1 (Sandal 1923)

269 वेदोऽखिलो धर्ममूलं स्मृतिशीले च तद्विदाम् ।
आचारश्चैव साधूनामात्मनस्तुष्टिरेव च ॥ *Manusmṛti* 2.6 (Kaundinyayana 2014)
*vedo'khilo dharmamūlaṃ smṛtiśīle ca tadvidām* ।
*ācāraścaiva sādhūnāmātmanastuṣṭireva ca* ॥

270 पुराणन्यायमीमांसाधर्मशास्त्राङ्गमिश्रिताः । वेदाः स्थानानि विद्यानां धर्मस्य च चतुर्दश ॥ *Yājñavalkya Smṛti* 1.3 (Pansikar 1936)
*purāṇanyāyamīmāṃsādharmaśāstrāṅgamiśritāḥ* । *vedāḥ sthānāni vidyānāṃ dharmasya ca caturdaśa* ॥

271 धर्मशब्दः कर्तव्याकर्तव्यतयोर् विधिप्रतिषेधयोर् अदृष्टार्थोस् तद्विषयायां च क्रियायां दृष्टप्रयोगः।*Medhātithi* on *Manu* 1.2 (Dave 1972)
*dharmaśabdaḥ kartavyākartavyatayor vidhipratiṣedhayor adṛṣṭārthos tadviṣayāyāṃ ca kriyāyāṃ dṛṣṭaprayogaḥ* |

272 धर्मरूपोपदेशाच्च यत्तद्विपरीतमधर्मोऽसावित्यर्थात्सिध्यति | अतो धर्माधर्मावुभावपि शास्त्रस्य विषय इत्युक्तं भवति | तत्राष्टकाकरणं धर्मो ब्रह्महत्यादिवर्जनं च धर्मः, अष्टकानामकरणमधर्मो ब्रह्महत्यायाश्च करणमधर्मः - अयं धर्माधर्मयोर्विवेकः | Medhātithi on *Manu* 1.2 (Dave 1972)
*dharmarūpopadeśācca yattadviparītamadharmo'sāvityarthātsidhyati | ato dharmādharmāvubhāvapi śāstrasya viṣaya ityuktaṃ bhavati | tatrāṣṭakākaraṇaṃ dharmo brahmahatyādivarjanaṃ ca dharmaḥ, aṣṭakānāmakaraṇamadharmo brahmahatyāyāśca karaṇamadharmaḥ - ayaṃ dharmādharmayorvivekaḥ |*

273 यत्तु ब्रह्महत्यादिरूपाऽधर्मकीर्तनमप्यत्र तत्प्रायश्चित्तविधिरूपधर्मविषयत्वेन न स्वतन्त्रतया || Kullūka Bhaṭṭa on *Manu* 1.2 (Kaundinyayana 2014)
*yattu brahmahatyādirūpā'dharmakīrtanamapyatra tatprāyaścittavidhirūpadharmaviṣayatvena na svatantratayā ||*

274 यज्ञेन यज्ञमयजन्त देवास्तानि धर्माणि प्रथमान्यासन् | *Puruṣasūkta* verse 16. (Purusha Suktam n.d.)
*yajñena yajñamayajanta devāstāni dharmāṇi prathamānyāsan |*

275 अर्हसीति सामर्थ्यलक्षणया योग्यतया प्रवचनाधिकारमाचार्यस्याहुः - यतस्त्वं समर्थो धर्मान्वक्तुमतोऽधिकृतः सन्नध्येष्यसे ब्रूहीति | यो यत्राधिकृतस्तत्तेन कर्तव्यमिति सामर्थ्यगम्यं ब्रूहीत्यध्येषणापदमध्याह्रियते || Medhātithi on *Manu* 1.2 (Dave 1972)
*arhasīti sāmarthyalakṣaṇayā yogyatayā pravacanādhikāramācāryasyāhuḥ - yatastvaṃ samartho dharmānvaktumato'dhikṛtaḥ sannadhyeṣyase brūhīti | yo yatrādhikṛtastattena kartavyamiti sāmarthyagamyaṃ brūhītyadhyeṣaṇāpadamadhyāhriyate ||*

276 वस्तुतस्तु कार्यं धर्मः तत्त्वार्थो ब्रह्म तदुभयं वेदार्थस्तद्वित् अन्यथा ज्ञानकाण्डस्य अप्रामाण्यापत्तिः कृत्स्नवेदार्थावित्त्वापत्तेश्च । प्रभो इत्युभयकथने सामर्थ्यमुक्तम् ।। Rāghavānanda Sarasvatī on *Manu* 1.3 (Dave 1972)
*vastutastu kāryaṃ dharmaḥ tattvārtho brahma tadubhayaṃ vedārthastadvit anyathā jñānakāṇḍasya aprāmāṇyāpattiḥ kṛtsnavedārthāvittvāpatteśca* | *prabho ityubhayakathane sāmarthyamuktam* ||

277 धर्माऽधर्मव्यवस्थापनसमर्थत्वात्प्रभो इति संबोधनम् ।। Kullūka Bhaṭṭa on *Manu* 1.3 (Kaundinyayana 2014)
*dharmā'dharmavyavasthāpanasamarthatvātprabho iti saṃbodhanam* ||

278 अतश्च निरवशेषपदार्थपरिज्ञानातिशययोगाद् धर्मप्रवचनसामर्थ्यं सिद्धवद् उपादाय, प्रभो इत्य् आमन्त्रणम् | Medhātithi on *Manu* 1.3 (Dave 1972)
*ataśca niravaśeṣapadārthaparijñānātiśayayogād dharmapravacanasāmarthyaṃ siddhavad upādāya, prabho ity āmantraṇam* |

279 तद्विज्ञानार्थं स गुरुमेवाभिगच्छेत्समित्पाणिः श्रोत्रियं ब्रह्मनिष्ठम् ॥ *Muṇḍaka Upaniṣad* 1.2.12 (Gambhirananda 1958)
*tadvijñānārthaṃ sa gurumevābhigacchetsamitpāṇiḥ śrotriyaṃ brahmaniṣṭham* ||

280 *Jaimini*'s *Mīmāṁsā Sūtra* 1.1.1 defines *dharma* as those actions indicated by the injunctions of the *Veda* (Sandal 1923).

281 *Manu* 2.10 says 'The *Veda* should be known as the "revealed word", and the *dharmaśāstra* as the "recollections"; in all matters, these two do not deserve to be criticised, as it is

out of these that *dharma* shone forth (G. Jha 1920).' Also, *Bhagavad Gītā* 16.24 (Gambhirananda 1998) notes that śāstra is the authority as regards the determination of what is to be done and what is not to be done. Commentators on *Gītā* like Śrī Rāmānujācārya and Śrī Madhusudhana Saraswati note that the term 'śāstra' stands for not only *Veda* but also for *dharmashastras* like *Smṛtis, Itihāsa,* and *Purāṇas*.

282 प्रवृत्तिश् च क्रिया निवृत्तिश् च क्रियेति | न हि परिस्पन्दनमानसाधनसाध्यम् एवानुष्ठानम् उच्यते | किं तर्हि | प्राप्ते तद्रूपे तन्निवृत्तिरपि | Medhātithi on *Manu* 1.3 (Dave 1972)
*pravṛttiś ca kriyā nivṛttiś ca kriyeti | na hi parispandanamānasādhanasādhyam evānuṣṭhānam ucyate | kiṃ tarhi | prāpte tadrūpe tannivṛttirapi |*

283 त्वयैव केवलेनैवंविधो वेद आगमितोऽतस्तस्य यः कार्यरूपस्तत्त्वार्थस्तं वेत्सि जानीषे | Medhātithi on *Manu* 1.3 (Dave 1972)
*tvayaiva kevalenaivaṃvidho veda āgamito 'tas tasya yaḥ kāryarūpas tattvārthas tam vetsi jānīṣe |*

284 मेधातिथिस्तु कर्ममीमांसावासनया वेदस्य कार्यमेव तत्त्वरूपोऽर्थस्तं वेत्तीति कार्यतत्त्वार्थविदिति व्याचष्टे। Kullūka Bhaṭṭa on *Manu* 1.3
*tvayaiva kevalenaivaṃvidho veda āgamito›tastasya yaḥ kāryarūpastattvārthastaṃ vetsi jānīṣe* ।

285 कार्यतत्त्वार्थवित् कार्यं धर्मः तदेव वेदस्य तात्पर्यविषयत्वात्तत्वं तद्वेत्तीति तथेति मेधातिथिः। वस्तुतस्तु कार्यं धर्मः तत्त्वार्थो ब्रह्म तदुभयं वेदार्थस्तद्वित् अन्यथा ज्ञानकाण्डस्य अप्रामाण्यापत्तिः कृत्स्नवेदार्थवित्त्वापत्तेश्च । Rāghavānanda Sarasvatī on *Manu* 1.3
*kāryatattvārthavit kāryaṃ dharmaḥ tadeva vedasya tātparyaviṣayatvāttatvaṃ tadvettīti tatheti medhātithiḥ* ।
*vastutastu kāryaṃ dharmaḥ tattvārtho brahma tadubhayaṃ*

*vedārthastadvit anyathā jñānakāṇḍasya aprāmāṇyāpattiḥ kṛtsnavedārthāvittvāpatteśca* ।

286 *Taittirīya Upaniṣad* 3.1.1 says: 'From which all the creatures are born, being born by which they sustain and into which they merge back, Know that as Brahman.'

287 *Brahmasūtra* 1.1.2 says '(Brahman is that) from which the origin etc., (i.e. the origin, sustenance and dissolution) of this (world proceed).'

288 कार्यमनुष्ठेयमग्निष्टोमादि तत्त्वं ब्रह्म सत्यं ज्ञानमनन्तं ब्रह्मेत्यादिवेदान्तवेद्यं तदेवाऽर्थः प्रतिपाद्यभागस्तं वेत्तीति कार्यतत्त्वार्थवित्। Kullūka Bhaṭṭa on *Manu* 1.3
*kāryamanuṣṭheyamagniṣṭomādi tattvaṃ brahma satyaṃ jñānamanantaṃ brahmetyādivedāntavedyaṃ tadevā'rthaḥ pratipādyabhāgastaṃ vettīti kāryatattvārthavit* ।

289 कार्य धर्मस्तस्य तत्त्वं पारमार्थ्यं तस्यार्थः प्रयोजनमभ्युदयसिद्धिरूपं तत्त्वमेको वेत्सि Nandana on *Manu* 1.3
*kārya dharmastasya tattvaṃ pāramārthyaṃ tasyārthaḥ prayojanamabhyudayasiddhirūpaṃ tattvameko vetsi*

290 अस्य सर्वस्य प्रत्यक्षश्रुतस्य स्मृत्याद्यनुमेयस्य Kullūka Bhaṭṭa on *Manu* 1.3 (Kaundinyayana 2014)
*asya sarvasya pratyakṣaśrutasya smṛtyādyanumeyasya*

291 सर्वस्य प्रत्यक्षाक्षरस्यानुमेयाक्षरस्य च | *sarvasya pratyakṣākṣarasyānumeyākṣarasya ca* | Medhātithi on *Manu* 1.3 (Dave 1972). He further uses the example of a mantra-text regarding chopping of grass to illustrate this point. He says: 'similarly, when we read the mantra-text, "I am chopping grass,

the seat of the Gods," we at once infer, on the basis of the indicative power of the words of that text, the Vedic injunction that "the said text is to be employed in the chopping of grass;" this mantra is found in that section of the *Veda* which deals with the *Darśa-pūrṇamāsa sacrifice*, and the *chopping of grass* is laid down as to be done in course of that sacrifice; but there is no such direct injunction indicating that "the chopping should be done with such and such a mantra" and the above-mentioned mantra-text is found to be capable, by its very form, of indicating the *chopping of grass*; while as regards its being connected in a general way, with the sacrifice, this follows the fact of its occurring in the same "context" as the injunction of that sacrifice; and it is by virtue of its own indicative force that it comes to be employed in the chopping of grass.... The text thus inferred is regarded as "*Veda*", by virtue of the fact that it owes its existence to the force of two other Vedic texts—*viz*., the text laying down the *Darśapūrṇamāsa* and the Mantra-text referred to above.' (G. Jha 1920)

292 वेदमूलाः स्मृतय इति ज्ञापयितुम् | Medhātithi on *Manu* 1.3 (Dave 1972)
*vedamūlāḥ smṛtaya iti jñāpayitum* |

293 यद्यपि च मुनिभिर्वेदादेव धर्मान् ब्रूहीत्युक्तः तथापि न मन्त्रब्राह्मणलक्षणाद् वेदाद् धर्मावगतिः, किं तर्हि पुराणादीनां धर्मोपयोगित्वं प्रसिद्धम् | न्यायमीमांसेति चैकं विद्यास्थानम् | पुराणम् इति चेतिहासपुराणयोर्ग्रहणम् | धर्मशाश्त्रं स्मृतिः | अङ्गानि षट् शीक्षादीनि | वेदाश् चत्वारः | एवं चतुर्दश |Viśvarūpa's *Bālakrīḍā* commentary on *Yājñavalkya Smṛti* 1.2-3 (Sastri 1922–1924)
*yadyapi ca munibhirvedādeva dharmān brūhītyuktaḥ tathāpi na mantrabrāhmaṇalakṣaṇād vedād dharmāvagatiḥ, kiṃ tarhi purāṇādīnāṃ dharmopayogitvaṃ prasiddham*

*| nyāyamīmāṃseti caikaṃ vidyāsthānam | purāṇam iti cetihāsapurāṇayorgrahaṇam | dharmaśāśtraṃ smṛtiḥ | aṅgāni ṣaṭ śīkṣādīni | vedāś catvāraḥ | evaṃ caturdaśa |*

294 व्युत्पाद्यते च वेदशब्दः | विदन्त्यनन्यप्रमाणवेद्यं धर्मलक्षणमर्थमस्मादिति 'वेदः' | तच्च वेदनमेकैकस्माद्वाक्याद्भवति, न यावानृग्वेदादिशब्दवाच्योऽध्यायानुवाकसमूहः |.....कृत्स्नोऽधिगन्तव्य इति कृत्स्नग्रहणं सकलवेदवाक्याध्ययनप्राप्त्यर्थम् | अन्यथा कतिचिद्वाक्यान्यधीत्य कृती स्यात्, न पुनः कृत्स्नं वेदम् इति | Medhātithi on *Manu* 2.6 (Dave 1972)
*vyutpādyate ca vedaśabdaḥ | vidantyananyapramāṇavedyaṃ dharmalakṣaṇamarthamasmāditi 'vedaḥ' | tacca vedanamekaikasmādvākyādbhavati, na yāvānṛgvedādiśabdavācyo'dhyāyānuvākasamūhaḥ|..... kṛtsno'dhigantavya iti kṛtsnagrahaṇaṃ sakalavedavākyādhyayanaprāptyartham | anyathā katicidvākyānyadhītya kṛtī syāt, na punaḥ kṛtsnaṃ vedam iti |*

295 अनन्ता वै वेदाः| (*anantā vai vedāḥ|) Taittirīya Brāhmaṇa* 3.10.11.4 (Sarma 2004-2005)

296 स्वयंभुवो नित्यस्याकृतकस्यापौरुषेयस्य... Medhātithi on *Manu* 1.3 (Dave 1972)
*svayaṃbhuvo nityasyākṛtakasyāpauruṣeyasya*

297 स्वयंभुवोऽपौरुषेयस्य Kullūka Bhaṭṭa on *Manu* 1.3 (Kaundinyayana 2014)
*svayaṃbhuvo'pauruṣeyasya*

298 स्वयंभुवः प्रजापतेः Sarvajñanārāyaṇa on *Manu* 1.3 (Dave 1972)
*svayaṃbhuvaḥ prajāpateḥ*

299 अनन्ता वै वेदाः| *Taittirīya brāhmaṇa* 3.10.11.4 (Sarma 2004-2005)
*anantā vai vedāḥ* |

300 अप्रमेयस्य दुरधिगमार्थस्य अनेनार्थतोऽप्यचिन्त्यत्वमुक्तम् । Rāghavānanda Sarasvatī on *Manu* 1.3 (Dave 1972)
*aprameyasya duradhigamārthasya anenārthato'pyacintyatvamuktam* |

301 अप्रमेयस्य अपर्यन्तस्य । Nandana on *Manu* 1.3 (Dave 1972)
*aprameyasya aparyantasya*

302 अप्रमेयस्य कल्प्यस्य प्रायशः स्मृतिवाक्यमूलस्य | न हि प्रत्यक्षेण प्रमीयते | अतोऽप्रेमेयस्येत्युच्यते | Medhātithi on *Manu* 1.3 (Dave 1972)
*aprameyasya kalpyasya prāyaśaḥ smṛtivākyamūlasya | na hi pratyakṣeṇa pramīyate | ato'premeyasyetyucyate* |

303 मीमांसादिन्यायनिरपेक्षतयाऽनवगम्यमानप्रमेयस्य। Kullūka Bhaṭṭa on *Manu* 1.3 (Kaundinyayana 2014)
*mīmāṃsādinyāyanirapekṣatayā'navagamyamānaprameyasya* |

304 अप्रमेयस्य प्रमाणान्तरागोचरस्य Sarvajñanārāyaṇa on *Manu* 1.3 (Dave 1972)
*aprameyasya pramāṇāntarā'gocarasya*

305 पदद्वयेन बाह्यान्तःकरणाविषयतया महत्त्वस्य ख्यापनेनाचार्यः प्रोत्साह्यते | त्वयैव केवलेनैवंविधो वेद आगमितोऽतस्तस्य यः कार्यरूपस्तत्त्वार्थस्तं वेत्सि जानीषे | Medhātithi on *Manu* 1.3 (Dave 1972)
*padadvayena bāhyāntaḥkaraṇāviṣayatayā mahattvasya khyāpanenācāryaḥ protsāhyate | tvayaiva kevalenaivaṃvidho veda āgamito'tastasya yaḥ kāryarūpastattvārthastaṃ vetsi jānīṣe* |

306 अस्य विधानस्य सर्वस्य चतुर्विधस्य भूतग्रामस्य उद्भिदस्वेदजाण्डजजरायुजस्येत्यर्थः । Rāmacandra on *Manu* 1.3 (Dave 1972) *asya vidhānasya sarvasya caturvidhasya bhūtagrāmasya udbhidasvedajāṇḍajajarāyujasyetyarthaḥ* ।

307 अस्येति प्रत्यक्षाभिनयेन जगन्निर्दिश्यते | सर्वस्यास्य जगतो यद्विधानं निर्माणं तत्स्वयंभुवः संबन्धि | अचिन्त्यमद्‌तरूपं विचित्रमतिमहदप्रमेयं न शक्यं सर्वेण ज्ञातुम् | तथा ऋषिः | "को अद्धा वेद क इह प्रवोचत् कुत आजाता कुत इयं विसृष्टिरिति"| किमिदं जगत्सर्वमुपादानमपेक्ष्य जायत उत नैर्माणिकमात्रम्, यथा बुद्धस्य दर्शनम् | किमीश्वरेच्छाधीनमुत केवलकर्मवशजमुत स्वाभाविकमप्रमेयम् | तथा किं महदादिक्रमेणोत्पद्यत उत द्व्यणुकादिक्रमेण | अस्य त्वं कार्यं तत्त्वमर्थं च वेत्सि | Medhātithi on *Manu* 1.11 (Dave 1972) *asyeti pratyakṣābhinayena jagannirdiśyate | sarvasyāsya jagato yadvidhānaṃ nirmāṇaṃ tatsvayaṃbhuvaḥ saṃbandhi | acintyamadbhutarūpaṃ vicitramatimahadaprameyaṃ na śakyaṃ sarveṇa jñātum | tathā ṛṣiḥ | "ko addhā veda ka iha pravocat kuta ājātā kuta iyaṃ visṛṣṭiriti"| kimidaṃ jagatsarvamupādānamapekṣya jāyata uta nairmāṇikamātram, yathā buddhasya darśanam | kimīśvarecchādhīnamuta kevalakarmavaśajamuta svābhāvikamaprameyam | tathā kiṃ mahadādikrameṇotpadyata uta dvyaṇukādikrameṇa | asya tvaṃ kāryaṃ tattvamarthaṃ ca vetsi* |

308 *Sāṅkhya Darśana* speaks about *puruṣas* which are pure-conscious entities without movement and *prakṛti* which is the primordial material cause of the universe. The creation or evolution of the universe happens when *puruṣa* comes into contact with *prakṛti*. *Prakṛti* is made up of three *guṇas*: sattva, rajas, and tamas, and is in an unmanifested state with the guṇas in equilibrium when it is not in contact with any

*puruṣa*. When it comes into contact with *puruṣa*, the contact results in disequilibrium in the three *guṇas* giving rise to evolution of the universe through the evolution of twenty-three evolutes in a particular order. Thus, *prakṛti* is the cause or *kāraṇa* and these twenty-three evolutes are the products or *kārya*. The twenty-three evolutes include: mahat or buddhi (the intelligence principle), *ahaṁkāra* (the ego principle), the *manas* (the mind), five *jnana indrīyas* (faculties of knowledge), five *karma indrīyas* (faculties of action), five *tanmatras* (subtle elements), and five *mahabhutas* (great gross elements). The mahat is produced from *prakṛti*, *ahaṁkāra* is produced from mahat, *tanmātras* arise from *ahaṁkāra*, and the *mahābhūtas* arise from *tanmātras*. The *indrīyas* also arise from *ahaṁkāra*. From the *pañcabhūtas,* everything in this universe is created.

309 'कार्यं' महतोऽहंकारोऽविशेषास्तन्मात्राण्यहंकारस्य, तन्मात्राणां विशेषाः पञ्चमहाभूतानि, अहंकारस्येन्द्रियाण्येकादश | विशेषाणामपि पिण्डः कार्यं ब्रह्मादिस्तम्बपर्यन्ताः| Medhātithi on *Manu* 1.11 (Dave 1972)
*'kāryaṃ' mahato'haṃkāro'viśeṣāstanmātrāṇyahaṃkārasya, tanmātrāṇāṃ viśeṣāḥ pañcamahābhūtāni, ahaṃkārasyendriyāṇyekādaśa | viśeṣāṇāmapi piṇḍaḥ kāryaṃ brahmādistambaparyantāḥ|*

310 तत्त्वं स्वभावो यथा महतो मूर्तिमात्रत्त्वम्|.... अहंकारस्य तत्त्वम् अस्मिप्रत्ययमात्रत्वम् | Medhātithi on *Manu* 1.11 (Dave 1972)
*tattvaṃ svabhāvo yathā mahato mūrtimātrattvam|.... ahaṃkārasya tattvam asmipratyayamātratvam |*

311 अर्थः प्रयोजनम् | पुरुषार्थमिदं वस्त्वनेन प्रकारेण पुरुषायोपयुज्यते इमं चार्थं साधयति | Medhātithi on *Manu* 1.11 (Dave 1972)
*arthaḥ prayojanam | puruṣārthamidaṃ vastvanena prakāreṇa*

*puruṣāyopayujyate imaṃ cārthaṃ sādhayati* |

312 चोदनालक्षणार्थो धर्मः । *Mīmāṁsā Sūtra* 1.1.1 (Sandal 1923)
*codanālakṣaṇo artho dharmaḥ* ।

313 वेदोऽखिलो धर्ममूलं स्मृतिशीले च तद्विदाम् ।
आचारश्चैव साधूनामात्मनस्तुष्टिरेव च ॥ *Manusmṛti* 2.6 (Kaundinyayana 2014)
*vedo'khilo dharmamūlaṃ smṛtiśīle ca tadvidām* ।
*ācāraścaiva sādhūnāmātmanastuṣṭireva ca* ॥

श्रुतिस्मृत्योदितं धर्ममनुतिष्ठन् हि मानवः ।
इह कीर्तिमवाप्नोति प्रेत्य चाऽनुत्तमं सुखम् ॥ *Manusmṛti* 2.9 (Kaundinyayana 2014)
*śrutismṛtyoditaṃ dharmamanutiṣṭhan hi mānavaḥ* ।
*iha kīrtimavāpnoti pretya cā'nuttamaṃ sukham* ॥

श्रुतिस्तु वेदो विज्ञेयो धर्मशास्त्रं तु वै स्मृतिः ।
ते सर्वार्थेष्वमीमांस्ये ताभ्यां धर्मो हि निर्बभौ ॥*Manusmṛti* 2.10 (Kaundinyayana 2014)

*śrutistu vedo vijñeyo dharmaśāstraṃ tu vai smṛtiḥ* ।
*te sarvārtheṣvamīmāṃsye tābhyāṃ dharmo hi nirbabhau* ॥

314 यः कश्चित् कस्य चिद्धर्मो मनुना परिकीर्तितः ।
स सर्वोऽभिहितो वेदे सर्वज्ञानमयो हि सः ॥ *Manusmṛti 2.7* (Kaundinyayana 2014)
*yaḥ kaścit kasya ciddharmo manunā parikīrtitaḥ* ।
*sa sarvo'bhihito vede sarvajñānamayo hi saḥ* ॥

315 अस्य सर्वस्य प्रत्यक्षश्रुतस्य स्मृत्याद्यनुमेयस्य *Kullūka Bhaṭṭa* on *Manu* 1.3 (Kaundinyayana 2014)

*asya sarvasya pratyakṣaśrutasya smṛtyādyanumeyasya*

316 सर्वत्र च प्रत्यक्षश्रुतिभिर्मन्वादिस्मृतिनां व्यतिषङ्गः, क्वचिन्मन्त्रेण क्वचिद्देवतया क्वचिद् द्रव्यविधिभिः | *Medhātithi* on *Manu* 2.6 (Dave 1972)
*sarvatra ca pratyakṣaśrutibhirmanvādismṛtinām vyatiṣaṅgaḥ, kvacinmantreṇa kvaciddevatayā kvacid dravyavidhibhiḥ |*

317 ....इत्येवमादि बहुविकल्पं विचारयन्ति विवरणकाराः | एतावांस्तु निर्णयः | वैदिकमेतदनुष्ठानम्, स्मार्तानां वैदिकैर्विधिभिर्व्यतिषङ्गावगमादनुष्ठातृणां च तद् दृष्ट्वानुष्ठानात् | व्यतिषङ्गश्च दर्शितः | क्वचिद्वैदिकमङ्गं प्रधानं स्मार्तं, क्वचिदेतदेव विपरीतं क्वचिदुत्पत्तिः क्वचिदधिकारः क्वचिदर्थवाद इति | एवं सर्व एव स्मार्ता वैदिकैर्व्यतिषक्ताः | Medhātithi on *Manu* 2.6 (Dave 1972)
.... *ityevamādi bahuvikalpaṃ vicārayanti vivaraṇakārāḥ | etāvāṃstu nirṇayaḥ | vaidikametadanuṣṭhānam, smārtānāṃ vaidikairvidhibhirvyatiṣaṅgāvagamādanuṣṭhātṝṇāṃ ca tad dṛṣṭvānuṣṭhānāt | vyatiṣaṅgaśca darśitaḥ | kvacidvaidikamaṅgaṃ pradhānaṃ smārtaṃ, kvacidetadeva viparītaṃ kvacidutpattiḥ kvacidadhikāraḥ kvacidarthavāda iti | evaṃ sarva eva smārtā vaidikairvyatiṣaktāḥ |*

318 The translation has been taken from Ganganath Jha's entry 'Comparative notes by various authors' under *Manusmṛti* verse 2.6 which cites Viśvarūpa's *Bālakrīḍā* commentary on *Yājñavalkya Smṛti* 1.7. [https://www.wisdomlib.org/hinduism/book/manusmriti-with-the-commentary-of-medhatithi/d/doc145579.html]

अत्राभिधीयते | नैवं स्वोत्प्रेक्षितविकल्पजालैः स्मृतीनामप्रामाण्यारोपणं युक्तम् | स्वयं हि मन्वादिभिरुक्तं "स सर्वोऽभिहितो वेदे», "वेदो धर्ममूलम्", "आम्नायप्रामाण्यादाचारः," "द्वितीयस्तदनुव्याख्या

स्मार्तः", वेदः स्मृतिः सदाचारः" इत्यादि | न चैवंरूपाभ्युपगमातिक्रमेण मूलान्तरान्वेषणं युक्तम् | युक्तश्चायमभ्युपगमोऽस्मिन्नर्थे प्रमाणान्तराभावात्, "चोदनालक्षण एव धर्मः" इति नियमो यतः | न च भ्रान्त्यादिकल्पनोपपत्तिः, वेदवित्परिग्रहविरोधात् | नाप्यन्यमूलत्वे तत्परिग्रहोपपत्तिः चैत्यवन्दनादिवत् | भ्रान्त्यादिकल्पने वा वेदेऽप्यवेदताप्रसङ्गः | न चासंभाव्यं वेदमूलत्वं, "वेदविदो हि मन्वादयः" इति स्मरणात् | न चैतद् भ्रान्तेः, स्मर्तृत्वस्मरणवत् | अतः सूक्तं वेदमूलत्वम् | आह च |.... ननु तदेव वेदमूलत्वं दुरुपपादमित्युक्तम् | उक्ता हि सर्वथा वेदस्य मूलत्वानुपपत्तिः | न तत् सम्यगुक्तं प्रमाणतो हि मूलत्वोपपत्तेः | उपलभ्यते हि स्मृतीनां तन्मूलत्वम् | विध्यर्थान्यथानुपपत् तिलभ्यत्वात् | तथा हि "स्वाध्यायोऽध्येयः" इत्युक्ते, "विद्यां चाध्यापयेत्" इति द्वयस्यानुपपत्त्यान्यो विधिस्तत्र प्रक्लप्यते | "विद्यामध्यापयेत्" इति हि विधिरात्मोपपादनायाध्ययनं प्रयुङ्क्ते | अध्ययनविधिरपि तत्प्रयुक्त्यैवोपपन्नानुष्ठानोऽधिकारान्तरकल्पनामन्तरेणौदासीन् यं प्रतिपद्यते | न चाध्यापयिताध्येतारमनुपनीयाध्यापयितुं क्षमह् | तत्र विधिद्वयोपपत्त्यर्थं विध्यन्तरानुमित्या "ब्राह्मणादीन् उपनयीत" इति |
*Viśvarūpa*'s *Bālakrīḍā* commentary on *Yājñavalkya Smṛti* 1.7 (Sastri 1922–1924)

*atrābhidhīyate | naivaṃ svotprekṣitavikalpajālaiḥ smṛtīnāmaprāmāṇyāropaṇaṃ yuktam | svayaṃ hi manvādibhiruktaṃ "sa sarvo'bhihito vede", "vedo dharmamūlam", "āmnāyaprāmāṇyādācāraḥ," "dvitīyastadanuvyākhyā smārtaḥ", vedaḥ smṛtiḥ sadācāraḥ" ityādi | na caivaṃrūpābhyupagamātikrameṇa mūlāntarānveṣaṇaṃ yuktam | yuktaścāyamabhyupagamo'sminnarthe pramāṇāntarābhāvāt, "codanālakṣaṇa eva dharmaḥ" iti niyamo yataḥ | na ca bhrāntyādikalpanopapattiḥ, vedavitparigrahavirodhāt | nāpyanyamūlatve tatparigrahopapattiḥ caityavandanādivat | bhrāntyādikalpane vā vede'pyavedatāprasaṅgaḥ | na cāsaṃbhāvyaṃ vedamūlatvaṃ, "vedavido hi manvādayaḥ" iti smaraṇāt | na caitad bhrānteḥ, smartṛtvasmaraṇavat | ataḥ sūktaṃ vedamūlatvam | āha ca |.... nanu tadeva vedamūlatvaṃ durupapādamityuktam | uktā hi sarvathā vedasya mūlatvānupapattiḥ | na tat samyaguktaṃ pramāṇato hi mūlatvopapatteḥ | upalabhyate hi smṛtīnāṃ tanmūlatvam | vidhyarthānyathānupapattilabhyatvāt | tathā hi "svādhyāyo'dhyeyaḥ" ityukte, "vidyāṃ cādhyāpayet" iti dvayasyānupapattyānyo vidhistatra praklapyate | "vidyāmadhyāpayet" iti hi vidhirātmopapādanāyādhyayanaṃ prayuṅkte | adhyayanavidhirapi tatprayuktyaivopapannānuṣṭhāno' dhikārāntarakalpanāmantareṇaudāsīnyaṃ pratipadyate | na cādhyāpayitādhyetāramanupanīyādhyāpayituṃ kṣamah | tatra vidhidvayopapattyarthaṃ vidhyantarānumityā "brāhmaṇādīn upanayīta" iti |*

319 Ganganath Jha's Comparative notes by various authors under *Manu* 2.6 includes the following quotations from *Nṛsiṃhaprasāda* and *Smṛticandrikā* which uphold the authoritativeness of *Manu* and other *Smṛti*s. [https://www.wisdomlib.org/hinduism/book/*Manusmṛti*-with-the-commentary-of-medhatithi/d/doc145579.html]

Dalapatirāya, the author of *Nṛsiṃhaprasāda*, *Saṁskārasāra* writes:

How can any authority attach to the smṛtis of Manu and others, which being of human origin are open to the suspicion of the possibility of all those defects to which human writers are liable; and for this reason these cannot be regarded as authoritative in the same manner as the *Vedas* are, whose authority is above suspicion.—The answer to this is that inasmuch as these smṛtis are found to be mere reproductions

> of what is contained in the *Veda*, they must be regarded as duly authoritative. The very name 'smṛti', 'Recollection', implies that they only reproduce what the authors have learnt elsewhere; and as Manu and others are known to have been learned in the *Veda*, it stands to reason that knowing as they did that the *Veda* was the sole authority on *dharma*, when they proceeded to note down for the benefit of others what the laws were that regulated *dharma*, they could not but have drawn upon the *Veda*. It is true that they are found to contain many rules that we cannot trace to the *Veda* as known to us; but if they were mere reproductions of whatever is found in the *Veda*, no one would care for them. So we are led to the inference that as on most of the points dealt with by them, their assertions are found to be based on Vedic texts, the other points also must have had their source in the *Veda*; but in those Vedic texts that have become lost to us. We have the *Veda* itself testifying to the trustworthy character of at least one smṛti-writer, Manu—'Whatever Manu has said is wholesome.'

Likewise, Devana Bhaṭṭa, the author of *Smṛticandrikā* observes:

> The ordinances composed by Manu and other writers, being based on the *Veda*, are our sole authority on *dharma*. That the smṛtis have their source in the *Veda* is deduced from the fact that they only expound what is contained in the *Veda*. Says Bhṛgu—'Whatever *dharma* has been expounded by Manu has all been set forth in the *Veda*.' Śaṅkara also says that 'the smṛtis have their source in the *Veda*.' But this refers to only what the smṛti says regarding spiritual matters, and not to what they lay down regarding temporal matters; as is distinctly declared in the Purāṇa—'All these (smṛtis) have their source in the *Veda*—save those portions that deal with visible (temporal) matters.'

320 *Ādi Śaṅkarācārya* in *Vivekacūḍāmaṇi* Verse 25 defines *śraddhā* thus: 'Acceptance by firm judgment as true of what the Scriptures and the Guru instruct, is called by sages *śraddhā* or faith, by means of which the Reality is perceived (Madhavananda, Vivekachudamani of Sri Sankaracharya 1921).' The key phrase he uses is '*satya-budhya-avadhāraṇa*'– ability and conviction to embrace truth.

321 अहिंसा सत्यमस्तेयं शौचमिन्द्रियनिग्रहः ।
एतं सामासिकं धर्मं चातुर्वर्ण्येऽब्रवीन् मनुः ॥ *Manusmṛti* 10.63
(Kaundinyayana 2014)
*ahiṃsā satyamasteyaṃ śaucamindriyanigrahaḥ* ।
*etaṃ sāmāsikaṃ dharmaṃ cāturvarṇye'bravīn manuḥ* ॥

322 यत्र नार्यस्तु पूज्यन्ते रमन्ते तत्र देवताः ।
यत्रैतास्तु न पूज्यन्ते सर्वास्तत्राऽफलाः क्रियाः ॥ *Manusmṛti* 3.56
(Kaundinyayana 2014)
*yatra nāryastu pūjyante ramante tatra devatāḥ* ।
*yatraitāstu na pūjyante sarvāstatrā'phalāḥ kriyāḥ* ॥

323 तपस्तप्त्वाऽसृजद् यं तु स स्वयं पुरुषो विराट् ।
तं मां वित्ताऽस्य सर्वस्य स्रष्टारं द्विजसत्तमाः ॥ *Manusmṛti* 1.33
(Kaundinyayana 2014)
*apastaptvā'sṛjad yaṃ tu sa svayaṃ puruṣo virāṭ* ।
*taṃ māṃ vittā'sya sarvasya sraṣṭāraṃ dvijasattamāḥ* ॥

324 इदं शास्त्रं तु कृत्वाऽसौ मामेव स्वयमादितः ।
विधिवद् ग्राहयामास मरीच्यादींस्त्वहं मुनीन् ॥ *Manusmṛti* 1.58
(Kaundinyayana 2014)
*idaṃ śāstraṃ tu kṛtvā'sau māmeva svayamāditaḥ* ।
*vidhivad grāhayāmāsa marīcyādīṃstvahaṃ munīn* ॥

325 श्रुतिस्तु वेदो विज्ञेयो धर्मशास्त्रं तु वै स्मृतिः ।
ते सर्वार्थेष्वमीमांस्ये ताभ्यां धर्मो हि निर्बभौ ॥ *Manusmṛti* 2.10 (Kaundinyayana 2014)
*śrutistu vedo vijñeyo dharmaśāstraṃ tu vai smṛtiḥ* ।
*te sarvārtheṣvamīmāṃsye tābhyāṃ dharmo hi nirbabhau* ॥

326 यद्वै किञ्च मनुरवदत्तद्भेषजम् *Taittirīya Saṁhitā* 2.2.10.2 (Taittiriya Samhita- Searchable Text n.d.)

*yadvai kiñca manuravadattadbheṣajam*

327 अमितौजा अक्षीणवाग्विभवः | अमितमनन्तमजो वीर्यमभिधानसामर्थ्यमस्येति | Medhātithi on *Manu* 1.4 (Datta 2022)
*amitaujā akṣīṇavāgvibhavaḥ* | *amitamanantamajo vīryamabhidhānasāmarthyamasyeti* |

328 अमितमपरिच्छेद्यमोजः सामर्थ्यं ज्ञानतत्त्वाऽभिधानादौ यस्य स तथा । अत एव सर्वज्ञसर्वशक्तितया महर्षीणामपि प्रश्नविषयः । Kullūka Bhaṭṭa on *Manu* 1.4 (Kaundinyayana 2014)
*amitamaparicchedyamojaḥ sāmarthya jñānatattvā'bhidhānādau yasya sa tathā* । *ata eva sarvajñasarvaśaktitayā maharṣīṇāmapi praśnaviṣayaḥ* ।

329 ओजः सर्वार्थो धर्म्मः तद् बीजं वा विज्ञानमप्रतिहतं सर्व्वार्त्थेष्वस्य सोयममितौजाः महात्मभिः । Bhāruḍhī on *Manu* 1.4 (Shivarajappa 2020)
*ojaḥ sarvārtho dharmmaḥ tad bījaṃ vā vijñānamapratihataṃ sarvvārttheṣvasya soyamamitaujāḥ mahātmabhiḥ* ।

330 अमितबलः(*amitabalaḥ*)Sarvajñanārāyaṇa on *Manu* 1.4 (Datta 2022)

331 अमितौजा धर्मब्रह्मणोर्वेदने शक्तः Rāghavānanda Sarasvatī on *Manu* 1.4 (Datta 2022)
*amitaujā dharmabrahmaṇorvedane śaktaḥ*

332 अत्र यदुच्यते 'यदि मनुनाऽयं ग्रन्थः कृतः परापदेशो न युक्तः - स तैः पृष्टः प्रत्युवाचेति | "अहं पृष्टः प्रत्यब्रवमिति" न्याय्यम् | अथान्य एव ग्रन्थस्य कर्ता मानवव्यपदेशः कथमिति' Medhātithi on *Manu* 1.4 (Dave 1972)
*atra yaducyate 'yadi manunā'yaṃ granthaḥ kṛtaḥ parāpadeśo na yuktaḥ - sa taiḥ pṛṣṭaḥ pratyuvāceti | "ahaṃ pṛṣṭaḥ pratyabravamiti" nyāyyam | athānya eva granthasya kartā mānavavyapadeśaḥ kathamiti'*

333 तदचोद्यं | प्रायेण ग्रन्थकाराः स्वमतं परापदेशेन ब्रुवते- "अत्राह," "अत्र परिहरन्ति" इति नैवम् "अहं तैः पृष्टः" इति....अथवा भृगुप्रोक्ता संहितेयं | मानवी तु स्मृतिरूपनिबद्धेति मानवव्यपदेशः| Medhātithi on *Manu* 1.4 (Dave 1972)
*tadacodyaṃ | prāyeṇa granthakārāḥ svamataṃ parāpadeśena bruvate- "atrāha," "atra pariharanti" iti naivam "ahaṃ taiḥ pṛṣṭaḥ" iti....athavā bhṛguproktā saṃhiteyaṃ | mānavī tu smṛtirūpanibaddheti mānavavyapadeśaḥ |*

334 कर्माण्यपि जैमिनिः फलाऽर्थत्वात् | *( karmāṇyapi jaiminiḥ phalā'rthatvāt |) Mīmāṁsāsutra* 3.1.4 Cited by Kullūka Bhaṭṭa in his commentary on Manu 1.4 (Kaundinyayana 2014)

335 तदुपर्यपि बादरायणः सम्भवात् ॥(*taduparyapi bādarāyaṇaḥ sambhavāt|*) *Brahmasūtra* 1.3.26 4 Cited by Kullūka Bhaṭṭa in his commentary on Manu 1.4 (Kaundinyayana 2014)

336 प्रायेणाऽऽचार्याणामियं शैली यत्स्वाभिप्रायमपि परोपदेशमिव वर्णयन्ति । अत एव कर्माण्यपि जैमिनिः फलाऽर्थत्वादिति

जैमिनेरेव सूत्रम् । अतएव तदुपर्यपि बादरायणः संभवादिति बादरायणस्यैव शारीरकसूत्रम् । *Kullūka Bhaṭṭa* on *Manu* 1.4 (Kaundinyayana 2014)
*prāyeṇā"cāryāṇāmiyaṃ śailī yatsvābhiprāyamapi paropadeśamiva varṇayanti* । *ata eva karmāṇyapi jaiminiḥ phalā'rthatvāditi jaiminereva sūtram* । *ataeva taduparyapi bādarāyaṇaḥ saṃbhavāditi bādarāyaṇasyaiva śārīrakasūtram* ।

337 तथा तेन प्रागुक्तेन प्रकारेण | पृच्छ्यमानवस्तुप्रश्नविधिश्च प्रकारवचने तथाशब्देऽन्तर्भूतः| *Medhātithi* on *Manu* 1.4 (Dave 1972) *tathā tena prāguktena prakāreṇa* | *pṛcchyamānavastupraśnavidhiśca prakāravacane tathāśabde'ntarbhūtaḥ* |

338 तथा तेन प्रकारेण पूर्वोक्तेन न्यायेन प्रणतिभक्तिश्रद्धाऽतिशयादिना *Kullūka Bhaṭṭa* on *Manu* 1.4 (Kaundinyayana 2014) *tathā tena prakāreṇa pūrvoktena nyāyena praṇatibhaktiśraddhā'tiśayādinā*

339 सा त्वस्मिन् परप्रेमरूपा । अमृतस्वरूपा च । *Nārada Bhakti Sūtra*s 1.2-3 (Sivananda 1957)
*sā tvasmin parapremarūpā* । *amṛtasvarūpā ca*

340 सा पराऽनुरक्तिरीश्वरे | *Śāṇḍilya Bhakti Sūtra*s 1.2 (Yati 1991)
*sā parā'nuraktirīśvare* |

341 *Ādi Śaṅkarācārya* in *Vivekacūḍāmaṇi* verse 25 defines *śraddhā* thus: 'Acceptance by firm judgment as true of what the Scriptures and the Guru instruct, is called by sages *śraddhā* or faith, by means of which the Reality is perceived (Madhavananda, Vivekachudamani of Sri Sankaracharya 1921).' The key phrase he uses is '*satya-budhya- avadhāraṇa*'-

ability and conviction to embrace truth.

342 'परार्थकारी सततं महात्मे' त्युच्यते | तेन यद्यपि स्वयं विदांसोऽधिगतयाथातथ्याः - अन्यथा महर्षित्वानुपपत्तेः, तथाऽपि परार्थमपृच्छन् | Medhātithi on *Manu* 1.4 (Dave 1972)
*parārthakārī satataṃ mahātme' tyucyate | tena yadyapi svayaṃ vidāṃso'dhigatayāthātathyāḥ - anyathā maharṣitvānupapatteḥ, tathā'pi parārthamapṛcchan |*

343 धर्मं चरत्येष महात्मेति । *Śaṅkara Bhāṣya* on *Brahmasūtra* 3.1.11 (Brahmasutra-bhashya n.d.)
*dharmaṃ caratyeṣa mahātmeti |*

344 मनुः प्रख्याततरप्रमाणभावः | एतेन यदुच्यते तल्लोकेनाद्रियते | प्रत्ययतोऽयं समुपास्यतेऽतः शास्त्रावतारार्थमुपाध्यायीकुर्मः | अस्माभिश्च पृच्छ्यमानः प्रमाणतरीकरिष्यते जनेनेति | अत एवार्च्य तान् सर्वानित्यर्चनमविरुद्धम् | अन्यथा शिष्यस्योपाध्यायात्कीदृश्यर्चेति |
Medhātithi on *Manu* 1.4 (Dave 1972)
*manuḥ prakhyātatarapramāṇabhāvaḥ | etena yaducyate tallokenādriyate | pratyayato'yaṃ samupāsyate'taḥ śāstrāvatārārthamupādhyāyīkurmaḥ | asmābhiśca pṛcchyamānaḥ pramāṇatarīkariṣyate janeneti | ata evārcya tān sarvānityarcanamaviruddham | anyathā śiṣyasyopādhyāyātkīdṛśyarceti |*

345 आप्तः खलु साक्षात्कृतधर्मा यथादृष्टस्यार्थस्य चिख्यापयिषया प्रयुक्त उपदेष्टा । *Vātsyāyana-Bhāṣya* on *Nyāyasutra* 1.1.7 (Tailanga 1896)
*āptaḥ khalu sākṣātkṛtadharmā yathādṛṣṭasyārthasya cikhyāpayiṣayā prayukta upadeṣṭā* |

346 सम्यक्शब्दः प्रतिवचनविशेषणम् | सम्यक् प्रत्युवाच | प्रसन्नेन मनसा

न क्रोधादियोगेन | Medhātithi on *Manu* 1.4 (Dave 1972)
*samyakśabdaḥ prativacanaviśeṣaṇam | samyak pratyuvāca | prasannena manasā na krodhādiyogena |*

347 सम्यग्यथातत्त्वं *samyagyathātattvaṃ* Kullūka Bhaṭṭa on *Manu* 1.4 (Kaundinyayana 2014)

348 केनचित्परमकारुणिकेन दर्शितयोगमार्गः*Śaṅkara Bhāṣya* on *Muṇḍaka Upaniṣad* 3.1.2 (Mundakopanishadbhashyam n.d.)
*kenacitparamakāruṇikena darśitayogamārgaḥ*

349 ततस्तथा स तेनोक्तो महर्षिर् मनुना भृगुः ।
तानब्रवीदृषीन् सर्वान् प्रीतात्मा श्रूयतामिति ॥ *Manusmṛti* 1.60 (Kaundinyayana 2014)
*tatastathā sa tenokto maharṣir manunā bhṛguḥ* ।
*tānabravīdṛṣīn sarvān prītātmā śrūyatāmiti* ॥

350 श्रुतिस्मृत्योदितं धर्ममनुतिष्ठन् हि मानवः ।
इह कीर्तिमवाप्नोति चाऽनुत्तमं सुखम् ॥
श्रुतिस्तु वेदो विज्ञेयो धर्मशास्त्रं तु वै स्मृतिः ।
ते सर्वार्थेष्वमीमांस्ये ताभ्यां धर्मो हि निर्बभौ ॥ *Manusmṛti* 2.9-10 (Kaundinyayana 2014)
*śrutismṛtyoditaṃ dharmamanutiṣṭhan hi mānavaḥ* ।
*iha kīrtimavāpnoti pretya cā'nuttamaṃ sukham* ॥
*śrutistu vedo vijñeyo dharmaśāstraṃ tu vai smṛtiḥ* ।
*te sarvārtheṣvamīmāṃsye tābhyāṃ dharmo hi nirbabhau* ॥

351 The *Puruṣasūkta* is seen earliest in the *Ṛgveda*, as the 90th *sūkta* of its 10th *maṇḍala*, with 16 *mantras*. Later, it is seen in the *Vājasaneyisaṃhitā* of the Śuklayajurveda, the *Taittirīyāraṇyaka* of the *Kṛṣṇayajurveda*, the *Sāmaveda*, and the *Atharvaveda*, with some modifications and redactions.

References to Puruṣasūkta in this chapter is taken from *Srishti: Songs of Creation From the Vedas* by Koti Sreekrishna and Hari Ravikumar (2015)

352 In the context of *varṇas*, David Frawley writes: 'In this Vedic idea, human society follows the same organic order as the human body, which mirrors the order of the entire universe. Like the human body, human society should be one in nature, but differentiated according to functions. Just as the human body is one organism that has different limbs and organs with specialized activities necessary for the health and survival of the whole, so too, human society should have a similar organic differentiation, with different professions working together for the good of all (Frawley 2014).'

353 Max Müller, for example, writes, 'There can be little doubt, for instance, that the 90th hymn of the 10th book (Puruṣasūkta)… is modern both in its character and in its diction (Müller 1859, 570-571).' Likewise,Henry Thomas Colebrooke writes, 'It has a decidedly more modern tone, and must have been composed after the Sanskrit language had been refined (Colebrooke 1837).'

354 *Taittirīya Saṃhitā* 7.1.1.4-6 says: 'Prajāpati desired, "May I have offspring." He meted out the trivṛt from his mouth. After it the god Agni was created, the gāyatri metre, the rathamtara sāman, of men the brāhmana, of cattle the goat…From the breast and arms he meted out the pañcadaśa ṣṭoma. After it the god Indra was created, the triṣṭubh metre, the bṛhat sāman, of men the rājanya, of cattle the sheep… From the middle he meted out the saptadaśa ṣṭoma. After it the All-gods as deities were created, the jagati metre, the vairupa sāman, of

men the vaiśya, of cattle cows.... From his feet he meted out the ekavimśa ṣṭoma. After it the anuṣṭubh metre was created, the vairaja sāman, of men the śūdra, of cattle the horse. (Keith 1914).'

355 And *Jaiminīya Brāhmaṇa* 1.68-69 says: 'Prajāpati (and nothing else) existed here in the beginning. Now Prajāpati was the (vital) power mind. He desired: "May I become manifold. May I procreate. May I become abundant". He created from his top, from his head, the trivṛt laud, the gāyatri metre, the rathamtara melody, the deity Agni, the human being brāhmana, the animal goat...He created from both his arms and from his breast the Fifteenfold laud, the Triṣṭubh metre, the bṛhat melody, the deity Indra, the human being kṣatriya, the animal horse.... He created from his belly, from his middle, the Seventeenfold laud, the jagati metre, the vāmadevya melody, the deity All-gods, the human being vaiśya and the animal cow.... He created from his two feet, from his support, the Twenty-onefold laud, the anuṣṭubh metre, the yajñāyajñīya melody, no deity at all, the human being śūdra and the animal sheep (Bodewitz 1990).'

356 ब्राह्मणोऽस्य मुखमासीद् बाहू राजन्यः कृतः ।
ऊरू तदस्य यद्वैश्यः पद्भ्यां शूद्रो अजायत ।। *Puruṣasūkta* verse 12. (Purusha Suktam n.d.)
*brāhmaṇoSsya mukhamāsīd bāhū rājanya: kṛta:* |
ūrū tadasya yadvaiśya: padbhyāṃ śūdro ajāyata ||

357 यत्पुरुषेण हविषा देवा यज्ञमतन्वत | *Puruṣasūkta* verse 6. (Purusha Suktam n.d.)
*yatpuruṣeṇa haviṣā devā yajñamatanvata* |

358 चातुर्वर्ण्यं मया सृष्टं गुणकर्मविभागशः ।
तस्य कर्तारमपि मां विद्ध्यकर्तारमव्ययम् ॥ *Bhagavad Gītā* 4.13 (Gambhirananda 1998)
*cāturvarṇyaṃ mayā sṛṣṭaṃ guṇakarmavibhāgaśaḥ* ।
*tasya kartāramapi māṃ viddhyakartāramavyayam* ॥

359 ब्राह्मणक्षत्रियविशां शूद्राणां च परन्तप ।
कर्माणि प्रविभक्तानि स्वभावप्रभवैर्गुणै: ॥ ॥ *Bhagavad Gītā* 18.41 (Gambhirananda 1998)
*brāhmaṇakṣatriyaviśāṃ śaūdrāṇāṃ ca parantapa* ।
*karmāṇi pravibhaktāni svabhāvaprabhavairguṇai:* ॥

360 विप्रक्षत्रियविट्शूद्रा मुखबाहूरुपादजा: ।
वैराजात् पुरुषाज्जाता य आत्माचारलक्षणा: ॥ *Bhāgavata Purāṇa* 11.17.13 (Śrīmad-Bhāgavatam (Bhāgavata Purāṇa) n.d.)
*viprakṣatriyaviṭśūdrā mukhabāhūrupādajā:* ।
*vairājāt puruṣājjātā ya ātmācāralakṣaṇā:* ॥

361 जन्मान्तरकृतसंस्कारः प्राणिनां वर्तमानजन्मनि स्वकार्याभिमुखत्वेन अभिव्यक्तः स्वभावः, सः प्रभवो येषां गुणानां ते स्वभावप्रभवाः गुणाः ; गुणप्रादुर्भावस्य निष्कारणत्वानुपपत्तेः । 'स्वभावः कारणम्' इति च कारणविशेषोपादानम् । *Ādi Śaṅkarācārya* on *Bhagavad Gītā* 18.41 (Srimad-Bhagavadgita-bhashya n.d.)
*janmāntarakṛtasaṃskāraḥ prāṇināṃ vartamānajanmani svakāryābhimukhatvena abhivyaktaḥ svabhāvaḥ, saḥ prabhavo yeṣāṃ guṇānāṃ te svabhāvaprabhavāḥ guṇāḥ; guṇaprādurbhāvasya niṣkāraṇatvānupapatteḥ* । *'svabhāvaḥ kāraṇam' iti ca kāraṇaviśeṣopādānam* ।

362 तत्र सात्त्विकस्य सत्त्वप्रधानस्य ब्राह्मणस्य 'शमो दमस्तपः'इत्यादीनि कर्माणि, सत्त्वोपसर्जनरजःप्रधानस्य क्षत्रियस्य शौर्यतेजःप्रभृतीनि कर्माणि, तमउपसर्जनरजःप्रधानस्य वैश्यस्य कृष्यादीनि

कर्माणि, रजउपसर्जनतमःप्रधानस्य शूद्रस्य शुश्रूषैव कर्म इत्येवं गुणकर्मविभागशः चातुर्वर्ण्यं मया सृष्टम् इत्यर्थः । *Ādi Śaṅkarācārya* on *Bhagavad Gītā* 4.13 (Srimad-Bhagavadgita-bhashya n.d.)

*tatra sāttvikasya sattvapradhānasya brāhmaṇasya 'śamo damastapaḥ' ityādīni karmāṇi, sattvopasarjanarajaḥpradhānasya kṣatriyasya śauryatejaḥprabhṛtīni karmāṇi, tamaupasarjanarajaḥpradhānasya vaiśyasya kṛṣyādīni karmāṇi, rajaupasarjanatamaḥpradhānasya śūdrasya śuśrūṣaiva karma ityevaṃ guṇakarmavibhāgaśaḥ cāturvarṇyaṃ mayā sṛṣṭam ityarthaḥ* ।

अथवा ब्राह्मणस्वभावस्य सत्त्वगुणः प्रभवः कारणम्, तथा क्षत्रियस्वभावस्य सत्त्वोपसर्जनं रजः प्रभवः, वैश्यस्वभावस्य तमउपसर्जनं रजः प्रभवः, शूद्रस्वभावस्य रजउपसर्जनं तमः प्रभवः, प्रशान्त्यैश्वर्येहामूढतास्वभावदर्शनात् चतुर्णाम् । *Ādi Śaṅkarācārya* on *Bhagavad Gītā* 18.41 (Srimad-Bhagavadgita-bhashya n.d.)

*athavā brāhmaṇasvabhāvasya sattvaguṇaḥ prabhavaḥ kāraṇam, tathā kṣatriyasvabhāvasya sattvopasarjanaṃ rajaḥ prabhavaḥ, vaiśyasvabhāvasya tamaupasarjanaṃ rajaḥ prabhavaḥ, śūdrasvabhāvasya rajaupasarjanaṃ tamaḥ prabhavaḥ, praśāntyaiśvaryehāmūḍhatāsvabhāvadarśanāt caturṇām* ।

363 ब्राह्मणानां सितो वर्णः क्षत्रियाणां तु लोहितः ।
वैश्यानां पीतको वर्णः शूद्राणामसितस्तथा ॥ *Mahābhārata* 12.181.5 (Mahabharata: Critical Edition Prepared by Scholars at Bhandarkar Oriental Research Institute BORI n.d.)

*brāhmaṇānāṃ sito varṇaḥ kṣatriyāṇāṃ tu lohitaḥ* ।
*vaiśyānāṃ pītako varṇaḥ śūdrāṇāmasitastathā* ॥

364 शमो दमस्तप: शौचं सन्तोष: क्षान्तिरार्जवम् ।
मद्भक्तिश्च दया सत्यं ब्रह्मप्रकृतयस्त्विमा: ॥
तेजो बलं धृति: शौर्यं तितिक्षौदार्यमुद्यम: ।
स्थैर्यं ब्रह्मण्यमैश्वर्यं क्षत्रप्रकृतयस्त्विमा: ॥
आस्तिक्यं दाननिष्ठा च अदम्भो ब्रह्मसेवनम् ।
अतुष्टिरर्थोपचयैर्वैश्यप्रकृतयस्त्विमा: ॥
शुश्रूषणं द्विजगवां देवानां चाप्यमायया ।
तत्र लब्धेन सन्तोष: शूद्रप्रकृतयस्त्विमा: ॥ *Bhagavada Purāṇa* 11.17.16-19 (Śrīmad-Bhāgavatam (Bhāgavata Purāṇa) n.d.)
*śamo damastapa: śaucaṃ santoṣa: kṣāntirārjavam* ।
*madbhaktiśca dayā satyaṃ brahmaprakṛtayastvimā:* ॥
*tejo balaṃ dhṛti: śauryaṃ titikṣaudāryamudyama:* ।
*sthairyaṃ brahmaṇyamaiśvaryaṃ kṣatraprakṛtayastvimā:* ॥
*āstikyaṃ dānaniṣṭhā ca adambho brahmasevanam* ।
*atuṣṭirarthopacayairvaiśyaprakṛtayastvimā:* ॥
*śuśrūṣaṇaṃ dvijagavāṃ devānāṃ cāpyamāyayā* ।
*tatra labdhena santoṣa: śūdraprakṛtayastvimā:* ॥

365 चातुर्वर्ण्यं मया सृष्टं गुणकर्मविभागशः ।
तस्य कर्तारमपि मां विद्ध्यकर्तारमव्ययम् ॥ *Bhagavad Gītā* 4.13 (Gambhirananda 1998)
*cāturvarṇyaṃ mayā sṛṣṭaṃ guṇakarmavibhāgaśaḥ* ।
*tasya kartāramapi māṃ viddhyakartāramavyayam* ॥

366 गुणविभागेन कर्मविभागः । Ānandagiriṭīkā on Śaṅkarācārya's commentary on (Anandagiri Tika on Gita Bhashya n.d.).
*guṇavibhāgena karmavibhāgaḥ* ।

367 शमो दमस्तपः शौचं क्षान्तिरार्जवमेव च ।
ज्ञानं विज्ञानमास्तिक्यं ब्रह्मकर्म स्वभावजम् ॥
शौर्यं तेजो धृतिर्दाक्ष्यं युद्धे चाप्यपलायनम् ।
दानमीश्वरभावश्च क्षत्रकर्म स्वभावजम् ॥

कृषिगौरक्ष्यवाणिज्यं वैश्यकर्म स्वभावजम् ।
परिचर्यात्मकं कर्म शूद्रस्यापि स्वभावजम् ॥ *Bhagavad Gītā* 18.42-44 (Gambhirananda 1998)

*śamo damastapaḥ śaucaṃ kṣāntirārjavameva ca* ।
*jñānaṃ vijñānamāstikyaṃ brahmakarma svabhāvajam* ॥
*śauryaṃ tejo dhṛtirdākṣyaṃ yuddhe cāpyapalāyanam* ।
*dānamīśvarabhāvaśca kṣatrakarma svabhāvajam* ॥
*kṛṣigaurakṣyavāṇijyaṃ vaiśyakarma svabhāvajam* ।
*paricaryātmakaṃ karma śūdrasyāpi svabhāvajam* ॥

368 अध्यापनमध्ययनं यजनं याजनं तथा ।
दानं प्रतिग्रहं चैव ब्राह्मणानामकल्पयत् ॥
प्रजानां रक्षणं दानमिज्याऽध्ययनमेव च ।
विषयेष्वप्रसक्तिश्च क्षत्रियस्य समासतः ॥
पशूनां रक्षणं दानमिज्याऽध्ययनमेव च ।
वणिक्पथं कुसीदं च वैश्यस्य कृषिमेव च ॥
एकमेव तु शूद्रस्य प्रभुः कर्म समादिशत् ।
एतेषामेव वर्णानां शुश्रूषामनसूयया ॥ *Manusmṛti* 1.88-91 (Kaundinyayana 2014)

*adhyāpanamadhyayanaṃ yajanaṃ yājanaṃ tathā* ।
*dānaṃ pratigrahaṃ caiva brāhmaṇānāmakalpayat* ॥
*prajānāṃ rakṣaṇaṃ dānamijyā'dhyayanameva ca* ।
*viṣayeṣvaprasaktiśca kṣatriyasya samāsataḥ* ॥
*paśūnāṃ rakṣaṇaṃ dānamijyā'dhyayanameva ca* ।
*vaṇikpathaṃ kusīdaṃ ca vaiśyasya kṛṣimeva ca* ॥
*ekameva tu śūdrasya prabhuḥ karma samādiśat* ।
*eteṣāmeva varṇānāṃ śuśrūṣāmanasūyayā* ॥

369 यैः कर्मभिः प्रचरितैः शुश्रूष्यन्ते द्विजातयः ।
तानि कारुककर्माणि शिल्पानि विविधानि च ॥ *Manusmṛti* 10.100 (Kaundinyayana 2014)

*yaiḥ karmabhiḥ pracaritaiḥ śuśrūṣyante dvijātayaḥ* ।

*tāni kārukakarmāṇi śilpāni vividhāni ca* ||

370 ब्राह्मणोऽस्य मुखमासीद् बाहू राजन्य: कृत: ।
ऊरू तदस्य यद्वैश्य: पद्भ्यां शूद्रो अजायत ।। *Puruṣasūkta* verse 12. (Purusha Suktam n.d.)
*brāhmaṇoSsya mukhamāsīd bāhū rājanya: kṛta:* ।
*ūrū tadasya yadvaiśya: padbhyāṃ śūdro ajāyata* ।।

371 Ānandagiriṭīkā on *Chāndogyopaniṣad* 5.10.7 observes that good actions refer to *svakarma* i.e. *varṇāśrama dharma.*

372 तद्य इह रमणीयचरणा अभ्याशो ह यत्ते रमणीयां योनिमापद्येरन्ब्राह्मणयोनिं वा क्षत्रिययोनिं वा वैश्ययोनिं वाथ य इह कपूयचरणा अभ्याशो ह यत्ते कपूयां योनिमापद्येरञ्श्वयोनिं वा सूकरयोनिं वा चण्डालयोनिं वा ॥ *Chāndogya Upaniṣad* verse 5.10.7 (Lokeswarananda 1998)
*tadya iha ramaṇīyacaraṇā abhyāśo ha yatte ramaṇīyāṃ yonimāpadyeranbrāhmaṇayoniṃ vā kṣatriyayoniṃ vā vaiśyayoniṃ vātha ya iha kapūyacaraṇā abhyāśo ha yatte kapūyāṃ yonimāpadyerañśvayoniṃ vā sūkarayoniṃ vā caṇḍālayoniṃ vā* ||

373 वर्णा आश्रमाश्च स्वधर्मनिष्ठाः प्रेत्य कर्मफलमनुभूय ततः शेषेण विशिष्टदेशजातिकुलरूपायुःश्रुतवृत्तवित्तसुखमेधसो जन्म प्रतिपद्यन्ते ।।
*Gautama Dharmasūtra* 11.29 (Olivelle 2000).
*varṇā āśramāśca svadharmaniṣṭhāḥ pretya karmaphalamanubhūya tataḥ śeṣeṇa viśiṣṭadeśajātikularūpāyuḥśrutavṛttavittasukhamedhaso janma pratipadyante* ।।

374 धर्मचर्यया जघन्यो वर्णः पूर्वं पूर्वं वर्णमापद्यते जातिपरिवृत्तौ ॥
अधर्मचर्यया पूर्वो वर्णो जघन्यं जघन्यं वर्णमापद्यते जातिपरिवृत्तौ ॥

Āpastamba Dharmasūtra 2.11.10-11 (Olivelle 2000)
*dharmacaryayā jaghanyo varṇaḥ pūrvaṃ pūrvaṃ varṇamāpadyate jātiparivṛttau ||*
*adharmacaryayā pūrvo varṇo jaghanyaṃ jaghanyaṃ varṇamāpadyate jātiparivṛttau ||*

375 Though svakarma in a generic sense refers to all actions a person performs in life, it specifically refers to one's svadharma which is a combination of sāmānya *dharma* which is universal values and varṇā-āśrama *dharma* which are duties especially applicable to the person. If one leads a life by performing actions in alignment to one's svadharma, then it will lead to positive results. If one's actions are in violation of svadharma, then it will lead to negative results.

376 The references to higher or lower varṇa is a reference made in ritualistic and spiritual context of a jivatma who pursues mokṣa through a journey of series of births and deaths and rebirths. Birth and station in life which are most conductive to a person's journey towards mokṣa is considered higher, while conditions where obstructions to such spiritual journey are numerous, they are considered lower. Such descriptions are not to be understood as moral or ethical judgments. They are not judgements based on ethics, character, value-system, intelligence and other such traits, or socio-political-economic power. Moreover, even within the framework of varṇa, brāhmaṇas are called 'high' only in ritualistic sense. kṣatriyas, vaiśyas, and śūdras respectively occupy highest position in terms of political power, economic power, and demographic power.

377 कर्मणा जायते जन्तुः कर्मणैव प्रलीयते । सुखं दुःखं भयं शोकं कर्मणैव

प्रपद्यते ॥ १७ ॥ कर्मणेन्द्रो भवेज्जीवो ब्रह्मपुत्रः स्वकर्मणा । स्वकर्मणा हरेर्दासो जन्मादिरहितो भवेत् ॥ १८ ॥ स्वकर्मणा सर्वसिद्धिममरत्वं लभेदध्रुवम् । लभेत्स्वकर्मणा विष्णोः सालोक्यादिचतुष्टयम् ॥ १९ ॥ कर्मणा ब्राह्मणत्वं च मुक्तत्वं च स्वकर्मणा । सुरत्वं मनुजत्वं च राजेन्द्रत्वं लभेन्नरः ॥ २० ॥ कर्मणा च मुनीन्द्रत्वं तपस्वित्वं च कर्मणा । कर्मणा क्षत्रियत्वं च वैश्यत्वं च स्वकर्मणा ॥ २१ ॥ कर्मणा चैव शूद्रत्वमनत्यजत्वं स्वकर्मणा । स्वकर्मणा च म्लेच्छत्वं लभते नात्र संशयः ॥ २२ ॥ स्वकर्मणा जङ्गमत्वं स्थावरत्वं स्वकर्मणा ।स्वकर्मणा च शैलत्वं वृक्षत्वं च स्वकर्मणा ॥ २३॥ स्वकर्मणा पशुत्वं च पक्षित्वं च स्वकर्मणा । स्वकर्मणा क्षुद्रजन्तुः कृमित्वं च स्वकर्मणा ॥ २४॥ स्वकर्मणा च सर्पत्वं गन्धर्वत्वं स्वकर्मणा । स्वकर्मणा राक्षसत्वं किन्नरत्वं स्वकर्मणा ॥ २५॥ स्वकर्मणा च यक्षत्वं कूष्माणण्डत्वं स्वकर्मणा । स्वकर्मणा च प्रेतत्वं वेतालत्वं स्वकर्मणा ॥ २६ ॥ भूतत्वं च पिशाचत्वं डाकिनीत्वं स्वकर्मणा । दैत्यत्वं दानवत्वं चाप्यसुरत्वं स्वकर्मणा ॥२७॥ कर्मणा पुण्यवाञ्जीव महापापी स्वकर्मणा । कर्मणा सुन्दरोऽरोगी महारोगी च कर्मणा ॥ २८ ॥ कर्मणा चाङ्गहीनत्वं बधिरश्च स्वकर्मणा । कर्मणा चान्धः काणश्च कुत्सितश्च स्वकर्मणा ॥ २९॥ कर्मणा नरकं यान्ति जीवाः स्वर्गं स्वकर्मणा । कर्मणा शक्रलोकं च सूर्यलोकं स्वकर्मणा ।। ३० ।। कर्मणा चन्द्रलोकं च वह्निलोकं स्वकर्मणा । कर्मणा वायुलोकं च कर्मणा वरुणालयम् ॥ ३१॥ तथा कुबेरलोकं च नरो याति स्वकर्मणा । कर्मणा ध्रुवलोकं च शिवलोकं स्वकर्मणा ॥ ३२ ॥ नक्षत्रलोकं च सत्यलोकं स्वकर्मणा । जनोलोकं तपोलोकं महर्लोकं स्वकर्मणा ॥ ३३॥ स्वकर्मणा च पातालं ब्रह्मलोकं स्वकर्मणा । कर्मणा भारतं पुण्यं सर्वेषामीप्सितं परम् ॥ ३४॥ कर्मणा याति वैकुण्ठं गोलोकं च निरामयम् । कर्मणा चिरजीवी च क्षणायुश्च स्वकर्मणा ॥ ३५ ॥ कर्मणा कोटिकल्पायुः क्षीणायुश्च स्वकर्मणा । जीवसंसारमात्रायुर्गर्भे मृत्युः स्वकर्मणा॥३६॥ *Brahmavaivarta Purāṇa* 2.24.17-36 (Nagar 2005)

*karmaṇā jāyate jantuḥ karmaṇaiva pralīyate* | *sukhaṃ duḥkhaṃ bhayaṃ śokaṃ karmaṇaiva prapadyate* ‖ *17* ‖ *karmaṇendro bhavejjīvo brahmaputraḥ svakarmaṇā*

*| svakarmaṇā harerdāso janmādirahito bhavet || 18 || svakarmaṇā sarvasiddhimamaratvaṃ labhedadhruvam | labhetsvakarmaṇā viṣṇoḥ sālokyādicatuṣṭayam || 19 || karmaṇā brāhmaṇatvaṃ ca muktatvaṃ ca svakarmaṇā | suratvaṃ manujatvaṃ ca rājendratvaṃ labhennaraḥ || 20 || karmaṇā ca munīndratvaṃ tapasvitvaṃ ca karmaṇā | karmaṇā kṣatriyatvaṃ ca vaiśyatvaṃ ca svakarmaṇā || 21 || karmaṇā caiva śūdratvamanatyajatvaṃ svakarmaṇā | svakarmaṇā ca mlecchatvaṃ labhate nātra saṃśayaḥ || 22 || svakarmaṇā jaṅgamatvaṃ sthāvaratvaṃ svakarmaṇā | svakarmaṇā ca śailatvaṃ vṛkṣatvaṃ ca svakarmaṇā || 23 || svakarmaṇā paśutvaṃ ca pakṣitvaṃ ca svakarmaṇā | svakarmaṇā kṣudrajantuḥ kṛmitvaṃ ca svakarmaṇā || 24 || svakarmaṇā ca sarpatvaṃ gandharvatvaṃ svakarmaṇā | svakarmaṇā rākṣasatvaṃ kinnaratvaṃ svakarmaṇā || 25 || svakarmaṇā ca yakṣatvaṃ kūṣmāṇaṇḍatvaṃ svakarmaṇā | svakarmaṇā ca pretatvaṃ vetālatvaṃ svakarmaṇā || 26 || bhūtatvaṃ ca piśācatvaṃ ḍākinītvaṃ svakarmaṇā | daityatvaṃ dānavatvaṃ cāpyasuratvaṃ svakarmaṇā ||27|| karmaṇā puṇyavāñjīva mahāpāpī svakarmaṇā | karmaṇā sundaro'rogī mahārogī ca karmaṇā || 28 || karmaṇā cāṅgahīnatvaṃ badhiraśca svakarmaṇā | karmaṇā cāndhaḥ kāṇaśca kutsitaśca svakarmaṇā || 29 || karmaṇā narakaṃ yānti jīvāḥ svargaṃ svakarmaṇā | karmaṇā śakralokaṃ ca sūryalokaṃ svakarmaṇā || 30 || karmaṇā candralokaṃ ca vahnilokaṃ svakarmaṇā | karmaṇā vāyulokaṃ ca karmaṇā varuṇālayam || 31 || tathā kuberalokaṃ ca naro yāti svakarmaṇā | karmaṇā dhruvalokaṃ ca śivalokaṃ svakarmaṇā || 32 || nakṣatralokaṃ ca satyalokaṃ svakarmaṇā | janolokaṃ tapolokaṃ maharlokaṃ svakarmaṇā || 33 || svakarmaṇā ca pātālaṃ brahmalokaṃ svakarmaṇā | karmaṇā bhārataṃ puṇyaṃ sarveṣāmīpsitaṃ param || 34 || karmaṇā*

*yāti vaikuṇṭhaṃ golokaṃ ca nirāmayam* । *karmaṇā cirajīvī ca kṣaṇāyuśca svakarmaṇā* ॥ *35* ॥ *karmaṇā koṭikalpāyuḥ kṣīṇāyuśca svakarmaṇā* । jīvasaṃsāramātrāyurgarbhe mṛtyuḥ svakarmaṇā ॥*36*॥

378 सर्ववर्णेषु तुल्यासु पत्नीष्वक्षतयोनिषु । आनुलोम्येन सम्भूता जात्या ज्ञेयास्त एव ते ॥ *Manusmṛti* 10.5 (Kaundinyayana 2014)
*sarvavarṇeṣu tulyāsu patnīṣvakṣatayoniṣu* ।
ānulomyena sambhūtā jātyā jñeyāsta eva te ॥

379 सवर्णापूर्वशास्त्रविहितायां यथर्तु गच्छतः पुत्रास्तेषां कर्मभिः संबन्धः|| Āpaśtamba Dharmasūtra 2.13.1. (Olivelle 2000)
*savarṇāpūrvaśāstravihitāyāṃ yathartu gacchataḥ putrāsteṣāṃ karmabhiḥ saṃbandhaḥ* ||

380 समानवर्णासु पुचाः सवर्णा भवन्ति ।। *Viṣṇusmṛti* 16.1. (Jolly 1881)
*samānavarṇāsu pucāḥ savarṇā bhavanti* ।।

381 सवर्णेभ्यः सवर्णासु जायन्ते हि सजातयः|| *Yājñavalkyasmṛti* 1.90 (Pansikar 1936)
*savarṇebhyaḥ savarṇāsu jāyante hi sajātayaḥ* ||

382 तत्र सवर्णासु सवर्णाः|| *Baudhāyana Dharmasūtra* 1.17.2. (Olivelle 2000)
*tatra savarṇāsu savarṇāḥ* ||

383 जायमानो वै ब्राह्मणस् त्रिभिर् ऋणवा जायते ब्रह्मचर्येनर्षिभ्यो यज्ञेन देवेभ्यः प्रजय पितृभ्य *Taittirīya Saṃhitā* 6.3.10.5 (Taittiriya Samhita- Searchable Text n.d.)
*jāyamāno vai brāhmaṇas tribhir ṛṇavā jāyate brahmacaryenarṣibhyo yajñena devebhyaḥ prajaya pitṛbhya*

384 आ ब्रह्मन्ब्राह्मणो ब्रह्मवर्चसी जायताम राष्ट्रे राजन्यः शूर इषव्योऽतिव्याधी महारथो जायतां *Shukla Yajurveda Vajasaneyi Samhita 22.22* (Weber 1852)
*ā brahmanbrāhmaṇo brahmavarcasī jāyatāma rāṣṭre rājanyaḥ śūra iṣavyo›tivyādhī mahāratho jāyatāṃ*

385 ब्राह्मण्यं देवि दुष्प्रापं निसर्गाद्ब्राह्मणः शुभे ।
क्षत्रियो वैश्यशूद्रौ वा निसर्गादिति मे मतिः ॥ *Mahābhārata Anuśāsanaparva* 131.6 *(Mahabharata: Critical Edition* Prepared by Scholars at Bhandarkar Oriental Research Institute BORI n.d.)
*brāhmaṇyaṃ devi duṣprāpaṃ nisargādbrāhmaṇaḥ śubhe* ।
*kṣatriyo vaiśyaśūdrau vā nisargāditi me matiḥ* ॥

386 This verse is only found in Southern editions of Mahābhārata. ब्राह्मणो हि महद्दैवं जातिमात्रेण जायते । *Mahābhārata Aśvamedhikāparva* 98.82 (Krishnacharya and Vyasacharya 1910)
*brāhmaṇo hi mahaddaivaṃ jātimātreṇa jāyate* ।

387 This verse is found only in Southern editions of Mahābhārata. उत्पत्तिरेव विप्रस्य मूर्तिधर्मस्य शाश्वती । *Mahābhārata Aśvamedhikāparva* 98.85 (Krishnacharya and Vyasacharya 1910)
*utpattireva viprasya mūrtidharmasya śāśvatī* ।

388 वर्णानामाश्रमाणां च जन्मभूम्यनुसारिणीः ।
आसन् प्रकृतयो नृणां नीचैर्नीचोत्तमोत्तमाः ॥ *Bhāgavata Purāṇa* 11.17.15 (Śrīmad-Bhāgavatam (Bhāgavata Purāṇa) n.d.)
*varṇānāmāśramāṇāṃ ca janmabhūmyanusāriṇī:* ।
*āsan prakṛtayo nṛṇāṃ nīcairnīcottamottamā:* ॥

389 ब्रह्मणे ब्राह्मणमालभते । क्षत्राय राजन्यम् । मरुद्भ्यो वैश्यम् । तपसे शूद्रम् | *Taittirīya Brāhmaṇa* 3.4.1.1 (Sayanacharya, 1863)
*brahmaṇe brāhmaṇamālabhate | kṣatrāya rājanyam | marudbhyo vaiśyam | tapase śūdram |*

390 'ब्रह्म' ब्राह्मणजात्यभिमानी देवः । तस्मै कश्चिद्ब्रह्मवर्च्चसयुक्तं 'ब्राह्मण'जातीयं पुरुषम्' आलभते' । क्षत्रिय जात्यभिमानी देवताय कश्चित् क्षत्रियजातीयं, देववैश्येभ्यो 'मरुद्भ्यः', मनुष्य 'वैश्यं', कृच्छचान्द्रायणादिदुःखरूपतपो देवाय दुःखेभ्यो जीवनं 'शूद्रं' । Sāyaṇācārya's commentary on *Taittirīya Brāhmaṇa 3.4.1.1* (Sayanacharya 1863)
*'brahma' brāhmaṇajātyabhimānī devaḥ | tasmai kañcidbrahmavarccasayuktaṃ 'brāhmaṇa'jātīyaṃ puruṣam' ālabhate' | kṣatriya jātyabhimānī devatāya kañcit kṣatriyajātīyaṃ, devavaiśyebhyo 'marudbhyaḥ', manuṣya 'vaiśyaṃ', kṛcchacāndrāyaṇādiduḥkharūpatapo devāya duḥkhebhyo jīvanaṃ 'śūdraṃ' |*

391 ब्रह्म वा इदमग्र आसीदेकमेव तदेकं सन्न व्यभवत् । तच्छ्रेयोरूपमत्यसृजत क्षत्रं यान्येतानि देवत्रा क्षत्राणीन्द्रो वरुणः सोमो रुद्रः पर्जन्यो यमो मृत्युरीशान इति । तस्मात्क्षत्रात्परं नास्ति तस्माद्ब्रह्मणः क्षत्रियमधस्तादुपास्ते राजसूये क्षत्र एव तद्यशो दधाति सैषा क्षत्रस्य योनिर्यद्ब्रह्म । तस्माद्यद्यपि राजा परमतां गच्छति ब्रह्मैवान्तत उपनिश्रयति स्वां योनिं य उ एनं हिनस्ति स्वां स योनिमृच्छति स पापीयान्भवति यथा श्रेयां सं हिंसित्वा ॥ *Bṛhadāraṇyaka Upaniṣad* 1.4.11 (Brihadaranyakopanishad-bhashyam n.d.)
*brahma vā idamagra āsīdekameva tadekaṃ sanna vyabhavat | tacchreyorūpamatyasṛjata kṣatraṃ yānyetāni devatrā kṣatrāṇīndro varuṇaḥ somo rudraḥ parjanyo yamo mṛtyurīśāna iti | tasmātkṣatrātparaṃ nāsti tasmādbrahmaṇaḥ kṣatriyamadhastādupāste rājasūye kṣatra eva tadyaśo dadhāti saiṣā kṣatrasya yoniryadbrahma | tasmādyadyapi rājā*

*paramatāṃ gacchati brahmaivāntata upaniśrayati svāṃ yoniṃ ya u enaṃ hinasti svāṃ sa yonimṛcchati sa pāpīyānbhavati yathā śreyāṃ saṃ hiṃsitvā* ॥

392 ब्रह्म वा इदमग्र आसीत् — यदग्निं सृष्ट्वा अग्निरूपापन्नं ब्रह्म — ब्राह्मणजात्यभिमानात् ब्रह्मेत्यभिधीयते — वै, इदं क्षत्रादिजातम्, ब्रह्मैव, अभिन्नमासीत् , एकमेव - न आसीत्क्षत्रादिभेदः । Ādi Śaṅkarācārya's commentary on *Bṛhadāraṇyaka Upaniṣad* 1.4.11 (Brihadaranyakopanishad-bhashyam n.d.)
*brahma vā idamagra āsīt—yadagniṃ sṛṣṭvā agnirūpāpannaṃ brahma — brāhmaṇajātyabhimānāt brahmetyabhidhīyate— vai, idaṃ kṣatrādijātam, brahmaiva, abhinnamāsīt, ekameva - na āsītkṣatrādibhedaḥ* ।

393 तदनु इन्द्रादिक्षत्रदेवताधिष्ठितानि मनुष्यक्षत्राणि सोमसूर्यवंश्यानि पुरूरवःप्रभृतीनि सृष्टान्येव द्रष्टव्यानि ; तदर्थ एव हि देवक्षत्रसर्गः प्रस्तुतः । Ādi Śaṅkarācārya's commentary on *Bṛhadāraṇyaka Upaniṣad* 1.4.11 (Brihadaranyakopanishad-bhashyam n.d.)
*tadanu indrādikṣatradevatādhiṣṭhitāni manuṣyakṣatrāṇi somasūryavaṃśyāni purūravaḥprabhṛtīni sṛṣṭānyeva draṣṭavyāni; tadartha eva hi devakṣatrasargaḥ prastutaḥ* ।

394 स नैव व्यभवत्स विशमसृजत यान्येतानि देवजातानि गणश आख्यायन्ते वसवो रुद्रा आदित्या विश्वेदेवा मरुत इति ॥ स नैव व्यभवत्स शौद्रं वर्णममृजत पूषणमियं वै पूषेयं हीदं सर्वं पुष्यति यदिदं किञ्च ॥
*Bṛhadāraṇyaka Upaniṣad* 1.4.12-13 (Madhavananda 1950)
*sa naiva vyabhavatsa viśamasṛjata yānyetāni devajātāni gaṇaśa ākhyāyante vasavo rudrā ādityā viśvedevā maruta iti* ॥
*sa naiva vyabhavatsa śaudraṃ varṇamamṛjata pūṣaṇamiyaṃ vai pūṣeyaṃ hīdaṃ sarvaṃ puṣyati yadidaṃ kiñca* ॥

395 स नैव व्यभवत्तच्छ्रेयोरूपमत्यसृजत धर्मं तदेतत्क्षत्रस्य क्षत्त्रं यद्धर्मस्तस्माद्धर्मात्परं नास्त्यथो अबलीयान्बलीयां समाशंसते धर्मेण यथा राज्ञैवं यो वै स धर्मः सत्यं वै तत्तस्मात्सत्यं वदन्तमाहुर्धर्मं वदतीति धर्मं वा वदन्तं सत्यं वदतीत्येतद्ध्येवैतदुभयं भवति ॥ *Bṛhadāraṇyaka Upaniṣad* 1.4.14 (Madhavananda 1950)
*sa naiva vyabhavattacchreyorūpamatyasṛjata dharmaṃ tadetatkṣatrasya kṣattraṃ yaddharmastasmāddharmātparaṃ nāstyatho abalīyānbalīyāṃ samāśaṃsate dharmeṇa yathā rājñaivaṃ yo vai sa dharmaḥ satyaṃ vai tattasmātsatyaṃ vadantamāhurdharmaṃ vadatīti dharmaṃ vā vadantaṃ satyaṃ vadatītyetaddhyevaitadubhayaṃ bhavati* ॥

396 तदेतद्ब्रह्म क्षत्रं विट्शूद्रस्तदग्निनैव देवेषु ब्रह्माभवद्ब्राह्मणो मनुष्येषु क्षत्रियेण क्षत्रियो वैश्येन वैश्यः शूद्रेण शूद्रस्तस्मादग्नावेव देवेषु लोकमिच्छन्ते ब्राह्मणे मनुष्येष्वेताभ्यां हि रूपाभ्यां ब्रह्माभवत् । *Bṛhadāraṇyaka Upaniṣad* 1.4.15 (Madhavananda 1950)
*tadetadbrahma kṣatraṃ viṭśūdrastadagninaiva deveṣu brahmābhavadbrāhmaṇo manuṣyeṣu kṣatriyeṇa kṣatriyo vaiśyena vaiśyaḥ śūdreṇa śūdrastasmādagnāveva deveṣu lokamicchante brāhmaṇe manuṣyeṣvetābhyāṃ hi rūpābhyāṃ brahmābhavat* ।

397 यत्तत् स्रष्ट ब्रह्म, तदग्निनैव, नान्येन रूपेण, देवेषु ब्रह्म ब्राह्मणजातिः, अभवत् ; ब्राह्मणः ब्राह्मणस्वरूपेण, मनुष्येषु ब्रह्माभवत् ; इतरेषु वर्णेषु विकारान्तरं प्राप्य, क्षत्रियेण — क्षत्रियोऽभवत् इन्द्रादिदेवताधिष्ठितः, वैश्येन वैश्यः, शूद्रेण शूद्रः । यस्मात्क्षत्रादिषु विकारापन्नम् , अग्नौ ब्राह्मण एव चाविकृतं स्रष्टृ ब्रह्म, तस्मादग्नावेव देवेषु देवानां मध्ये लोकं कर्मफलम् , इच्छन्ति, अग्निसम्बद्धं कर्म कृत्वेत्यर्थः ; तदर्थमेव हि तद्ब्रह्म कर्माधिकरणत्वेनाग्निरूपेण व्यवस्थितम् ; तस्मात्तस्मिन्नग्नौ कर्म कृत्वा तत्फलं प्रार्थयन्त इत्येतत् उपपन्नम् । ब्राह्मणे मनुष्येषु — मनुष्याणां पुनर्मध्ये कर्मफलेच्छायां नाग्न्यादिनिमित्तक्रियापेक्षा, किं तर्हि जातिमात्रस्वरूपप्रतिलम्भेनैव पुरुषार्थसिद्धिः । Ādi Śaṅkarācārya's

commentary on *Bṛhadāraṇyaka Upaniṣad* 1.4.15 (Madhavananda 1950)

*yattat sraṣṭṛ brahma, tadagninaiva, nānyena rūpeṇa, deveṣu brahma brāhmaṇajātiḥ, abhavat ; brāhmaṇaḥ brāhmaṇasvarūpeṇa, manuṣyeṣu brahmābhavat ; itareṣu varṇeṣu vikārāntaraṃ prāpya, kṣatriyeṇa — kṣatriyo'bhavat indrādidevatādhiṣṭhitaḥ, vaiśyena vaiśyaḥ, śūdreṇa śūdraḥ* । *yasmātkṣatrādiṣu vikārāpannam , agnau brāhmaṇa eva cāvikṛtaṃ sraṣṭṛ brahma, tasmādagnāveva deveṣu devānāṃ madhye lokaṃ karmaphalam , icchanti, agnisambaddhaṃ karma kṛtvetyarthaḥ ; tadarthameva hi tadbrahma karmādhikaraṇatvenāgnirūpeṇa vyavasthitam ; tasmāttasminnagnau karma kṛtvā tatphalaṃ prārthayanta ityetat upapannam* । *brāhmaṇe manuṣyeṣu — manuṣyāṇāṃ punarmadhye karmaphalecchāyāṃ nāgnyādinimittakriyāpekṣā, kiṃ tarhi jātimātrasvarūpapratilambhenaiva puruṣārthasiddhiḥ* ।

398 क्षत्रियो यदि वा वैश्यः शूद्रो वा राजसत्तम
ब्राह्मण्यं प्राप्नुयात्केन तन्मे व्याख्यातुमर्हसि ॥
तपसा वा सुमहता कर्मणा वा श्रुतेन वा
ब्राह्मण्यमथ चेदिच्छेत्तन्मे ब्रूहि पितामह ॥ *Mahābhārata Anuśāsanaparva* 28.2-3 (Mahabharata: Critical Edition Prepared by Scholars at Bhandarkar Oriental Research Institute BORI n.d.)

*kṣatriyo yadi vā vaiśyaḥ śūdro vā rājasattama*
*brāhmaṇyaṃ prāpnuyātkena tanme vyākhyātumarhasi ||*
*tapasā vā sumahatā karmaṇā vā śrutena vā*
*brāhmaṇyamatha cedicchettanme brūhi pitāmaha ||*

399 ब्राह्मण्यं तात दुष्प्रापं वर्णैः क्षत्रादिभिस्त्रिभिः
परं हि सर्वभूतानां स्थानमेतद्युधिष्ठिर॥

बह्वीस्तु संसरन्योनीर्जायमानः पुनः पुनः
पर्याये तात कस्मिंश्चिद्ब्राह्मणो नाम जायते || *Mahābhārata Anuśāsanaparva* 28.4-5 (Mahabharata: Critical Edition Prepared by Scholars at Bhandarkar Oriental Research Institute BORI n.d.)
*brāhmaṇyaṃ tāta duṣprāpaṃ varṇaiḥ kṣatrādibhistribhiḥ*
*paraṃ hi sarvabhūtānāṃ sthānametadyudhiṣṭhira* ||
*bahvīstu saṃsaranyonīrjāyamānaḥ punaḥ punaḥ*
*paryāye tāta kasmiṃścidbrāhmaṇo nāma jāyate* ||

400 मतङ्ग परमं स्थानं प्रार्थयन्नतिदुर्लभम् ||
मा कृथाः साहसं पुत्र नैष धर्मपथस्तव
अप्राप्यं प्रार्थयानो हि नचिराद्विनशिष्यसि ||
मतङ्ग परमं स्थानं वार्यमाणो मया सकृत्
चिकीर्षस्येव तपसा सर्वथा न भविष्यसि ||
तिर्यग्योनिगतः सर्वो मानुष्यं यदि गच्छति
स जायते पुल्कसो वा चण्डालो वा कदाचन ||
पुंश्चलः पापयोनिर्वा यः कश्चिदिह लक्ष्यते
स तस्यामेव सुचिरं मतङ्ग परिवर्तते ||
ततो दशगुणे काले लभते शूद्रतामपि
शूद्रयोनावपि ततो बहुशः परिवर्तते ||
ततस्त्रिंशद्गुणे काले लभते वैश्यतामपि
वैश्यतायां चिरं कालं तत्रैव परिवर्तते ||
ततः षष्टिगुणे काले राजन्यो नाम जायते
राजन्यत्वे चिरं कालं तत्रैव परिवर्तते ||
ततः षष्टिगुणे काले लभते ब्रह्मबन्धुताम्
ब्रह्मबन्धुश्चिरं कालं तत्रैव परिवर्तते ||
ततस्तु द्विशते काले लभते काण्डपृष्ठताम्
काण्डपृष्ठश्चिरं कालं तत्रैव परिवर्तते ||
ततस्तु त्रिशते काले लभते द्विजतामपि
तां च प्राप्य चिरं कालं तत्रैव परिवर्तते ||
ततश्चतुःशते काले श्रोत्रियो नाम जायते

श्रोत्रियत्वे चिरं कालं तत्रैव परिवर्तते ॥
तदैव क्रोधहर्षौ च कामद्वेषौ च पुत्रक
अतिमानातिवादौ तमाविशन्ति द्विजाधमम् ॥
तांश्चेज्जयति शत्रून्स तदा प्राप्नोति सद्गतिम्
अथ ते वै जयन्त्येनं तालाग्रादिव पात्यते ॥
मतङ्ग संप्रधार्यैतद्यदहं त्वामचूचुदम्
वृणीष्व काममन्यं त्वं ब्राह्मण्यं हि सुदुर्लभम् ॥ *Mahābhārata Anuśāsanaparva* 29.2-16 (Mahabharata: Critical Edition Prepared by Scholars at Bhandarkar Oriental Research Institute BORI n.d.)

*mataṅga paramaṃ sthānaṃ prārthayannatidurlabham ||*
*mā kṛthāḥ sāhasaṃ putra naiṣa dharmapathastava*
*aprāpyaṃ prārthayāno hi nacirādvinaśiṣyasi ||*
*mataṅga paramaṃ sthānaṃ vāryamāṇo mayā sakṛt*
*cikīrṣasyeva tapasā sarvathā na bhaviṣyasi ||*
*tiryagyonigataḥ sarvo mānuṣyaṃ yadi gacchati*
*sa jāyate pulkaso vā caṇḍālo vā kadācana ||*
*puṃścalaḥ pāpayonirvā yaḥ kaścidiha lakṣyate*
*sa tasyāmeva suciraṃ mataṅga parivartate ||*
*tato daśaguṇe kāle labhate śūdratāmapi*
*śūdrayonāvapi tato bahuśaḥ parivartate ||*
*tatastriṃśadguṇe kāle labhate vaiśyatāmapi*
*vaiśyatāyāṃ ciraṃ kālaṃ tatraiva parivartate ||*
*tataḥ ṣaṣṭiguṇe kāle rājanyo nāma jāyate*
*rājanyatve ciraṃ kālaṃ tatraiva parivartate ||*
*tataḥ ṣaṣṭiguṇe kāle labhate brahmabandhutām*
*brahmabandhuściraṃ kālaṃ tatraiva parivartate ||*
*tatastu dviśate kāle labhate kāṇḍapṛṣṭhatām*
*kāṇḍapṛṣṭhaściraṃ kālaṃ tatraiva parivartate ||*
*tatastu triśate kāle labhate dvijatāmapi*
*tāṃ ca prāpya ciraṃ kālaṃ tatraiva parivartate ||*
*tataścatuḥśate kāle śrotriyo nāma jāyate*

*śrotriyatve ciraṃ kālaṃ tatraiva parivartate ||*
*tadaiva krodhaharṣau ca kāmadveṣau ca putraka*
*atimānātivādau tamāviśanti dvijādhamam ||*
*tāṃścejjayati śatrūnsa tadā prāpnoti sadgatim*
*atha te vai jayantyenaṃ tālāgrādiva pātyate ||*
*mataṅga saṃpradhāryaitadyadahaṃ tvāmacūcudam*
*vṛṇīṣva kāmamanyaṃ tvaṃ brāhmaṇyaṃ hi sudurlabham ||*

401 छन्दोदेव इति ख्यातः स्त्रीणां पूज्यो भविष्यसि || *Mahābhārata Anuśāsanaparva* 30.14 (Mahabharata: Critical Edition Prepared by Scholars at Bhandarkar Oriental Research Institute BORI n.d.)
*chandodeva iti khyātaḥ strīṇāṃ pūjyo bhaviṣyasi |*

402 प्राणांस्त्यक्त्वा मतङ्गोऽपि प्राप तत्स्थानमुत्तमम् | *Mahābhārata Anuśāsanaparva* 30.15 (Mahabharata: Critical Edition Prepared by Scholars at Bhandarkar Oriental Research Institute BORI n.d.)
*prāṇāṃstyaktvā mataṅgo'pi prāpa tatsthānamuttamam |*

403 'If a person abandons the status of a brāhmaṇa and follows the *dharma* of a kṣatriya, he is dislodged from the status of a brāhmaṇa and is reborn as a kṣatriya. The status of a brāhmaṇa is extremely difficult to obtain. However, because of greed and confusion, a brāhmaṇa may always resort to the work of vaiśyas and this shows extreme folly. A brāhmaṇa can thus become a vaiśya and a vaiśya can become a śūdra. A brāhmaṇa can be dislodged from his own *dharma* and can become a śūdra. Such a brāhmaṇa is dislodged from his varṇa and becomes an outcast.... He is reborn as a śūdra. An immensely fortunate kṣatriya or vaiśya can also deviate from his own *dharma* and tasks and follow the tasks meant

for a śūdra. Dislodged from this own position, he causes a confusion of *varṇas*. In this way, brāhmaṇas, kṣatriyas and vaiśyas can become śūdras…. However, by performing the acts associated with virtuous conduct, a śūdra can obtain the status of a brāhmaṇa and a vaiśya that of a kṣatriya. Following the law and the ordinances, a śūdra must make efforts to serve and attend to the needs of the superior *varṇas*. Without any distraction, a śūdra must always remain established in this path of the virtuous…. A śūdra who desires to become a vaiśya must not eat pointless meat. He must be truthful in speech…. A vaiśya must thus tend to the three fires. Such a vaiśya is pure and obtains greatness by being born in a family of kṣatriyas. If such a vaiśya is born as a kṣatriya, observes all the sacraments from the time of birth, performs virtuous deeds and observes all the vows, thereafter, he becomes a brāhmaṇa…' Mahābhārata Anuśāsanaparva chapter 131 (Debroy, The Mahabharata, Volume 9 2015).

404 ब्राह्मण्यं काचिद्देवता । सा यस्मिन्नेव देहेऽभिव्यक्ता भवति ते ब्राह्मणा इत्युच्यन्ते । अत एव शापादिना शूद्रत्वं चण्डालत्वमनुग्रहेण ब्रह्मत्वमिति । सा चोपनयनेन देहे समायाति । *Subodhinī* on *Bhāgavata Purāṇa* 2.1.37 (Vallabhacharya 1986)
*brāhmaṇyaṃ kāciddevatā* । sā yasminneva dehe›bhivyaktā bhavati te brāhmaṇā ityucyante । *ata eva śāpādinā śūdratvaṃ caṇḍālatvamanugraheṇa brahmatvamiti* । sā copanayanena dehe samāyāti ।

405 निर्गुणं निर्मलं ब्रह्म यत्र तिष्ठति स द्विजः ॥
एते योनिफला देवि स्थानभागनिदर्शकाः| *Mahābhārata Anuśāsanaparva* 131.51-52 (Mahabharata: Critical Edition Prepared by Scholars at Bhandarkar Oriental Research Institute BORI n.d.)

*nirguṇaṃ nirmalaṃ brahma yatra tiṣṭhati sa dvijaḥ ||*
*ete yoniphalā devi sthānabhāganidarśakāḥ |*

406 पुरुषे ह वा अयमादितो गर्भो भवति । यदेतद्रेतस्तदेतत्सर्वेभ्योऽङ्गेभ्यस्तेजः सम्भूतमात्मन्येवात्मानं बिभर्ति तद्यथा स्त्रियां सिञ्चत्यथैनज्जनयति तदस्य प्रथमं जन्म ॥ तत्स्त्रिया आत्मभूयं गच्छति यथा स्वमङ्गं तथा । तस्मादेनां न हिनस्ति सास्यैतमात्मानमत्र गतं भावयति ॥ सा भावयित्री भावयितव्या भवति तं स्त्री गर्भं बिभर्ति सोऽग्र एव कुमारं जन्मनोऽग्रेऽधि भावयति । स यत्कुमारं जन्मनोऽग्रेऽधि भावयत्यात्मानमेव तद्भावयत्येषां लोकानां सन्तत्या एवं सन्तता हीमे लोकास्तदस्य द्वितीयं जन्म ॥ सोऽस्यायमात्मा पुण्येभ्यः कर्मभ्यः प्रतिधीयते । अथास्यायमितर आत्मा कृतकृत्यो वयोगतः प्रैति स इतः प्रयन्नेव पुनर्जायते तदस्य तृतीयं जन्म ॥ *Aitareyopaniṣad* 2.1.1-4 (Aitereyoupanishad-bhashyam n.d.)
*puruṣe ha vā ayamādito garbho bhavati* | *yadetadretastadetatsarvebhyo'ṅgebhyastejaḥ sambhūtamātmanyevātmānaṃ bibharti tadyathā striyāṃ siñcatyathainajjanayati tadasya prathamaṃ janma* || *tatstriyā ātmabhūyaṃ gacchati yathā svamaṅgaṃ tathā* | *tasmādenāṃ na hinasti sāsyaitamātmānamatra gataṃ bhāvayati* || sā bhāvayitrī bhāvayitavyā bhavati taṃ strī garbhaṃ bibharti so›gra eva kumāraṃ janmano›gre›dhi bhāvayati | *sa yatkumāraṃ janmano'gre'dhi bhāvayatyātmānameva tadbhāvayatyeṣāṃ lokānāṃ santatyā evaṃ santatā hīme lokāstadasya dvitīyaṃ janma* || *so'syāyamātmā puṇyebhyaḥ karmabhyaḥ pratidhīyate* | *athāsyāyamitara ātmā kṛtakṛtyo vayogataḥ praiti sa itaḥ prayanneva punarjāyate tadasya tṛtīyaṃ janma* ||

407 पतिर्भार्यां सम्प्रविश्य गर्भो भूत्वेह जायते ।
जायायास्तद् धि जायात्वं यदस्यां जायते पुनः ॥ *Manusmṛti* 9.8 (Kaundinyayana 2014)
*patirbhāryāṃ sampraviśya garbho bhūtveha jāyate* |
*jāyāyāstad dhi jāyātvaṃ yadasyāṃ jāyate punaḥ* ||

408 तस्या वेदिरुपस्थो लोमानि बर्हिश्चर्माधिषवणे समिद्धो मध्यतस्तौ मुष्कौ स यावान्ह वै वाजपेयेन यजमानस्य लोको भवति तावानस्य लोको भवति... *Bṛhadāraṇyaka Upaniṣad* 6.4.3 (Brihadaranyakopanishad-bhashyam n.d.)
*tasyā vedirupastho lomāni barhiścarmādhiṣavaṇe samiddho madhyatastau muṣkau sa yāvānha vai vājapeyena yajamānasya loko bhavati tāvānasya loko bhavati...*

409 Though the verse appears as 8.26 in (Dutt 1908), it is present as verse 8.19 in *Pārāśaramādhava, Prāyaścittakāṇḍam* (Tripati 2019): चित्रकर्म यथाऽनेकैरङ्गैरुन्मील्यते शनैः । ब्राह्मण्यमपि तद्वद्धि संस्कारैर्मन्त्रपूर्वकैः ॥
*citrakarma yathā'nekairaṅgairunmīlyate śanaiḥ* ।
*brāhmaṇyamapi tadvaddhi saṃskārairmantrapūrvakaiḥ* ॥

410 जन्मशारीरविद्ययाभिराचारेण श्रुतेन च।
धर्मेण च यथोक्तेन ब्राह्मणत्वं विधीयते ।
चित्रकर्म यथाऽनेकैरङ्गैरुन्मील्यते शनैः ।
ब्राह्मण्यमपि तद्वत् स्यात् संस्कारैर्विधिपूर्वकैः ॥ Verse from Aṅgirā cited in *Pārāśaramādhava* commentary on *Pārāśarasmṛti* 8.26 (Tripati 2019)
*janmaśārīravidyayābhirācāreṇa śrutena ca* ।
*dharmeṇa ca yathoktena brāhmaṇatvaṃ vidhīyate* ।
*citrakarma yathā'nekairaṅgairunmīlyate śanaiḥ* ।
*brāhmaṇyamapi tadvat syāt saṃskārairvidhipūrvakaiḥ* ॥

411 स्वाध्यायेन व्रतैर्होमैस्त्रैविद्येनेज्यया सुतैः ।
महायज्ञैश्च यज्ञैश्च ब्राह्मीयं क्रियते तनुः ॥ *Manusmṛti* 2.28 (Kaundinyayana 2014)
*svādhyāyena vratairhomaistraividyenejyayā sutaiḥ* ।
*mahāyajñaiśca yajñaiśca brāhmīyaṃ kriyate tanuḥ* ॥

It is to be noted that most traditional commentators have interpreted the phrase *'brāhmīyaṃ kriyate tanuḥ'* as 'the body is made fit to attain Brahman'. This while being correct does not capture the complete meaning. The phrase is actually a direct reference to the complete manifestation of the divine varṇa essence that is present in an individual since birth in an unmanifest state and which has now become fully manifest as a result of the performance of saṃskāras and other ritual activities. Medhatithi is perhaps hinting at this when he says '"Godliness" (i.e. *brāhmīyaṃ*) meant here is that which consists in being transformed into the very essence of God (G Jha 1920)'.

412 *Atri Saṃhitā* verse 140 says, 'By birth, one is known as a brāhmaṇa; and by the purificatory rites, he is called a dvija (twice-born). He attains to the dignity of a vipra by learning (of *veda*); and by these three (together), to that of a śrotriya (Dutt 1908).' This verse is reiterated in *Padma Purāṇa* 46.129 as well.

413 We find a reference to the term *brahmabaṃdhu* in Amarakośa in the *Nānārthavarga. Kṣīrasvāmin* in his commentary on *Amarakośa* defines *brahmabaṃdhu* as a person who is *brāhmaṇa* by birth only, but who has forsaken brāhmaṇa duties (Devi 2017). The term *vrātya* refers to a *brāhmaṇa* by birth who has not even undergone saṃskāras. *Manu* 2.30 says: 'not having received the sacrament at the proper time, become excluded from *sāvitrī* (initiation), and thereby come to be known as *vrātyas*, despised by all good men (G. Jha 1920).' The *patita* is a person who has fallen from his *varṇa* due to performance of criminal actions in violation of *dharma*. Medhātithi in his commentary on *Manu* 3.150 defines *patita*

as 'one who commits any one of the five "great sins". (G. Jha 1920)'. The five heneious offences called as *Mahāpātaka* are described in *Manu* 11.54 thus: 'Brāhmaṇa-slaying, wine-drinking, theft, intercourse with the Preceptor's wife,are called the 'heinous offences,' as also association with these (G. Jha 1920).

414 Taittirīya Saṃhitā 7.1.1.6 has said Śūdra is not eligible for Yajña because Śūdra is not born after any Devatās (Keith 1914). This indicates that the ritual state of shudra is such that they are ineligible for vaidika karmas including upanayana. It may be noted that while the Taittirīya Saṃhitā says Śūdras are not born after Devatās, other Vedic texts associate Śūdra Varna with Pūṣan or Tapa. However, there is no contradiction here. The Taittirīya Saṃhitā phrase "not born after Devatas" merely indicates that Śūdras are not born after Devatās such as Indra, Marutas, etc. which makes them ineligible for vaidika karmas. Instead, the Śūdra ritual state is such that it is manifest at birth itself and though there is a general ineligibility for vaidika karmas, they are eligible for certain vedic rituals such as the *Aṣṭakā,* the *Pārvaṇa-śrāddha* and the *Vaiśvadeva* offerings which have all been prescribed for the Śūdra, a point noted by Medhātithi in his commentary on Manu 10.127. They are further eligible for other ritualistic practices such as sāmānya-dharma, śūdra-dharma, bhakti, etc.

415 I thank Angirasa Shreshta who is a practitioner-scholar with special interest in Srauta and Shaiva Siddhanta for bringing this section from Jaiminiya Brahmana to my attention and also for painstakingly explaining the various nuances expounded in the text.

416 तस्यो एव द्वे सवने बृहतीं संपद्येते । यथैव पुरा तृतीयसवनं तथा तृतीयसवनम् । एकान्नसप्ततिः प्रातस्सवनस्य स्त्रोत्रियाः । ताष् षट्चत्वारिंशद् बृहत्यस् संपद्यन्ते । या हि तिस्रो गायत्र्यस् ते द्वे बृहत्यौ । न ताष् षट्चत्वारिंशद् बृहत्यस् संपद्यन्ते । तद् एतद् आयद् एव प्रातस्सवनं बृहतीम् अभिसंपद्यते । यस्माद् आयद् एव प्रातस्सवनं बृहतीम् अभिसंपद्यते तस्माद् ब्राह्मणो जायमान एव लोकी जायते । तं वा त्वै चरणेन भूयांसं कुरुते तं वा कनीयांसम् ॥ Jaiminīya Brāhmaṇa 1.244 (Vira and Chandra 1986)
*tasyo eva dve savane bṛhatīṃ saṃpadyete | yathaiva purā tṛtīyasavanaṃ tathā tṛtīyasavanam | ekānnasaptatiḥ prātassavanasya strotriyāḥ | tāṣ ṣaṭcatvāriṃśad bṛhatyas saṃpadyante | yā hi tisro gāyatryas te dve bṛhatyau | na tāṣ ṣaṭcatvāriṃśad bṛhatyas saṃpadyante | tad etad āyad eva prātassavanaṃ bṛhatīm abhisaṃpadyate | yasmād āyad eva prātassavanaṃ bṛhatīm abhisaṃpadyate tasmād brāhmaṇo jāyamāna eva lokī jāyate | taṃ vā tvai caraṇena bhūyāṃsaṃ kurute taṃ vā kanīyāṃsam ||*

417 The translation by Bodewitz while being good, it does not capture the full nuances of the idea put forward by the Śruti. Particularly, consider the section '*tasmādbrāhmaṇo jāyamāna eva lokī jāyate | taṃ vā tvai caraṇena bhūyāṃsaṃ kurute taṃ vā kanīyāṃsam*'. A more meaninful translation of the section would be, 'Therefore, the brāhmaṇa, having taken birth (jāyamāna), is born as (jāyate) the possessor of this world (lokī). [However], he by his conduct (caraṇena) makes (kurute) this [birth] greater (bhūyāṃsaṃ) or inferior (kanīyāṃsam).' The idea that a brāhmaṇa is by birth a possessor of the world indicates the ritually exalted state of a brāhmaṇa from birth itself. Despite such an exalted state, a brāhmaṇa becomes greater only through conduct which further adds to the brahmanya already present in him since birth. This is what the

Śruti is indicating when it compares a brāhmaṇa to the gāyatri verse which though exalted in itself, it needs to be accumulated together to become equal to bṛhati (also means great). Without such accumulation of brāhmaṇya through performance of actions conducive to such accumulation (namely brāhmaṇa *dharma*), one will cause one's brāhmaṇya to be dissipated slowly, thus attaining an inferior condition including losing one's varṇa completely.

418 O Goddess, wherever pure Brahman devoid of qualities exists, such a person is a brāhmaṇa with the fruits of birth serving the purpose of classification — Mahābhārata Anuśāsanaparva *131.51-52.*

419 दृष्ट्वा गर्भमनुप्राप्तां भार्यां स च महानृषिः
उवाच तां सत्यवतीं दुर्मना भृगुसत्तमः ||
व्यत्यासेनोपयुक्तस्ते चरुर्व्यक्तं भविष्यति
व्यत्यासः पादपे चापि सुव्यक्तं ते कृतः शुभे ||
मया हि विश्वं यद्ब्रह्म त्वच्चरौ संनिवेशितम्
क्षत्रवीर्यं च सकलं चरौ तस्या निवेशितम् ||
त्रिलोकविख्यातगुणं त्वं विप्रं जनयिष्यसि
सा च क्षत्रं विशिष्टं वै तत एतत्कृतं मया ||
व्यत्यासस्तु कृतो यस्मात्त्वया मात्रा तथैव च
तस्मात्सा ब्राह्मणश्रेष्ठं माता ते जनयिष्यति ||
क्षत्रियं तूग्रकर्माणं त्वं भद्रे जनयिष्यसि
न हि ते तत्कृतं साधु मातृस्नेहेन भामिनि || *Mahābhārata Anuśāsanaparva* 4.35-40 (Mahabharata: Critical Edition Prepared by Scholars at Bhandarkar Oriental Research Institute BORI n.d.)
*dṛṣṭvā garbhamanuprāptāṃ bhāryāṃ sa ca mahānṛṣiḥ*
*uvāca tāṃ satyavatīṃ durmanā bhṛgusattamaḥ* ||
*vyatyāsenopayuktaste carurvyaktaṃ bhaviṣyati*

*vyatyāsaḥ pādape cāpi suvyaktaṃ te kṛtaḥ śubhe ||*
*mayā hi viśvaṃ yadbrahma tvaccarau saṃniveśitam*
*kṣatravīryaṃ ca sakalaṃ carau tasyā niveśitam ||*
*trilokavikhyātaguṇaṃ tvaṃ vipraṃ janayiṣyasi*
*sā ca kṣatraṃ viśiṣṭaṃ vai tata etatkṛtaṃ mayā ||*
*vyatyāsastu kṛto yasmāttvayā mātrā tathaiva ca*
*asmātsā brāhmaṇaśreṣṭhaṃ mātā te janayiṣyati ||*
*kṣatriyaṃ tūgrakarmāṇaṃ tvaṃ bhadre janayiṣyasi*
*na hi te tatkṛtaṃ sādhu mātṛsnehena bhāmini ||*

420 *Pratilōmavivāha* describes a hypogamous marriage between a woman belonging to a higher varṇa and a man belonging to a lower varṇa relative to the respective woman.

421 यज्ञेन यज्ञमयजन्त देवास्तानि धर्माणि प्रथमान्यासन् ।
ते ह नाकं महिमानः सचन्त यत्र पूर्वे साध्याः सन्ति देवाः ॥
*Puruṣasūkta* verse 16. (Purusha Suktam n.d.)
*yajñena yajñamayajanta devāstāni dharmāṇi prathamānyāsan* ।
*te ha nākaṃ mahimānaḥ sacanta yatra pūrve sādhyāḥ santi devāḥ* ॥

422 स नैव व्यभवत्तच्छ्रेयोरूपमत्यसृजत धर्मं तदेतत्क्षत्रस्य क्षत्त्रं यद्धर्मस्तस्माद्धर्मात्परं नास्ति *Bṛhadāraṇyaka Upaniṣad* 1.4.14 (Brihadaranyakopanishad-bhashyam n.d.)
*sa naiva vyabhavattacchreyorūpamatyasṛjata dharmaṃ tadetatkṣatrasya kṣattraṃ yaddharmastasmāddharmātparaṃ nāsti*

423 अतस्तदभिमानोऽविद्वान् तद्विशेषानुष्ठानाय ब्रह्मक्षत्रविट्छूद्रनिमित्तविशेषमभिमन्यते; तानि च निसर्गत एव कर्माधिकारनिमित्तानि ॥ । Ādi Śaṅkarācārya's commentary on *Bṛhadāraṇyaka Upaniṣad* 1.4.14 (Brihadaranyakopanishad-bhashyam n.d.)

*atastadabhimāno'vidvān tadviśeṣānuṣṭhānāya brahmakṣatraviṭchūdranimittaviśeṣamabhimanyate; tāni ca nisargata eva karmādhikāranimittāni* ॥

424 ब्रह्मणा सृष्टा वर्णाः कर्मार्थम्; तच्च कर्म धर्माख्यं सर्वानेव कर्तव्यतया नियन्तृ पुरुषार्थसाधनं च Ādi Śaṅkarācārya's commentary on *Bṛhadāraṇyaka Upaniṣad* 1.4.15 (Brihadaranyakopanishad-bhashyam n.d.)
*brahmaṇā sṛṣṭā varṇāḥ karmārtham; tacca karma dharmākhyaṃ sarvāneva kartavyatayā niyantṛ puruṣārthasādhanaṃ ca*

425 अध्यापनमध्ययनं यजनं याजनं तथा ।
दानं प्रतिग्रहं चैव ब्राह्मणानामकल्पयत् ॥ *Manusmṛti* 1.88 (Kaundinyayana 2014)
*adhyāpanamadhyayanaṃ yajanaṃ yājanaṃ tathā* ।
*dānaṃ pratigrahaṃ caiva brāhmaṇānāmakalpayat* ॥

426 अर्थकामेष्वसक्तानां धर्मज्ञानं विधीयते । *Manusmṛti* 2.13 (Kaundinyayana 2014)
arthakāmeṣvasaktānāṃ dharmajñānaṃ vidhīyate ।

427 तं हि स्वयम्भूः स्वादास्यात् तपस्तप्त्वाऽऽदितोऽसृजत् ।

हव्यकव्याऽभिवाह्याय सर्वस्यास्य च गुप्तये ॥
यस्याऽऽस्येन सदाऽश्नन्ति हव्यानि त्रिदिवौकसः ।
कव्यानि चैव पितरः किं भूतमधिकं ततः ॥ *Manusmṛti* 1.94-95 (Kaundinyayana 2014)
*taṃ hi svayambhūḥ svādāsyāt tapastaptvā'dito'sṛjat* ।
*havyakavyā'bhivāhyāya sarvasyāsya ca guptaye* ॥
*yasyā''syena sadā'śnanti havyāni tridivaukasaḥ* ।
*kavyāni caiva pitaraḥ kiṃ bhūtamadhikaṃ tataḥ* ॥

428 सकर्मत्वाद्वहतेः । तेन च कर्मणा सर्वस्य त्रैलोक्यस्य गुप्तिः परिपालनं भवति । इतः प्रदानं देवा उपजीवन्ति । ते च शीतोष्ण वर्षैरोषधीः पचन्ति पाचयन्ति । अतः परस्परोपकाराद्गुप्तिः।। Medhātithi's commentary on *Manusmṛti* 1.94 (Dave 1972)
*sakarmatvādvahateḥ* । *tena ca karmaṇā sarvasya trailokyasya guptiḥ paripālanaṃ bhavati* । *itaḥ pradānaṃ devā upajīvanti* । *te ca śītoṣna varṣairoṣadhīḥ pacanti pācayanti* । *ataḥ parasparopakārādguptiḥ* ।।

429 उत्पत्तिरेव विप्रस्य मूर्तिर्धर्मस्य शाश्वती ।
स हि धर्मार्थमुत्पन्नो ब्रह्मभूयाय कल्पते ॥ *Manusmṛti* 1.98 (Kaundinyayana 2014)
*utpattireva viprasya mūrtirdharmasya śāśvatī* ।
*sa hi dharmārthamutpanno brahmabhūyāya kalpate* ॥

430 एतयर्चा विसंयुक्तः काले च क्रियया स्वया ।
ब्रह्मक्षत्रियविड्योनिर्गर्हणां याति साधुषु ॥ *Manusmṛti* 2.80 (Kaundinyayana 2014)
*etayarcā visaṃyuktaḥ kāle ca kriyayā svayā* ।
*brahmakṣatriyaviḍyonirgarhaṇāṃ yāti sādhuṣu* ॥

431 न तिष्ठति तु यः पूर्वां नोपास्ते यश्च पश्चिमाम् ।
स शूद्रवद् बहिष्कार्यः सर्वस्माद् द्विजकर्मणः ॥ *Manusmṛti* 2.103 (Kaundinyayana 2014)
*na tiṣṭhati tu yaḥ pūrvāṃ nopāste yaśca paścimām* ।
*sa śūdravad bahiṣkāryaḥ sarvasmād dvijakarmaṇaḥ* ॥

432 अनागतां तु ये पूर्वामनतीतां तु पश्चिमाम् । संध्यां नोपासते विप्राः कथं ते ब्राह्मणाः स्मृताः ।।
सायंप्रातः सदा संध्यां ये विप्रा नो उपासते । कामं तान्धार्मिको राजा शूद्रकर्मसु योजयेदिति ।। Baudhāyana Dharmasūtra 2.7.15 (Olivelle 2000)

*anāgatāṃ tu ye pūrvāmanatītāṃ tu paścimām* । *saṃdhyāṃ nopāsate viprāḥ kathaṃ te brāhmaṇāḥ smṛtāḥ* ।। *sāyaṃprātaḥ sadā saṃdhyāṃ ye viprā no upāsate* । kāmaṃ tāndhārmiko rājā śūdrakarmasu yojayediti ।।

433 Though the verse appears as 8.11 in (Dutt 1908), it is present as verse 8.3 in *Pārāśaramādhava, Prāyaścittakāṇḍam* (Tripati 2019): सावित्र्याश्चापि गायत्र्याः संध्योपास्त्यग्निकार्ययोः |अज्ञानात्कृषिकर्त्तारो ब्राह्मणा नामधारकाः|| *sāvitryāścāpi gāyatryāḥ saṃdhyopāśtyagnikāryayoḥ* | *ajñānātkṛṣikarttāro brāhmaṇā nāmadhārakāḥ* ||

434 प्रजापतिर् वावेदम् अग्र आसीत् । जनो ह वै प्रजापतिर् देवता । सो ऽकामयत बहुस् स्याम प्रजायेय भूमानं गच्छेयम् इति । स शीर्षत एव मुखतस् त्रिवृतं स्तोमम् असृजत गायत्रीं छन्दो रथन्तरं सामाग्निं देवतां ब्राह्मणं मनुष्यम् अजं पशुम् । तस्माद् ब्राह्मणो गायत्री छन्दा आग्नेयो देवतया । तस्माद् उ मुखं प्रजानाम् । मुखाद् ध्य् एनम् असृजत ॥ सो ऽकामयत प्रैव जायेयेति । स बाहुभ्याम् एवोरसः पञ्चदशं स्तोमम् असृजत त्रिष्टुभं छन्दो बृहत् सामेन्द्रं देवतां राजन्यं मनुष्यम् अश्वं पशुम् । तस्माद् राजन्यस् त्रिष्टुप्छन्दा ऐन्द्रो देवतया । तस्माद् उ बाहुभ्यां वीर्यं करोति । बाहुभ्यां ह्य् एनम् उरसो वीर्याद् असृजत || सो ऽकामयत प्रैव जायेयेति ॥ स उदराद् एव मध्यतस् सप्तदशं स्तोमम् असृजत जगतीं छन्दो वामदेव्यं साम विश्वान् देवान् देवतां वैश्यं मनुष्यं गां पशुम् । तस्माद् वैश्यो जगतीछन्दा वैश्वदेवो देवतया । तस्माद् उ प्रजनिष्णुः । उदराद् ध्य् एनं प्रजननाद् असृजत || सो ऽकामयत प्रैव जायेयेति । स पद्भ्याम् एव प्रतिष्ठाया एकविशं स्तोमम् असृजतानुष्टुभं छन्दो यज्ञायज्ञीयं साम न कां चन देवतां शूद्रं मनुष्यम् अविं पशुम् । तस्माच् शूद्रो ऽनुष्टुप्छन्दा वेश्मपतिदेवः । । Jaiminīya Brāhmaṇa 69-1.68 (Vira and Chandra 1986)

*prajāpatir vāvedam agra āsīt* । *jano ha vai prajāpatir devatā* । *so'kāmayata bahus syāma prajāyeya bhūmānaṃ gaccheyam iti* । *sa śīrṣata eva mukhatas trivṛtaṃ stomam asṛjata gāyatrīṃ chando rathantaraṃ sāmāgniṃ devatāṃ brāhmaṇaṃ manuṣyam ajaṃ paśum* । *tasmād brāhmaṇo gāyatrī chandā āgneyo devatayā* । *tasmād u mukhaṃ prajānām* । *mukhād dhy enam asṛjata* । *so-kāmayata praiva jāyeyeti* । *sa bāhubhyām evorasaḥ pañcadaśaṃ stomam asṛjata triṣṭubhaṃ chando bṛhat sāmendraṃ devatāṃ rājanyaṃ manuṣyam aśvaṃ paśum* । *tasmād rājanyas triṣṭupchandā aindro devatayā* । *tasmād u bāhubhyāṃ vīryaṃ karoti* । *bāhubhyāṃ hy enam uraso vīryād asṛjata* || *so'kāmayata praiva jāyeyeti* । *sa udarād eva madhyatas saptadaśaṃ stomam asṛjata jagatīṃ chando vāmadevyaṃ sāma viśvān devān devatāṃ vaiśyaṃ manuṣyaṃ gāṃ paśum* । *tasmād vaiśyo jagatīchandā vaiśvadevo devatayā* । *tasmād u prajaniṣṇuḥ* । *udarād dhy enaṃ prajananād asṛjata* || *so'kāmayata praiva jāyeyeti* । *sa padbhyām eva pratiṣṭhāyā ekaviśaṃ stomam asṛjatānuṣṭubhaṃ chando yajñāyajñīyaṃ sāma na kāṃ cana devatāṃ śūdraṃ manuṣyam aviṃ paśum* । *tasmāc śūdro 'nuṣṭupchandā veśmapatidevaḥ* ।

435 धर्मेप्सवस्तु धर्मज्ञाः सतां वृत्तमनुष्ठिताः ।
मन्त्रवर्जं न दुष्यन्ति प्रशंसां प्राप्नुवन्ति च ॥
यथायथा हि संवृत्तमातिष्ठत्यनसूयकः।
तथातथेमं चाऽमुं च लोकं प्राप्नोत्यनिन्दितः ॥ *Manusmṛti* 10.127-128 (Kaundinyayana 2014)
*dharmepsavastu dharmajñāḥ satāṃ vṛttamanuṣṭhitāḥ* ।
*mantravarjaṃ na duṣyanti praśaṃsāṃ prāpnuvanti ca* ॥
*yathāyathā hi sadvṛttamātiṣṭhatyanasūyakaḥ* ।
*tathātathemaṃ cā'muṃ ca lokaṃ prāpnotyaninditaḥ* ॥

436 भार्यारतिः शुचिर्भृत्यभर्ता श्राद्धक्रियारतः |
नमस्कारेण मन्त्रेण पञ्चयाज्ञान्न हापयेत् || *Yajñavalkyasmṛti* 1.121 (Pansikar 1936)
*bhāryāratiḥ śucirbhṛtyabhartā śrāddhakriyārataḥ* |

*namaskāreṇa mantreṇa pañcayājñānna hāpayet* ||

437 Theodore Benke in his work *The Śūdrācāraśiromani of Krsna Śesa: A 16th Century Manual of Dharma for Śūdras* (2010, 11-12) gives a list of 49 śūdra-*dharma* texts which were composed between 1360-1660 to specifically address the ritualistic and spiritual requirements of the śūdra varṇa: 1. *Śatśūdrācāraśiromani of Kṛṣṇa Śeṣa* 2. *Śūdrakamalākara of Kamalākarabhaṭṭa* 3. *Śūdradharmoddyota of Gāgābhaṭṭa* 4. *Śūdrakṛtyavicāraṇatattva of Raghunandana* 5. *Śūdrācāracintāmaṇi of Vācaspatimiśra 6. Acāracandrikā* 7. *Śūdrīpaddhati or Śrīdharapaddhati* 8. *Śūdrotpatti* 9. *Śūdrakarmavṛtti* 10. *Śūdrācārasamgraha or Saccūdrāhnika* 11. *Śūdrasmṛti*12. *Śūdrāhnikācāra* 13. *Śūdrāhnikācārasāra of Yādavendra Śarman* 14. *Śūdrakṛtya of Lālabahādur* 15. *Śūdraśānti* 16. *Smṛtikaumudī of Viśveśvarabhaṭṭa* 17. *Śūdrapaddhati of Apipāla* 18. *Śūdrapaddhati of Gopāla* 19. *Śūdrakuladīpikā of Rāmānandaśarman* 20. *Śūdrasamkara* 21. *Śūdrācārasaṁgraha of Navarasaundaryabhaṭṭa* 22. *Śūdrāhnikācāra of Śrīgarbha* 23. *Śūdrapañcasaṁskāravidhi of Kaśyapa* 24. *Śūdrācāra* 25. *Śūdrasatkarmacandrikā* 26. *Śūdrapañcasamskāraprayoga* 27. *Śūdravivāhapaddhati of Śivarāma Rāvala* 28. *Śūdradharmanirṇaya* 29. *Śūdrāhnika of Dhanapati* 30. *Śūdrasamskṛtapratimāsamseḍha* 31. *Śūdratarpaṇa* 32. *Śūdrottarakriyāprayoga* 33. *Śūdravāstuśānti* 34. *Śūdrānām ekādāśāhaprayoga* 35. *Śūdrasamskāranirṇaya* 36. *Śūdraśrāddhapaddhati* 37. *Śūdrasthālipākaprayoga or Agnimukha* 38. *Śūdraśrāddhaprayoga* 39. *Śūdrapaddhati of Śankaradaivavit* 40. *Śūdraṣaṭkarmacandrikā* 41. *Śūdrasamskāradīpikā of Gopālabhaṭṭa* 42. *Śūdradharmanirūpaṇa* 43. *Śūdrajapavidhāna* 44. *Śūdrānām ekoddiṣṭavidha* 45. *Śūdraviveka of Rāmaśaṁkara* 46.

*Śūdrapaddhati of Kṛṣṇarāja* 47. *Saccūdrasatkarmadarpaṇa* 48. *Śūdrācārapaddhati of Rāmadattaṭhakkura* 49. *Śūdrācāravivekapaddhati of Goṇḍimiśra*

438 एते चतुर्णां वर्णानामापद्धर्माः प्रकीर्तिताः ।
यान् सम्यगनुतिष्ठन्तो व्रजन्ति परमां गतिम् ॥ *Manusmṛti* 10.130 (Kaundinyayana 2014)

*ete caturṇāṃ varṇānāmāpaddharmāḥ prakīrtitāḥ* ।
*yān samyaganutiṣṭhanto vrajanti paramāṃ gatim* ॥

439 एतेषां जातिविहितानां कर्मणां सम्यगनुष्ठितानां स्वर्गप्राप्तिः फलं स्वभावतः*Gītābhāṣya of Śaṅkarācārya on* (Srimad-Bhagavadgita-bhashya n.d.)
*eteṣāṃ jātivihitānāṃ karmaṇāṃ samyaganuṣṭhitānāṃ svargaprāptiḥ phalaṃ svabhāvataḥ*

440 स भगवान् सृष्ट्वेदं जगत्, तस्य च स्थितिं चिकीर्षुः, मरीच्यादीनग्रे सृष्ट्वा प्रजापतीन्, प्रवृत्तिलक्षणं धर्मं ग्राहयामास वेदोक्तम् । ततोऽन्यांश्च सनकसनन्दनादीनुत्पाद्य, निवृत्तिलक्षणं धर्मं ज्ञानवैराग्यलक्षणं ग्राहयामास । द्विविधो हि वेदोक्तो धर्मः, प्रवृत्तिलक्षणो निवृत्तिलक्षणश्च, जगतः स्थितिकारणम् । प्राणिनां साक्षादभ्युदयनिःश्रेयसहेतुर्यः स धर्मो ब्राह्म णाद्यैर्वर्णिभिराश्रमिभिश्च श्रेयोर्थिभिः अनुष्ठीयमानो दीर्घेण कालेन । Introductory section, *Gītābhāṣya of Śaṅkarācārya* (Srimad-Bhagavadgita-bhashya n.d.)
*sa bhagavān sṛṣṭvedaṃ jagat, tasya ca sthitiṃ cikīrṣuḥ, marīcyādīnagre sṛṣṭvā prajāpatīn, pravṛttilakṣaṇaṃ dharmaṃ grāhayāmāsa vedoktam* । *tato'nyāṃśca sanakasanandanādīnutpādya, nivṛttilakṣaṇaṃ dharmaṃ jñānavairāgyalakṣaṇaṃ grāhayāmāsa* । *dvividho hi vedokto dharmaḥ, pravṛttilakṣaṇo nivṛttilakṣaṇaśca, jagataḥ sthitikāraṇam* । *prāṇināṃ*

*sākṣādabhyudayaniḥśreyasaheturyaḥ sa dharmo rāhmaṇādyairvarṇibhirāśramibhiśca śreyorthibhiḥ anuṣṭhīyamāno dīrgheṇa kālena* ।

441 This Appendix was first published on Pragyata Magazine, January, 2022-https://pragyata.com/antaraprabhava-in-surendra-kumars-visuddha-manusm%e1%b9%9bti-a-critical-assessment-in-light-of-its-avowedly-revisionist-interpretation/

442 The translations and paraphrasing of Dr Kumar's arguments from Hindi into English are by this author.

443 Bhāruci says: अन्तरं ब्राह्मणादिवर्ण्णमध्ये तत्र प्रभवः येषां तदन्तरप्रभवा अनुलोमप्रतिलोमा वर्ण्णेभ्यो जात्यन्तरप्रभूता अश्वतरवत्। (S and S 2020, 3)
*antaraṃ brāhmaṇādivarṇṇamadhye tatra prabhavaḥ yeṣāṃ tadantaraprabhavā anulomapratilomā varṇṇebhyo jātyantaraprabhūtā aśvataravat* ।

444 Medhātithi says: अन्तरं तन्मध्यम् । द्वयोर्जात्योः सङ्करादेकाऽप्यपरिपूर्णा जातिः । अन्तरे प्रभव उत्पत्तिर्येषां तेऽन्तरप्रभवाः अनुलोमप्रतिलोमा मूर्धावसिक्ताम्बष्ठक्षत्तृवैदेहकादयः । (Dave 1972, 8)

*antaraṃ tanmadhyam* । *dvayorjātyoḥ saṅakarādekā'pyaparipūrṇā jātiḥ* । *antare prabhava utpattiryeṣāṃ te'ntaraprabhavāḥ anulomapratilomā mūrdhāvasiktāmbaṣṭhakṣattṛvaidehakādayaḥ*

445 Govindarāja says: तथा ब्राह्मणक्षत्रियादिसङ्करजातानां अनुलोमप्रतिलोमानां यावत् कृत्स्नं कृत्वा… (Dave 1972, 10)
*tathā brāhmaṇakṣatriyādisaṅkarajātānāṃ*

*anulomapratilomānāṃ yāvat kṛtsnaṃ kṛtvā…*

446 Kullūka-Bhaṭṭa says: तेषामन्तरप्रभवाणां च सङ्कीर्णजातीनां चापि अनुलोमप्रतिलोमजातानाम्… (Kaundinyayana 2014, 75)
*teṣāmantaraprabhavāṇāṃ ca saṃkīrṇajātīnāṃ cāpi anulomapratilomajātānām…*

447 तस्मिन् देशे य आचारः पारम्पर्यक्रमागतः ।
वर्णानां सान्तरालानां स सदाचार उच्यते ॥ *Manusmṛti* 2.18 (Kaundinyayana 2014)
*tasmin deśe ya ācāraḥ pāramparyakramāgataḥ* ।
*varṇānāṃ sāntarālānāṃ sa sadācāra ucyate* ॥

448 मातृदोषविगर्हितान् *Manusmṛti* 10.6 (Kaundinyayana 2014)
*mātṛdoṣavigarhitān*

449 क्षत्रियाच् छूद्रकन्यायां क्रूराऽऽचारविहारवान् । *Manusmṛti* 10.9 (Kaundinyayana 2014)
*kṣatriyāc chūdrakanyāyāṃ krūrā"cāravihāravān* ।

450 चण्डालश्चाऽधमो नृणाम् *Manusmṛti* 10.16 (Kaundinyayana 2014)
*caṇḍālaścā'dhamo nṛṇām*

451 द्विजातयः सवर्णासु जनयन्त्यव्रतांस्तु यान् ।
तान् सावित्रीपरिभ्रष्टान् व्रात्यानिति विनिर्दिशेत् ॥ *Manusmṛti* 10.20 (Kaundinyayana 2014)
*dvijātayaḥ savarṇāsu janayantyavratāṃstu yān* ।
*tān sāvitrīparibhraṣṭān vrātyāniti vinirdiśet* ॥

452 पापाऽऽत्मा भूर्जकण्टकः *Manusmṛti* 10.21 (Kaundinyayana 2014)
*pāpā"tmā bhūrjakaṇṭakaḥ*

453 अप्यधिकदूषितान् *Manusmṛti* 10.29 (Kaundinyayana 2014)
*apyadhikadūṣitān*

454 सजातिजाऽनन्तरजाः षट् सुता द्विजधर्मिणः ।
शूद्राणां तु सधर्माणःसर्वेऽपध्वंसजाः स्मृताः ॥ *Manusmṛti* 10.41 (Kaundinyayana 2014)
*sajātijā'nantarajāḥ ṣaṭ sutā dvijadharmiṇaḥ* ।
śūdrāṇāṃ tu sadharmāṇaḥ sarve›padhvaṃsajāḥ smṛtāḥ ॥

455 अहिंसा सत्यमस्तेयं शौचमिन्द्रियनिग्रहः ।
एतं सामासिकं धर्मं चातुर्वर्ण्येऽब्रवीन् मनुः ॥ *Manusmṛti* 10.63 (Kaundinyayana 2014)
*ahiṃsā satyamasteyaṃ śaucamindriyanigrahaḥ* ।
*etaṃ sāmāsikaṃ dharmaṃ cāturvarṇye'bravīn manuḥ* ॥

456 सामासिकं समस्तस्य सर्वमनुष्यभेदजातेरुक्तम्, न ब्राह्मणादिजातिविभागेन । Medhātithi on *Manusmṛti* 10.63 (Dave 1972)
*sāmāsikaṃ samastasya sarvamanuṣyabhedajāteruktam, na brāhmaṇādijātivibhāgena* ।

प्रकरणसामर्थ्यात् सङ्कीर्णानामप्ययं धर्मो वेदितव्यः । Kullūka-Bhaṭṭa on *Manusmṛti* 10.63 (Kaundinyayana 2014)
*prakaraṇasāmarthyāt saṅkīrṇānāmapyayaṃ dharmo veditavyaḥ*

प्रकरणसामर्थ्याच्च चातुर्वर्ण्यग्रहणस्यान्तरप्रभवे दर्शनार्थत्वे...
*Govindarāja* on *Manusmṛti* 10.63 (Dave 1972)
*prakaraṇasāmarthyācca cāturvarṇyagrahaṇasyāntaraprabhave darśanārthatve...*

एवं च प्रकरणसामर्थ्यात् चातुर्वर्ण्यान्तरप्रभवानामप्यहिंसादिपुरुषधर्मो

विज्ञेयः । Bhāruci on *Manusmṛti* 10.63 (Dave 1972)
*evaṃ ca prakaraṇasāmarthyāt cāturvarṇyāntaraprabhavānāmapyahiṃsādipuruṣadharmo vijñeyaḥ* ।

457 यथा विवाहादौ कङ्कणबन्धनादि माङ्गलिकत्वेन यत्क्रियते, या च कन्यायास्तदहर्विवाहयिष्यणायाः प्रख्यातवृक्षयक्षचतुष्पथादिपूजा देशभेदेन, तथा चूडासङ्ख्या देशभेदश्च, या चातिथ्यादीनां गुर्वादीनां चानुवृत्तिः प्रियहितवचनाभिवादनाभ्युत्थानादिरूपा, तथा पृश्निसूक्तं तृणपाणयोऽधीयते अश्वमेधमश्वं यथा समर्पयन्तः । Medhātithi on *Manusmṛti* 2.6 (Dave 1972)
*yathā vivāhādau kaṅkaṇabandhanādi māṅgalikatvena yatkriyate, yā ca kanyāyāstadaharvivāhayiṣyaṇāyāḥ prakhyātavṛkṣayakṣacatuṣpathādipūjā deśabhedena, tathā cūḍāsaṅkhyā deśabhedaśca, yā cātithyādīnāṃ gurvādīnāṃ cānuvṛttiḥ priyahitavacanābhivādanābhyutthānādirūpā, tathā pṛśnisūktaṃ tṛṇapāṇayo'dhīyate aśvamedhamaśvaṃ yathā samarpayantaḥ* ।

458 वर्णधर्मान् निबोधत । *Manusmṛti* 2.25 (Kaundinyayana 2014)
*varṇadharmānnibodhata* ।

459 एष वोऽभिहितो धर्मो ब्राह्मणस्य चतुर्विधः ।
पुण्योऽक्षयफलः प्रेत्य राज्ञां धर्मं निबोधत ॥ *Manusmṛti* 6.97 (Kaundinyayana 2014)
*eṣa vo'bhihito dharmo brāhmaṇasya caturvidhaḥ* ।
*puṇyo'kṣayaphalaḥ pretya rājñāṃ dharmaṃ nibodhata* ॥

460 चत्वारो ब्राह्मणस्योक्ता आश्रमाः श्रुतिचोदिताः ।
क्षत्रियस्य त्रयः प्रोक्ता द्वावेको वैश्यशूद्रयोः ॥ *Yogī-Yājñavalkya* 1.29 (Shri Yoga Yajnyavalkya n.d.) is quoted as is in *Parāśara*

*Mādhava (Ācāra khaṇḍa)* (Tripati, Parasharamadhava: Acharakhandam 2019)
*catvāro brāhmaṇasyoktā āśramāḥ śruticoditāḥ* ।
*kṣatriyasya trayaḥ proktā dvāveko vaiśyaśūdrayoḥ* ॥

चत्वार आश्रमाश्चैते ब्राह्मणस्य प्रकीर्त्तिताः ।
गार्हस्थ्यं ब्रह्मचर्यञ्च वानप्रस्थं त्रयोऽश्रमाः ॥
क्षत्रियस्यापि कथिता य आचारा द्विजस्य हि ।
ब्रह्मचर्यञ्च गार्हस्थ्यमाश्रमद्वितयं विशः ॥
गार्हस्थ्यमुचितन्त्वेकं शूद्रस्य क्षणदाचर ॥ A verse from *Vāmanapurāṇa* as quoted in *Parāśara Mādhava (Ācāra khaṇḍa)* (Tripati, Parasharamadhava: Acharakhandam 2019) which differs slightly from the *Vāmanapurāṇa* 15.61-63 (Gupta, et al. 1968) in its word usage but essentially gives same import.
*catvāra āśramāścaite brāhmaṇasya prakīrttitāḥ* ।
*gārhasthyaṃ brahmacaryañca vānaprasthaṃ trayo'śramāḥ* ॥
*kṣatriyasyāpi kathitā ya ācārā dvijasya hi* ।
*brahmacaryañca gārhasthyamāśramadvitayaṃ viśaḥ* ॥
*gārhasthyamucitantvekaṃ śūdrasya kṣaṇadācara* ॥

461 चातुर्वर्ण्यं त्रयो लोकाश् चत्वारश् चाऽऽश्रमाः पृथक् ।
भूतं भव्यं भविष्यं च सर्वं वेदात् प्रसिध्यति ॥ *Manusmṛti* 12.97 (Kaundinyayana 2014)
*cāturvarṇyaṃ trayo lokāś catvāraś cā''śramāḥ pṛthak* ।
*bhūtaṃ bhavyaṃ bhaviṣyaṃ ca sarvaṃ vedāt prasidhyati* ॥

462 स्वेस्वे धर्मे निविष्टानां सर्वेषामनुपूर्वशः ।
वर्णानामाश्रमाणां च राजा सृष्टोऽभिरक्षिता ॥ *Manusmṛti* 7.35 (Kaundinyayana 2014)
*svesve dharme niviṣṭānāṃ sarveṣāmanupūrvaśaḥ* ।
*varṇānāmāśramāṇāṃ ca rājā sṛṣṭo'bhirakṣitā* ॥

463 वर्णधर्मान् निबोधत । *Manusmṛti* 2.25 (Kaundinyayana 2014)
*varṇadharmānnibodhata* ।

464 एष धर्मविधिः कृत्स्नश् चातुर्वर्ण्यस्य कीर्तितः । *Manusmṛti* 10.131 (Kaundinyayana 2014)
*eṣa dharmavidhiḥ kṛtsnaś cāturvarṇyasya kīrtitaḥ* ।

465 ब्राह्मणः क्षत्रियो वैश्यस् त्रयो वर्णा द्विजातयः ।
चतुर्थ एकजातिस् तु शूद्रो नाऽस्ति तु पञ्चमः ॥ *Manusmṛti* 10.4 (Kaundinyayana 2014)
*brāhmaṇaḥ kṣatriyo vaiśyas trayo varṇā dvijātayaḥ* ।
*caturtha ekajātis tu śūdro nā'sti tu pañcamaḥ* ॥

466 मुखबाहूरुपज्जानां या लोके जातयो बहिः ।
म्लेच्छवाचश् चाऽऽर्यवाचः सर्वे ते दस्यवः स्मृताः ॥ *Manusmṛti* 10.45 (Kaundinyayana 2014)
*mukhabāhūrupajjānāṃ yā loke jātayo bahiḥ* ।
*mlecchavācaś cā"ryavācaḥ sarve te dasyavaḥ smṛtāḥ* ॥

467 धर्मेप्सवस् तु धर्मज्ञाः सतां वृत्तमनुष्ठिताः ।
मन्त्रवर्जं न दुष्यन्ति प्रशंसां प्राप्नुवन्ति च ॥ *Manusmṛti* 10.127 (Kaundinyayana 2014)
*dharmepsavas tu dharmajñāḥ satāṃ vṛttamanuṣṭhitāḥ* ।
*mantravarjaṃ na duṣyanti praśaṃsāṃ prāpnuvanti ca* ॥

468 एषोऽनापदि वर्णानामुक्तः कर्मविधिः शुभः ।
आपद्यपि हि यस् तेषां क्रमशस् तं निबोधत ॥ *Manusmṛti* 9.336 (Kaundinyayana 2014)
*eṣo'nāpadi varṇānāmuktaḥ karmavidhiḥ śubhaḥ* ।
*āpadyapi hi yas teṣāṃ kramaśas taṃ nibodhata* ॥

469 एते चतुर्णां वर्णानामापद्धर्माः प्रकीर्तिताः ।
यान् सम्यगनुतिष्ठन्तो व्रजन्ति परमां गतिम् ॥ *Manusmṛti* 10.130
(Kaundinyayana 2014)
*ete caturṇāṃ varṇānāmāpaddharmāḥ prakīrtitāḥ* ।
*yān samyaganutiṣṭhanto vrajanti paramāṃ gatim* ॥

470 कुलक्षये प्रणश्यन्ति कुलधर्माः सनातनाः।
धर्मे नष्टे कुलं कृत्स्नमधर्मोऽभिभवत्युत।।
अधर्माभिभवात् कृष्ण प्रदुष्यन्ति कुलस्त्रियः।
स्त्रीषु दुष्टासु वार्ष्णेय जायते वर्णसङ्करः।।
सङ्करो नरकायैव कुलघ्नानां कुलस्य च।
पतन्ति पितरो ह्येषां लुप्तपिण्डोदकक्रियाः।।
दोषैरेतैः कुलघ्नानां वर्णसङ्करकारकैः।
उत्साद्यन्ते जातिधर्माः कुलधर्माश्च शाश्वताः।। *Bhagavad Gītā* 1.40-43
(Gambhirananda 1998)
*kulakṣaye praṇaśyanti kuladharmāḥ sanātanāḥ* ।
*dharme naṣṭe kulaṃ kṛtsnamadharmo'bhibhavatyuta* ।।
*adharmābhibhavāt kṛṣṇa praduṣyanti kulastriyaḥ* ।
*strīṣu duṣṭāsu vārṣṇeya jāyate varṇasaṅkaraḥ* ।।
*saṅkaro narakāyaiva kulaghnānāṃ kulasya ca* ।
*patanti pitaro hyeṣāṃ luptapiṇḍodakakriyāḥ* ।।
*doṣairetaiḥ kulaghnānāṃ varṇasaṅkarakārakaiḥ* ।
*utsādyante jātidharmāḥ kuladharmāśca śāśvatāḥ* ।।

Translation: From the ruin of the family are totally destroyed the traditional rites and duties of the family. When rites and duties are destroyed, vice overpowers the entire family also. O Kṛṣṇa, when vice predominates, the women of the family become corrupt. O descendent of the Vṛṣṇi, when women become corrupted, it results in the intermingling of castes. And the intermingling in the family leads the ruiners of the family verily into hell. The forefathers of these fall down (into hell) because of being deprived of the offerings of rice-balls and water. Due to these misdeeds of the ruiners of the family, which cause intermingling of castes, the traditional rites and duties of the castes and families become destroyed (Gambhirananda 1998).

471 उत्सीदेयुरिमे लोका न कुर्यां कर्म चेदहम्।
सङ्करस्य च कर्ता स्यामुपहन्यामिमाः प्रजाः।। *Bhagavad Gītā* 3.24
(Gambhirananda 1998)
*utsīdeyurime lokā na kuryāṃ karma cedaham* |
*saṅkarasya ca kartā syāmupahanyāmimāḥ prajāḥ* ||

472 ब्राह्मणः क्षत्रियो वैश्यस्त्रयो वर्णा द्विजातयः।
चतुर्थ एकजातिस्तु शूद्रो नाऽस्ति तु पञ्चमः॥ *Manusmṛti* 10.4
(Kaundinyayana 2014)
*brāhmaṇaḥ kṣatriyo vaiśyastrayo varṇā dvijātayaḥ* |
*caturtha ekajātistu śūdro nā'sti tu pañcamaḥ* ||

473 मुखबाहूरुपज्जानां या लोके जातयो बहिः।
म्लेच्छवाचश् चाऽऽर्यवाचः सर्वे ते दस्यवः स्मृताः॥ *Manusmṛti* 10.45
(Kaundinyayana 2014)
*mukhabāhūrupajjānāṃ yā loke jātayo bahiḥ* |
*mlecchavācaś cā''ryavācaḥ sarve te dasyavaḥ smṛtāḥ* ||

474 व्यभिचारेण वर्णानामवेद्यावेदनेन च।
स्वकर्मणां च त्यागेन जायन्ते वर्णसङ्कराः॥ *Manusmṛti* 10.24
(Kaundinyayana 2014)
*vyabhicāreṇa varṇānāmavedyāvedanena ca* |
*svakarmaṇāṃ ca tyāgena jāyante varṇasaṅkarāḥ* ||

475 शनकैस् तु क्रियालोपादिमाः क्षत्रियजातयः।
वृषलत्वं गता लोके ब्राह्मणाऽदर्शनेन च॥

पौण्ड्रकाश् चौड्रद्रविडाः काम्बोजा यवनाः शकाः ।
पारदाः पह्लवाश् चीनाः किराता दरदाः खशाः ॥ *Manusmṛti* 10.43-44 (Kaundinyayana 2014)

śanakais tu kriyālopādimāḥ kṣatriyajātayaḥ ।
*vṛṣalatvaṃ gatā loke brāhmaṇā'darśanena ca* ॥

*pauṇḍrakāś cauḍradraviḍāḥ kāmbojā yavanāḥ śakāḥ* ।
*pāradāḥ pahlavāś cīnāḥ kirātā daradāḥ khaśāḥ* ॥

476 सर्वस्याऽस्य तु सर्गस्य गुप्त्यर्थं स महाद्युतिः ।
मुखबाहूरुपज्जानां पृथक् कर्माण्यकल्पयत् ॥

अध्यापनमध्ययनं यजनं याजनं तथा ।
दानं प्रतिग्रहं चैव ब्राह्मणानामकल्पयत् ॥

प्रजानां रक्षणं दानमिज्याऽध्ययनमेव च ।
विषयेष्वप्रसक्तिश् च क्षत्रियस्य समासतः ॥

पशूनां रक्षणं दानमिज्याऽध्ययनमेव च ।
वणिक्पथं कुसीदं च वैश्यस्य कृषिमेव च ॥

एकमेव तु शूद्रस्य प्रभुः कर्म समादिशत् ।
एतेषामेव वर्णानां शुश्रूषामनसूयया ॥ *Manusmṛti* 1.87-91 (Kaundinyayana 2014)

*sarvasyā'sya tu sargasya guptyarthaṃ sa mahādyutiḥ* ।
*mukhabāhūrupajjānāṃ pṛthak karmāṇyakalpayat* ॥

*adhyāpanamadhyayanaṃ yajanaṃ yājanaṃ tathā* ।
*dānaṃ pratigrahaṃ caiva brāhmaṇānāmakalpayat* ॥

*prajānāṃ rakṣaṇaṃ dānamijyā'dhyayanameva ca* ।
*viṣayeṣvaprasaktiś ca kṣatriyasya samāsataḥ* ॥

*paśūnāṃ rakṣaṇaṃ dānamijyā'dhyayanameva ca* ।
*vaṇikpathaṃ kusīdaṃ ca vaiśyasya kṛṣimeva ca* ॥

*ekameva tu śūdrasya prabhuḥ karma samādiśat* ।
*eteṣāmeva varṇānāṃ śuśrūṣāmanasūyayā* ॥

477 वैश्यशूद्रोपचारं च सङ्कीर्णानां च सम्भवम् ।
आपद्धर्मं च वर्णानां प्रायश्चित्तविधिं तथा ॥ *Manusmṛti* 1.116
(Kaundinyayana 2014)
*vaiśyaśūdropacāraṃ ca saṅkīrṇānāṃ ca sambhavam* ।
*āpaddharmaṃ ca varṇānāṃ prāyaścittavidhiṃ tathā* ॥

478 वैश्यशूद्रोपचारं च सङ्कीर्णानां च सम्भवम् ।
आपद्धर्मं च वर्णानां प्रायश्चित्तविधिं तथा ॥ *Manusmṛti* 1.116
(Kaundinyayana 2014)
*vaiśyaśūdropacāraṃ ca saṅkīrṇānāṃ ca sambhavam* ।
*āpaddharmaṃ ca varṇānāṃ prāyaścittavidhiṃ tathā* ॥

## ALSO BY THIS AUTHOR

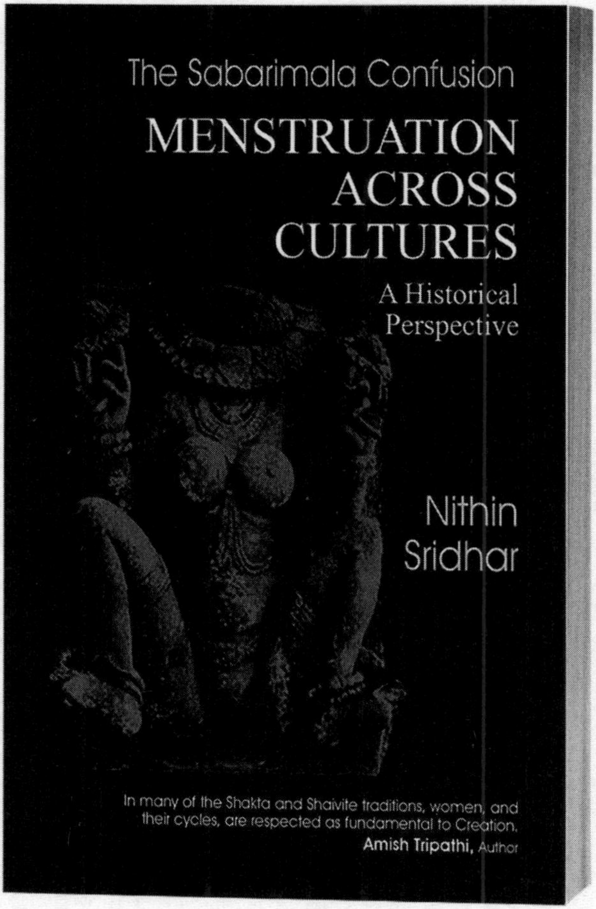
The Sabarimala Confusion
MENSTRUATION ACROSS CULTURES
A Historical Perspective
Nithin Sridhar
In many of the Shakta and Shaivite traditions, women, and their cycles, are respected as fundamental to Creation.
Amish Tripathi, Author